JAVA
PROGRAMMER'S LIBRARY

Suleiman "Sam" Lalani

Kris Jamsa, Ph.D.

JAMSA
P·R·E·S·S ®
...a computer user's best friend ®

Published by
Jamsa Press
2975 S. Rainbow, Suite I
Las Vegas, NV 89102
U.S.A.

For information about the translation or distribution of any Jamsa Press book, please write to Jamsa Press at the address listed above.

Java Programmer's Library

Printed in the United States of America.
98765432

ISBN 1-884133-26-6

Publisher	***Technical Advisor***	***Cover Design***
Debbie Jamsa	Phil Schmauder	Marianne Helm
Publisher's Assistant	***Cover Photograph***	***Proofer***
Janet Lawrie	O'Gara/Bissell	Tammy Funk
		Jeanne Smith
Indexer	***Copy Editor***	Rosemary Paseo
Linda Linssen	Tammy Funk	
	Rosemary Paseo	

TABLE OF CONTENTS

CHAPTER 1

INTRODUCING JAVA

Welcome to the *Java Programmer's Library*. When we first sat back and thought about doing this book, our goal was to create one product that gave programmers everything they would need to be instantly productive with Java. We thought that it would be wonderful if we could give programmers real-world programs they could incorporate into their client's Web sites within minutes. We also wanted to provide powerful code fragments that programmers could quickly cut-and-paste into their own applets. Lastly, we wanted to create some high-end applications (such as a Java-based chat program) that let programmers see the true power of Java applets.

After months and months of coding, we knew that you would more than like our code. We've produced several practical applets that Web sites may use on a daily basis. We developed some high-tech applications based on other Internet protocols such as FTP. But most importantly, we created several really cool applets (like the **Magnifier** presented in Chapter 29, the **Eraser** presented in Chapter 46, and the scaleable **LED Clock** presented in Chapter 33). If you are really into coding, you will rank these applets high on your cool meter.

But our complete package did not come together until we decided to include Sun's Official Java Developer's Kit for Windows 95 and Windows NT on our CD-ROM. So, in addition to giving you over 10,000 lines of real-world Java code, the CD-ROM that accompanies this book also includes the Java compiler, debugger, appletviewer, and even sample applets that were developed at Sun! In short, the *Java Programmer's Library* is your complete Java package!

Note: If you are not using Windows 95 or Windows NT, don't worry, later in this chapter we will tell you how you can download the Java Developer's Kit for your system from Sun's Web site.

INSTALLING THE JAVA DEVELOPER'S KIT

Installing the Java Developer's Kit (or JDK) from this book's companion CD-ROM is very easy. To begin, Sun provides the JDK in a single self-extracting executable file whose name we have simplified on the CD as JDK101.EXE (for Java Developer's Kit version 1.01). When you run the program, it will extract all the files for the Java Developer's Kit (from itself) into a directory named Java on your hard disk. To install the JDK, perform these steps:

1. If you are using Windows 95, select the Start menu Run option. Windows 95, in turn, will display the Run dialog box. Type **command** and press ENTER.

2. If you are using Windows NT, select the Program Manager's File menu Run option. Windows NT, in turn, will display the Run dialog box. Type **command** and press ENTER.

3. From the command prompt, use the following change directory command to select the root directory as your current directory:

    C:\WINDOWS> **CD \ ** <ENTER>

4. Insert the CD-ROM from the *Java Programmer's Library* into your CD-ROM drive.

5. Without changing your current drive from your hard drive, type in the program name JDK101 preceded by your CD-ROM drive letter, a colon, and a back slash and press ENTER. For example, if your CD-ROM drive is drive D:, you would type the following:

    C:\> **D:\JDK101** <ENTER>

Note: *When you install the Java Developer's Kit on your hard disk, the installation program will create the Java directory within the current directory. In most cases, you will want to put the Java directory within your disk's root directory. If, for some reason, you install Java into the wrong directory, simply remove the Java directory using the DELTREE command and run the JDK101.EXE a second time, but in the correct directory.*

Note: *If you download the Java Developer's Kit from Sun, the name of your self extracting file will differ from the name we are using on the CD. If you are using Windows 95 or Windows NT, the file will use a long filename.*

As the program runs, it will place all the Java Developer's Kit files onto your hard drive. Specifically, the program will create the subdirectories listed in Table 1.

Subdirectory	Contents
java	The main directory
java\lib	Contains the Java class libraries, primarily the file classes.zip from which the Java compiler extracts classes during compilation.
java\bin	Contains the executable Java programs, such as the compiler, debugger, and the appletviewer.
java\include	Contains C++ header files that correspond to various Java classes.

Table 1 Subdirectories the Java installation creates on your disk.

After you install the Java Developer's Kit onto your hard disk, you need to modify the two environment variables before you can use the Kit's programs:

PATH   Use the PATH command to add the directory **C:\JAVA\BIN** to your command path.

HOME   Use the SET command to assign the HOME entry to the drive and directory that contains the JAVA directory files, such as **SET HOME=C:**

Edit your system's AUTOEXEC.BAT file and update the PATH command to include the C:\JAVA\BIN directory. Next, add a SET command that assigns the HOME variable the directory path of your Java files.

Note: *Sun offers a very liberal license agreement with respect to your rights to use and distribute the Java Developer's Kit. Read the license agreement closely. In fact, we've included a copy of the agreement on the CD-ROM in a file named LICENSE.TXT.*

USING THE JAVA PROGRAMMER'S LIBRARY APPLETS

If you examine the CD-ROM disk that accompanies this book you will find a directory on the disk named JavaBook. Within the JavaBook directory, you will find subdirectories named CHAP01, CHAP02, CHAP03, and so on up to CHAP51. Each of these chapters contains the Java applets, image files, and sound files you need to run the applet presented in a specific chapter of this book. For example, Chapter 29 presents a Magnify applet that lets you use your mouse to magnify or zoom in on a screen image as shown in Figure 1.

Figure 1 Using the Magnify applet to zoom in on a screen object.

To run the Chapter 29 Magnify applet, you would perform these steps:

1. Select your CD-ROM drive as the current drive by typing the drive letter and colon and press ENTER (such as D: <ENTER >)

2. Use the CD command to change your directory to JAVABOOK\CHAP21 as shown here:

    D:\> CD \JAVABOOK\CHAP21 <ENTER>

3. Use the *appletviewer* and the HTML file *ex.html* that resides in the directory to view the applet as shown here:

    D:\JAVABOOK\CHAP21> appletviewer ex.html <ENTER>

To end the applet, simply close the applet window. Using these three steps, you can run all of this book's programs right from your CD-ROM. However, because the CD-ROM may take longer to load the image files, you may eventually want to copy the files to your hard disk.

COMPILING AN APPLET

Our goal is that you will experiment with each of the applets this book presents. When you decide to edit a Java applet, you will need to copy the applet and its support files (such as the image and sound files) to your hard disk. To better organize your files, consider creating a directory on your hard disk named *JavaBook*. Next, within the directory, use subdirectory names that correspond to the book's chapter numbers; just as we did on the CD-ROM. After you create the directory and copy the files, you can use your text editor to edit the applet source code which resides in the file that uses the *.java* extension, such as *hello_java.java*. Next, to compile your applet, use the *javac* command as shown here:

    C:\JavaBook\CHAP2> javac hello_java.java <ENTER>

After you compile the applet, you can run it using the appletviewer and the corresponding HTML file:

    C:\JavaBook\CHAP2> appletviewer ex.html <ENTER>

3

MORE INFORMATION ON JAVA PROGRAMMING

As you search the bookstore, you won't find a shortage of books that discuss Java. One of the best descriptions of the Java programming language, however, is free. You can download the *Java Language Specification*, which is a several hundred page manual that discusses the language in detail, from Sun's Web site discussed next. In addition, you will find complete descriptions of the Java API (application program interfaces) whose descriptions of the functions are several hundred pages long!

CHECK OUT SUN'S WEB SITE REGULARILY

Make it a habit to visit Sun's Web site on a regular basis: **http://java.sun.com**

From Sun's Web site, you can download the Java Developer's Kit for other systems, such as the Mac or UNIX. In addition, you will find tons of Java documentation and sample applets. If you are serious about Java programming, visit the Sun site at least once a week.

EXPERIMENT, EXPERIMENT, AND EXPERIMENT

Our goal in providing you with the applets in this book is for you to experiment with them and to put them to use. As you work through the book, we think that you will find many of the applications are a lot of fun. Take time to implement our suggested enhancements. If you come up with something cool and you put it on your Web site, let us know and we'll come check it out. We want you to use our source code within your applets. Put the code to good use.

kjamsa@jamsa.com

slalani@jamsa.com

LEARNING MORE ABOUT JAVA

Rather than spend more time in this chapter discussing reasons why you need and should want to learn Java, we thought it was better just to show you. So, let's get started. If you are new to Java, turn to Chapter 1 and get started. If you have been around the block with Java, pick your chapter of choice and dive in. Oh yeah, remember to have fun. We had a great time putting this book together for you.

CHAPTER 2

HELLO, JAVA!
DISPLAYING MESSAGES TO THE SYSTEM CONSOLE

In Chapter 1, "Introducing Java," you learned how to create and compile a Java applet. In this chapter, you will use a simple Java program to examine statements you'll encounter in each of the programs this and other Java books present. In short, this chapter lays your Java programming foundation. By the time you finish this chapter, you will understand the following key concepts:

◆ Java is an object-oriented programming language that makes extensive use of classes.

◆ A *class* is a data structure that defines an object's data and *methods* (functions that manipulate the object's data).

◆ The Java Developer's Kit (JDK) provides class libraries (called *packages*), whose objects you can quickly integrate into your applications.

◆ A Java package contains one or more related classes. For example, the *Graphics* package contains the *Color*, *Button*, *Font*, and *Image* classes.

◆ Within your programs, you use one or more *import* statements to tell the Java compiler which packages your program requires.

◆ A Java applet is a class which inherits from the *Applet* class.

◆ When a browser runs a Java applet, the first applet function the browser executes is *init*. Think of the Java *init* function as similar to the *main* function which executes first in C/C++ programs.

◆ A Java applet can display output to an applet window or to a system console.

◆ To help you debug (remove errors from) a Java applet, you may display status messages to the system console.

◆ To perform console I/O within a Java applet, you use the *System* class.

◆ To display text to the console window, a Java applet uses the *System.out* object.

UNDERSTANDING THE SYSTEM CONSOLE

As you learned in Chapter 1, to run a Java applet, you can use a Web browser or the Java *appletviewer*. Normally, you will use the *appletviewer* to test and debug your applets. When you use the *appletviewer* to run a Java applet, the applet can display its output within a window (which is most common) and also to the system console. In the days of mini computers, the system console corresponded to a printer that stood next to the computer. When programs sent messages to the console, a computer operator (a person) would read and respond. Such console messages might ask the operator to mount a magnetic tape or a specific disk drive.

For PCs running an operating system such as Windows 95 or Windows NT, the console corresponds to a window containing the command prompt within which you executed the *appletviewer*. As discussed, you will normally use display messages to the system console to help you test and debug your programs. Therefore, when you use the common browsers (such as Netscape) to run the applet, the messages the applet writes to the system console normally do not appear.

Java is an object-oriented (or class-based) programming language. Every operation a Java applet performs is based on class object. To display messages to the system console, your applets will use the *System* class.

UNDERSTANDING HELLO, JAVA!

This chapter presents the **Hello, Java!** applet, which displays messages to the system console. Our primary goal in presenting the **Hello, Java!** program is to provide you with a simple program you can test, change, and compile. Also, as your programs become more complex, you may want to display messages to the console to help you debug your program.

When you run the **Hello, Java!** applet, Java will open a window and display the console message, **Hello, Java!**, as shown in Figure 2.

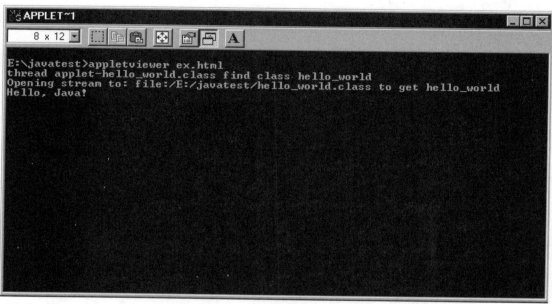

Figure 2 Displaying the Hello, Java! message to the system console.

THE HTML FILE

For users to access your Java applet as they surf the Web, you must include the applet within an HTML file. As you learned in Chapter 1, you use the HTML **applet** tag to specify the applet's class file. Use the following HTML entry to test the **Hello, Java!** applet. In this case, the **applet** tag specifies the applet's class and the applet window size (330 by 170 pixels):

```
<applet code=hello_java.class width=330 height=170> </applet>
```

Because the **Hello, Java!** applet displays its message to the console and not the applet window, the applet window will remain empty. To end the applet, simply close the applet window.

LOOKING AT HELLO, JAVA!

The following Java code implements the **Hello, Java!** applet. Even though the applet is small, it contains all the necessary pieces you will use for each Java program you create:

```
//********************************************************************
// hello_java.java
//********************************************************************

import java.applet.*;

//********************************************************************

public class hello_java extends Applet
  {
    public void init()
      {
        System.out.println("Hello, Java!");
      }
  }
```

BREAKING APART HELLO, JAVA!

Java is an object-oriented programming language based on classes. A *class* is a programming data structure within which you can group an object's data and functions (methods) that operate on the data. For example, the data within a *window* class might contain the window's size and screen location. Likewise, the methods within the *window* class might include functions that display, size, and move the window. When you create a Java applet, you can define your own classes within the applet, or you can use existing classes from a class library (*packages*) that resides within a file on your disk.

One of the features that makes the Java programming language so powerful is that you can use the objects you create for one applet within another. In addition, your Java applets can use classes written by other programmers. Programmers store existing classes within class libraries. In fact, each Java applet you create will use a special *Applet* class.

Before your Java applet can use an existing class, you must tell the Java compiler which packages the applet requires and the specific classes within each package. To tell the Java compiler which classes your applet uses, you use the Java *import* statement.

UNDERSTANDING JAVA CLASSES AND PACKAGES

Java is an object-oriented, or class-based, programming language. In short, a class is simply a data structure that groups an object's data and methods. When you create a Java applet, you can define classes within the applet itself or within a class-library-file that contains one or more class definitions. The Java documentation refers to a class library as a package. In other words, a Java package contains one or more class definitions. To use the classes a package defines within your applet, you use the *import* statement.

Every Java program usually starts with one or more *import* statements. For example, the **Hello, Java!** applet begins with the following *import* statement:

```
import java.applet.*;
```

In the case of the **Hello, Java!** applet, the *import* statement tells the Java compiler that the program will use one or more of the classes the *java.applet* package defines.

Think of an *import* statement as similar to *#include* statements in C/C++. Just as *#include* statements tell the C/C++ compiler the names of files that contain class and constant definitions, the *import* statement tells the Java compiler the names of files that contain your applet's class libraries.

USING JAVA PACKAGES

 Java packages, or class libraries, contain one or more class definitions. To save disk space, Java stores the Windows 95 version of its standard packages in a compressed file named *classes.zip*. When you compile an applet, the Java compiler knows how to extract the class libraries from this zip file. Normally, you will find this file in the **java\lib** subdirectory. Take time now to look at the package files within the **lib** subdirectory as well as in the *classes.zip* file.

Java packages use the *class* file extension, such as *java.lang.String.class*. If you unzip the *classes.zip* file, you will find files with the class extension. The class library *java.lang.String.class*, for example, will reside in the *String.class* file within the **java\lang** subdirectory.

Within your Java applets, you will make extensive use of packages provided with the Java Developer's Kit (JDK) as discussed in Chapter 1. To use a class that is defined within a package, your Java applets must specify an *import* statement. As you examine Java applets, you will find one or more *import* statements at the start of an applet. The following *import* statement, for example, informs the Java compiler that an applet uses the *AudioClip* class:

```
import java.applet.AudioClip
```

Note that like the C/C++ *#include* statement, you don't place a semicolon at the end of an *import* statement.

When you create an instance of a class, the Java compiler first looks in the current file to see if it defines the class. If the class is not defined in the current file, the compiler then examines the files that the applet has imported. If the compiler has still not found the class, the compiler then looks in other class files that reside in the same directory as the current file.

As you have learned, to use the classes a Java package defines, an applet must use one or more *import* statements. Depending on the number of a package's classes you are using, you can individually list the classes or you can use the asterisk (*) to eliminate your need to enumerate each class. For example, the following *import* statements list the classes they use:

```
import java.util.Date
import java.applet.AudioClip
```

To simplify code within the **Hello, Java!** applet, the *import* statement uses the asterisk following the *applet* package name, as opposed to the specific classes:

```
import java.applet.*
```

As you examine Java programs, you will find that most programs use the asterisk in this way to specify classes.

Defining the Applet Class

Every Java applet you create must define an *Applet* class. Normally, after an applet specifies its *import* statements, the applet will declare its *Applet* class. The *Applet* class definition specifies the class name. For example, to define its *Applet* class, the **Hello, Java!** applet uses the following statement:

```
public class hello_java extends Applet
```

In this case, the statement defines *hello_java* as the *Applet* class name. The *public* keyword tells the Java compiler that objects outside the current file can use the *hello_java* class. In this case, when the HTML browser loads the applet, the browser itself will use functions defined within the *hello_java* class. All public classes must reside in their own source file, which has the same name as the class and uses the *.java* extension.

The *extends* keyword tells the Java compiler that the *hello_java* class extends an existing class. In this case, the *hello_java* class adds either data or methods to the existing *Applet* class. Think of extending a Java class as similar to class inheritance within C++. In this case, the *hello_java* class inherits the *Applet* class data and methods. Specifically, the *hello_java* class extends the *Applet* class by providing an *init* function, which will be discussed next.

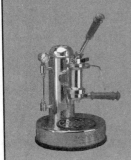

UNDERSTANDING JAVA CLASS APPLET NAMES

As you have learned, you use the HTML **applet** tag to include a Java applet within a Web page. The name you specify within the **applet** tag must match the name you specify within the statement that defines the *Applet* class name. When you compile your applet, the Java compiler will create a file whose name matches the class name you specify for the *Applet* class. In the case of the **Hello, Java!** applet (which resides in the file *hello_java.java*), the Java compiler will create a class file named *hello_java.class*.

Extending the Applet Class

After you define the *Applet* class name, you define its class-member functions. In the case of the **Hello, Java!** applet, the only class-member function is the *init* function.

As it turns out, when a Web browser (or the *appletviewer*) runs a Java applet, the applet's execution starts with the *init* function. Think of the Java *init* function as being similar to the *main* function in C/C++. Just as C/C++ programs start their execution with the *main* function, Java applets start their execution with the *init* function, which can, in turn, call other functions. However, unlike the C/C++, when the Java *init* function ends, the applet does not end.

The **Hello, Java!** applet uses the following statement to define the *init* function:

```
public void init()
```

The *public* keyword tells the Java compiler that another object (in this case, the browser) will call the *init* function from outside of the *Applet* class. The *void* keyword tells the Java compiler that the *init* function does not return any values to the browser. As you can see, the *init* function does not use any parameters. Note that, unlike C++, Java does not use the *void* keyword within the parentheses to indicate no parameters. Instead, you simply use the empty parameters, as shown.

UNDERSTANDING THE INIT FUNCTION

When a browser executes a Java applet, the first statements the browser executes reside within the *init* function. Each Java applet you create, therefore, can have an *init* function if you want to initialize your member variables. The following statements illustrate the format of an *init* function:

```
public void init()
    {
        // Statements
    }
```

The *public* keyword lets items outside of the *Applet* class (in this case, the browser) call the *init* function. The *void* keyword informs the Java compiler that the function does not return a value. In this case, the empty parameters tell you that the function does not use parameters.

Printing to the System Console

The **Hello, Java!** applet is quite simple. In fact, it uses only one statement to display the Hello, Java! message to the system console:

```
System.out.println("Hello, Java!");
```

To display the message, the applet uses the *println* member function of the *System* class *out* object. The *java.lang* package defines the *System* class. As it turns out, the Java compiler imports the *java.lang* package automatically, so you don't have to include it using import statements.

As you debug an applet, there may be times when you will need to display a numeric value, such as a loop count or user response. In such cases, you simply pass the numeric value to the *println* function as a parameter as long as you add the numeric value to a string. The *println* function, in turn, will convert the number to its corresponding ASCII characters. For example, the following statement uses *println* to display the number 5:

```
int i = 5;
System.out.println("Number of items: " + i);
```

When the applet runs, it will display the following message to the system console:

```
Number of items: 5
```

ENHANCEMENTS YOU CAN MAKE TO HELLO, JAVA!

Because the **Hello, Java!** applet is uncomplicated, it limits the enhancements you might make. However, take time now to change the message the *println* function displays to the system console. Compile the program to integrate your change and then try out the applet. Next, add an integer variable (such as the variable *i* just shown) and use the *println* function to display the value.

Putting It All Together

The **Hello, Java!** applet is easy to create and use. However, by using the applet, you learned many key concepts. In Chapter 3, you will add more classes to the *Applet* class, which will let your applet display output to the applet window, as opposed to the console window. Before you continue with Chapter 3, however, make sure you have learned the following key concepts:

- ☑ To simplify your programming, the Java developers provide class libraries that define objects you can use in your program.

- ☑ Java developers refer to class libraries as *packages*.

- ☑ All Java programs use one or more *import* statements to tell the Java compiler which pre-defined Java packages your program uses.

- ☑ Using an *import* statement, you can list the specific objects you will use from a package, or you can use the asterisk (*) to avoid having to list each object.

- ☑ Java programs that users access using HTML pages are applets.

- ☑ Each Java applet object *extends* (inherits) the base *Applet* object, which the Java compiler provides.

- ☑ All programs have a function that is the first to execute. For Java applets, the first instructions that execute reside in the *init* function of the main *Applet* object.

- ☑ Java programs normally display their output to the corresponding applet window. However, when they are run using the *appletviewer,* they can also display output to the system console.

- ☑ The console is the window that contains the command prompt from which you started the *appletviewer.* The *appletviewer* command always runs from a console. If you run the *appletviewer* using a graphical menu, the operating system opens a console window.

CHAPTER 3

HELLO, JAVA! II
DEFINING A CLASS WITHIN AN APPLET AND DISPLAYING MESSAGES TO THE APPLET WINDOW

When a Java applet runs, it can display messages to an applet window or to a system-console window. In Chapter 2, you learned how to display messages to the system console using the *System* class. Normally, you will only display messages to the system console when you debug your applet. In this chapter, you will learn how to display messages to the applet window. Each of the applets you create throughout the rest of this book will display messages to the applet window. In addition, this chapter shows you how to define a class within an applet. By the time you finish this chapter, you will understand the following key concepts:

- To define a class within an applet, you define class members within braces {} following the *class* keyword.

- Like C++ classes, Java class members are either data or methods (functions that operate on the data).

- If you precede a class definition with the *public* keyword, objects outside of the applet (such as the browser) can access the class. If you omit the *public* keyword, only classes that reside in the same source file as the class can use the class.

- After you define a class, you declare variables of the class type. However, to create an instance of the class type (an object), you must use the *new* operator.

- Like C++ classes, Java supports class-constructor functions that run each time you create a class object (using the *new* operator).

- Unlike C++, Java does not provide a *delete* operator that destroys an object you created using *new*. Instead, Java performs its own "garbage collection" to destroy unused objects.

- A class-constructor function has the same name as the class.

- When Java performs its garbage collection of unused objects, Java calls the object's class-specific *finalize* function.

- When Java recognizes that an object is no longer in use, Java destroys the object, freeing the memory the object consumed. In addition, Java automatically destroys your objects when your applet ends.

- To display text messages or drawings to the applet window, you use the *Graphics* class.

- The *drawString* function displays text messages on the applet window.

- The *paint* function redraws the applet window following a change in size, movement of the window, change in window content, and so on.

USING HELLO, JAVA! II

In Chapter 2, you learned how to display text messages to the system-console window. As you will learn, Java applets display most output to the applet window. Unlike the system-console window, the applet window is graphical, which lets you display text as well as images. To display output to the applet window, you use graphics functions that Java provides. The **Hello, Java!** II applet uses the Java graphics functions to display a message to an applet window.

When you run the **Hello, Java!** II applet, Java will open an applet window and display the message inside the window, as shown in Figure 3.

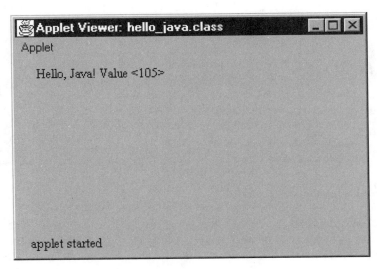

Figure 3 Displaying a message within an applet window.

Within the applet window, the **Hello, Java II!** applet displays the following message:

> Hello, Java! Value <105>

In Figure 3, the *appletviewer* displays the text "Applet" and "applet started" which appear within the window. In this case, the status message "applet started" tells you the applet has started and is currently running. As you will learn, using the *showStatus* function, your applets can change the status message to any text they desire (or to no message). The *appletviewer* displays the "Applet" text to provide you with a pull-down menu that lets you control applet characteristics. Using this pull-down menu, for example, you can reload the applet, clone a copy of the applet, or change the applet's security.

THE HTML FILE

Like all applets, you run **Hello, Java!** II from within a browser or the *appletviewer*. Use the following HTML file to access the **Hello, Java!** II applet:

```
<applet code=hello_java.class width=330 height=170> </applet>
```

The HTML applet entry is the same entry you used in Chapter 2 to access the **Hello, Java!** applet. As you can see, the entry uses the *hello_java.class* applet, whose name matches that of the **Hello, Java!** applet class you created in Chapter 2. To prevent Java from overwriting one applet with another, and to ensure your browser runs the correct applet, make sure you keep your applets in separate directories on your disk.

LOOKING AT HELLO, JAVA! II

The **Hello, Java!** II applet builds on the concepts you learned in Chapter 1:

- To use Java class libraries (packages), your applet must import the package.

- To create an applet, you extend the *Applet* class.

- Within an applet, the first function Java runs is *init*.

To write its output to the applet window, the applet uses a *Graphics* object and the *paint* function. Also, the applet defines a class, in this case named *something,* and then creates an object instance of that class type. The following code implements the **Hello, Java! II** applet:

```
//**************************************************************
// hello_java.java
//**************************************************************

import java.applet.*;
import java.awt.Graphics;


//**************************************************************

public class hello_java extends Applet
   {
     public void paint(Graphics g)
       {
         something s;
         s = new something(105);

         g.drawString("Hello, Java! Value " + s, 20, 20);
       }
   }


//**************************************************************

class something
   {
     private int value;

     //————————————————————————

     public something(int value)
       {
         this.value = value;
       }

     //————————————————————————

     public String toString()
       {
         String s;
         s = "<" + value + ">";
         return s;
       }
   }
```

WHAT HAPPENED TO THE INIT FUNCTION?

In Chapter 1, you learned that when Java runs an applet, the first function Java calls is *init*. If you examine the statements for the **Hello, Java!** II applet, however, you will find that there is no *init* function. Keep in mind, that, when you create a Java applet, you extend the *Applet* class. The *Applet* class itself defines an *init* function. If you do not specify an *init* function within your applet, Java will run the *Applet* class *init* function instead.

HOW THE HELLO, JAVA! II APPLET RUNS

As discussed, the **Hello, Java!** II applet does not provide an *init* function at which the browser can start the applet's processing. Instead, in this case, after the applet starts, the browser calls the *paint* function to update the applet window. As you can see, the **Hello, Java!** II applet redefines the *paint* function, which lets the applet display a message within the applet window. As a result, when the browser calls the *paint* function, the applet's *paint* function runs, which in turn, displays the applet's message. The applet could have also displayed its message from within the *init* function. However, if the user later sized, moved, or covered the applet window, the message would have been lost. The only way to ensure that an applet window's contents are up-to-date is to redefine the *paint* function in this way.

BREAKING APART HELLO, JAVA! II

As you learned in Chapter 2, most Java applets start with one or more *import* statements that define the class libraries (packages) they use. The **Hello, Java!** II applet uses two Java packages:

```
import java.applet.*;
import java.awt.Graphics;
```

To create an applet, you must extend the *Applet* class, defined in the *java.applet* package. Likewise, to display messages to the applet window, the applet will use the *Graphics* class, which is defined in the *java.awt.Graphics* package.

Extending the Applet

After the applet imports the *Applet* and *Graphics* packages, it extends the *Applet* class, just as the applet did in Chapter 2:

```
public class hello_java extends Applet
```

When you run a program or Java applet within a window, you can size, move, or cover the window's contents (with a different window). When you later display the window, the program, or Java applet, must redraw the window's contents. Depending on the window's contents, the steps the program must perform to redraw the window will differ. For example, in the case of the **Hello, Java!** II applet, the program must simply redisplay the text message. On the other hand, if an applet's window contains text and graphics, the program must redraw each image.

As it turns out, each time an applet must redraw its applet-window contents, the *Applet* class calls a special function named *paint*. By redefining the *paint* function, the applet can control what items it redraws within the applet window. The **Hello, Java!** II applet, for example, redefines the *paint* function to display its text message:

```
public void paint(Graphics g)
```

The *paint* function receives a parameter that is a *Graphics* object. The *Graphics* object is the graphics context and contains attributes such as the current window color, font, font size, and so on.

In addition to showing you how to display text to an applet window, this applet also shows you how to define and use a class. In this case, the applet creates a class named *something* to which it assigns the value 105 to a class member. As you can see, within the *paint* function, the applet declares an object of the *something* class, and then uses the *new* operator to create the object instance:

```
something s;
s = new something(105);
```

The first statement declares the variable *s* an object of type *something*. Unlike C++, the declaration does not create an instance of the object. Instead, you must use the *new* operator to create an instance of the object. In this case, when the applet uses *new* to create the object instance, the applet specifies the object's initial value, in this case, 105, within parenthesis. As you will learn, Java uses the class-constructor function to assign the initial value to a class member.

To declare and create an instance of the *something* class, the **Hello, Java! II** applet uses two statements. The applet, however, could have declared and created the object using only one statement, as shown here:

```
something s = new something(105);
```

Displaying the Hello, Java! Message

After the applet defines the object, it uses the *drawString* function to display the "Hello, Java!" message, as well as the object's value, to the applet window.

```
g.drawString("Hello, Java! Value " + s, 20, 20);
```

As you can see, *drawString* is a class method (function) you access using the *Graphics* object *g*. The *drawString* function uses three parameters. The first parameter specifies the *String* object, whose contents (letters, numbers, and symbols) you want to display within the applet window. The second and third parameters are integer values that specify the x-and-y coordinates within the applet window where you want the message to begin. The x-coordinate specifies the number of pixels from the applet window's left edge, and the y-coordinate specifies the number of pixels from the window's top. The x-and-y coordinates specify the starting point of the string's baseline (bottom-left corner).

In this case, *drawString's* string parameter consists of an actual string within quotes, plus the object *s*. As you will learn, the object *s* provides a special function named *toString* that converts its contents to a string. By converting the object's contents to a character string, the applet can use the *drawString* function to display the object's value (which, in this case, is 105).

Taking a Look at the something Class

The purpose in presenting the *something* class within the **Hello, Java! II** applet is to show you the format you will follow to define and use class objects within your applets. As you will see, the *something* class is quite simple, but you can use it to learn several key concepts.

To define a class within your applet, you specify the *class* keyword followed by the class name, as shown here:

```
class something
```

In this case, because the *something* class is used only within the applet, its definition did not include the *public* keyword. If you want to use the *something* class outside of the applet, you need to place the class definition within its own source file, and you need to precede the *class* keyword with the *public* keyword. The filename has to be the same as the classname, followed by the ".java" extension.

Declaring the something Class Data Members

As you know, a class is a data structure that contains one or more members. Class members are either data or methods (functions that operate on the data). The *something* class, for example, has only one data member and it is named *value*:

```
private int value;
```

In this case, the *value* member stores an integer value. The *private* keyword that precedes the variable's name tells the Java compiler that only member functions of the *something* class can access the *value* member.

Declaring the something Class Methods

Following the class-member variable declaration, you will find the class-member functions. In this case, the *something* class defines two functions: the constructor function *something*, and the *toString* function that converts an object's integer value to a character string for display.

When you create class objects, you can initialize member variables using a *constructor function*. A constructor function is a special class function whose purpose is to initialize class-member variables among other things. The constructor function always has the same name as the class. For example, the constructor function for the *something* class is named *something*. Also, the constructor function never returns a value to its caller, and is always declared *public*. The following statements define the constructor function for the *something* class:

```
public something(int value)
   {
     this.value = value;
   }
```

In this applet, the constructor function receives an integer parameter that the constructor assigns to the *value* class member. The applet passes the value to the constructor when you create the class object by using the *new* operator:

```
s = new something(105);
```

As you can see, the constructor function assigns the value 105 to the *value* member. Note that, in this case, the constructor parameter is named *value,* and the class member to which the constructor is assigning the value is also named *value*. When parameter and class member names conflict in this way, you need to distinguish between them. One way to distinguish between the parameter and class member names is simply to change the parameter name, as shown here:

```
public something(int initial_value)
   {
     value = initial_value;
   }
```

A second way to distinguish between the parameter and class-member names is to use the *this* keyword. When you specify the *this* keyword followed by a period and a member name, the Java compiler knows you are referring to the class member variable.

Before the Java *Graphics* functions can display an object's value, the value must be a character string. As it turns out, when a Java function needs an object's value as a *String* object, the function calls the object's *toString* function. The *toString* function, in turn, converts the object's value to a *String* object and returns the *String* to the calling function. Within your class definition, you must define the *toString* function. The following *toString* function, for example, builds a *String* by placing the *something* class *value* member's value within left and right brackets, such as <105>, and then returns the *String* to the calling function:

```
public String toString()
  {
    String s;
    s = "<" + value + ">";
    return s;
  }
```

As you can see, the function first declares a *String* variable *s*. Next, the function assigns to the string object *s* a left bracket, the value, and a right bracket. Using the *return* statement, *toString* returns the string to the calling function. Note that the *toString* function does not receive any parameters. Remember, unlike C++ functions that use the *void* keyword to indicate they do not receive parameters, Java functions simply use the empty parentheses.

As you will recall, the *something* class member variable *value* is type *int*. As it turns out, Java provides a built-in equivalent of a *toString* function for the fundamental types, such as *int*, *float*, and so on. In the case of the *toString* function, when it uses the variable *value* within the following *String* expression, Java uses its built-in functions to convert the variable's value from *int* to *String*:

```
s = "<" + value + ">";
```

UNDERSTANDING DESTRUCTOR FUNCTIONS

When you create an instance of a class object by using the *new* operator, Java calls the class-constructor function. Using the constructor function, your applet can initialize class-member variables. As you learned, the constructor function uses the same name as the class, is declared *public*, and does not return a value:

```
public something(int initial_value)
  {
    value = initial_value;
  }
```

Unlike C++, Java does not support destructor functions. Instead of letting the programmer manage memory (or in the opinion of many "forcing" the programmer to be responsible for memory management), Java performs all memory management. When Java determines that an applet no longer uses a specific object, Java discards the object. If one of your classes has processing it absolutely must perform before Java discards an object, you can define a *finalize* function that performs the class-specific processing. Unfortunately, because Java decides when to perform its garbage collection, you don't know when the function will run and in what order (as compared to other objects).

ENHANCEMENTS YOU CAN MAKE TO HELLO, JAVA! II

Although the **Hello, Java! II** applet is still quite simple, you can experiment with the applet to better understand classes and applet windows. To get a better understanding of how Java handles text strings within an applet window, change the x and y coordinates the applet passes to the *drawString* function. Also, modify the string to make it bigger than the window's width and see what happens. Then, change the *toString* function to convert the number into a readable format; for example, given the value 105, the function would return a *String* containing "one hundred and five."

PUTTING IT ALL TOGETHER

The **Hello, Java! II** applet has shown you how to display text within an applet window, and how to add a class to your applet. In Chapter 4, you will learn how to use fonts within an applet window. Before you continue with Chapter 4, however, make sure that you understand the following key concepts:

- ☑ To define a class within an applet, you define class members within braces, following the *class* keyword. To use the class only within the applet, you do not have to precede the class with the *public* keyword.

- ☑ After you define a class, you declare variables of the class type and then use the *new* operator to create an instance of the class type (an object).

- ☑ Like C++ classes, Java supports a class-constructor function that runs each time you create a class object (by using the *new* operator).

- ☑ A class-constructor function has the same name as the class. Constructor functions are *public* and do not return a value. Constructor functions may receive multiple parameters.

- ☑ Java does not provide *delete* operator, as does C++, to destroy objects when you no longer need them. Instead, Java performs its own garbage collection, deleting objects when they are no longer in use. When Java destroys an object, Java runs the corresponding *finalize* function.

- ☑ To display text messages or drawings to the applet window, you use the *Graphics* class.

- ☑ The *drawString* function displays text messages on the applet window.

- ☑ The *paint* function redraws the applet window following a change in size, movement of the window, change in window content, and so on.

- ☑ The *toString* method contains code to convert an object to a string. Java automatically calls this method when you add an object to a string.

- ☑ A *Graphics* object contains the current graphics context, which includes such attributes as the current font, window size, and window color.

- ☑ Whenever the applet redraws its window, the applet calls the *paint* function.

- ☑ Using the *Graphics* class *drawString* method, you can display a text message within an applet window.

CHAPTER 4

FONT LIST
LISTING THE AVAILABLE SYSTEM FONTS

In Chapter 3, you learned how to add a class to a Java applet and how to display output to an applet window. Using the *Graphics* class *drawString* function, your applet displayed the "Hello, Java!" message by using the default font, font size, and color. In this chapter, you will learn how to select the font, change the font's size, and set its color. Across the World Wide Web, Java applets make extensive use of fonts. By the time you finish this chapter, you will understand the following key concepts:

♦ Java applets often need to determine information about the current system. To help applets get the information they need, Java provides the *Toolkit* class.

♦ Using the *Toolkit* class *getFontList*, the **Font List** applet determines the available system fonts.

♦ To define a specific font, font size, and font attribute (such as italic), you create a *Font* object. Then, using the *Graphics* class *setFont* method, you select the font for use.

♦ Using the *Graphics* class *setColor* method, you can choose the color you desire.

♦ An array is a data structure that can hold multiple items of the same type. In Java, you do not specify the array size when you declare an array.

♦ Like C/C++, Java uses the value zero for the first array index.

♦ The Java *for* statement is identical to that of C/C++.

♦ The *final* keyword before a variable declaration tells the Java compiler that the variable's value will not change.

USING FONT LIST

If you are using Windows or a similar operating environment, you may have many fonts installed on your system. Unfortunately, Java applications can't access your system fonts. Instead, Java provides a set of default fonts your applets can use to display text. Depending on your version of the Java interpreter, the fonts on your system may differ slightly from those of another user. To help you identify the fonts you have available, you can run this chapter's **Font List** applet. When you run the **Font List** applet, Java will open an applet window, and within the window, will list your system's available fonts, as shown in Figure 4.1.

Figure 4.1 Displaying a list of the fonts available on the system.

Because the current Java implementations only support a limited number of fonts, the **Font List** will only display a limited number of font names. In fact, if your list of Java fonts becomes long, you will need to change the applet to display the font names using a smaller font so the applet can fit more font names into the applet window.

In addition to writing the font list to the applet window, the **Font List** applet also lists the fonts to a system-console window, as shown in Figure 4.2. As the applet lists a font to the system-console, the applet precedes the font name with its corresponding number.

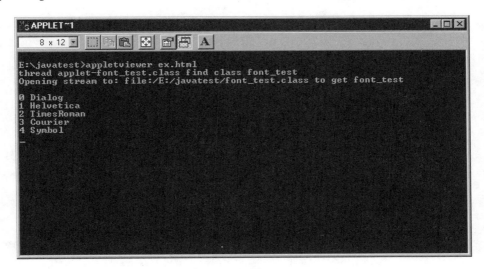

Figure 4.2 The debug statements listing the fonts retrieved by the getFontList function.

THE HTML FILE

To access the **Font List** applet, use the following HTML entry:

```
<applet code=font_list.class width=330 height=170> </applet>
```

LOOKING AT FONT LIST

As you learned in Chapter 3, using the *drawString* function, your applets can display text messages to the applet window. The **Font List** applet uses the *drawString* function to write each font's name to the applet window. In fact, before the applet writes a font name, the applet selects the corresponding font, so the applet can use it to write the font name. The applet writes each name to the applet window using a 30-point font.

To start, the applet uses the Java *Toolkit* class to obtain the list of fonts available on your system. Then, the applet uses a *for* statement to loop through an array that contains the font names. The following code implements the **Font List** applet:

```
//*************************************************************
// font_list.java
//*************************************************************

import java.applet.*;
import java.awt.Graphics;
```

```
import java.awt.Color;
import java.awt.Toolkit;
import java.awt.Font;

//***********************************************************************

public class font_list extends Applet
  {
    final int fontsize = 30;

    //───────────────────────────────────

    public void paint(Graphics g)
      {
        Toolkit toolkit = Toolkit.getDefaultToolkit();

        String fontlist[] = toolkit.getFontList();

        System.out.println("");

        for (int i = 0; i < fontlist.length; i++)
          {
            System.out.println(i + " " + fontlist[i]);

            Font font = new Font(fontlist[i], i%4, fontsize);
              // The second parameter selects one of four available styles:
              //     PLAIN, BOLD, ITALIC, BOLD+ITALIC

            g.setFont(font);
            g.setColor(Color.blue);
            g.drawString(fontlist[i], 20, fontsize*(i+1));
          }
      }
  }
```

BREAKING APART FONT LIST

The code for the **Font List** applet starts by importing several packages provided in the Java Developers Kit (JDK):

```
import java.applet.*;
import java.awt.Graphics;
import java.awt.Color;
import java.awt.Toolkit;
import java.awt.Font;
```

The **Font List** applet uses the *applet* and *Graphics* packages you have used in previous chapters. In addition, the applet uses the *Color*, *Toolkit*, and *Font* packages. As you may note, four of the packages are defined in the *java.awt* package (awt is an acronym for *Abstract Windowing Toolkit*). You could, for simplicity, replace the last four *import* statements with the following statement:

```
import java.awt.*;
```

As you will remember, using the asterisk (*) tells the Java compiler that your applet will use one, some, or all of the classes defined in *java.awt*.

Extending the Applet

Following the import statements, the applet extends the *Applet* class:

```
public class font_list extends Applet
```

In this case, the applet name is *font_list*. As before, the applet inherits attributes from the *Applet* class.

As discussed, the **Font List** applet displays the names of your available fonts within the applet window. To display the font names, the applet uses a 30-point font. The **Font List** applet uses the *fontsize* variable to store the font size:

```
final int fontsize = 30;
```

The *final* keyword tells the Java compiler that the value of this attribute is final, or in other words, constant. When you declare a variable as final, your applet cannot later change the variable's value. When you work with fonts, you specify their size in terms of points. Each point corresponds to 1/72 of an inch. A 72-point font, therefore, is a 1-inch font. A 36-point font is half an inch, and so on.

As you will recall from Chapter 3, when an applet needs to redraw its applet window, the applet calls the *paint* function. By redefining the *paint* function, an applet can control which elements are redrawn. The **Font List** applet redefines the *paint* function, so that the function rewrites the names of the system fonts to the window each time the window is redrawn, as shown here:

```
public void paint(Graphics g)
```

As in **Hello, Java! II**, this applet uses the *Graphics* object *g* to store the graphics content (window size, current font, and so on).

To determine the available fonts, the applet uses the *Toolkit* class. The *Toolkit* class has many methods. For the **List Fonts** applet, however, you need only to retrieve the default toolkit, as shown here:

```
Toolkit toolkit = Toolkit.getDefaultToolkit();
```

As you can see, the statement declares an object *toolkit* of type *Toolkit* and assigns it to the value returned by the *getDefaultToolkit* method of the *Toolkit* class. There is only one toolkit per system, and the *getDefaultToolKit* method gives the applet access to it.

UNDERSTANDING THE TOOLKIT CLASS

The *Toolkit* class is an abstract class that you can use to get information about your system, such as the available fonts, screen resolution, and screen size. To access the *Toolkit* object, your applet must call the *getDefaultToolkit* function, using the function's return as a reference to the object. In addition to the *getFontList* function used in the **Font List** applet, you may want to use the *getScreenResolution* function which returns the screen's resolution dots per inch, or the *getScreenSize* function that returns a *Dimension* object, whose member variables specify the screen's width and height.

WHY YOU DID NOT NEED TO USE THE NEW OPERATOR

The **Font List** applet declares the variable *toolkit* as a *Toolkit* object, and then assigns to the variable the value returned by the *Toolkit.getDefaultToolkit()* method. In Chapter 3, you learned that to create an object, you must first declare the object variable and then use the *new* operator to create an object instance. In this case, however, you are not creating a new object. Instead, you are using the existing *Toolkit* object. Therefore, your application does not use the *new* operator. Instead, your applet simply assigns the function value to the object *toolkit*, which, in turn, lets the object access the toolkit.

After the applet has access to the toolkit, the applet uses the toolkit's *getFontList* method to obtain the list of available fonts:

```
String fontlist[] = toolkit.getFontList();
```

The *getFontList* method returns an array of strings. The applet assigns the strings to the variable *fontlist,* which is an array of type *String*. When you declare an array in Java, you normally don't specify the size of the array! Instead, the **Font List** applet relies on the *getFontList* method to fill the array properly. The applet will use the array's *length* member variable to determine the number of elements the array contains. For example, the applet uses the following *for* statement to loop through the font names that the array contains:

```
for (int i = 0; i < fontlist.length; i++)
```

The Java *for* loop is exactly the same as it is in C/C++. Note that arrays in Java, as in C/C++, are accessed from index 0.

Within the *for* loop, the applet first writes a debug statement to the console:

```
System.out.println(i + " " + fontlist[i]);
```

As you can see, the applet writes the font's number and a space, followed by the font name. Remember that when you add different objects to a string, Java converts the items to a string before performing the operation. As discussed, before the applet writes a font name to the applet window, the applet selects a corresponding font. To select a font, the applet creates a *Font* object, as shown here:

```
Font font = new Font(fontlist[i], i%4, size);
```

As you can see, the applet uses the *new* operator to create a font-object instance. The first parameter to the *Font* constructor is the name of the font. The second parameter specifies the font style: PLAIN, BOLD, ITALIC, and BOLD with ITALIC. To specify a font style, you can use the values 0, 1, 2, and 3, or you can specify the attribute names: *Font.PLAIN*, *Font.BOLD*, or *Font.ITALIC*. You can also combine the names, such as *Font.BOLD+Font.ITALIC*.

After the applet defines the font attributes, it uses the *setFont* function to change the graphics context:

```
g.setFont(font);
```

In a similar way, the applet uses the *setColor* method to change the current font color to blue:

```
g.setColor(Color.blue);
```

In this case, the applet uses the *blue* attribute of the *Color* class. As of this writing, the *Color* class contains thirteen color attributes: *white, lightGray, gray, darkGray, black, red, pink, orange, yellow, green, magenta, cyan,* and *blue.* You can create other colors by declaring a variable of the *Color* class and using the constructor to pass RGB values in the range 0-255. For example, the following statement defines a *Color* object by combining red, green, and blue colors:

```
Color color = new Color (255, 100, 50);
```

If you are only using one color, you move the *setColor* function call outside of the *for* loop. After setting the color within the graphics context, the applet can print the font name using the *drawString* function:

```
g.drawString(fontlist[i], 20, fontsize*(i+1));
```

In this case, the applet calculates the y-coordinate by using the font size and a multiple of the current index plus one. The applet adds one to the current index to compensate for the fact that Java array-index values start at zero.

ENHANCEMENTS YOU CAN MAKE TO FONT LIST

The **Font List** applet presents you with several new functions with which you can experiment. For example, you might vary the font-name messages by changing the message size, style, position, or color. In addition, you might create your own *Color* objects that use different combinations of red, green, and blue.

PUTTING IT ALL TOGETHER

The **Font List** applet presents many of the functions you will use to display text and to manage fonts. In Chapter 5, you will use the *drawString* function to create a marquee message that moves from right to left across your screen. Before you continue with Chapter 5, however, make sure that you understand the following key concepts:

☑ To help your applets learn specifics about the current system, Java provides the *ToolKit* class.

☑ By creating a *Font* object, an applet can tell the graphics context which font it wants to use.

☑ Using the *Color* class, you can define your own colors by combining values of red, green, and blue colors.

☑ An array is a data structure that can hold multiple values of the same type. For example, the **Font List** applet used a string array to hold the available system fonts.

☑ Like C++, the first index value for a Java array is zero.

☑ The *final* keyword lets an applet create constants whose values cannot change.

CHAPTER 5

SIMPLE MARQUEE
DISPLAYING A MARQUEE MESSAGE

In Chapter 4, you learned how to select a font, change the font's point size, and set the font color. You also learned how to make your own colors, use the *for* loop, and declare a *String* array. In this chapter, you will learn about threads, exceptions, and using a timed delay. Although the code for the **Simple Marquee** applet is quite easy, the code presents several advanced concepts. By the time you finish this chapter, you will understand the following key concepts:

◆ A Java applet consists of a set of instructions the browser executes to run the applet.

◆ A thread defines a set of instructions the browser can execute at the same time it runs the applet.

◆ By using one or more threads, a Java applet can perform two or more operations at the same time.

◆ A Java applet that uses more than one thread is a *multithreaded* applet.

◆ To create a thread which runs the applet's *run* function, the applet must support the *Runnable* interface. When you use the *Runnable* interface for a class, you tell Java that the class contains a *run* function.

◆ To create a thread object, you use the *Thread* class that is defined in the *java.lang* package, which Java imports automatically.

◆ To start a thread's execution, you call the thread's *start* method. The *start* method, in turn, will call the thread's *run* method, which you define within your applet. Unlike an *Applet* object, *Thread* objects do not have an *init* function which is executed first.

◆ The **Simple Marquee** applet uses the *Thread.sleep* method to create a time delay. Using the time delay, the applet controls how fast the marquee scrolls across the window.

◆ If the *Thread.sleep* method is interrupted during a time delay, it "throws" an exception the applet can detect using the *try* and *catch* statements.

USING SIMPLE MARQUEE

If you have ever stood in Times Square in New York, or watched the Times Square New Year's party, you may have seen the marquee message board, which constantly displays the latest news and information. In a similar way, the **Simple Marquee** applet displays a message that moves across the applet window from right to left.

When you run the **Simple Marquee** applet, Java will open a window and display the marquee, as shown in Figures 5.1 and 5.2. As you can see, **Simple Marquee** scrolls the "Hello, Java!" message across the applet window from right to left.

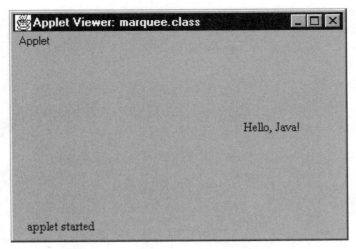

Figure 5.1 *First snapshot of the marquee.*

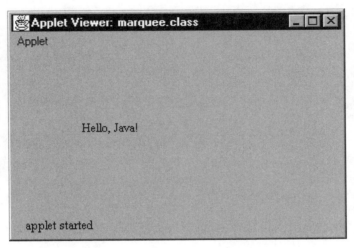

Figure 5.2 *Second snapshot of the marquee.*

The HTML File

To access the **Simple Marquee** applet, use the following HTML entry:

```
<applet code=marquee.class width=330 height=170> </applet>
```

Looking at Simple Marquee

In your previous applets, after you used the *drawString* method to display output to the applet window, the applet stopped. In other words, the applets did not have dynamic content that constantly changed. The **Simple Marquee** applet, on the other hand, runs constantly during the life of the applet to keep the marquee. The following code implements the **Simple Marquee** applet:

```
//********************************************************************
// marquee.java
//********************************************************************

import java.applet.*;
import java.awt.Graphics;

//********************************************************************

public class marquee extends Applet implements Runnable
  {
    int x = 0;
    int y = 0;
    int width = 0;

    Thread my_thread = null;

    //────────────────────────────────────────

    public void init()
      {
        x = size().width;
        y = size().height / 2;
        width = x;
      }

    //────────────────────────────────────────

    public void start()
      {
        my_thread = new Thread(this);
        my_thread.start();
      }

    //────────────────────────────────────────

    public void run()
      {
        while(true)
          {
            repaint();
            x -= 10;
            if(x < 0)
              x = width;

            try
              {
                Thread.sleep(100);
              }
            catch(InterruptedException e)
              {
              }
          }
      }
```

```
//————————————————————————

public void paint(Graphics g)
  {
    g.drawString("Hello, Java!", x, y);
  }
}
```

BREAKING APART SIMPLE MARQUEE

The **Simple Marquee** applet imports two packages. The first package contains the *Applet* class which you use to create an applet. The second package contains the *Graphics* class, which the applet uses to display the marquee message to the applet window:

```
import java.applet.*;
import java.awt.Graphics;
```

As it turns out, the applet also uses a third class: the *Thread* class which the *java.lang* package defines. When you compile your applet, the Java compiler includes the *java.lang* package automatically.

Extending the Applet

The applet declaration for **Simple Marquee** differs a little from what you have seen in the previous applets:

```
public class marquee extends Applet implements Runnable
```

As you can see, the applet includes the *implements* keyword and the *Runnable* interface name. In short, the applet needs the *Runnable* interface to support threads. The *Runnable* interface, for example, tells Java that your class contains a *run* function. Unlike C++, Java does not support multiple inheritance—which lets an object inherit attributes from two or more classes. However, Java does provide a way for you to use interfaces to define multiple classes which implement the same functions.

An *interface* is an abstract class definition, which means that you cannot declare a variable of this class. Instead, you define a class that *implements* this interface. In other words, when you define an *interface*, you give a name to a set of functions which are defined in the interface. In this applet, you will implement the *Runnable* interface.

As discussed, the *Runnable* interface tells Java the class has a *run* function. As such, to implement the *Runnable* interface, your applet must define the *run* function.

As you have learned, within a Java applet you may find an *init* and a *start* function. Java calls the *init* function first and when *init* is done, Java calls *start*. When your applet uses *Thread* objects, on the other hand, your applet must call the *Thread* object's *start* function, which, in turn, will call the *Thread* object's *run* function. Unlike Java applets, *Thread* objects do not have an *init* function that executes first.

At the start of a class definition, you will normally find the class-member variables. The *marquee* class declares three variables that specify the marquee's x-and-y window location, as well as the window width. In addition, the class declares the *Thread* object *my_thread*:

```
int x = 0;
int y = 0;

int width = 0;

Thread my_thread = null;
```

The init Function

As you have learned, the first function that executes within an applet is *init*. The **Simple Marquee** applet uses the *init* function to initialize the class member variables:

```
public void init()
  {
    x = size().width;
    y = size().height / 2;
    width = x;
  }
```

The *init* function uses the *size* function to get the width and height of the window. The *size* function is defined in the *Component* class. The applet can use the *size* function without an object (such as *some_object.size().width*) because *size* is defined in one of the parent classes to the *Applet* class. In other words, the *Applet* class inherits the *size* method from the *Component* class. Figure 5.3 illustrates the inheritance order that leads to the *Applet* class.

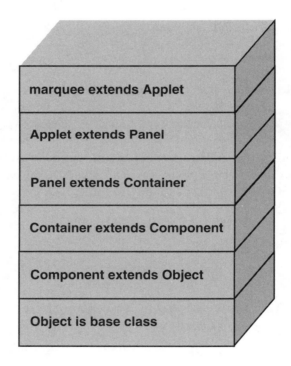

marquee extends Applet

Applet extends Panel

Panel extends Container

Container extends Component

Component extends Object

Object is base class

Figure 5.3 *The inheritance chain that leads to the Applet class.*

The *size* method returns an object of type *Dimension* which contains two attributes: *width* and *height*.

The *init* function sets the *x* variable to the width of the window, placing the message at the window's right edge. The function then assigns the *y* variable to half the height of the window, placing the message in the center of the applet window. Because the *x* variable already contains the applet-window width, the *init* function uses the *x* variable's value instead of calling the *size* function for a third time.

IMPLEMENTING A RUNNABLE INTERFACE

To run an applet as a thread, it must implement the *Runnable* interface. In short, that means the applet must include a *run* function. To start a *Thread* object, your applet calls the object's *start* function, which, in turn, calls the *run* function that you define within your applet. In the case of the **Simple Marquee** applet, the *run* function is the "work horse" which loops repeatedly to display the marquee message.

The start Function

As you have learned, the *init* function is the first code within your applet that Java runs. After the *init* function ends, Java calls the *start* function:

```
public void start()
  {
    my_thread = new Thread(this);
    my_thread.start();
  }
```

As you can see, the *start* function uses the *new* operator to create a *Thread* object. By passing the *Thread*-class constructor the parameter value *this*, the applet creates a thread that corresponds to the *marquee* class. Remember, the *this* keyword points to the current object. Then, the function starts the thread by calling the *Thread*-class *start* function. As discussed, the *Thread* object's *start* function, in turn, will call the *run* function which you define within your applet.

Note: *If you had not implemented the* **Runnable** *interface, Java would not let you create a new* **Thread** *object with the "this" parameter and the compiler would generate an error.*

The run Function

The *run* function is where most of the **Simple Marquee** applet's work gets done. The *Thread* object's *start* function calls the *run* function, which in turn, starts the *while* loop, which continually moves the marquee message across the screen. The function defines the *while* loop to run forever, or at least until the applet ends:

```
public void run()
  {
    while(true)
      {
        repaint();
        x -= 10;
        if(x < 0)
          x = width;

        try
          {
            Thread.sleep(100);
```

```
                }
            catch (InterruptedException e)
                {
                }
        }
    }
```

Within the loop, the *repaint* function insures the applet window's contents are up-to-date. Each time the loop calls the *repaint* function, *repaint,* in turn, calls the *paint* method. Within the *paint* method, the applet simply redraws the marquee message at its new coordinates. As you can see, the loop also decrements the *x* variable by 10 pixels. If *x* is less than zero (it has reached the left edge of the applet window), the loop resets *x* to the original window width (to the right-window edge).

Next, using the *Thread.sleep* method, the function delays its execution for one tenth-of-a-second. The *sleep* method argument specifies the number of milliseconds to sleep. If the *sleep* function is interrupted it throws an exception of type *InterruptedException.*

In Java, your applet must catch all exceptions. Therefore, you must place the code that contains exceptions inside the *try* block, which is followed by *catch* statements. Each *catch* statement must specify the statements you want the applet to perform, should the exception occur. In the case of the **Simple Marquee** applet, the *catch* statement catches and then ignores the interrupt exception. Depending on your applet's code, there may be times when you have multiple *catch* statements:

```
try
  {
    // statements that may generate the exception
  }
catch (object1)
  {
    // statements to process the exception
  }
catch (object2)
  {
    // statements to process the exception
  }
```

In this case, the code tests for two different exceptions. When the exception occurs, Java will match the exception to the corresponding *catch* statement and will execute the statements that correspond to the *catch.*

Note: *Exceptions are not unique to Java. In fact, the use of exceptions is beginning to grow within C++ programs. For a detailed description of exceptions, turn to the book* **Rescued by C++, Second Edition***, Jamsa Press, 1996.*

The paint Function

Finally, the *paint* function displays the marquee message as it moves across the window. As previously discussed, the *run* function's *while* loop calls the *repaint* function with each iteration. The *repaint* function, in turn, calls *paint.* As you can see, the function uses the class variables *x* and *y* to specify the message's screen position:

```
public void paint (Graphics g)
  {
    g.drawString("Hello, Java!", x, y);
  }
```

ENHANCEMENTS YOU CAN MAKE TO SIMPLE MARQUEE

Because of its use of threads, the **Simple Marquee** applet is more complex than your previous applets. To enhance the applet, first change the message. Next, experiment with the *Thread.sleep* function to change the rate at which the marquee moves across the window. Lastly, change the y-coordinate with each iteration of the loop so that the marquee moves up and down as well as left to right. If you are an advanced Java programmer, you might add a second thread that wakes up to change the message color every 60 seconds.

PUTTING IT ALL TOGETHER

The **Simple Marquee** applet introduced you to threads and exceptions. In Chapter 6, you will change the marquee applet to get information, such as the message text, from the HTML file. Before you continue with Chapter 6, however, make sure that you understand the following key concepts:

☑ A thread defines a set of instructions the browser can execute at the same time it runs the applet. You create thread objects within your applet using the *Thread* class.

☑ By using one or more threads, a Java applet can perform two or more operations at the same time.

☑ To create a thread object, you use the *Thread* class that is defined in the *java.lang* package, which Java imports automatically.

☑ To run your applet as a thread, you must implement the *Runnable* interface, and define a *run* function.

☑ After the *init* function ends, the browser calls the *start* function which you can use to start your thread. The thread's *start* function, in turn, calls the *run* method.

☑ An exception is an error that your program can detect and then process accordingly. To detect an exception within your program, you must use *try* and *catch* statements.

☑ Using the *Thread.sleep* function, your applets can create a time delay. The function's parameter specifies the number of milliseconds you want it to sleep.

☑ If the *Thread.sleep* function is interrupted it throws the *InterruptedException* exception that your applet must catch.

Chapter 6

Modifiable Marquee
Controlling the Marquee Using HTML

In Chapter 5, you learned how to create thread objects and to use the thread's *start* and *run* functions. In addition, you also learned about exceptions and how to use the *Thread.sleep* function to create a time delay. In this chapter, you will learn how to access settings specified in the HTML file, which contains the applet. Using such HTML settings, you can obtain the marquee text, the font information, the time delay that specifies how fast the marquee message moves across the applet window, and much more. In short, by getting information from the HTML file in this way, you can create generic applets that end users can easily customize. By the time you finish this chapter, you will understand the following key concepts:

- Using the **param** entry, you can place parameters for a Java applet within an HTML file.

- Java always treats the parameter values you specify within an HTML file as character strings.

- Within your applet, you access the HTML parameters using the *getParameter* function.

- If the HTML file does not define a specified parameter, the *getParameter* function returns the *null* value.

- To convert an integer parameter from its string representation, your applet uses the *Integer.parseInt* function.

Using Modifiable Marquee

At first glance, the **Modifiable Marquee** applet seems very similar to the **Simple Marquee** applet that you examined in Chapter 5. When you run the **Modifiable Marquee** applet, Java will open a window and display the marquee, as shown in Figures 6.1 and 6.2.

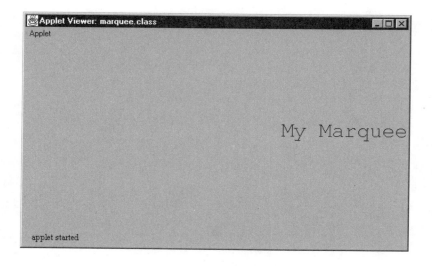

Figure 6.1 *First snapshot of the modifiable marquee.*

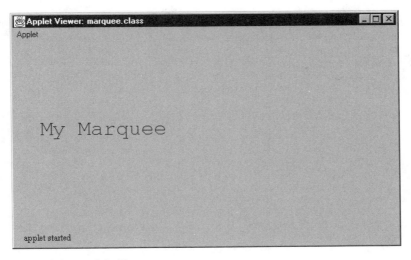

Figure 6.2 *Second snapshot of the modifiable marquee.*

The difference between the two marquee applets, however, occurs behind the scenes. By using **param** entries within the HTML file, the user can control the message the applet displays, as well as the font, and font size.

The HTML File

Because the HTML for the **Modifiable Marquee** applet includes the param entries, this HTML is slightly more complex than those you have seen so far:

```
<applet code=marquee.class width=330 height=170>
<param name=message        value="My Marquee">
<param name=font           value=Courier>
<param name=point size     value=30> </applet>
```

Looking at Modifiable Marquee

In Chapter 5, the **Simple Marquee** applet used message-text, a font, and a font size that the user could not change without editing and compiling the Java applet. In other words, each of these items were hard-coded into the program's source code. Although the **Simple Marquee** applet worked, it is difficult, at best, for an end user to change that applet.

In contrast, the **Modifiable Marquee** applet gets this information from the HTML file. Therefore, an end user can change the applet's text, font, and font size by simply editing the HTML entries. The following code implements the **Modifiable Marquee** applet:

```
//**********************************************************
// marquee.java
//**********************************************************

import java.applet.*;
import java.awt.Graphics;
import java.awt.Font;


//**********************************************************
```

```java
public class marquee extends Applet implements Runnable
  {
    int x = 0;
    int y = 0;
    int width = 0;

    Thread my_thread = null;

    String message = "Hello, Java!";
    String font_to_use = "TimesRoman";
    int point_size = 10;

    //————————————————————

    public void init()
      {
        get_defaults();

        String parameter;

        parameter = getParameter("MESSAGE");
        if (parameter != null)
          message = parameter;

        parameter = getParameter("FONT");
        if (parameter != null)
          font_to_use = parameter;

        parameter = getParameter("POINT_SIZE");
        if (parameter != null)
          point_size = Integer.parseInt(parameter);
      }

    //————————————————————

    public void start()
      {
        my_thread = new Thread(this);
        my_thread.start();
      }

    //————————————————————

    void get_defaults()
      {
        y = size().height / 2;
        width = size().width;
        if (x > width)
          x = width;
      }

    //————————————————————

    public void run()
```

```
        {
          while (true)
            {
              repaint();
              x -= 10;
              if (x < 0)
                x = width;

              try
                {
                  Thread.sleep(100);
                }
              catch (InterruptedException e)
                {
                }
            }
        }

      //————————————————————————

      public void paint(Graphics g)
        {
          get_defaults();
          Font font = new Font(font_to_use, Font.PLAIN, point_size);
          g.setFont(font);
          g.drawString(message, x, y);
        }
    }
```

BREAKING APART MODIFIABLE MARQUEE

Because the **Modifiable Marquee** applet lets the user control the font and font size, the applet imports the *java.awt.Font* package, which was not required by the **Simple Marquee** applet:

```
import java.applet.*;
import java.awt.Graphics;
import java.awt.Font;
```

The Applet

As you can see, like the **Simple Marquee** applet, the **Modifiable Marquee** applet extends the *Applet* class and implements a *Runnable* interface:

```
public class marquee extends Applet implements Runnable
```

In addition to specifying the message's x and y coordinates and the applet window width, and declaring a *Thread* object, the applet also declares and initializes variables for which the applet will search the HTML file for user-specified values:

```
int x = 0;
int y = 0;
```

```
   int width = 0;

   Thread my_thread = null;

   String message = "Hello, world";
   String font_to_use = "TimesRoman";
   int point_size = 10;
```

As you can see, the code specifies default values for variables whose values the user can modify using the HTML param entries: *message* contains the marquee message; *font_to_use* contains the font with which the applet displays the message; and *point_size* contains the point size at which applet displays the message.

The init Function

As you have learned, the *init* function is the applet's first function to execute. Within the *init* function, an applet will normally initialize key variables. In the case of the **Modifiable Marquee** applet, the *init* function uses the *getParameter* function to get user-specified values from the HTML file:

```
public void init()
  {
    get_defaults();

    String parameter;

    parameter = getParameter("MESSAGE");
    if(parameter != null)
      message = parameter;

    parameter = getParameter("FONT");
    if (parameter != null)
      font_to_use = parameter;

    parameter = getParameter("POINT_SIZE");
    if (parameter != null)
      point_size = Integer.parseInt(parameter);
  }
```

The *init* function first calls the applet-defined *get_defaults* function, which initializes the message's x and y coordinates, as well as the applet-window width. Then, the function declares the *parameter* variable as a *String*. The function will use this variable with the *getParameter* function to get each of the parameter values from the HTML file. As briefly discussed, Java treats each of the parameter values in the HTML file as a character string.

The *init* function first uses the *getParameter* function to determine if the user has specified a value for the marquee message. In this case, the argument the applet passes to the *getParameter* function must match the parameter name that appears in the HTML file's param entry (in this case, MESSAGE). If the parameter exists in the HTML file, the *getParameter* function will return the value as a *String* object. If the parameter does not exist, the parameter will return the null value. Note that the parameter name is not case sensitive.

Next, the *init* function uses the *getParameter* function to get the value for the *FONT* parameter.

Because the *POINT_SIZE* parameter is an integer value, the applet must convert the string value that the *getParameter* function returns to an integer using the *Integer.parseInt* method:

```
   point_size = Integer.parseInt(parameter);
```

In this case, the *Integer.parseInt* method converts the *String* parameter to an *int* value, which the applet, in turn, assigns to the variable *point_size*.

Do not confuse the type *Integer* with the fundamental *int* type. The *Integer* object is one of the objects called *wrappers* by Java. The reason for having wrappers is to have objects that not only contain the fundamental objects, but also include special conversion functions. In addition to the *Integer* object, Java implements the following types as wrappers:

- Boolean
- Character
- Double
- Float
- Integer
- Long

Notice that some of these wrappers differ from the fundamental types only by an uppercase first letter. For example, *Float* is the wrapper object, whereas *float* is a fundamental type. The *Character* object, for example, contains functions to check for case (*isUpperCase* function), check for a digit (*isDigit* function), or convert to uppercase (*toUpperCase* function). Java implements these functions as *public* and *static* so your applets can use them without having to create an object instance.

USING getPARAMETER TO ACCESS USER-DEFINED HTML ENTRIES

As you design Java applets, keep in mind that your applets should be easy for end users to customize. In other words, if the user wants to change the applet's appearance, the user should be able to make some changes without needing a Java programmer. Ideally, your applet should let the user specify values within the applet's HTML entry. Then, using the *getParameter* function, your applet can determine if the user has defined a specific entry. If the user has specified a setting value within the HTML file, the applet should use the value; otherwise, the applet should use a default value. By allowing the user to customize your applets using HTML, your applets will provide the user with greater flexibility.

The Start Function

Like the **Simple Marquee** applet discussed in Chapter 5, the **Modifiable Marquee** uses the *start* function to run the applet's thread:

```
public void start()
  {
     my_thread = new Thread(this);
     my_thread.start();
  }
```

As before, the *start* function creates a *Thread* object and then starts the thread's execution.

The get_defaults Function

The *get_defaults* function uses the *size* method, discussed in Chapter 5, to get the height and width of the applet window to initialize the variables *x*, *y*, and *width*:

```
void get_defaults()
  {
    y = size().height / 2;
    width = size().width;
    if (x > width)
      x = width;
  }
```

When an end user runs your applet within a window, it is possible that the user may size the window. Therefore, the *paint* function calls *get_defaults* each time it runs. If the user was working within the window, its width and height may have changed. By constantly checking the window size in this way, the applet better handles dynamic changes.

The run Function

As was the case with the **Simple Marquee** applet, the *run* function is responsible for moving the marquee message across the applet window:

```
public void run()
  {
    while (true)
      {
        repaint();
        x -= 10;
        if (x < 0)
          x = width;

        try
          {
            Thread.sleep(100);
          }
        catch (InterruptedException e)
          {
          }
      }
  }
```

As you can see, the *run* function continually loops, decrementing the message's x-coordinate with each iteration. When the x-coordinate reaches zero, the function resets the coordinate to the width of the window. See Chapter 5 for more details.

The paint Function

As discussed in Chapter 5, the *run* function calls *repaint* with each iteration of its *while* loop. The *repaint* function, in turn, calls the *paint* function shown next to display the message. This *paint* function, however, differs from that shown in Chapter 5 in that it uses the parameter values the user specified within the HTML file:

```
public void paint(Graphics g)
  {
    get_defaults();
    Font font = new Font(font_to_use, Font.PLAIN, point_size);
    g.setFont(font);
    g.drawString(message, x, y);
  }
```

To start, the *paint* function calls the *get_defaults* function to determine the applet-window size. Next, the function creates a new font using either the parameters specified in the HTML file or the applet's default settings. The function then uses the *setFont* function to set the graphics context to use this font. Then, the function displays the message at the current x and y coordinates using the *drawString* function.

ENHANCEMENTS YOU CAN MAKE TO MODIFIABLE MARQUEE

In **Modifiable Marquee**, the applet recreates the font every time the *paint* function runs. However, keep in mind that the parameters don't change during the life of the applet because the HTML file is static. Modify the applet so that it creates the font within the *init* function. In this way, the applet creates the font only once. Next, change the applet to let the user specify the color parameter in the HTML file.

PUTTING IT ALL TOGETHER

The **Modifiable Marquee** applet shows you how to get parameters from the applet's HTML file. As you create Java applets, use the techniques this program illustrates to build applets that are easier for the end user to modify. In Chapter 7, you will change the marquee program to display its message around the outside edges of the applet window. In other words, the message will move up the lsft edge, across the top of the window, down the right edge, and then across the bottom of the window. Before you continue with Chapter 7, however, make sure you understand the following key concepts:

- ☑ Within your HTML file, you can specify parameter values your applet can access.

- ☑ By supporting HTML parameters, your Java applets are easier for end users to modify.

- ☑ To access the HTML parameters from within your applet, you use the *getParameter* function.

- ☑ If the user did not specify a parameter value within the HTML file, the *getParameter* function will return the null value for that parameter.

- ☑ The *getParameter* function returns all values as *String* objects. To convert a *String* representation of an integer value to a numeric value, use the *Integer.parseInt* function.

CHAPTER 7

RECTANGULAR MARQUEE
DISPLAYING A MARQUEE AROUND THE SCREEN

In Chapter 6, you created a marquee program that used user-defined HTML parameters to customize its processing. In this chapter, you will again enhance the marquee. In this case, however, you will create the **Rectangular Marquee** applet, whose message moves around the edges of the applet window. In other words, the marquee message will travel up the left edge, across the top of the applet window, down the window's right side, and then across the bottom of the window. Much of the processing the **Rectangular Marquee** applet performs is similar to processing you've examined in the last two chapters. However, the applet introduces some subtle concepts you will use extensively in other applets throughout this book. By the time you finish this chapter, you will understand the following key concepts:

- By using a *char* array as opposed to a *String*, your applet can control the marquee message on a letter-by-letter basis; that is essential, since the message changes direction at each window corner.

- Java lets you create and run a thread without declaring a *Thread* object.

- Using the *new* operator, your applet can allocate space to store an array's elements.

- To move the marquee message around the applet-window corners, the applet must keep track of the coordinates of the window's upper-left corner, as well as the window's height and width.

USING THE RECTANGULAR MARQUEE

As discussed, the **Rectangular Marquee** applet moves the marquee message around the edges of the applet window. When you run the **Rectangular Marquee** applet, Java will open a window and display the marquee message, as shown in Figures 7.1 and 7.2.

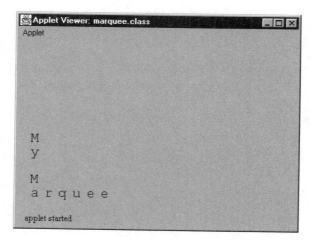

Figure 7.1 First snapshot of the rectangular marquee.

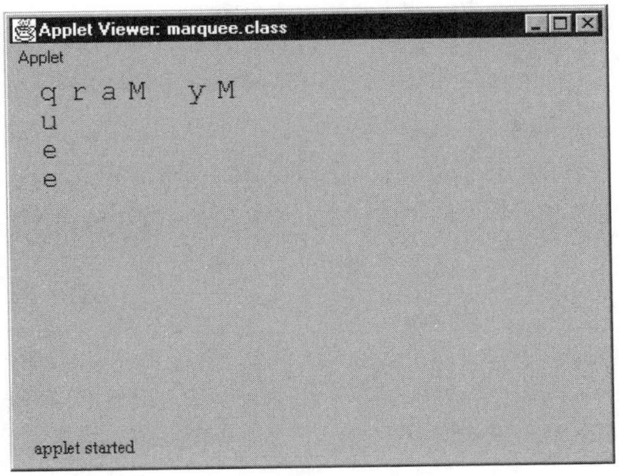

Figure 7.2 Second snapshot of the rectangular marquee.

THE HTML FILE

As was the case with the **Modifiable Marquee** applet, the **Rectangular Marquee** applet also supports HTML-based parameters for the message, font, and point size. In addition, the applet supports the delay parameter that controls how fast the marquee moves across the applet window:

```
<applet code=marquee.class width=400 height=250>
<param name=message     value="My Marquee">
<param name=font        value=Courier>
<param name=point_size value=20>
<param name=delay       value=125>
</applet>
```

LOOKING AT RECTANGULAR MARQUEE

The following Java code implements the **Rectangular Marquee** applet which displays its message around the outer edges of an applet window:

```
//*****************************************************************
// marquee.java
//*****************************************************************

import java.applet.*;
import java.awt.Graphics;
import java.awt.Font;


//*****************************************************************

public class marquee extends Applet implements Runnable
    {
      int width = 0;
      int height = 0;
      int length = 0;
```

```java
    int delay = 0;

    int point_size = 10;
    String message = "Hello, Java!";
    String font_to_use = "TimesRoman";

    char char_array[];
    int offset_x[];
    int offset_y[];

    //————————————————————————————

    public void init()
      {
        String parameter;

        parameter = getParameter("MESSAGE");
        if (parameter != null)
          message = parameter;

        parameter = getParameter("FONT");
        if (parameter != null)
          font_to_use = parameter;

        parameter = getParameter("POINT_SIZE");
        if (parameter != null)
          point_size = Integer.parseInt(parameter);

        parameter = getParameter("DELAY");
        if (parameter != null)
          delay = Integer.parseInt(parameter);

        length = message.length();
        char_array = new char[length];
        message.getChars(0, length, char_array, 0);
        offset_x = new int[length];
        offset_y = new int[length];
      }

    //————————————————————————————

    public void start()
      {
        (new Thread(this)).start();
      }

    //————————————————————————————

    void get_defaults()
      {
        width = size().width;
        height = size().height;
      }

    //————————————————————————————
```

```
public void re_draw()
  {
    repaint();

    try
      {
         Thread.sleep(delay);
      }
    catch (InterruptedException e)
      {
      }
  }

//—————————————————————

public void run ()
  {
    while (true)
      {
        //———————————————————
        // Go up on the left side.
        //———————————————————
        for (int y1 = height - point_size; y1 > point_size;
             y1 -= point_size)
          {
            int j = -1;

            for (int i = 0; i < length; i++)
              {
                if (y1 + i * point_size > height - point_size)
                  {
                    if (j < 0)
                      j = i;

                    offset_y[i] = height - point_size;
                    offset_x[i] = (i - j + 2) * point_size;
                  }
                else
                  {
                    offset_y[i] = y1 + i * point_size;
                    offset_x[i] = point_size;
                  }
              }

            re_draw();
          }

        //———————————————————
        // Go right at the top.
        //———————————————————
        for (int x1 = point_size; x1 < width; x1 += point_size)
          {
            int j = -1;
```

```
                for (int i = 0; i < length; i++)
                  {
                    if (x1 - i * point_size < point_size * 2)
                      {
                        if (j < 0)
                          j = i;

                        offset_y[i] = (i - j + 1) * point_size;
                        offset_x[i] = point_size;
                      }
                    else
                      {
                        offset_y[i] = point_size;
                        offset_x[i] = x1 - i * point_size;
                      }
                  }

            re_draw();
          }

    //————————————————————————————
    // Go down on the right side.
    //————————————————————————————
    for (int y1 = point_size * 2; y1 < height - point_size;
         y1 += point_size)
      {
        int j = -1;

        for (int i = 0; i < length; i++)
          {
            if (y1 - i * point_size < point_size)
              {
                if (j < 0)
                  j = i;

                offset_y[i] = point_size;
                offset_x[i] = width - (i-j+2) * point_size;
              }
            else
              {
                offset_y[i] = y1 - i * point_size;
                offset_x[i] = width - point_size;
              }
          }

        re_draw();
      }

    //————————————————————————————
    // Go left at the bottom.
    //————————————————————————————
    for (int x1 = width - point_size; x1 > point_size;
         x1 -= point_size)
```

```
                {
                    int j = -1;
                    for (int i = 0; i < length; i++)
                    {
                        if (x1 + i * point_size > width - point_size * 2)
                        {
                            if (j < 0)
                                j = i;

                            offset_y[i] = height - (i-j+1) * point_size;
                            offset_x[i] = width - point_size;
                        }
                        else
                        {
                            offset_y[i] = height - point_size;
                            offset_x[i] = x1 + i * point_size;
                        }
                    }

                    re_draw();
                }
            }
        }

//————————————————————————

    public void paint(Graphics g)
    {
        get_defaults();
        Font font = new Font(font_to_use, Font.PLAIN, point_size);
        g.setFont(font);

        for (int i = 0; i < message.length(); i++)
            g.drawChars(char_array, i, 1, offset_x[i], offset_y[i]);
    }
}
```

Breaking Apart the Rectangular Marquee

The **Rectangular Marquee** applet imports the same packages as the previous **Modifiable Marquee** applet:

```
import java.applet.*;
import java.awt.Graphics;
import java.awt.Font;
```

Extending the Applet

Like the previous two marquee applets, the **Rectangular Marquee** applet extends the *Applet* class by implementing a *Runnable* interface:

```
public class marquee extends Applet implements Runnable
```

Next, the applet declares the variables to store the applet-window's width and height:

```
int width = 0;
int height = 0;
```

The previous marquee applets stored the message as a character string. To display the message, the applets used the *drawString* function. Because the **Rectangular Marquee** must be able to display the message moving up-and-down, left-to-right, right-to-left, or, at times, moving in two directions, the applet must display the marquee message one character at a time. As you will learn, the applet stores the message text within an array of characters. The *length* variable specifies the number of characters in the message.

As briefly discussed, the **Rectangular Marquee** applet lets the user specify the time delay as an HTML-based parameter. The *delay* variable stores the millisecond delay interval:

```
int length = 0;
int delay = 0;
```

Like the **Modifiable Marquee** applet, this applet defines a default message, font, and point size:

```
String message = "Hello, Java!";
String font_to_use = "TimesRoman";
int point_size = 10;
```

As discussed, to display the marquee message, the **Rectangular Marquee** applet needs to access individual characters within the message. Therefore, rather than using a character string, the applet stores the message using an array of individual characters. The following statement declares the variable *char_array* as an array:

```
char char_array[];
```

Note that the array declaration does not specify an array size. Later, after the application knows the number of characters the message contains, the applet will use the *new* operator to allocate space to store the array.

To display characters as they move around the applet window, the applet must know each character's x and y coordinates. To track each character's position, the applet uses the following arrays:

```
int offset_x[];
int offset_y[];
```

The init Function

Like the **Modifiable Marquee** applet, the **Rectangular Marquee** applet uses the *init* function to obtain user-specified values from the HTML file. Note that this applet also lets the user specify the time delay as an HTML parameter:

```
public void init()
  {
    String parameter;

    parameter = getParameter("MESSAGE");
    if (parameter != null)
      message = parameter;
```

```
    parameter = getParameter("FONT");
    if (parameter != null)
        font_to_use = parameter;

    parameter = getParameter("POINT_SIZE");
    if (parameter != null)
        point_size = Integer.parseInt(parameter);

    parameter = getParameter("DELAY");
    if (parameter != null)
        delay = Integer.parseInt(parameter);
```

After the applet knows the message text, it must break apart the string into characters. To start, the applet uses the *length* method to determine the length of the string (the number of characters the string contains):

```
length = message.length();
```

Using the string length with the *new* operator, the applet can allocate space for the character array:

```
char_array = new char[length];
```

After the applet allocates space for the character array, it can use the *String* object's *getChars* method to assign the string characters to the array of characters. The *getChars* function parameters specify the index of the first string character you want, the index of the last character, the destination array of characters, and the starting offset in the destination array:

```
message.getChars(0, length, char_array, 0);
```

As discussed, the applet uses two arrays to track each character's x and y coordinates. Again, using the *new* operator, the applet allocates space for the arrays:

```
offset_x = new int[length];
offset_y = new int[length];
```

The start Function

The **Rectangular Marquee** *start* function is slightly different than what you have used before. Here, the applet combines the two steps taken in previous programs into one step. Using this technique, the applet does not have to create a *Thread* variable:

```
public void start()
    {
      (new Thread(this)).start();
    }
```

In the previous applets, the *start* function created a *Thread* object and then called the Thread object's *start* method to run the thread. After the thread was running, the applet did not use the *Thread* object again. In this case, rather than declaring a *Thread* object, the applet simply creates a *Thread* object that it runs without saving the object to a variable.

The get_defaults Function

As before, the *get_defaults* function returns the applet's windows height and width:

```
void get_defaults()
  {
    width = size().width;
    height = size().height;
  }
```

To ensure it knows the correct window size, the *paint* function will call the *get_defaults* function each time it draws the window's contents.

The redraw Function

Within the *redraw* function, the applet calls the *repaint* function to update the applet windows, and then delays for the number of milliseconds specified in the *delay* variable. Remember, that applet obtains the value for the *delay* variable from the HTML file:

```
public void re_draw()
  {
    repaint();

    try
      {
        Thread.sleep(delay);
      }
    catch (InterruptedException e)
      {
      }
  }
```

The run Function

The *run* function is the key to the **Rectangular Marquee** applet. Within the *run* function, you will find the code that makes the string move up the applet window's left side, move right across the top of the window, move down along the window's right side, and then move left across the bottom of the window. The *run* function does not actually display the characters; that's done within the *paint* function. Instead, the *run* function determines each character's screen position, and stores the corresponding x and y coordinates within the *offset_x* and *offset_y* arrays.

To start, examine the code that moves the message up the applet window's left side. The following *for* loop starts at the bottom of the window and moves up, toward the top-left corner. The loop moves the message characters in increments based on the font's point size:

```
for (int y1 = height - point_size; y1 > point_size; y1 -= point_size)
```

Using a second *for* loop, the applet steps through each character in the array to determine the character's x and y coordinates. In this case, if the character goes off the top, then the applet needs to make the character move to the right along the top of the window. The variable *j* keeps track of which character is at the corner's turning point:

```
int j = -1;
```

```
for (int i = 0; i < length; i++)
  {
    if (y1 + i * point_size > height - point_size)
      {
        if (j < 0)
          j = i;

        offset_y[i] = height - point_size;
        offset_x[i] = (i - j + 2) * point_size;
      }
    else
      {
        offset_y[i] = y1 + i * point_size;
        offset_x[i] = point_size;
      }
  }
```

After the applet calculates each character's x and y offset, the applet redraws the string:

```
re_draw();
```

The applet uses similar code to move the message characters in each direction. In other words, the applet determines each character's x and y coordinates and then redraws the message.

The paint Function

The *paint* function actually displays the message characters on the screen. To display the message, the function loops through the character array, using each character's x and y coordinate to position the character:

```
public void paint(Graphics g)
  {
    get_defaults();
    Font font = new Font(font_to_use, Font.PLAIN, point_size);
    g.setFont(font);

    for (int i = 0; i < message.length(); i++)
        g.drawChars(char_array, i, 1, offset_x[i], offset_y[i]);
  }
```

ENHANCEMENTS YOU CAN MAKE TO THE RECTANGULAR MARQUEE

The **Rectangular Marquee** applet currently displays its message around the applet window's outer edges. Modify the program to move right across the window and then left one row down, moving the message down one row at a time until the message reaches the bottom of the window. Then, reverse the code so the message moves back up toward the top of the window. Next, change the *paint* function so that each character changes color as the string is redrawn. The current applet assumes that the length of the string does not span three sides at once. Modify the applet to support a very long string.

PUTTING IT ALL TOGETHER

The **Rectangular Marquee** applet shows you how to work with text messages on a character-by-character basis. In later chapters, you will learn how to create bitmap fonts that your applet can rotate. In this way, you can rotate the characters as they move up, across, or down an edge of the applet window. In Chapter 8, you will learn how to display simple graphics within an applet window. Before you continue with Chapter 8, however, make sure you understand the following key concepts:

☑ To manipulate message text a character at a time, you must store the message within an array of characters.

☑ To allocate space to store a character array, you use the *new* operator.

☑ Using the *new* operator, you can create and run a *Thread* object in one step.

☑ To determine the number of characters a *String* object contains, you can use the *length* method.

☑ Using an array of the x-and-y offsets, an applet can track the window position for each character in an array of characters.

CHAPTER 8

FREE SAMPLES
BLINKING GRAPHICS CAPTURE THE USER'S ATTENTION

In several of the applets you created in the previous chapters, you made extensive use of the *Graphics* class *drawString* function to display text within an applet window. In this chapter, you will use *Graphics* class functions to perform simple line graphics within the applet window. Although the applet's code is quite simple, it will provide the foundation you will use to create more complex applets in the future. By the time you finish this chapter, you will understand the following key concepts:

◆ To perform graphics operations within your applet, you use the *Graphics* class.

◆ Using the *lineDraw* function, you can draw lines within an applet window.

◆ By interconnecting the lines the applet draws using the *lineDraw* function, your applet can draw complex shapes.

◆ By blinking even a simple graphic, your applet can capture the user's attention quickly.

◆ Using the *FontMetrics* class, an applet can determine a string's width in pixels; this is very important when you mix text and graphics within an applet window.

USING FREE SAMPLES

The **Free Samples** applet uses the Java *Graphics* class to draw a blinking star within the applet window. When you run the **Free Samples** applet, Java will open an applet window displaying a blinking star that contains a text message, as shown in Figure 8.

Figure 8 Displaying a blinking star that contains a text message.

The primary purpose of the **Free Samples** applet is to show you how to create simple line illustrations using the Java *Graphics* library. However, you might combine the blinking star with an existing homepage to capture the user's attention. In later chapters, you will learn how to combine Java graphics with a background image.

THE HTML FILE

The **Free Samples** applet focuses on the code you use to perform graphics. Therefore, the applet does not support HTML parameters. Using the techniques you have learned from previous chapters, you can change the applet to get its text message and size from HTML parameters. For now, use the following HTML entry to access the **Free Samples** applet:

```
<applet code=star.class width=400 height=400> </applet>
```

LOOKING AT FREE SAMPLES

Several of the previous applets you have created used the Java *Graphics* class to display text. The **Free Samples** applet uses *Graphics* class functions to display text and line-based graphics. The following code implements the **Free Samples** applet:

```
//***************************************************************
// star.java
//***************************************************************

import java.applet.*;
import java.awt.*;


//***************************************************************

public class star extends Applet implements Runnable
   {
     boolean blink = false;

     //———————————————————————————

     public void start()
       {
         (new Thread(this)).start();
       }

     //———————————————————————————

     public void run()
       {
         while (true)
           {
             repaint();

             try
               {
                 Thread.sleep(500);
               }
```

```
            catch (InterruptedException e)
                {
                }
        }
    }

    //————————————————————————————

    public void paint(Graphics g)
        {
        if (blink)
            {
                g.setColor(Color.red);
                blink = false;
            }
        else
            {
                g.setColor(Color.blue);
                blink = true;
            }

        int width = size().width;
        int height = size().height;

        Font font = new Font("TimesRoman", Font.BOLD, 20);
        g.setFont(font);

        FontMetrics font_metrics = g.getFontMetrics();

        g.drawString("Free", (width-font_metrics.stringWidth("Free"))/2,
                    height/2);
        g.drawString("Samples", (width-
                    font_metrics.stringWidth("Samples"))/2,
                    height/2+20);

        g.drawLine(width/2, (height*9)/10, (width*3)/8, (height*5)/8);
        g.drawLine((width*3)/8, (height*5)/8, width/10, height/2);
        g.drawLine(width/10, height/2, (width*3)/8, (height*3)/8);
        g.drawLine((width*3)/8, (height*3)/8, width/2, height/10);
        g.drawLine(width/2, height/10, (width*5)/8, (height*3)/8);
        g.drawLine((width*5)/8, (height*3)/8, (width*9)/10, height/2);
        g.drawLine((width*9)/10, height/2, (width*5)/8, (height*5)/8);
        g.drawLine((width*5)/8, (height*5)/8, width/2, (height*9)/10);
        }
    }
```

BREAKING APART FREE SAMPLES

The **Free Samples** applet imports two packages: the *java.applet* package provides the classes the applet needs to extend the *Applet* class, and the *java.awt* package provides the *Graphics* and *Font* classes:

```
import java.applet.*;
import java.awt.*;
```

Extending the Applet

Like the previous marquee applets, the **Free Samples** applet extends the *Applet* class by implementing a *Runnable* interface:

```
public class star extends Applet implements Runnable
```

As discussed, the code for the **Free Samples** applet is quite simple. In fact, the applet uses only one variable that specifies whether or not the star is blinking. If the *blink* variable is true, the applet draws the star using a red color. If the *blink* variable is false, the applet draws the star using a blue color. By using different colors to redraw the star, the applet causes the star to blink:

```
boolean blink = false;
```

Because the applet does not have variables to initialize, the applet does not provide the *init* function. Instead, when the browser runs the applet, the first function to execute is the *start* function discussed next.

The start Function

In the previous chapters, your applets used a *Thread* object to move a marquee message across the applet window. In a similar way, the **Free Samples** applet uses a *Thread* object to blink the star. When the browser executes the *start* function, the applet creates and runs the thread:

```
public void start()
   {
     (new Thread(this)).start();
   }
```

The run Function

Within the *start* function just shown, the applet creates and starts the *Thread* object, which, in turn, will blink the star. The applet uses the thread's *run* function, shown here, to blink the star forever, or until the applet ends:

```
public void run()
   {
       while (true)
         {
           repaint();

           try
             {
                Thread.sleep(500);
             }
           catch (InterruptedException e)
             {
             }
         }
   }
```

As you can see, the *run* function uses a *while* statement that will loop forever. Within the loop, the function calls the *repaint* function to update the applet window. Next, the applet uses the *Thread.sleep* function to delay one-half of a second (500 milliseconds). If the *Thread.sleep* function is interrupted, it generates an exception that the *catch* statement catches and ignores.

The paint Function

The **Free Samples** applet *paint* function performs most of the applet's processing. As you saw, the thread's *run* function calls *repaint* with each iteration of the loop, which in turn calls *paint*. The *paint* function, in turn, draws the star and "Free Samples" text within the applet window.

The *paint* function creates the blinking star by toggling the star's color between blue and red. Therefore, the first processing the applet performs is to determine which color it should use. The *paint* function determines the star's color by examining the *blink* variable. If the *blink* variable is true, *paint* uses the color red. Otherwise, if the *blink* variable is false, *paint* uses the color blue:

```
if (blink)
  {
     g.setColor(Color.red);
     blink = false;
  }
else
  {
     g.setColor(Color.blue);
     blink = true;
  }
```

Next, the *paint* function uses the *size* method to determine the applet window's width and height:

```
int width = size().width;
int height = size().height;
```

As discussed, the **Free Samples** applet combines text and graphics. As you can see, the applet uses a 20-point, bold, TimesRoman font. In addition, the applet uses the *getFontMetrics* method to determine the font's pixel width:

```
Font font = new Font("TimesRoman", Font.BOLD, 20);
g.setFont(font);

FontMetrics font_metrics = g.getFontMetrics();

g.drawString("Free", (width-font_metrics.stringWidth("Free"))/2, height/2);
g.drawString("Samples", (width-font_metrics.stringWidth("Samples"))/2,
            height/2+20);
```

The *FontMetrics* object provides the applet with font information, such as the width of a string in pixels. By knowing a string's pixel width, the applet can center the string. As you can see, to center a string, the applet subtracts the string's pixel width from the width of the window and then divides the result by 2. To center a string vertically within a window, the applet uses one-half of window height.

Lastly, the *paint* function uses a series of calls to the *drawLine* function to draw lines that define the four-sided star. If you examine Figure 8, you will find that the four-sided star consists of eight lines. Therefore, the applet uses eight calls to the *drawLine* function to create the star:

```
g.drawLine(width/2, (height*9)/10, (width*3)/8, (height*5)/8);
g.drawLine((width*3)/8, (height*5)/8, width/10,  height/2);
g.drawLine(width/10,  height/2, (width*3)/8, (height*3)/8);
g.drawLine((width*3)/8, (height*3)/8, width/2, height/10);
g.drawLine(width/2, height/10, (width*5)/8, (height*3)/8);
g.drawLine((width*5)/8, (height*3)/8, (width*9)/10, height/2);
g.drawLine((width*9)/10,  height/2, (width*5)/8, (height*5)/8);
g.drawLine((width*5)/8, (height*5)/8, width/2, (height*9)/10);
```

The *drawLine* function's first two parameters specify the line's starting x and y coordinates. The next two parameters specify the line's ending x and y coordinates. Notice that the ending coordinates of one *drawLine* call become the beginning coordinate of the next *drawLine* call, with the last call ending where the first call began.

The *run* function uses the *width* and *height* variables to determine the coordinates so it can draw the star correctly, regardless of the window size.

ENHANCEMENTS YOU CAN MAKE TO FREE SAMPLES

The **Free Samples** applet creates the blinking effect by toggling the star's color from red to blue. To start, change the program so it uses three colors to blink the star instead of two. Next, modify the applet's HTML file to include parameters for the text string the applet displays. Then, within your applet, use the *getParameter* method to obtain the message text. Also, modify the applet so that it changes the size of the font, depending on the current window size. Lastly, use the background color to erase the star and its text, and then use a different color to redisplay both, which may give the image a more realistic appearance of blinking.

PUTTING IT ALL TOGETHER

The **Free Samples** applet shows you how to perform simple graphics within an applet window. In Chapter 9 you will learn how to integrate a background image into your Java applet. Before you continue with Chapter 9, however, make sure you understand the following key concepts:

- ☑ The *lineDraw* function lets you draw a line within the applet window. To use the function, your applet specifies the line's starting and ending x and y coordinates.

- ☑ By using the *lineDraw* function to connect lines, you can create complex shapes within an applet window.

- ☑ To blink an object within a window, an applet simply changes the object's color at specific intervals.

- ☑ The *FontMetrics* class provides an applet with information about the current font. The **Free Samples** applet, for example, used the *stringWidth* function to determine the width of a text string that the applet then used to center the string within the window.

CHAPTER 9

"VIVA LAS VEGAS"
USING AN IMAGE WITH A FANCY TITLE

In Chapter 8, you learned how to create simple graphics within the applet window. As your applets become more complex, however, you will want to place background images within the applet window. You may later overwrite the images using fonts or other graphics. In this chapter, you will learn how to place a background image within the applet window. In addition, the applet will demonstrate how you create a fancy title whose letters change color continually. By the time you finish this chapter, you will understand the following key concepts:

- To place a background image, (such a GIF picture) within an applet window, you can use the Java *drawImage* function.

- To display an image within an applet window, your applet must create an *Image* object.

- Using the *showStatus* function, your applets can display status-bar messages.

- By tracking the applet window's height and width, your applet can ensure it displays the background image at the correct size.

- To display a *String* object's contents one letter at a time, using a different color, your application can use the *charWidth* function.

USING "VIVA LAS VEGAS"

The "**Viva Las Vegas**" applet sets the stage for advanced applets that you will create in the future. By examining the "**Viva Las Vegas**" code, you will learn how to display a background image within the applet window. In addition, you will learn how to create your own applet title, which appears beneath the image. When you run the "**Viva Las Vegas**" applet, Java will open an applet window and display the image with its title, as shown in Figure 9.

Figure 9 An image with a fancy title.

59

As you can see, by simply integrating a background image into the applet window, you quickly change your applet's look and feel. Within minutes, you can change the "**Viva Las Vegas**" applet to display a picture of your company, your product, or even yourself!

THE HTML FILE

The purpose of the "**Viva Las Vegas**" applet is to teach you how to display a background image within the applet window. To access the applet, use the following HTML entries:

```
<applet code=las_vegas.class width=560 height=350> </applet>
```

However, the applet does let the user specify the text message that appears within the title by using HTML-based parameters. In this case, the HTML does not specify any parameter values. When the applet uses the getParameter function to search the HTML file for parameters, the function will return the *null* value. As a result, the program will use its default values.

LOOKING AT "VIVA LAS VEGAS"

In Chapter 8, you used the *Graphics* library to display simple line graphics within the applet window. The "**Viva Las Vegas**" applet also uses the *Graphics* library—this time to display an applet-window background image. In addition to displaying the background image, the applet scrolls a red character through the title that appears near the bottom of the applet window. The following code implements the "**Viva Las Vegas**" applet:

```
//****************************************************************
// las_vegas.java
//****************************************************************

import java.applet.*;
import java.awt.*;


//****************************************************************

public class las_vegas extends Applet implements Runnable
   {
     Graphics g;

     Image background;
     int width;
     int height;
     boolean done_loading_image = false;

     Thread my_thread = null;
     String message = "Las Vegas";
     boolean thread_running = false;

     int message_length;
     char char_array[];

     //—————————————————————————————
```

```
public void init()
  {
    g = getGraphics();

    background = getImage(getCodeBase(), "vegas.gif");

    Image offScrImage = createImage(size().width, size().height);
    Graphics offScrGC = offScrImage.getGraphics();
    offScrGC.drawImage(background, 0, 0, this);

    String parameter = getParameter("MESSAGE");
    if (parameter != null)
      message = parameter;

    message_length = message.length();
    char_array = new char[message_length];
    message.getChars(0, message_length, char_array, 0);
  }

//—————————————————————————

public void start()
  {
    if (my_thread == null)
      my_thread = new Thread(this);
  }

//—————————————————————————

public void run_thread()
  {
    if (!thread_running)
      {
        my_thread.start();
        thread_running = true;
      }
  }

//—————————————————————————

void delay()
  {
    try
      {
        Thread.sleep(500);
      }
    catch (InterruptedException e)
      {
      }
  }

//—————————————————————————
```

```
   public void run()
     {
       repaint();

       int red_character = 0;

       Font font = new Font("TimesRoman", Font.BOLD, 20);
       g.setFont(font);

       FontMetrics font_metrics = g.getFontMetrics();

       int string_width = font_metrics.stringWidth(message);
       int string_height = font_metrics.getHeight();

       while (true)
         {

           int x = (width - string_width)/2;

           g.setColor(Color.black);
           g.fillRect(x, height+10, string_width, string_height);

           for (int i = 0; i < message_length; i++)
             {
               if (i == red_character)
                 g.setColor(Color.red);
               else
                 g.setColor(Color.white);

               g.drawChars(char_array, i, 1, x, height+30);
               x += font_metrics.charWidth(char_array[i]);
             }

           if (++red_character == message_length)
             red_character = 0;
           else
             while (char_array[red_character] == ' ')
               red_character++;

           delay();
         }
     }

   //————————————————————————————————————

   public boolean imageUpdate(Image img, int infoflags, int x, int y,
                       int w, int h)
     {
       if (infoflags == ALLBITS)
         {
           width = background.getWidth(this);
           height = background.getHeight(this);
```

```
            resize(width, height+40);

            done_loading_image = true;
            repaint();

            run_thread();

            return false;
        }
      else
        return true;
    }


    //————————————————————

    public void paint(Graphics g)
      {
        if (!done_loading_image)
          showStatus("Las Vegas:  loading image");

        else
          {
            showStatus("Las Vegas:  done");
            g.drawImage(background, 0, 0, null);
          }
      }
  }
```

BREAKING APART "VIVA LAS VEGAS"

The "**Viva Las Vegas**" applet imports two packages. The *java.applet* package provides the classes the applet needs to extend the *Applet* class; the *java.awt* package provides the *Graphics* and *Font* classes:

```
import java.applet.*;
import java.awt.*;
```

Extending the Applet

Because the "**Viva Las Vegas**" applet displays the dynamic title bar, whose letters constantly change, the applet uses a *Thread* object. Like the previous marquee applets, the "**Viva Las Vegas**" applet extends the *Applet* class and implements a *Runnable* interface:

```
public class star extends Applet implements Runnable
```

Next, the applet defines the class variables. Because the applet uses the graphics context in multiple functions, the applet defines a *Graphics* object as global to the class:

```
Graphics g;
```

To store the background image, the applet uses an *Image* object named *background*:

```
Image background;
```

The *width* and *height* variables store the width and the height of the image:

```
int width;
int height;
```

Several functions need to know when the applet has finished loading the background image. The *done_loading_image* lets the functions quickly determine whether the image is still loading. If the variable is true, the applet has loaded the image. If, on the other hand, the variable is false, the applet has not loaded the image:

```
boolean done_loading_image = false;
```

As briefly discussed, the "**Viva Las Vegas**" applet uses a *Thread* object to continuously change the letters of the applet's title. The applet uses the *Thread* object *my_thread* to start a thread that loops continuously through the letters in the title and draws them in a different color. The applet uses the *thread_running* variable to determine whether or not the *Thread* object is running. If the *thread_running* variable contains the true value, the thread is running. Otherwise, if the variable is false, the applet has not yet started the thread:

```
Thread my_thread = null;
boolean thread_running = false;
```

Finally, the applet defines a *String* object to store the applet title. To display the title one letter at a time, the applet stores the title within an array of characters. The *message_length* variable stores the number of characters the title contains:

```
String message = "Las Vegas";

int message_length;
char char_array[];
```

The init Function

As you have learned, the *init* function is the first applet function to run. Most applets use *init* to initialize key variables. To start, the applet uses the *getGraphics* function to get the graphics context:

```
g = getGraphics();
```

The *getGraphics* function is a member of the *Component* class, which, as you learned in Chapter 5, is one of the parent classes to the *Applet* class. For more information on the *Applet* class inheritance hierarchy, turn to Chapter 5.

Next, the applet uses the *getImage* method to retrieve the background image, which is stored in the file vegas.gif:

```
background = getImage(getCodeBase(), "vegas.gif");
```

The *getImage* and the *getCodeBase* functions are methods of the *Applet* class. The *getCodeBase* function returns the applet's base URL (unique resource locator). For example, the applet's URL might be *www.jamsa.com*. The applet passes the URL as the first parameter to the *getImage* function to tell the function where to retrieve the image. The second parameter to the *getImage* function specifies the image's filename.

The *getImage* function requires the URL because most applets are running on the World Wide Web. To retrieve the image file, the browser must know the site (URL) and the image's filename.

The *getImage* function does not actually load the image into the applet window. Rather, the function provides an object the applet can later use to draw the image within the applet window.

To display the background image, the applet has several choices. First, the applet can draw the image right within the applet window. Unfortunately, drawing the image within the applet window in this way causes considerable flashing. Also, the function that draws the image, *drawImage*, returns to the applet immediately and does not wait for the image to finish loading. The function's immediate return causes a problem when you want the image to finish loading before applet starts to run. To "get around" these problems, the "**Viva Las Vegas**" applet creates the image off screen (outside of the applet window), and then uses the *drawImage* function to display the image after it is complete.

To start, the applet creates the off-screen image using the *createImage* function. The *createImage* function is a *Component*-class method, and takes the image dimensions as its parameters. For the "**Viva Las Vegas**" applet, the image's dimensions are the same as the applet window:

```
Image offScrImage = createImage(size().width, size().height);
```

Next, the applet needs the graphics context for the off-screen image. To get the graphics context, the applet uses the *Image*-class *getGraphics* method:

```
Graphics offScrGC = offScrImage.getGraphics();
```

Finally, the applet uses the *drawImage* function to display the image within the applet window. The parameters to the *drawImage* function specify the image, the image's top-left x and y coordinates, and an *ImageObserver* class:

```
offScrGC.drawImage(background, 0, 0, this);
```

ImageObserver is an interface defined in the *java.awt.image* package. The applet uses the *this* keyword as the *ImageObserver* parameter, which means the applet must contain the *ImageObserver* interface functions. As it turns out, there is only one function in the *ImageObserver* interface, the *imageUpdate* function, which, as you will see, the applet defines.

As discussed, the applet lets the user specify the message that appears in the applet's fancy title. Using the *getParameter* function, the applet can retrieve the user's HTML setting:

```
String parameter = getParameter("MESSAGE");
if (parameter != null)
   message = parameter;
```

Lastly, because the applet works with the fancy title characters individually, the applet assigns the message text to an array of characters:

```
message_length = message.length();
char_array = new char[message_length];
message.getChars(0, message_length, char_array, 0);
```

The start Function

As discussed in previous chapters, the browser calls the *start* function after the *init* function is done. Within the *start* function, the applet creates a thread. Notice, however, that we do not start the thread. Instead, the applet will start the thread after the image has finished loading:

```
public void start()
  {
    if (my_thread == null)
      my_thread = new Thread(this);
  }
```

The run_thread Function

As just discussed, the applet does not start the *Thread* object, which updates the fancy title until the applet has loaded the background image. Then, after the image is loaded, the applet calls the *run_thread* function, which, in turn, starts the thread. The *run_thread* function uses the *thread_running* variable to double check that the thread is not already running. If the thread is not running, the function starts the thread:

```
public void run_thread()
  {
    if (!thread_running)
      {
        my_thread.start();
        thread_running = true;
      }
  }
```

The reason the *run_thread* function must check whether the *Thread* object is running is because the *ImageUpdate* function calls *run_thread* each time it updates the image. The first time that *imageUpdate* calls *run_thread*, the function should start the *Thread* object. After that, *run_thread* should simply return to the calling function.

The delay Function

Like the marquee applets, the "**Viva Las Vegas**" applet uses the *Thread.sleep* function to delay execution for half a second. In this case, the applet uses the *Thread* object to update the fancy title that appears beneath the background image. As before, the applet places the function within a *try* block. If the *Thread.sleep* function is interrupted, the *catch* block catches and ignores the *InterruptedException* exception:

```
void delay()
  {
    try
      {
        Thread.sleep(500);
      }
    catch(InterruptedException e)
      {
      }
  }
```

The run Function

After the image is loaded and the *Thread* object has started, thread's *start* function calls the *run* function. The *run* function, in turn, displays the message text centered horizontally at the bottom of the applet window.

To start, the *run* function makes sure that the image is on the screen by calling *repaint*:

```
repaint();
```

As discussed, the applet highlights one character in the title at a time by using a red font. To track which character is currently red, the applet uses the *red_character* variable:

```
int red_character = 0;
```

The applet then uses a *while* statement to update the title-message text forever, or at least until the applet ends:

```
while (true)
```

Within the *while* loop, the applet first sets the font, determines the size of the title text in pixels, and then determines the x coordinate that will center the title horizontally:

```
Font font = new Font("TimesRoman", Font.BOLD, 20);
g.setFont(font);

FontMetrics font_metrics = g.getFontMetrics();

int string_width = font_metrics.stringWidth(message);
int string_height = font_metrics.getHeight();

int x = (width - string_width)/2;
```

If you examine Figure 9, you will find that the applet displays the title text within a rectangular box. The following statements create the black box:

```
g.setColor(Color.black);
g.fillRect(x, height+10, string_width, string_height);
```

As you can see, the function uses the *setColor* font to select the color black. Next, the *fillRect* function draws the black box. The *fillRect* parameters specify the box's top-left x and y coordinates, the box width, and the box height.

After drawing the black rectangle, the applet draws each of the title characters in white, except for the one red character, to which the *red_character* variable points:

```
for (int i = 0; i < message_length; i++)
  {
    if (i == red_character)
       g.setColor(Color.red);
    else
       g.setColor(Color.white);
```

```
        g.drawChars(char_array, i, 1, x, height+30);
        x += font_metrics.charWidth(char_array[i]);
    }
```

To place the characters at the correct location within the box, the applet uses the *charWidth* function. As you can see, the applet increments the x coordinate of the next character based on the width of the character just drawn.

Next, the function increments the *red_character* variable so the next iteration of the *while* loop draws the next character in red. After the applet draws the title's last character in red, the applet starts over at the title's first character. Also, note that the applet skips blank characters:

```
if (++red_character == message_length)
    red_character = 0;
else
    while (char_array[red_character] == ' ')
        red_character++;
```

Finally, the applet calls the *delay* function to delay the applet for one-half of a second:

```
delay();
```

The imageUpdate Function

To use the *ImageObserver* class, the applet must implement the *imageUpdate* function. As it turns out, each time the *drawImage* function runs, it creates a thread that in turn calls *imageUpdate*. As you can see, the *imageUpdate* function uses six parameters: the image, the information flag (which specifies how much of the image has been drawn), the image's top-left x and y coordinates, and the image's width and height:

```
public boolean imageUpdate(Image img, int infoflags, int x, int y, int w,
                           int h)
```

As it turns out, the last parameter the applet passes to *drawImage* function controls whether or not it calls the *imageUpdate* function. If the parameter is null, *drawImage* does not call *imageUpdate*. If the applet passes the parameter value *this* to *drawImage*, the function will call the *imageUpdate* function defined by the current class. If your applet has multiple classes, the applet can pass a reference to the class whose *imageUpdate* function the applet wants *drawImage* to call.

The applet declares the *imageUpdate* function as *public* so the thread started by *drawImage* can call it. The function returns a *boolean* (true or false) value that specifies whether the function should be called again for the next block of the image.

The function uses the *infoflag* parameter to determine how much of the image has been drawn. When the *infoflags* parameter is equal to the *ALLBITS* constant, the image is done. The *ALLBITS* constant is defined in the *ImageObserver* interface:

```
if (infoflags == ALLBITS)
  {
    width = background.getWidth(this);
    height = background.getHeight(this);

    resize(width, height+40);
```

```
        done_loading_image = true;
        repaint();

        run_thread();

        return false;
      }
  else
    return true;
```

When the image is done, the applet performs several operations. First, the applet determines the image's width and height, and resizes the applet window to hold the image and the fancy title (height+40 pixels). Next, the applet sets the *done_loading_image* variable to true and repaints the screen. Lastly, the applet starts the thread that will draw the fancy-title characters, and returns *false* so *drawImage* does not call this function again.

The *resize* function deserves special mention here. Because the applets in Web pages cannot be resized, you should only use the *resize* function when you run the applet from the *appletviewer*, and not from an HTML browser such as Netscape on the Web.

When you use the *appletviewer*, you can pass the applet window's width and height to the applet, and the applet will resize the window correctly. If you are running the applet from within a browser, the *resize* function will have no effect.

The paint Function

Within the *paint* function, the applet draws the image on the screen, provided the image has already been loaded. If the image has not been loaded yet, the applet displays a status message so stating:

```
public void paint(Graphics g)
  {
    if (!done_loading_image)
      showStatus("Las Vegas:  loading image");
    else
      {
        showStatus("Las Vegas:  done");
        g.drawImage(background, 0, 0, null);
      }
  }
```

The *showStatus* function displays a message in the applet-window status bar. When you run the applet from an HTML page on the Web, this status message will appear in the browser's status bar, if there is one.

If the image has been drawn, the applet will not use the *drawImage* function to call the *imageUpdate* function again. Therefore, the applet passes the *drawImage* function a *null* value for the *ImageObserver* parameter.

Enhancements You Can Make to "Viva Las Vegas"

Your first modifications to the "Viva Las Vegas" applet should be to change the image and message text. Next, change the direction the applet moves the red character. In other words, move the red character right to left instead of left to right. You might also use multiple colors to draw the letters. Lastly, change the message-text display to appear as a marquee within the black box.

Putting It All Together

In this chapter, you learned how to place a background image within the applet window. In addition, you created a fancy applet title whose letters change color. In Chapter 10, you will create a Java applet that plays music. Before you continue with Chapter 10, however, make sure you understand the following key concepts:

☑ To draw an image within the applet window, you use the *drawImage* function. Note, however, that the function does not finish the loading before it returns to the calling program.

☑ To eliminate flashing when you display a background image, build the image outside of the applet window and then display the image.

☑ The *imageUpdate* function tells the applet when the image has finished loading.

☑ To resize a window for an applet you are running, using the *appletviewer*, you can use the *resize* function. Because an applet cannot size a browser window, you should not use the *resize* function for applets you run using HTML pages displayed on the Web.

☑ The *showStatus* function lets your applets display status-bar messages.

☑ Using the *charWidth* function, an applet can determine a character's pixel-width based on the current font.

☑ Using the *drawChars* function, an applet can draw a character at a specific location.

CHAPTER 10

Welcome to Joe's Bar
Using Audio Class to Play Music

In Chapter 9, you learned how to place an image within the applet window. In this chapter, you will extend the "**Viva Las Vegas**" applet to use an audio clip to play background music. By combining images and music in this way, your applet quickly takes on a professional flair. In short, the **Welcome to Joe's Bar** applet is your first multimedia applet! By the time you finish this chapter, you will understand the following key concepts:

- To play an audio clip within your applet, you use the *AudioClip* class.

- The *getAudioClip* function loads an audio clip from a file.

- Using the *AudioClip* class *loop* method, your applet can play an audio clip continuously.

- When your applet displays an image, you can fit the image to the applet window's width and height specified in the HTML file.

USING WELCOME TO JOE'S BAR

The **Welcome to Joe's Bar** applet combines images and music. When you run the applet, Java will open an applet window and display the image and its title, as shown in Figure 10. In addition, Java will play the audio-clip's background music.

Figure 10 *Displaying an image with a fancy title.*

THE HTML FILE

The HTML file for the **Welcome to Joe's Bar** applet defines the applet window's width and height and the title text, as well as the delay interval the applet waits between drawing the title's letters in red:

```
<applet code=audio.class width=420 height=260>
<param name=message value="Joe's Bar">
<param name=delay value=100>
</applet>
```

LOOKING AT WELCOME TO JOE'S BAR

In Chapter 9, you created the "**Viva Las Vegas**" applet that displayed an image with a fancy title. The **Welcome to Joe's Bar** applet enhances the previous applet by adding code to playback an audio clip. The following code implements the **Welcome to Joe's Bar** applet:

```java
//***********************************************************************
// audio.java
//***********************************************************************

import java.applet.*;
import java.awt.*;


//***********************************************************************

public class audio extends Applet implements Runnable
  {
    Graphics g;
    Image background;

    int delay_amount = 500;
    Thread my_thread = null;

    boolean done_loading_image = false;
    boolean thread_running = false;

    String message = "Default String";

    int width;
    int height;
    int message_length;
    char char_array[];

    //————————————————————————————————————

    public void init()
      {
        g = getGraphics();

        background = getImage(getCodeBase(), "joes_bar.gif");

        String parameter;
```

```java
      parameter = getParameter("MESSAGE");
      if (parameter != null)
        message = parameter;

      parameter = getParameter("DELAY");
      if (parameter != null)
        delay_amount = Integer.parseInt(parameter);

      width = size().width;
      height = size().height;

      Image offScrImage = createImage(width, height);
      Graphics offScrGC = offScrImage.getGraphics();
      offScrGC.drawImage(background, 0, 0, width, height, this);

      message_length = message.length();
      char_array = new char[message_length];
      message.getChars(0, message_length, char_array, 0);
    }

//————————————————————

public void start()
  {
    if (my_thread == null)
      my_thread = new Thread(this);
  }

//————————————————————

public void run_thread()
  {
    if (!thread_running)
      {
        my_thread.start();
        thread_running = true;
      }
  }

//————————————————————

void delay()
  {
    try
      {
        Thread.sleep(delay_amount);
      }
    catch (InterruptedException e)
      {
      }
  }

//————————————————————
```

```java
   public void run()
     {
       repaint();

       int red_character = 0;
       AudioClip clip = getAudioClip(getCodeBase(), "bar.au");
       clip.loop();

       Font font = new Font("TimesRoman", Font.BOLD, 20);
       g.setFont(font);

       FontMetrics font_metrics = g.getFontMetrics();

       int string_width = font_metrics.stringWidth(message);
       int string_height = font_metrics.getHeight();

       while (true)
         {
           int x = (width - string_width)/2;

           g.setColor(Color.black);
           g.fillRect(x, height+10, string_width, string_height);

           for (int i = 0; i < message_length; i++)
             {
               if (i == red_character)
                 g.setColor(Color.red);
               else
                 g.setColor(Color.white);

               g.drawChars(char_array, i, 1, x, height+30);
               x += font_metrics.charWidth(char_array[i]);
             }

           if (++red_character == message_length)
             red_character = 0;
           else
             while (char_array[red_character] == ' ')
               red_character++;

           delay();
         }
   }

//————————————————————————————————

public boolean imageUpdate(Image img, int infoflags, int x, int y,
                           int w, int h)
   {
     if (infoflags == ALLBITS)
       {
         resize(width, height+40);

         done_loading_image = true;
```

```
            repaint();

            run_thread();

            return false;
          }
        else
          return true;
    }


    //—————————————————————————————

    public void paint(Graphics g)
      {
        if (!done_loading_image)
          showStatus("Joe's Bar: loading image");

        else
          {
            showStatus("Joe's Bar: done");
            g.drawImage(background, 0, 0, width, height, this);
          }
      }
  }
```

BREAKING APART WELCOME TO JOE'S BAR

Much of this applet's code is identical to the "**Viva Las Vegas**" applet you created in the previous chapter. Therefore, this section will only discuss the differences between the two programs.

To start, the applet uses the *delay_amount* variable to store the time delay the applet waits before drawing a title character in red. As previously discussed, the applet's HTML file provides a value for the *delay_amount* variable:

```
int delay_amount = 500;
```

The init Function

Within the *init* function, the applet uses the *getParameter* function to get the value for the *delay_amount* variable from the HTML file. Next, the applet uses the *Integer.parseInt* function to convert the *String* parameter to an integer value:

```
parameter = getParameter("DELAY");
if (parameter != null)
  delay_amount = Integer.parseInt(parameter);
```

Next, to fit the background image within the applet-window's width and height (which is specified in the HTML file), the applet uses the *size* function to determine the window's dimensions:

```
width = size().width;
height = size().height;
```

The applet then creates an off-screen image using the applet-window's size. As you will learn, the applet uses a *drawImage* function that differs from the one that you created in the previous chapter. The new function uses two more parameters, which specify the width and height of the area within which the applet must fit the image:

```
Image offScrImage = createImage(width, height);
Graphics offScrGC = offScrImage.getGraphics();
offScrGC.drawImage(background, 0, 0, width, height, this);
```

The delay Function

The *delay* function also differs slightly from the function you created in the previous chapter. In the previous chapter, the *Thread.sleep* function used a hard-coded value of one-half second. In this applet, the function delays the amount specified by the *delay_amount* variable:

```
Thread.sleep(delay_amount);
```

As discussed, the applet gets the delay amount from a user-defined parameter within the applet's HTML file.

The run Function

Within the *run* function, the applet loads and plays the audio clip. To start, the applet uses the *getAudioClip* function to load the audio clip from a file on disk or the web. As before, the *getCodeBase* function returns the applet's base URL. By combining the applet's URL with the audio-clip filename, the *getAudioClip* function locates the audio clip across the Web. After the applet loads the audio clip, the applet uses the *AudioClip*-class *loop* method to play the audio clip continuously:

```
AudioClip clip = getAudioClip(getCodeBase(), "bar.au");
clip.loop();
```

The imageUpdate Function

Because the applet does not use the image width and height to size the applet window, the *imageUpdate* function becomes simpler, as shown here:

```
public boolean imageUpdate(Image img, int infoflags, int x, int y, int w,
int h)
  {
   if (infoflags == ALLBITS)
     {
        resize(width, height+40);

        done_loading_image = true;
        repaint();

        run_thread();

        return false;
     }
   else
     return true;
  }
```

In this case, the applet resizes the window to add room for the title at the bottom of the window. If, however, you are running the applet from within a browser, as opposed to the *appletviewer*, the applet cannot use the *resize* function. In that case, rather than resize the window in this way, you must make sure that the image fits within the window (minus the 40 pixels the title consumes).

The paint Function

If the image has been loaded, the *paint* function displays the image using the applet-window's width and height:

```
public void paint(Graphics g)
  {
    if (!done_loading_image)
      showStatus("Joe's Bar:  loading image");
    else
      {
        showStatus("Joe's Bar:  done");
        g.drawImage(background, 0, 0, width, height, null);
      }
  }
```

ENHANCEMENTS YOU CAN MAKE TO WELCOME TO JOE'S BAR

By combining text, graphics, and sound, the **Welcome to Joe's Bar** applet is your first multimedia applet. Take time now to change the audio clip the applet plays, as well as the image the applet displays. In addition, change the applet window's width and the height within the HTML file and watch how the applet shrinks or expands the image.

PUTTING IT ALL TOGETHER

The **Welcome to Joe's Bar** applet shows you how to play an audio clip within a Java applet. In addition, the applet shows how you fit an image within an applet window's width and height. In Chapter 11, you will use the **Neon Las Vegas** applet to display neon lights that flash on the outer edges of the applet window. Before you continue with Chapter 11, however, make sure you understand the following key concepts:

- ☑ Using the *AudioClip* class, your applet can load and play an audio clip.

- ☑ To load an audio clip from a file, your applet uses the *getAudioClip* method.

- ☑ To play the audio clip continuously, as background music, use the *AudioClip*-class *loop* method. The function, in turn, will play the audio clip infinitely.

- ☑ By changing the *drawImage* function slightly, you can fit an image to the width and height of an applet window, as specified within an HTML file.

CHAPTER 11

NEON LAS VEGAS
DISPLAYING NEON LIGHTS AROUND AN IMAGE

In Chapter 10, you learned how to load and play an audio clip within a Java applet. In addition, you learned how to size an image to fit into the applet window. In this chapter, you will learn how to draw neon lights around an image. By the time you finish this chapter, you will understand the following key concepts:

◆ To store an object's x and y coordinates, you can use the *Coordinate* class.

◆ Using the *Graphics*-class *drawOval* and *fillOval* functions, your applets can draw circles and fill the circles using the current color.

◆ By flashing circles around an image, your application can create the effect of neon lights.

USING NEON LAS VEGAS

The **Neon Las Vegas** applet builds upon several of the previous applets. As you will find, the applet loads a background image and displays the fancy title, whose letters change color continuously. In addition, the applet surrounds the applet window with flashing Vegas-like neon lights. When you run the **Neon Las Vegas** applet, Java will open a window and display the image with the neon lights, as shown in Figure 11.

Figure 11 *Displaying an image surrounded by flashing neon lights.*

THE HTML FILE

The **Neon Las Vegas** HTML file lets the user define the applet window's width and height, the title text, the time delay the applet waits between drawing the title-text letters in red, the diameter size of each bulb in the neon lights, and the bulb spacing in pixels:

```
<applet code=neon.class width=480 height=300>
<param name=message        value="This is Las Vegas!!">
<param name=delay          value=200>
<param name=bulb_size      value=15>
<param name=bulb_spacing value=20>
</applet>
```

LOOKING AT NEON LAS VEGAS

The previous applet, **Welcome to Joe's Bar**, displayed an image with a fancy title and played an audio clip in the background. The **Neon Las Vegas** applet adds neon lights around the image. The following code implements the **Neon Las Vegas** applet:

```
//*************************************************************
// neon.java
//*************************************************************

import java.applet.*;
import java.awt.*;

//*************************************************************

class Coordinate
  {
    public int x;
    public int y;

    public Coordinate(int x, int y)
      {
        this.x = x;
        this.y = y;
      }
  }

//*************************************************************

public class neon extends Applet implements Runnable
  {
    Graphics g;
    FontMetrics font_metrics;
    Image background;

    int bulb_size = 10;
    int bulb_spacing = 20;
    int delay_amount = 500;
    int off_bulb = 0;
```

```
      Thread my_thread = null;
      boolean done_loading_image = false;
      boolean thread_running = false;

      String message = "Las Vegas";

      int width;
      int height;
      int message_length;
      int string_x;
      int string_y;
      int string_width;
      int string_height;
      char char_array[];

      Coordinate coordinate[];

      int total_bulbs;

      //————————————————————————————————

      public void init()
        {
          g = getGraphics();

          background = getImage(getCodeBase(), "vegas.gif");

          String parameter;

          parameter = getParameter("MESSAGE");
          if (parameter != null)
            message = parameter;

          parameter = getParameter("DELAY");
          if (parameter != null)
            delay_amount = Integer.parseInt(parameter);

          parameter = getParameter("BULB_SIZE");
          if (parameter != null)
            bulb_size = Integer.parseInt(parameter);

          parameter = getParameter("BULB_SPACING");
          if (parameter != null)
            bulb_spacing = Integer.parseInt(parameter);

          width = size().width;
          height = size().height;

          Image offScrImage = createImage(width, height);
          Graphics offScrGC = offScrImage.getGraphics();
          offScrGC.drawImage(background, 0, 0, width, height, this);

          message_length = message.length();
          char_array = new char[message_length];
```

```
        message.getChars(0, message_length, char_array, 0);
        Font font = new Font("TimesRoman", Font.BOLD, 20);
        g.setFont(font);
        font_metrics = g.getFontMetrics();

        string_width = font_metrics.stringWidth(message);
        string_height = font_metrics.getHeight();

        string_x = (width + bulb_spacing*2 - string_width)/2;
        string_y = height + 30 + bulb_spacing*2;

        resize(width+bulb_spacing*2, height+40+bulb_spacing*2);

        get_bulb_coordinates();
    }

//————————————————————————

public void start()
    {
        if (my_thread == null)
          my_thread = new Thread(this);
    }

//————————————————————————

public void run_thread()
    {
        if (!thread_running)
          {
             my_thread.start();
             thread_running = true;
          }
    }

//————————————————————————

void delay ()
    {
        try
          {
             Thread.sleep(delay_amount);
          }
        catch (InterruptedException e)
          {
          }
    }

//————————————————————————

void get_bulb_coordinates()
    {
        total_bulbs = 2*width/bulb_spacing + 2*height/bulb_spacing + 4;
```

```
        coordinate = new Coordinate[total_bulbs];
        int current_bulb = 0;

        int x;
        int y;
        int end;

        //————————————————————————
        // top
        //————————————————————————
        y = (bulb_spacing-bulb_size)/2;
        end = width + bulb_spacing;
        for (x = (bulb_spacing - bulb_size)/2; x < end; x += bulb_spacing)
          coordinate[current_bulb++] = new Coordinate(x, y);


        //————————————————————————
        // right
        //————————————————————————
        x = width + bulb_spacing + (bulb_spacing-bulb_size)/2;
        end = height + bulb_spacing;
        for (y = (bulb_spacing - bulb_size)/2; y < end; y += bulb_spacing)
          coordinate[current_bulb++] = new Coordinate(x, y);


        //————————————————————————
        // bottom
        //————————————————————————
        y = height + bulb_spacing + (bulb_spacing-bulb_size)/2;
        end = bulb_spacing;
        for (x = width + bulb_spacing + (bulb_spacing - bulb_size)/2;
           x > end; x -= bulb_spacing)
          {
            coordinate[current_bulb++] = new Coordinate(x, y);
          }


        //————————————————————————
        // left
        //————————————————————————
        x = (bulb_spacing - bulb_size)/2;
        end = (bulb_spacing - bulb_size)/2;
        for (y = height + bulb_spacing + (bulb_spacing - bulb_size)/2;
           y > end; y -= bulb_spacing)
          {
            coordinate[current_bulb++] = new Coordinate(x, y);
          }
      }


  //————————————————————————————————

void draw_bulbs()
   {
     int bulb_counter = 0;

     g.setColor(Color.red);
     for (int i = 0; i < total_bulbs; i++)
```

```
              {
          if (++bulb_counter == 5)
            bulb_counter = 0;
          if (bulb_counter == off_bulb)
            {
               g.setColor(Color.lightGray);
               g.fillOval(coordinate[i].x, coordinate[i].y, bulb_size,
                          bulb_size);
               g.setColor(Color.red);
               g.drawOval(coordinate[i].x, coordinate[i].y, bulb_size,
                          bulb_size);
            }
          else
            g.fillOval(coordinate[i].x, coordinate[i].y, bulb_size,
                       bulb_size);
        }

    if (++off_bulb == 5)
      off_bulb = 0;
  }

//————————————————————————————

public void run ()
  {
     repaint();

     int red_character = 0;
     AudioClip clip = getAudioClip(getCodeBase(), "bar.au");
     clip.loop();

     try
       {
         while (!done)
           {
             int x = string_x;

             g.setColor(Color.black);
             g.fillRect(x, height+10+bulb_spacing*2, string_width,
                        string_height);

             for (int i = 0; i < message_length; i++)
               {
                  if (i == red_character)
                    g.setColor(Color.red);
                  else
                    g.setColor(Color.white);

                  g.drawChars(char_array, i, 1, x, string_y);
                  x += font_metrics.charWidth(char_array[i]);
               }

             if (++red_character == message_length)
               red_character = 0;
```

83

```
                   else
                     while (char_array[red_character] == ' ')
                       red_character++;

                 draw_bulbs();
                 delay();
             }
        }
      finally
        {
        }
    }

//————————————————————

  public boolean imageUpdate(Image img, int infoflags, int x, int y,
                             int w, int h)
    {
     if (infoflags == ALLBITS)
       {
         done_loading_image = true;
         repaint();

         run_thread();

         return false;
       }
     else
       return true;
  }

//————————————————————

  public void paint(Graphics g)
    {
      if (!done_loading_image)
        showStatus("Neon:  loading image");
      else
        {
        showStatus("Neon:  done");
        g.drawImage(background, bulb_spacing, bulb_spacing, width,
                    height, null);
        }
    }
}
```

BREAKING APART NEON LAS VEGAS

Much of the **Neon Las Vegas** applet is similar to the **Welcome to Joe's Bar** applet presented in the previous chapter. Therefore, this section will only discuss the differences between the two programs.

To start, the program declares a new class, called *Coordinate*, that contains x-and-y coordinates, which are both *public*. Using *Coordinate*-class objects, an applet can store an object's x and y coordinates. The class-constructor function uses its parameter values to initialize the coordinate variables:

```
class Coordinate
  {
    public int x;
    public int y;

    public Coordinate(int x, int y)
      {
        this.x = x;
        this.y = y;
      }
  }
```

Notice that the constructor function's parameters are named *x* and *y*, as are the class-member variables. To differentiate between the two, the constructor accesses the class variables using the *this* keyword.

Within its data members, the applet declares a *FontMetrics* object the applet can use to determine a string's width and height. The applet uses the string's width and height to center the title text at the bottom of the image, and also to move the *red_character* from one letter to the next:

```
FontMetrics font_metrics;
```

As you can see in Figure 11, the applet displays round light bulbs around the applet window. The *bulb_size* variable contains the diameter of each bulb, and the *bulb_spacing* variable contains the pixel space between bulbs:

```
int bulb_size = 10;
int bulb_spacing = 20;
```

As the applet flashes its neon lights, the applet turns four successive lights on and one light off. The *off_bulb* variable holds the index of the bulb that is off. With each iteration of the applet's *while* loop, the applet increments the *off_bulb* index to point to the next bulb:

```
int off_bulb = 0;
```

If you examine Figure 11, you will see that the applet displays a title beneath the image. The *string_x* and *string_y* variables contain the x and y baseline coordinates of the first letter of the title text:

```
int string_x;
int string_y;
```

The *string_width* and *string_height* variables contain the title-text's width and height. The applet uses the width and height information to center the title under the image:

```
int string_width;
int string_height;
```

The applet uses the *coordinate* array to store the x-and-y coordinates of each bulb that surrounds the window. The applet calculates the bulb coordinates one time, and then uses the coordinates within the *run* function to paint the bulbs around the applet window:

```
Coordinate coordinate[];
```

The *total_bulbs* variable contains the number of bulbs that appear around the image. The applet uses the bulb count to create the array of coordinates, as well as to draw the bulbs around the window:

```
int total_bulbs;
```

Initializing the Applet

Within the *init* function, the applet adds code to get the *BULB_SIZE* and *BULB_SPACING* parameters from the HTML file. Because both of these values are integers, the applet uses the *Integer.parseInt* function to convert the strings:

```
parameter = getParameter("BULB_SIZE");
if (parameter != null)
  bulb_size = Integer.parseInt(parameter);

parameter = getParameter("BULB_SPACING");
if (parameter != null)
  bulb_spacing = Integer.parseInt(parameter);
```

Next, the *init* function includes code to determine the size and the coordinates for the title text it displays at the bottom of the image. To get this information, the applet selects its desired font and then uses a *FontMetrics* object to determine the text's width and height:

```
Font font = new Font("TimesRoman", Font.BOLD, 20);
g.setFont(font);

font_metrics = g.getFontMetrics();

string_width = font_metrics.stringWidth(message);
string_height = font_metrics.getHeight();
```

To calculate the actual image width, the applet must now consider the two columns of bulbs:

```
string_x = (width + bulb_spacing*2 - string_width)/2;
```

Likewise, to calculate the image height, the applet must consider the two rows of bulbs. In addition, the applet specifies the y-coordinate of the string to be 30 pixels below the bottom of the image. Therefore, to calculate the string's y coordinate, the applet uses the following expression:

```
string_y = height + bulb_spacing*2 + 30;
```

To include spacing for the bulbs and space for the message, the applet resizes the window. To provide space for the message, the applet adds 40 pixels to the message height:

```
resize(width+bulb_spacing*2, height+40+bulb_spacing*2);
```

You can only use the *resize* function to resize the applet window when you are running the applet from within the applet viewer. If you are running the applet from within a browser, the *resize* function may not work. To change the applet so you can run it within a browser, you have two choices: you must make the window larger (by 40 pixels in width and height) or you must make the image smaller (by 40 pixels). To change the applet, remove the *resize* function call. Next, within the *paint* function, change the *drawImage* function call to subtract *bulb_spacing**2 from the image's height and width.

Lastly, the *init* function calls the *get_bulb_coordinates* function to calculate the x-and-y coordinates for each bulb that surrounds the image:

```
get_bulb_coordinates();
```

Getting the Bulb Coordinates

As just discussed, the *get_bulb_coordinates* function calculates each bulb's x-and-y coordinates. To start, the function calculates the total number of bulbs. Each bulb requires the number of pixels specfied by the *bulb_spacing* variable. Therefore, to calculate the number of bulbs the width of the image contains, you divide the width by the bulb spacing:

```
width_number_of_bulbs = width/bulb_spacing;
```

Because there are bulbs on the top and the bottom, the function multiplies the result by 2. As it turns out, the function can use a similar equation to determine the number of bulbs for the image height. Lastly, the function adds four bulbs for the image corners. The final expression to calculate the number of bulbs becomes the following:

```
total_bulbs = 2*width/bulb_spacing + 2*height/bulb_spacing + 4;
```

After the function knows the number of bulbs, it can allocate an array of *Coordinates* to hold each bulb's x-and-y coordinates:

```
coordinate = new Coordinate[total_bulbs];
```

To calculate each bulb's coordinates, the function moves around the window, one bulb at a time. The function uses the *current_bulb* variable to keep track of the current bulb:

```
int current_bulb = 0;
```

As the function calculates the coordinates for each bulb, it must track the *x-and-y* coordinates, as well as the *end* of each row or column of bulbs (the left, top, right, and bottom lines of bulbs):

```
int x;
int y;
int end;
```

As the function calculates the coordinates for the top row of bulbs, the *y*-coordinate stays the same. Because the applet places the bulb inside the applet window, leaving a little space above the bulb, the applet can calculate the top row's y-coordinate as follows:

```
y = (bulb_spacing-bulb_size)/2;
```

The loop will calculate coordinates for the first bulb to one less than the end bulb. The function stops before the end bulb because the end bulb is actually the first bulb for the right column of bulbs:

```
end = width + bulb_spacing;
```

The *for* statement loops through the *x*-coordinates, starting at the left-most bulb and going to one less than the end bulb. The *for* loop's increment corresponds to the bulb spacing:

```
for (x = (bulb_spacing - bulb_size)/2; x < end; x += bulb_spacing)
```

With each iteration through the loop, function calculates a bulb's *x* and *y* coordinate. Then, the function creates a new *Coordinate* object to store the coordinates and places the object into the coordinate array. As the function stores the coordinates, it increments the *current_bulb* index in preparation for the next bulb:

```
coordinate[current_bulb++] = new Coordinate(x, y);
```

The function then calculates the right-side, bottom, and left-side bulb coordinates in a similar fashion. Notice that each loop goes to one less than the end, because the end bulb is the beginning of the next loop.

Drawing the Bulbs

The *draw_bulbs* function actually draws the bulbs around the image. Using the coordinates array that contains each bulb's x-and-y coordinates, the function simply loops through the array drawing the lights at the corresponding coordinates.

As discussed, however, the applet draws four bulbs on and then one bulb off. To keep track of which of the five bulbs is off, the function uses the *bulb_counter* variable. During the first loop, the first bulb is off and the next four bulbs are on. With the second loop, the second bulb is off and the other four bulbs are on. The function repeats for each of the bulbs. After the function turns off the fifth bulb, it starts over, turning off the first bulb again:

```
int bulb_counter = 0;
```

All the bulbs that are on are the color red. The function uses the *Graphics*-class *setColor* function to specify the bulb color:

```
g.setColor(Color.red);
```

Using a *for* statement, the function loops through each bulb:

```
for (int i = 0; i < total_bulbs; i++)
```

As discussed, the applet draws bulbs working in groups of five. The applet uses the *bulb_counter* variable to track the current bulb. When the *bulb_counter* variable gets to five, the function resets the counter to zero:

```
if (++bulb_counter == 5)
    bulb_counter = 0;
```

When the applet encounters a bulb that should be off, it draws a red circle filled with the light-gray color. The *drawOval* and *fillOval* function parameters specify the bulb's x-and-y coordinates, as well as the bulb's width and height. In this case, because the width and height are the same, the oval is a circle:

```
if (bulb_counter == off_bulb)
  {
    g.setColor(Color.lightGray);
    g.fillOval(coordinate[i].x, coordinate[i].y, bulb_size, bulb_size);
```

```
        g.setColor(Color.red);
        g.drawOval(coordinate[i].x, coordinate[i].y, bulb_size, bulb_size);
    }
```

To draw a bulb that is on, the applet simply draws a red-filled circle:

```
    g.fillOval(coordinate[i].x, coordinate[i].y, bulb_size, bulb_size);
```

As the function draws its current set of five bulbs, one of the bulbs is off. The function uses the *off_bulb* variable to track the bulb that is currently turned off. When the off bulb is the fifth bulb, the function resets the *off_bulb* variable to zero:

```
    if (++off_bulb == 5)
      off_bulb = 0;
```

Summarizing Changes to the Rest of the Program

The only differences in the *run* function from the previous chapter are:

- The *Font* and the *FontMetrics* objects now reside in the *init* function.

- The *draw_bulbs* function call occurs before the delay.

- The *resize* function was removed from the *imageUpdate* function because the applet now resizes the window in the *init* function.

Enhancements You Can Make to Neon Las Vegas

The current **Neon Las Vegas** applet calculates the bulb coordinates at the start of the applet, and the coordinates then remain constant. If the user sizes the applet window, errors may occur. To start, change the program so that, should the user resize the window, the applet will recalculate all the bulb coordinates. Next, change the code to rotate the bulbs in the counter-clockwise direction. Lastly, consider using multiple colors for the bulbs—something like **Christmas in Las Vegas**.

Putting It All Together

The **Neon Las Vegas** applet showed you how to draw neon lights around an image. More importantly, the applet provided you with techniques you can use to center items within an applet window. In Chapter 12, you will place buttons the user can select with their mouse on the applet window. Specifically, the **Pushbutton Music** applet creates a simple jukebox. Before you continue with Chapter 12, however, make sure you understand the following key concepts:

- ☑ By creating your own *Coordinate* class, your applet can store an object's x-and-y coordinates.

- ☑ The *drawOval* and *fillOval* functions let your applets draw empty and filled ovals.

- ☑ If the height and width of your oval are the same, the *drawOval* and *fillOval* functions will create a circle.

- ☑ Using the *setColor* function, you can control the color used by the *drawOval* and *fillOval* functions.

CHAPTER 12

PUSHBUTTON MUSIC
RESPONDING TO USER BUTTON SELECTIONS

Each of the Java applets you have created thus far have been one-directional, meaning the applet displayed images to the user, or played sounds the user could hear. In each case, the user did not truly interact with the applet. With the **Pushbutton Music** applet, however, all that changes. In this chapter, you will create an applet with which the user can interact. In short, the applet will display three buttons on which the user can click his or her mouse. When the user selects a button, the applet will play a specific audio clip. By the time you finish this chapter, you will understand the following key concepts.

- Using the *Panel* class, an applet can display buttons on which the user can click their mouse.

- To create a button on a panel, an applet uses the *Button* class.

- Each button you place on a panel has a corresponding action. When the user selects the button, the applet's *action* function automatically runs.

- By examining the parameters Java passes to the *action* function, the applet can determine which button the user selected.

- Using the *AudioClip* class *stop* method, an applet can stop the playback of the current audio clip.

USING PUSHBUTTON MUSIC

The **Pushbutton Music** applet extends previous applets to include three buttons, which the user can select with their mouse. When the user clicks their mouse on a button, the applet will play a specific audio clip. If the applet is playing an audio clip, and the user clicks their mouse on a different button, the applet will stop playing the current audio clip and will start playing the newly-selected clip. When you run the **Pushbutton Music** applet, Java will open an applet window and display the image with a title and three buttons, as shown in Figure 12. To "try out" this applet, click on one of the buttons, and the associated audio clip will play.

Figure 12 Displaying an image with a title and three buttons.

THE HTML FILE

The **Pushbutton Music** applet HTML file lets the user specify the title text and the time delay the applet waits between changing a title-text character to red:

```
<applet code=audio.class width=480 height=300>
<param name=message value="Joe's Bar">
<param name=delay value=100>
</applet>
```

LOOKING AT PUSHBUTTON MUSIC

As your Java applets become more complex, they will need to support user interaction. The **Pushbutton Music** applet provides your first step toward interactive applets. Using a panel of buttons, the applet defines actions that correspond to each button. When the user clicks their mouse on a button, the applet performs the corresponding processing. The following code implements the **Pushbutton Music** applet:

```
//*****************************************************************
// audio.java
//*****************************************************************

import java.applet.*;
import java.awt.*;

//*****************************************************************

public class audio extends Applet implements Runnable
   {
     Graphics g;
     Image background;

     int delay_amount = 500;
     Thread my_thread = null;

     AudioClip clip;

     boolean done_loading_image = false;
     boolean thread_running = false;

     String message = "Las Vegas";

     int width;
     int height;
     int message_length;
     char char_array[];

     //──────────────────────────────────────

     public void init()
       {
         g = getGraphics();

         String parameter;
```

```
        background = getImage(getCodeBase(), "piano.gif");

        parameter = getParameter("MESSAGE");
        if (parameter != null)
          message = parameter;

        parameter = getParameter("DELAY");
        if (parameter != null)
          delay_amount = Integer.parseInt(parameter);

        width = size().width;
        height = size().height;

        Image offScrImage = createImage(width, height);
        Graphics offScrGC = offScrImage.getGraphics();
        offScrGC.drawImage(background, 0, 0, width, height, this);

        message_length = message.length();
        char_array = new char[message_length];
        message.getChars(0, message_length, char_array, 0);

        Panel panel = new Panel();
        add("Buttons", panel);
        panel.add(new Button("A"));
        panel.add(new Button("B"));
        panel.add(new Button("C"));

        resize(width, height+40);
      }


//———————————————————————————————

   public boolean action(Event event, Object event_object)
      {
        if (event_object.equals("A"))
          {
            clip.stop();
            clip = getAudioClip(getCodeBase(), "button_a.au");
            clip.loop();
          }
        else if (event_object.equals ("B"))
          {
            clip.stop();
            clip = getAudioClip(getCodeBase(), "button_b.au");
            clip.loop();
          }
        else if (event_object.equals("C"))
          {
            clip.stop();
            clip = getAudioClip(getCodeBase(), "button_c.au");
            clip.loop();
          }

        return true;
      }
```

```
//——————————————————————

public void start()
  {
    if (my_thread == null)
      my_thread = new Thread(this);
  }

//——————————————————————

public void run_thread()
  {
    if (!thread_running)
      {
        my_thread.start();
        thread_running = true;
      }
  }

void delay()
  {
    try
      {
        Thread.sleep(delay_amount);
      }
    catch (InterruptedException e)
      {
      }
  }

//——————————————————————

public void run()
  {
    repaint();

    int red_character = 0;

    clip = getAudioClip(getCodeBase(), "button_a.au");
    clip.loop();

    Font font = new Font("TimesRoman", Font.BOLD, 20);
    g.setFont(font);

    FontMetrics font_metrics = g.getFontMetrics();

    int string_width = font_metrics.stringWidth(message);
    int string_height = font_metrics.getHeight();

    while (true)
      {
        int x = (width - string_width)/2;

        g.setColor(Color.black);
        g.fillRect(x, height+10, string_width, string_height);
```

93

```
                    for (int i = 0; i < message_length; i++)
                      {
                        if (i == red_character)
                          g.setColor(Color.red);
                        else
                          g.setColor(Color.white);

                        g.drawChars(char_array, i, 1, x, height+30);
                        x += fm.charWidth(char_array[i]);
                      }

                    if (++red_character == message_length)
                      red_character = 0;
                    else
                      while (char_array[red_character] == ' ')
                        red_character++;

                    delay();
                  }
              }

    //————————————————————————————

    public boolean imageUpdate(Image img, int infoflags, int x, int y,
                               int w, int h)
      {
        if (infoflags == ALLBITS)
          {
            done_loading_image = true;
            repaint();

            run_thread();

            return false;
          }
        else
          return true;
      }

    //————————————————————————————

    public void paint(Graphics _g)
      {
        if (!done_loading_image)
          showStatus("Pushbutton:  loading image");
        else
          {
            showStatus("Pushbutton:  done");
            g.drawImage(background, 0, 0, width, height, null);
          }
      }
  }
```

Breaking Apart Pushbutton Music

The **Pushbutton Music** applet program adds only one variable to the class variables you have been using within the previous applets. The applet uses the *AudioClip*-class *clip* variable to hold the current audio clip:

```
AudioClip clip;
```

The init Function

Within the *init* function, the applet creates a panel within the applet window. A *panel* is a generic container. In this case, the applet will use the panel to hold three buttons. To create a panel, the applet creates a *Panel* object. Next, the applet uses the *add* function to add the panel to the applet window:

```
Panel panel = new Panel();
add("Buttons", panel);
```

After the applet adds the panel to the applet window, it creates new buttons and adds them to the panel. To add a button to the panel, the applet calls the *Panel* object *add* method. In this case, the applet assigns the three buttons the labels *A*, *B*, and *C*:

```
panel.add(new Button("A"));
panel.add(new Button("B"));
panel.add(new Button("C"));
```

The code to add buttons to your applet window hides many behind-the-scenes operations. In short, the *Applet* class extends the *Panel* class which, in turn, extends the *Container* class. The *Container* class, in turn, contains an *add* function you can use to add objects to a container. When you add an object to a container, Java uses a *LayoutManager* object to control how and where the objects are placed. By default, Java uses *FlowLayout* as the *LayoutManager* which centers objects at the top of the container; hence the locations of the buttons within the applet window shown in Figure 12.

The action Function

As it turns out, any time the user performs an operation on a user-interface component, Java calls the component container's *action* function. In this case, the applet is the container for the mouse operations the user performs on the buttons. As such, when the user clicks his or her mouse on a button, Java calls the *action* function and passes the *action* function two parameters, which specify the event that generated the action and the object on which the action occurred. Later in this book, you will examine the *Event* class in detail. For now, the applet need only examine the *object* parameter:

```
public boolean action(Event event, Object event_object)
```

To determine which button the user clicked, the applet checks the *event_object* parameter. The object's *equals* method checks for equality between the object and the specified parameter. In other words, using the *equals* function, the applet can compare the *event_object* parameter to a button's label. If the *equals* function returns true, the applet knows which button the user selected.

When the applet determines the correct button, the applet stops the current audio clip, and loads and starts the audio clip that corresponds to the selected button. The applet returns the true value to Java to inform Java that it has handled the event:

```
if (event_object.equals("A"))
  {
    clip.stop();
    clip = getAudioClip(getCodeBase(), "button_a.au");
    clip.loop();
  }
else if(event_object.equals("B"))
  {
    clip.stop();
    clip = getAudioClip(getCodeBase(), "button_b.au");
    clip.loop();
  }
else if(event_object.equals("C"))
  {
    clip.stop();
    clip = getAudioClip(getCodeBase(), "button_c.au");
    clip.loop();
  }

return true;
```

As you know, the applet uses a *Thread* object to continuously update the fancy title. When the user clicks their mouse on a button, Java creates a second thread that processes the event. After the thread completes the event processing and returns the true value to Java, the thread terminates. The applet's orginal thread, which is displaying the fancy title, is never disturbed.

The remainder of the **Pushbutton Music** applet's functions are identical to functions already discussed in previous chapters. Therefore, this chapter will not discuss them.

ENHANCEMENTS YOU CAN MAKE TO PUSHBUTTON MUSIC

The **Pushbutton Music** applet provides your foundation for creating interactive applets. To start, change the applet to support four or five buttons, each with a unique audio clip. Next, change the applet to get the audio clip filenames from the HTML file. Lastly, use a method other than *clip.loop* to play back the audio file.

PUTTING IT ALL TOGETHER

The **Pushbutton Music** applet shows you how to create a Java applet that interacts with the user. In Chapter 13, the **Cyber Zoo** applet will extend this applet, letting the user click their mouse on various animal images to play back the corresponding animal sound. Before you continue with Chapter 13, however, make sure you understand the following key concepts:

☑ Using the *Panel* class, an applet can create a container within the applet window.

☑ The *Panel* class inherits from the *Container* class, so applets can use it to hold objects.

☑ The **Pushbutton Music** applet uses a *Panel* class object to hold buttons.

☑ To add *Button*-class objects to a panel, an applet should use the *Panel* object's *add* method.

☑ The *action* function responds to actions on the buttons. When the user clicks their mouse on a button, Java calls the *action* function.

☑ Using the *action* function's second parameter, an applet can determine on which object the action occurred.

CHAPTER 13

CYBER ZOO
GRAPHICS, SOUNDS, AND MOUSE OPERATIONS

In Chapter 12, you created the **Pushbutton Music** applet, which let the user select audio clips from a panel of buttons. By responding to mouse operations, the **Pushbutton Music** applet was your first truly interactive applet. In this chapter, you will use the **Cyber Zoo** applet to learn how to capture mouse clicks within an applet. In short, the Cyber Zoo presents pictures of several different animals. As you click your mouse on an animal, the applet plays back an audio clip of the animal's sound. By the time you finish this chapter, you will understand the following key concepts:

- To capture the user's press of a mouse button, your applet uses the *mouseDown* function.

- When the user presses the mouse button down, Java calls the *mouseDown* function, passing the function x-and-y coordinates of the location at which the user pressed the mouse button.

- When the user releases the mouse button down, Java calls the *mouseUp* function, passing the function x-and-y coordinates of the location at which the user pressed the mouse button.

- When the user moves the mouse with the button down, Java calls the *mouseDrag*.

- When the user simply moves the mouse, without pressing a mouse button down, Java calls the *mouseMove* function.

- To play an audio clip one time (as opposed to looping the clip), you use the *AudioClip* object *play* method.

- By knowing the x-and-y coordinates of objects within the applet window, an applet can determine on which item the user clicked the mouse.

USING CYBER ZOO

When you run the **Cyber Zoo** applet, Java will open an applet window and display an image that contains nine animals, as shown in Figure 13. To "experience" this applet, click your mouse on one of the animals. The **Cyber Zoo** applet, in turn, will play the animal's corresponding audio clip.

THE HTML FILE

The purpose of the **Cyber Zoo** applet is to show you how an applet can respond to mouse operations. Therefore, the applet does not support HTML-based parameters. Use the following HTML file to access the applet:

```
<applet code=animals.class width=576 height=360> </applet>
```

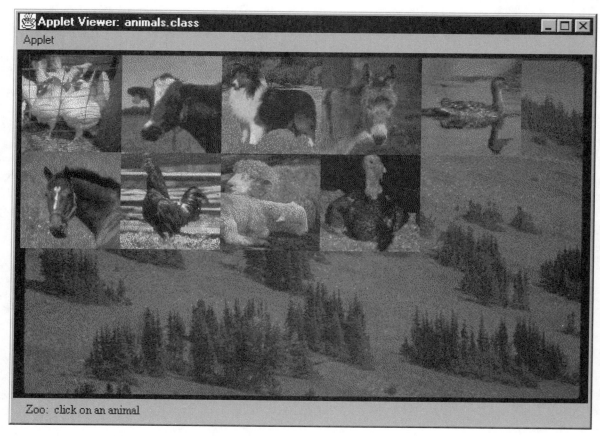

Figure 13 *Displaying the Cyber Zoo image of nine animals.*

LOOKING AT CYBER ZOO

In Chapter 12, you used the **Pushbutton Music** applet to respond to button selections for buttons that reside in a *Panel* object. Although the applet supported user interaction, it's interface was quite simplistic. In the **Cyber Zoo** applet, on the other hand, you will examine code that responds to mouse clicks on objects that your applet can disperse across the applet window. The following code implements the **Cyber Zoo** applet:

```
//*************************************************************
// animals.java
//*************************************************************

import java.applet.*;
import java.awt.*;

//*************************************************************

public class animals extends Applet
  {
    final int TOTAL_ANIMALS = 9;

    int max_rows;
    boolean done_loading_image = false;
```

```
   int width;
   int height;

   Graphics g;
   Image background;
   Image animal_gif[];
   AudioClip clip;

   //—————————————————————

   public void init()
     {
        g = getGraphics();

        background = getImage(getCodeBase(), "cyberzoo.gif");

        width = size().width;
        height = size().height;

        Image offScrImage = createImage(width, height);
        Graphics offScrGC = offScrImage.getGraphics();
        offScrGC.drawImage(background, 0, 0, width, height, this);

        animal_gif = new Image[TOTAL_ANIMALS];
        for (int i = 0; i < TOTAL_ANIMALS; i++)
          animal_gif[i] = getImage(getCodeBase(),
                                   "animal" + (i+1) + ".gif");

        max_rows = (TOTAL_ANIMALS + 4) / 5;
     }

   //—————————————————————

   public boolean mouseDown(Event evt, int x, int y)
     {
        System.out.println("X " + x + " Y " + y);

        if (x < 500 && y < max_rows*100)
          {
             int index = (y/100)*5 + (x/100);
             if (index < TOTAL_ANIMALS)
               {
                  String filename = "animal" + (index+1) + ".au";
                  clip = getAudioClip(getCodeBase(), filename);
                  System.out.println("Playing " + filename);
                  clip.play();
               }
          }

        return true;
     }

   //—————————————————————
   public boolean imageUpdate(Image img, int infoflags, int x, int y,
                              int width, int height)
```

```
       {
         if (infoflags == ALLBITS)
           {
              done_loading_image = true;
              showStatus("Zoo:  click on an animal");
              repaint();
              return false;
           }
         else
           return true;
       }

      //————————————————————————

      public void paint(Graphics g)
        {
          if (!done_loading_image)
            showStatus("Zoo:  loading image");
          else
            {
              g.drawImage(background, 0, 0, width, height, this);

              for (int i = 0; i < max_rows; i++)
                for (int j = i*5; j < Math.min ((i+1)*5, TOTAL_ANIMALS); j++)
                  g.drawImage(animal_gif[j], (j-(i*5))*100+ 5, i*100+5,
                                  this);
            }
        }
    }
```

BREAKING APART CYBER ZOO

Much of the code within the **Cyber Zoo** applet is similar to that which you have examined in other applets. Therefore, this section will focus only on new concepts. Note, however, that because the **Cyber Zoo** applet does not use a *Thread* object to continually update a fancy title or to scroll a marquee message, the applet does not require the *Runnable* interface:

```
public class animals extends Applet
```

As shown in Figure 13, the **Cyber Zoo** applet displays nine animals within the applet window. The applet uses the TOTAL_ANIMALS constant to track the animal count:

```
final int TOTAL_ANIMALS = 9;
```

As you may recall, the *final* keyword tells the Java compiler that this variable's value will not change. Creating a constant using the *final* keyword is similar to using the *const* keyword in C++.

The **Cyber Zoo** applet displays the animal images in two rows, placing five animals on the top row, and four on the second. The applet uses *max_rows* to store the number of rows of animal pictures:

```
int max_rows;
```

Next, the applet declares variables to store the applet window's width and height, and a *boolean* value that indicates whether the applet has finished loading the image:

```
int width;
int height;

boolean done_loading_image = false;
```

Finally, the applet declares variables to store the graphics context, the background image, an array of animal images, and an audio clip object:

```
Graphics g;
Image background;
Image animal_gif[];
AudioClip clip;
```

Initializing the Applet

Like each of the previous applets, the **Cyber Zoo** applet uses the *init* function to initialize its key variables. After the applet loads the background image, the applet allocates an array to hold the individual animal images:

```
animal_gif = new Image[TOTAL_ANIMALS];
```

Next, the applet uses a *for* loop to load each animal image from a file. Notice that the animal-image filenames use a combination of strings and integers (such as animal1.gif). Remember, when you add an integer to a string, Java converts the integer to a string, and then concatenates (joins) the strings together:

```
for (int i = 0; i < TOTAL_ANIMALS; i++)
    animal_gif[i] = getImage(getCodeBase(), "animal" + (i+1) + ".gif");
```

Lastly, the applet calculates the number of rows of animals it must display:

```
max_rows = (TOTAL_ANIMALS + 4) / 5;
```

Responding to the Mouse-Down Action

Each time the user clicks a mouse within an applet, Java calls the *mouseDown* function. Java passes, as parameters, to the function, the event, and the x-and-y coordinates at which the user clicked the mouse:

```
public boolean mouseDown(Event evt, int x, int y)
```

To help you better understand the mouse-click processing, the **Cyber Zoo** applet uses a system-console window to display the x-and-y coordinates of each mouse event:

```
System.out.println("X " + x + " Y " + y);
```

The applet assumes the size of each animal image is 100 pixels wide by 100 pixels high. So, if the x-coordinate of a mouse event is greater than 500 (five animals across the window), the user did not click on an animal, and the applet ignores the mouse click. In addition, by using the *max_rows* variable, the applet can test the y-coordinate to make sure the user clicked the mouse within the rows of animals:

```
if (x < 500 && y < max_rows*100)
```

If the x-and-y coordinates of the mouse event are inside the rectangle that encompasses the animal images, the applet determines the index number that corresponds to the animal on which the user clicked their mouse:

```
int index = (y/100)*5 + (x/100);
```

If the user clicked on an animal, the applet creates the filename of the corresponding audio clip, displays out the filename to the console, and then plays the audio clip:

```
if (index < TOTAL_ANIMALS)
  {
    String filename = "animal" + (index+1) + ".au";
    clip = getAudioClip(getCodeBase(), filename);
    System.out.println("Playing " + filename);
    clip.play();
  }
```

Notice that the applet uses the *AudioClip* class *play* method to play the audio clip, and not the *loop* method that you have used in previous applets. The *play* method plays the audio clip once, while the *loop* method plays the clip continuously.

Lastly, the function returns the true value to inform Java that it handled the mouse click:

```
return true;
```

Painting the Images

Like many of the previous applets, the *paint* function displays the images within the applet window. Providing the background image has finished loading, the *paint* function first displays the background image:

```
g.drawImage(background, 0, 0, width, height, this);
```

Next, the *paint* function uses nested *for* loops to draw the animal images on top of the background image:

```
for (int i = 0; i < max_rows; i++)
  for (int j = i*5; j < Math.min ((i+1)*5, TOTAL_ANIMALS); j++)
```

The outer *for* loop steps through each row, and the inner loop draws five animals per row. Note that because the last row might not have five animals, the applet uses the *Math* class *min* function to stop the loop with the last animal.

To draw the animals within the applet window, the applet uses the variable *j* as an index to the current animal, and the variable *i* to determine the row number. Using the image size, animal index, and row number, the applet calculates each image's top-left x-and-y coordinates:

```
g.drawImage(animal_gif[j], (j-(i*5))*100+ 5, i*100+5, this);
```

ENHANCEMENTS YOU CAN MAKE TO CYBER ZOO

The current **Cyber Zoo** applet hard codes the number of animals within its source code. To start, add a parameter to the HTML file that specifies the number of animals.

Because the applet draws the animals within the applet window, some flashing appears on the screen. Modify the program to load the animal images on an off-screen image, and then display the image after is has been built. Building an image off-screen before you display the image is often called *double-buffering*.

PUTTING IT ALL TOGETHER

The **Cyber Zoo** applet shows you how to capture the mouse events, and then how to determine on which screen object the user clicked their mouse. As your Java applets become more complex, your ability to respond to mouse events is critical. In Chapter 14, using the **Animal I.D.** applet, you will expand the applet presented here to display pop-up animal-name boxes as the user moves their mouse over the animal images. Before you continue with Chapter 14, however, make sure you understand the following key concepts:

☑ To capture a mouse event within your applet, use the *mouseDown* function.

☑ When the user clicks their mouse within an applet window, Java calls the *mouseDown* function, specifying the x-and-y coordinates at which the user clicked the mouse.

☑ To play an audio clip only one time, use the *AudioClip*-class *play* method.

☑ By keeping track of screen-object coordinates, an applet can determine on which screen object the user clicked their mouse.

CHAPTER 14

ANIMAL I.D.
USING MESSAGE BOXES TO IDENTIFY SCREEN OBJECTS

In Chapter 13, the **Cyber Zoo** applet taught you how to capture mouse clicks within a Java applet. In this chapter, you will learn how to track the mouse movement across your applet window. The **Animal I.D.** applet extends the **Cyber Zoo** applet to display a small message box that contains the animal's name as the user moves the mouse over the animal image. As your Java applets become more complex, there will be times when the applet window contains many different objects. If the user needs to determine an object's purpose, the user can rest the mouse pointer on top of the object. The applet, in turn, will display a small message box that describes the object. By the time you finish this chapter, you will understand the following key concepts:

- To capture mouse movements within a Java applet, you use the *mouseMove* function.

- To display a filled rectangle within the applet window, you use the *Graphics*-class *fillRect* function.

- To control the *fillRect* function's fill color, use the *Graphics*-class *setColor* method.

USING ANIMAL I.D.

At first glance, the **Animal I.D.** applet appears identical to the **Cyber Zoo** applet you created in Chapter 13. When you run the **Animal I.D.** applet, Java will open an applet window and display the nine animal images. However, as you move your mouse over an animal image, the **Animal I.D.** applet will display a message box that contains the animal's name, as shown in Figure 14. If you click your mouse on an animal, the applet will play the animal's corresponding audio clip.

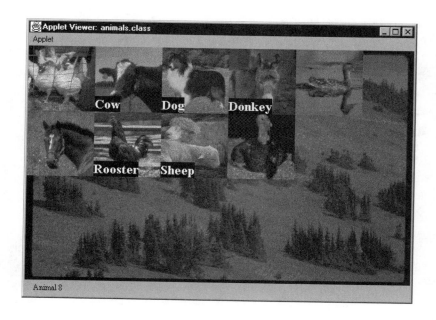

Figure 14 Displaying message boxes that identify screen objects.

THE HTML FILE

The purpose of the **Animal I.D.** applet is to show you how an applet can respond to mouse movement. Therefore, the applet does not support HTML-based parameters. Use the following HTML file to access the applet:

```
<applet code=animals.class width=576 height=360> </applet>
```

LOOKING AT ANIMAL I.D.

The previous **Cyber Zoo** applet displayed nine animal images over a background image. The **Animal I.D.** applet improves upon **Cyber Zoo** by letting the user display each animal's name. To display an animal name, the user simply moves the mouse pointer on top of the animal image. The applet, in turn, tracks the movement of the mouse to determine when the mouse pointer is over an animal image. The following code implements the **Animal I.D.** applet:

```java
//*************************************************************
// animals.java
//*************************************************************

import java.applet.*;
import java.awt.*;

//*************************************************************

public class animals extends Applet
   {
     final int TOTAL_ANIMALS = 9;

     Graphics g;
     Image background;
     Image animal_gif[];
     String description[];

     boolean done_loading_image = false;

     int max_rows;
     int width;
     int height;
     int current_item = 0;

     AudioClip clip;

     //————————————————————————————

     public void init()
       {
         g = getGraphics();

         background = getImage(getCodeBase(), "cyberzoo.gif");

         width = size().width;
         height = size().height;
```

105

```
        Image offScrImage = createImage(width, height);
        Graphics offScrGC = offScrImage.getGraphics();
        offScrGC.drawImage(background, 0, 0, width, height, this);

        animal_gif = new Image[TOTAL_ANIMALS];
        for (int i = 0; i < TOTAL_ANIMALS; i++)
          animal_gif[i] = getImage(getCodeBase(), "animal" + (i+1) +
                                    ".gif");

        get_descriptions();

        max_rows = (TOTAL_ANIMALS + 4) / 5;
    }

//————————————————————————

void get_descriptions()
    {
        description = new String[TOTAL_ANIMALS];

        description[0] = new String("Chicken");
        description[1] = new String("Cow");
        description[2] = new String("Dog");
        description[3] = new String("Donkey");
        description[4] = new String("Duck");
        description[5] = new String("Horse");
        description[6] = new String("Rooster");
        description[7] = new String("Sheep");
        description[8] = new String("Turkey");
    }

//————————————————————————

public boolean mouseMove(Event evt, int x, int y)
    {
        int where = 0;

        if (x < 500 && y < max_rows*100)
          {
            int index = (y/100)*5 + (x/100);
            if (index < TOTAL_ANIMALS)
              {
                where = index + 1;
                if (current_item != where)
                  {
                    System.out.println(description[index]);

                    Font font = new Font("TimesRoman", Font.BOLD, 20);
                    g.setFont(font);

                    FontMetrics font_metrics = g.getFontMetrics();

                    int string_width =
                     font_metrics.stringWidth(description[index]);
                    int string_height = font_metrics.getHeight();
```

```
                    int x2 = (x/100)*100;
                    int y2 = ((y+100)/100)*100;

                    g.setColor(Color.black);
                    g.fillRect(x2, y2-string_height, string_width,
                            string_height);

                    g.setColor(Color.white);
                    g.drawString(description[index], x2, y2-
                        font_metrics.getDescent());
                }
            }
        }

    current_item = where;

    if (current_item == 0)
        showStatus("");
    else
        showStatus("Animal " + current_item);

    return true;
    }

//————————————————————————

public boolean mouseDown(Event evt, int x, int y)
    {
    System.out.println("X " + x + " Y " + y);

    if (x < 500 && y < max_rows*100)
        {
        int index = (y/100)*5 + (x/100);
        if (index < TOTAL_ANIMALS)
            {
            String filename = "animal" + (index+1) + ".au";
            clip = getAudioClip(getCodeBase(), filename);
            System.out.println("Playing " + filename);
            clip.play();
            }
        }

    return true;
    }

//————————————————————————

public boolean imageUpdate(Image img, int infoflags, int x, int y,
                        int width, int height)
    {
    if (infoflags == ALLBITS)
```

```
                   {
                     done_loading_image = true;
                     repaint();
                     return false;
                   }
               else
                  return true;
            }


      //————————————————————————


      public void paint(Graphics g)
        {
          if (!done_loading_image)
            showStatus("Zoo:  loading image");
          else
            {
              g.drawImage(background, 0, 0, width, height, this);

              for (int i = 0; i < max_rows; i++)
                for (int j = i*5; j < Math.min ((i+1)*5, TOTAL_ANIMALS); j++)
                    g.drawImage(animal_gif[j], (j-(i*5))*100, i*100,
                                  this);
            }
        }
    }
```

BREAKING APART ANIMAL I.D.

Much of the **Animal I.D.** applet code is similar to that of the **Cyber Zoo** applet you examined in Chapter 13. Therefore, this section only examines the code that differs. To start, the applet adds two class variables. The first variable, *description*, is an array of character strings that contain the animal names:

```
String description[];
```

The second variable, *current_item*, contains the index to the last animal for which the applet displayed a description:

```
int current_item = 0;
```

Initializing the Applet

Within the *init* function, the applet calls the *get_descriptions* function to assign the animal names to the *description* array:

```
get_descriptions();
```

As you can see, the *get_description* function fills the array with nine *String* objects, each of which contains an animal name:

```
void get_descriptions()
  {
    description = new String[TOTAL_ANIMALS];

    description[0] = new String("Chicken");
    description[1] = new String("Cow");
    description[2] = new String("Dog");
    description[3] = new String("Donkey");
    description[4] = new String("Duck");
    description[5] = new String("Horse");
    description[6] = new String("Rooster");
    description[7] = new String("Sheep");
    description[8] = new String("Turkey");
  }
```

As you can see, the function uses the *new* operator to allocate space for each array element. The *String*-class constructor, in turn, assigns the animal name to the *String* object.

Displaying the Descriptions

As the user moves the mouse over an animal image, the applet displays a message box that contains the animal name. To capture the user's mouse movements, the applet uses the *mouseMove* function. As it turns out, each time the user moves the mouse, Java calls the *mouseMove* function, passing the mouse pointer's x-and-y coordinates as parameters to the function,.

Within the *mouseMove* function, the applet must determine if the user has moved a mouse over an animal image. Next, if the mouse is over an image, the applet must determine if the image is the same as the last image the mouse was over. In other words, as the user moves the mouse over an image, Java may call the *mouseMove* function several times. The *mouseMove* function, however, only needs to perform its processing the first time the user moves the mouse over the image.

To track the current image, the *mouseMove* function uses the *current_item* variable. When the user moves the mouse pointer over a mouse, the function determines the index value that corresponds to the image, and compares the index to the *current_item* variable. If the index and *current_item* are equal, the user is moving the mouse over the same image.

The *current_item* variable always contains a value that is one greater than the current index. That's because the applet uses the *current_item* value of zero to indicate there is no current item:

```
where = index + 1;
if (current_item != where)
```

To help you better understand the applet's processing, the applet writes debug statements to the system-console window. To center the animal name beneath the animal image, the applet creates a *Font* object, gets the *FontMetrics* object for the font, and then determines the description's width and height:

```
System.out.println(description[index]);

Font font = new Font("TimesRoman", Font.BOLD, 20);
```

109

```
g.setFont(font);

FontMetrics font_metrics = g.getFontMetrics();

int string_width = font_metrics.stringWidth(description[index]);
int string_height = font_metrics.getHeight();
```

The applet displays the animal's name at the bottom-left corner of the animal image. The applet stores the corner's x-and-y coordinates within the variables *x2* and *y2*, as shown here:

```
int x2 = (x/100)*100;
int y2 = ((y+100)/100)*100;
```

The applet displays the animal description within a black rectangle. To create the rectangle, the applet first selects the color black, and then uses the *fillRect* function to draw a rectangle whose size is determined by the *string_width* and the *string_height* variables:

```
g.setColor(Color.black);
g.fillRect(x2, y2-string_height, string_width, string_height);
```

To display the animal name within the black rectangle, the applet uses a white font:

```
g.setColor(Color.white);
g.drawString(description[index], x2, y2-fm.getDescent());
```

After the applet displays the description, it sets the *current_item* variable to the current image. In this way, the applet won't redraw the same description if the user continues to move the mouse over the current animal:

```
current_item = where;
```

Using the *showStatus* function, the applet displays status-bar messages that describe the current animal:

```
if (current_item == 0)
   showStatus("");
else
   showStatus("Animal" + current_item);
```

Lastly, the function returns the *true* value to inform Java the function has handled the mouse event:

```
return true;
```

The remainder of the **Animal I.D.** applet is the same as the **Cyber Zoo** applet you examined in Chapter 13.

ENHANCEMENTS YOU CAN MAKE TO ANIMAL I.D.

As you learned, the Animal I.D. applet hardcodes the animal descriptions within its source file. A better way for the applet to get the animal descriptions is to use HTML-based parameters. The applet uses the *current_item* variable to prevent the applet from redrawing an animal's name as the user moves the mouse over the current image. Unfortunately, if the user moves the mouse off the image and then back onto the image, the applet will redraw the animal name. Modify the applet to use an array that tracks which animal's name the applet has displayed. Next, use the array to redisplay animal names within the *paint* function in case the user covers the applet window with a second window. In this way, the applet can paint the window's contents correctly with the previous animal names displayed.

PUTTING IT ALL TOGETHER

The **Animal I.D.** applet shows you how to capture mouse movements within a Java applet. In Chapter 15, you will use the **Animal Popups** applet to display a message box when the user moves the mouse onto an animal image, and then to remove the box when the user moves the mouse off the image. Before you continue with Chapter 15, however, make sure you understand the following key concepts:

☑ Using the *mouseMove* function, your applets can capture mouse movements.

☑ Using the *Graphics*-class *fillRect* method, your applet can draw a box filled with the current color.

☑ Using the *Graphics*-class *setColor* method, your applet can specify the current color used by other *Graphics*-class functions, such as *fillRect*.

CHAPTER 15

ANIMAL POPUPS
POPUP MESSAGES THAT COME AND GO WITH THE MOUSE

In Chapter 14, you used the **Animal I.D.** applet to learn how to trap mouse movements within a Java applet. In this chapter, the **Animal Popups** applet builds upon the **Animal I.D.** applet to display the animal-name message box as the user moves the mouse onto the animal image, and to remove the message box as the user moves the mouse off the image. By the time you finish this chapter, you will understand the following key concepts:

- ◆ To display and later erase a message box as the user moves the mouse onto and off of an animal image, an applet simply tests for movements into and out of the image.

- ◆ Using the *Graphics* class *create* method, an applet can create a second graphics context that is based on the current context.

- ◆ Using the *Graphics* class *clipRect* function, your applet can define an area within the applet window where the applet's graphics functions will take place. If the applet performs any graphics operations outside of the clipping rectangle, they will be ignored by Java.

- ◆ When an applet removes an image that was previously displayed on top of a background image, the applet must restore the piece of the background image that was previously covered.

USING ANIMAL POPUPS

As discussed, the **Animal Popups** applet displays and later removes message boxes that contain animal names. You will use many of the concepts the applet presents in several future Java applets. For example, you will learn that when you remove a graphics image or text from on top of a background image, you need to redraw the parts of the background image that were previously covered. In addition, the **Animal Popups** applet shows you how to create a clipping rectangle that controls the area within the applet window where the applet can perform graphics operations.

When you run the **Animal Popups** applet, Java will open an applet window that contains nine animal images, as shown in Figure 15. To "experience" the **Animal Popups** applet, move your mouse onto an animal image. The applet, in turn, will display a popup message box that contains the animal's name. Next, as you move your mouse off the image, the applet will remove the message box. As before, if you click your mouse on an animal image, the applet will play back the animal's corresponding audio clip.

THE HTML FILE

The purpose of the **Animal Popup** applet is to show you how to update a background image as you review a graphics item that previously covered the image. Therefore, the applet does not support HTML-based parameters. Use the following HTML file to access the applet:

```
<applet code=animals.class width=520 height=324> </applet>
```

Figure 15 *Displaying a popup message box within an applet window.*

LOOKING AT ANIMAL POPUPS

The previous **Animal I.D.** applet let you display a message box as the user moved the mouse over a specific region within the applet window. The **Animal Popups** applet improves upon that applet by erasing the message box as the user moves the mouse out of the region. The following code implements the **Animal Popups** applet:

```
//****************************************************************
// animals.java
//****************************************************************

import java.applet.*;
import java.awt.*;

//****************************************************************

public class animals extends Applet
   {
     final int TOTAL_ANIMALS = 9;

     Graphics g;
     Image background;
     Image animal_gif[];
     String description[];

     boolean done_loading_image = false;
```

```java
    int max_rows;
    int width;
    int height;
    int current_item = 0;

    AudioClip clip;
    FontMetrics fm;

    //————————————————————————

    public void init()
      {
        g = getGraphics();

        Font font = new Font("TimesRoman", Font.BOLD, 20);
        g.setFont(font);

        font_metrics = g.getFontMetrics();

        background = getImage(getCodeBase(), "cyberzoo.gif");

        width = size().width;
        height = size().height;

        Image offScrImage = createImage(width, height);
        Graphics offScrGC = offScrImage.getGraphics();
        offScrGC.drawImage(background, 0, 0, width, height, this);

        animal_gif = new Image[TOTAL_ANIMALS];
        for (int i = 0; i < TOTAL_ANIMALS; i++)
          animal_gif[i] = getImage(getCodeBase(), "animal"+(i+1)+".gif");

        get_descriptions();

        max_rows = (TOTAL_ANIMALS + 4) / 5;
      }

    //————————————————————————

    void get_descriptions()
      {
        description = new String[TOTAL_ANIMALS];

        description[0] = new String("Chicken");
        description[1] = new String("Cow");
        description[2] = new String("Dog");
        description[3] = new String("Donkey");
        description[4] = new String("Duck");
        description[5] = new String("Horse");
        description[6] = new String("Rooster");
        description[7] = new String("Sheep");
        description[8] = new String("Turkey");
      }

    //————————————————————————
```

```
public boolean mouseMove(Event evt, int x, int y)
  {
    int where_clicked = 0;
    boolean erased = false;

    if (x < 500 && y < max_rows*100)
      {
        int index = (y/100)*5 + (x/100);
        if (index < TOTAL_ANIMALS)
          {
            where_clicked = index + 1;
            if (current_item != where_clicked)
              {
                if (current_item != 0)
                  {
                    erase_name(current_item - 1);
                    erased = true;
                  }
                System.out.println(description[index]);
                draw_name(index);
              }
          }
      }

    if (!erased && current_item != 0 && current_item != where_clicked)
      erase_name(current_item - 1);

    current_item = where_clicked;

    if (current_item == 0)
      showStatus("");
    else
      showStatus("Animal " + current_item);

    return true;
  }

//——————————————————————————

void erase_name(int index)
  {
    int string_width = font_metrics.stringWidth(description[index]);
    int string_height = font_metrics.getHeight();

    int x = (index%5) * 100;
    int y = (index/5) * 100;

    int x2 = (x/100)*100 + 50 - string_width/2;
    int y2 = ((y+100)/100)*100;

    Graphics g2;
    g2 = g.create();

    g2.clipRect(x2, y2-string_height, string_width, string_height);
```

```java
        g2.drawImage(background, 0, 0, width, height, null);
    }

    //————————————————————————

    void draw_name(int index)
    {
        int string_width = font_metrics.stringWidth(description [index]);
        int string_height = font_metrics.getHeight();

        int x = (index%5)*100;
        int y = (index/5)*100;

        int x2 = (x/100)*100 + 50 - string_width/2;
        int y2 = ((y+100)/100)*100;

        g.setColor(Color.black);
        g.fillRect(x2, y2-string_height, string_width, string_height);

        g.setColor(Color.white);
        g.drawString(description[index], x2, y2-font_metrics.getDescent());
    }

    //————————————————————————

    public boolean mouseDown(Event evt, int x, int y)
    {
        System.out.println("X " + x + " Y " + y);

        if (x < 500 && y < max_rows*100)
        {
            int index = (y/100)*5 + (x/100);
            if (index < TOTAL_ANIMALS)
            {
                String filename = "animal" + (index+1) + ".au";
                clip = getAudioClip(getCodeBase(), filename);
                System.out.println("Playing " + filename);
                clip.play();
            }
        }

        return true;
    }

    //————————————————————————

    public boolean imageUpdate(Image img, int infoflags, int x, int y,
                               int width, int height)
    {
        if (infoflags == ALLBITS)
        {
            done_loading_image = true;
            repaint ();
            return false;
        }
```

```
        else
          return true;
      }


    //————————————————————————————————

    public void paint(Graphics g)
        {
        if (!done_loading_image)
          showStatus("Zoo:  loading image");
        else
          {
            g.drawImage(background, 0, 0, width, height, this);
            g.setColor(Color.white);

            for (int i = 0; i < max_rows; i++)
              for (int j = i*5; j < Math.min ((i+1)*5, TOTAL_ANIMALS); j++)
                {
                  g.drawImage(animal_gif[j], (j-(i*5))*100+ 5, i*100+5,
                            this);

                  g.drawRect((j-(i*5))*100+ 5, i*100+5, 100, 100);
                }
          }
      }
    }
```

BREAKING APART ANIMAL POPUPS

The **Animal Popups** applet is very similar to the **Animal I.D.** applet you examined in Chapter 14. In fact, this applet adds only one variable to the class variables you examined in the previous applet. The applet uses a *FontMetrics* object to determine the size of the name whose message box the applet must display or erase:

```
FontMetrics font_metrics;
```

Initializing the Applet

In addition to the initialization you examined in the **Animal I.D.** applet's *init* function, the **Animal Popups** applet *init* function creates the *Font* object and the *FontMetrics* object, because the two objects do not change during the applet's execution:

```
Font font = new Font("TimesRoman", Font.BOLD, 20);
g.setFont(font);

font_metrics = g.getFontMetrics();
```

Capturing Mouse Movements

As you learned in Chapter 14, to capture mouse movements, your applet uses the *mouseMove* function. In the case of the **Animal Popups** applet, the *mouseMove* function must determine if the mouse has moved into or out of an animal's image area. If the user has moved the mouse into the image area, the function must display the animal's name. Likewise, if the user has moved the mouse out of an animal's image area, the function must erase the animal's name. The **Animal I.D.** applet presented the Java code to draw the animal's name within the *mouseMove* function, as shown in Chapter 14. In this applet, that piece of code now resides in its own function, called *draw_name*. In a similar way, the code to erase an animal's name resides in the *erase_name* function.

As was the case with the **Animal I.D.** applet, when the user moves the mouse pointer within an animal's area, the applet must first check to see if the mouse pointer has moved out of another animal's image. If the mouse pointer has moved from one image to another, the applet must erase the previous image name:

```
if (current_item != 0)
  {
     erase_name(current_item - 1);
     erased = true;
  }
```

As you may recall from Chapter 14, the *current_item* variable's value is always one greater than the index of the corresponding animal. Therefore, to erase the correct animal's name, the applet subtracts one from the *current_item* variable. To help you better understand the applet's processing, the applet displays debug messages to the system-console window before it display's the current animal's name:

```
System.out.println(description[index]);
draw_name(index);
```

If the user moved the mouse from one animal's area, but did not move the mouse onto a second animal, the applet simply needs to erase the animal's name:

```
if (!erased && current_item != 0 && current_item != where_clicked)
   erase_name(current_item - 1);
```

The remainder of the *mouseMove* function is the same as the function code you examined in Chapter 14.

Erasing an Animal's Name

When the user moves the mouse out of an animal's region, the applet calls the *erase_name* function to erase the animal's name and passes to it the index of the animal:

```
void erase_name(int index)
```

To start, the function determines the applet-window area within which the applet displayed the animal's name:

```
int string_width = font_metrics.stringWidth(description[index]);
int string_height = font_metrics.getHeight();

int x = (index%5)*100;
int y = (index/5)*100;

int x2 = (x/100)*100+50 - string_width/2;
int y2 = ((y+100)/100)*100;
```

As briefly discussed, when an applet removes an image from on top of a background image, the applet must redraw the part of the background image that was previously hidden. Rather than redraw the entire background image, the applet should redraw only the part that was previously obscured. To redraw part of an image, the applet first creates a copy of the graphics context:

```
Graphics g2;
g2 = g.create();
```

Next, the applet uses the *Graphics*-class *clipRect* function to define a clipping rectangle. In short, a clipping rectangle defines an area within the applet window within which the applet can perform graphics operations. If the applet tries to perform an operation outside of the clipping rectangle, Java ignores or clips that part of the graphic. In this case, the applet will restrict the clipping rectangle to the window area that previously contained the animal's name:

```
g2.clipRect(x2, y2-string_height, string_width, string_height);
```

After the applet defines the clipping rectangle, the applet can redraw the background image. Because the clipping rectangle defines the window area where graphics operations can take place, only the previously missing region of the background image is redrawn:

```
g2.drawImage(background, 0, 0, width, height, null);
```

If the applet had not made a copy of the graphics context, the clipping rectangle would remain in effect for the main graphics context, and no future graphics displayed outside the clipping rectangle would show up within the applet window. By making a copy of the graphics context, the clipping rectangle affects only the function calls made using the copy, such as the *drawImage* function call.

Drawing the Animal's Name

To display an animal's name, the applet calls the *draw_name* function. As you can see, the function does not return a value, and receives one parameter that specifies the index of the animal whose name the function is to draw:

```
void draw_name(int index)
```

To start, the *draw_name* function uses the name's width and height to determine the area within which it will draw the animal's name:

```
int string_width = font_metrics.stringWidth(description [index]);
int string_height = font_metrics.getHeight();

int x = (index%5)*100;
int y = (index/5)*100;

int x2 = (x/100)*100+50 - string_width/2;
int y2 = ((y+100)/100)*100;
```

After the function determines the region within which it will display the animal's name, the applet fills the region with a black rectangle:

```
g.setColor(Color.black);
g.fillRect(x2, y2-string_height, string_width, string_height);
```

The function then draws the animal's name, using a white font:

```
g.setColor(Color.white);
g.drawString(description[index], x2, y2-font_metrics.getDescent());
```

Note the use of the *getDescent* function, which returns the number of pixels below the baseline of the font. When you use *drawString*, the y-coordinate specifies the string's baseline. Because the *y2* variable contains the bottom of the rectangle, the function subtracts the font's descent to determine the baseline.

The paint Function

To help the user recognize an animal's image area, the *paint* function displays a white rectangle around each animal's image:

```
g.drawRect((j-(i*5))*100+ 5, i*100+5, 100, 100);
```

ENHANCEMENTS YOU CAN MAKE TO ANIMAL POPUPS

The current **Animal Popup** applet treats the message boxes as popups that come and go with the mouse. Depending on your applet's purpose, you may want to display all the animals names, and use a special font for the active animal. In this way, rather than erasing the name of the animal, you can change the name's appearance. You might, for example, display a red string when the mouse is in the animal's area, and a gray string when the mouse leaves the area. You could also use a different image when the mouse leaves the area, which would require that you have two images for each animal.

PUTTING IT ALL TOGETHER

The **Animal Popup** applet shows you how to use a clipping rectangle to control graphics operations. In Chapter 16, you will use the **Election Year** applet to learn how to track objects dispersed across the applet window. Before you continue with Chapter 16, however, make sure you understand the following key concepts:

☑ To create a second graphics context, use the *Graphics*-class *create* method.

☑ Using a second graphics context is convenient when you want to make temporary changes to the context, such as defining a temporary clipping rectangle.

☑ A clipping rectangle defines a region within the applet window where graphics operations can occur. If the applet performs graphics operations outside of the clipping rectangle, Java ignores them.

☑ To create a clipping rectangle, use the *Graphics*-class *clipRect* function.

☑ When an applet removes an image that was previously displayed on top of a background image, the applet must restore the piece of the background image that was previously covered.

CHAPTER 16

ELECTION YEAR
KEEPING TRACK OF COORDINATES OF ITEMS

In Chapter 15, you learned how to display and erase the descriptions of the items displayed on an image. As you may recall, each of the animal images you displayed in Chapter 15 were located on the screen at predefined places. In this chapter, you will again display and track multiple screen images. However, this time the images can reside at any location. Therefore, your applet must keep track of each image's screen coordinates. Luckily, the program defines a *Coordinate* class that makes tracking an object's x-and-y coordinates easy. By the time you finish this chapter, you will understand the following key concepts:

◆ Within your applet, you can keep track of an object's screen coordinates by using the *Coordinate* class.

◆ The *Coordinate* class members let your applet store an object's x-and-y coordinates.

◆ By knowing an object's s coordinates and size, your applet can determine when the user has moved the mouse on top of the object.

USING ELECTION YEAR

Across the Web, one of the most often visited Web sites is **http://www.whitehouse.gov**. To help the site's Webmaster jazz things up a little (or Java things up), we created the **Election Year** applet. When you run the **Election Year** applet, pictures of nine of the past presidents will appear as independent graphics that sit on top of an image of the White House, as shown in Figure 16. To use the **Election Year** applet, simply move your mouse onto an image of a president. The applet, in turn, will display the President's name, centered at the bottom of the picture. As you move your mouse off of the image, the applet removes the President's name.

Figure 16 Displaying an image with nine items in their own space.

THE HTML FILE

Use the following HTML file to run the **Election Year** applet:

```
<applet code=people.class width=640 height=400> </applet>
```

LOOKING AT ELECTION YEAR

As discussed, the previous **Animal Popups** applet displayed nine animals at fixed locations. Because the applet knew each animal's relative screen coordinates, it could determine when the user moved the mouse on top of the animal image. In the **Election Year** applet, however, the images can reside at any screen location. Therefore, the applet must track each image's screen coordinates individually. To track the image coordinates, the applet uses an array of coordinate values. Each entry in the array corresponds to the x-and-y location of an image's top-left corner. By knowing the image coordinates and size, the applet can determine when the user has moved the mouse onto and off of an image. The following code implements the **Election Year** applet:

```
//*********************************************************************
// people.java
//*********************************************************************

import java.applet.*;
import java.awt.*;


//*********************************************************************

class Coordinate
   {
     public int x;
     public int y;

     public Coordinate(int x, int y)
       {
         this.x = x;
         this.y = y;
       }
   }


//*********************************************************************

public class people extends Applet
   {
     final int TOTAL_PEOPLE = 9;

     Graphics g;
     Image background;
     Image person_gif[];
     String description[];

     boolean done_loading_image = false;
```

```
    int max_rows;
    int width;
    int height;
    int current_item = 0;

    FontMetrics font_metrics;
    Coordinate coordinate[];

    //————————————————————

    public void init()
      {
        g = getGraphics();

        Font font = new Font("TimesRoman", Font.BOLD, 15);
        g.setFont(font);

        font_metrics = g.getFontMetrics();

        background = getImage(getCodeBase(), "whitehse.gif");

        width = size().width;
        height = size().height;

        Image offScrImage = createImage(width, height);
        Graphics offScrGC = offScrImage.getGraphics();
        offScrGC.drawImage(background, 0, 0, width, height, this);

        person_gif = new Image[TOTAL_PEOPLE];
        for (int i = 0; i < TOTAL_PEOPLE; i++)
          person_gif[i] = getImage(getCodeBase(), "pres" + (i+1) + ".gif");

        get_descriptions_and_coordinates();

        max_rows = (TOTAL_PEOPLE + 4) / 5;
      }

    //————————————————————

    void get_descriptions_and_coordinates()
      {
        description = new String[TOTAL_PEOPLE];

        description[0] = new String("Reagan");
        description[1] = new String("Carter");
        description[2] = new String("Ford");
        description[3] = new String("Nixon");
        description[4] = new String("Johnson");
        description[5] = new String("Kennedy");
        description[6] = new String("Eisenhower");
        description[7] = new String("Truman");
        description[8] = new String("Roosevelt");
```

```java
      coordinate = new Coordinate[TOTAL_PEOPLE];

      coordinate[0] = new Coordinate(118, 102);
      coordinate[1] = new Coordinate(243, 27);
      coordinate[2] = new Coordinate(361, 103);
      coordinate[3] = new Coordinate(496, 150);
      coordinate[4] = new Coordinate(525, 28);
      coordinate[5] = new Coordinate(49, 238);
      coordinate[6] = new Coordinate(171, 220);
      coordinate[7] = new Coordinate(305, 282);
      coordinate[8] = new Coordinate(474, 290);
    }

  //————————————————————————————

  public boolean mouseMove(Event evt, int x, int y)
    {
      int mouse_location = 0;
      boolean erased = false;

      for (int i = 0; i < TOTAL_PEOPLE; i++)
        {
          if (x > coordinate[i].x && x < coordinate[i].x + 100 &&
              y > coordinate[i].y && y < coordinate[i].y + 100)
            {
              mouse_location = i + 1;
              if (current_item != mouse_location)
                {
                  if (current_item != 0)
                    {
                      erase_name(current_item - 1);
                      erased = true;
                    }
                  draw_name(i);
                  break;
                }
            }
        }

      if (!erased && current_item != 0 &&
          current_item != mouse_location)
        erase_name(current_item - 1);

      current_item = mouse_location;

      if (current_item == 0)
        showStatus("");
      else
        showStatus("Person " + current_item);

      return true;
    }

  //————————————————————————————
```

```
void erase_name(int index)
  {
    int string_width = font_metrics.stringWidth(description [index]);
    int string_height = font_metrics.getHeight();

    int x2 = coordinate[index].x +  50 - string_width/2;
    int y2 = coordinate[index].y + 100;

    Graphics g2;
    g2 = g.create();

    g2.clipRect(x2, y2-string_height, string_width, string_height);

    g2.drawImage(background, 0, 0, width, height, null);

    g2.drawImage(person_gif[index], coordinate[index].x,
                 coordinate[index].y, this);
  }

//——————————————————————

void draw_name(int index)
  {
    g.setColor(Color.black);

    int string_width = font_metrics.stringWidth(description[index]);
    int string_height = font_metrics.getHeight();

    int x2 = coordinate[index].x +  50 - string_width/2;
    int y2 = coordinate[index].y + 100;

    g.fillRect(x2, y2-string_height, string_width, string_height);

    g.setColor(Color.yellow);
    g.drawString(description [index], x2,
                 y2-font_metrics.getDescent ());
  }

//——————————————————————

public boolean imageUpdate(Image img, int infoflags, int x, int y,
                           int width, int height)
  {
    if (infoflags == ALLBITS)
      {
        done_loading_image = true;
        repaint();
        return false;
      }
    else
      return true;
  }

//——————————————————————
```

```
        public void paint(Graphics g)
          {
            if (!done_loading_image)
              showStatus("People:  loading image");

            else
              {
                g.drawImage(background, 0, 0, width, height, this);
                g.setColor(Color.white);

                for (int i = 0; i < TOTAL_PEOPLE; i++)
                  {
                    g.drawImage(person_gif[i], coordinate[i].x,
                                coordinate[i].y, this);

                    g.drawRect(coordinate[i].x, coordinate[i].y,
                               100, 100);
                  }
              }
          }
        }
```

BREAKING APART ELECTION YEAR

To track each image's x-and-y coordinates, the **Election Year** applet uses the *Coordinate* class introduced in Chapter 11:

```
  class Coordinate
    {
      public int x;
      public int y;

      public Coordinate(int x, int y)
        {
          this.x = x;
          this.y = y;
        }
    }
```

In this case, to track the coordinates for 9 images, the applet uses an array of *Coordinate* objects:

```
  Coordinate coordinate[];
```

Next, the applet modifies the *get_descriptions* function that you examined in Chapter 15's **Animal Popups** applet to get each image's screen coordinates also:

```
  void get_descriptions_and_coordinates()
```

Using the *new* operator, the applet creates 9 *Coordinate* items, assigning each object to the *coordinate* array. The applet uses the class-constructor function to initialize each x-and-y coordinate pair with the locations for a president's image:

```
  coordinate = new Coordinate[TOTAL_PEOPLE];
```

```
coordinate[0] = new Coordinate(118, 102);
coordinate[1] = new Coordinate(243, 27);
coordinate[2] = new Coordinate(361, 103);
coordinate[3] = new Coordinate(496, 150);
coordinate[4] = new Coordinate(525, 28);
coordinate[5] = new Coordinate(49, 238);
coordinate[6] = new Coordinate(171, 220);
coordinate[7] = new Coordinate(305, 282);
coordinate[8] = new Coordinate(474, 290);
```

As discussed, when the user moves the mouse onto an image, the applet displays the President's name. Likewise, when the user moves the mouse off the image, the applet erases the name. Within the *erase_name* function, the applet redraws the President after erasing the name, just in case the name happened to obscure any part of the image:

```
g.drawImage(person_gif[index], coordinate[index].x, coordinate[index].y,
        this);
```

As it turns out, within the *mouseMove* function, because you have the coordinates and the size of each item, it is now easier to determine which image the mouse is over. To determine the image, the function uses a *for* loop to loop through the *coordinate* array to test if the current mouse x-and-y coordinate falls within an image. After the function determines the current image, it erases the old name and displays the new one. As you can see, the function uses the *break* statement to exit the *for* loop:

```
for (int i = 0; i < TOTAL_PEOPLE; i++)
  {
    if (x > coordinate[i].x && x < coordinate[i].x + 100 &&
        y > coordinate[i].y && y < coordinate[i].y + 100)
      {
        mouse_location = i + 1;
        if (current_item != mouse_location)
          {
            if (current_item != 0)
              {
                erase_name(current_item - 1);
                erased = true;
              }
            draw_name(i);
            break;
          }
      }
  }
```

The *erase_name* and the *draw_name* functions are slightly different than those you examined in Chapter 15's **Animal Popups** applet. As you might guess, it's now easier to determine the x-and-y coordinates of the current name. Using the *current-item* index and the *coordinate* array, the functions can quickly determine the bottom-center of the image rectangle:

```
int string_width = font_metrics.stringWidth(description [index]);
int string_height = font_metrics.getHeight();

int x2 = coordinate[index].x +  50 - string_width/2;
int y2 = coordinate[index].y + 100;
```

In addition, because you know each image's screen coordinates, the *paint* function is also easier. As you can see, the function uses one *for* statement to loop through and display each image, as opposed to the nested *for* loops you used in the **Animal Popups** applet:

```
for (int i = 0; i < TOTAL_PEOPLE; i++)
  {
    g.drawImage(person_gif[i], coordinate[i].x, coordinate[i].y, this);
    g.drawRect(coordinate[i].x, coordinate[i].y, 100, 100);
  }
```

Enhancements You Can Make to Election Year

To modify the **Election Year** applet, first change the applet so that it gets the image, image coordinates, and image description for each item from the HTML file. Next, using techniques you learned in Chapter 15, you might associate a sound with each image. When the user clicks their mouse on the image, the sound file will play.

Putting It All Together

The **Election Year** applet shows you how to create and maintain an array of object coordinates in order to keep track of your items that appear in the applet window. In Chapter 17, you will use the Java *Math* package to access trigonometric functions, such as sine and cosine, which are essential to rotating graphics items. Before you continue with Chapter 17, however, make sure you understand the following key concepts:

- ☑ By using the *Coordinate* class, you can track an object's x-and-y coordinates.

- ☑ To track the coordinates for multiple objects, you simply create an array of *Coordinate* class objects.

- ☑ By knowing the coordinates and the size of a screen image, your applet can quickly determine when the user has moved the mouse onto the image.

CHAPTER 17

BOUNCING BALL
USING TRIGONOMETRIC FUNCTIONS WITH JAVA'S MATH PACKAGE

In Chapter 16, you used the **Election Year** applet to learn how to display images at coordinates that were independent of the other images. In this chapter, you will move away from the display of images and you will return to program-based graphics that rely on functions in the Java *Graphics* class. Specifically, the **Bouncing Ball** applet combines the *Graphics* class functions with the *Math* class trigonometric functions to create a ball that bounces from one letter to the next across the string of characters. By the time you finish this chapter, you will understand the following key concepts:

- By moving the ball in a semi-circle pattern, your applet can make the ball bounce from one letter to the next, across a character string.

- To draw a circle that is filled with a specific color, your applet uses the *fillArc* function.

- To determine the semi-circle pattern over which the ball is to bounce, the applet uses the *pi* constant, as defined in the *Math* class.

- To move an object across your screen smoothly, move the item using small intervals, and erase the old image before drawing the new one.

USING BOUNCING BALL

When you run the **Bouncing Ball** applet, you will see a window containing a string of characters with a ball that bounces from one letter to the next in a semi-circle pattern, as shown in Figure 17.

Figure 17 A ball bouncing across the letters of a string.

THE HTML FILE

The HTML file for the **Bouncing Ball** applet contains several parameters. The first parameter, MESSAGE, specifies the character string message the applet displays. The second parameter, POINT_SIZE, specifies the point size at which the applet displays the message on your screen.

The BALL_SIZE specifies the diameter of the bouncing ball, in pixels. The DELAY parameter contains the amount of time the applet takes to move the ball from one letter to the next. Lastly, DIVISIONS specifies the number of iterations the applet uses to draw the ball as it travels in its semi-circle pattern. In short, the greater the number of iterations to move the object across the semi-circle path, the smoother the object's movement will appear:

```
<applet code=ball.class width=200 height=100>
<param name=message      value="Swedish Ice Cream">
<param name=point_size value=100>
<param name=ball_size  value=20>
<param name=delay      value=300>
<param name=divisions  value=8>
</applet>
```

LOOKING AT BOUNCING BALL

As briefly discussed, the **Bouncing Ball** applet uses the Java *Graphics* and *Math* classes to bounce a ball from one letter of a string to another. When the ball reaches the end of the string, the ball moves back to the start of the string and repeats the same process of moving from left to right again. The following code implements the **Bouncing Ball** applet:

```
//*****************************************************************
// ball.java
//*****************************************************************

import java.applet.*;
import java.awt.*;

//*****************************************************************

public class ball extends Applet implements Runnable
  {
    Graphics g;

    FontMetrics font_metrics;

    int string_width;
    int string_height;

    Thread my_thread = null;
    String message = "JAMSA PRESS";
    int point_size = 20;

    int message_length;
    char char_array[];

    int ball_size = 10;
```

```java
    int delay_amount = 500;

    double decrement;

    int ball_x = 0;
    int ball_y = 0;

    //————————————————————————

    public void init()
      {
        g = getGraphics();

        String parameter;

        parameter = getParameter("MESSAGE");
        if (parameter != null)
          message = parameter;

        parameter = getParameter("POINT_SIZE");
        if (parameter != null)
          point_size = Integer.parseInt(parameter);

        parameter = getParameter("BALL_SIZE");
        if (parameter != null)
          ball_size = Integer.parseInt(parameter);

        parameter = getParameter("DELAY");
        if (parameter != null)
          delay_amount = Integer.parseInt(parameter);

        int divisions = 10;
        parameter = getParameter("DIVISIONS");
        if (parameter != null)
          divisions = Integer.parseInt(parameter);

        decrement = Math.PI / divisions;

        delay_amount /= divisions;

        message_length = message.length();
        char_array = new char[message_length];
        message.getChars(0, message_length, char_array, 0);

        Font font = new Font("TimesRoman", Font.BOLD, point_size);
        g.setFont(font);

        font_metrics = g.getFontMetrics();

        string_width = font_metrics.stringWidth(message);
        string_height = font_metrics.getHeight();

        resize(string_width, string_height*2);
      }
```

```
    //─────────────────────────────

    public void start()
      {
        (new Thread(this)).start();
      }

    //─────────────────────────────

    void delay()
      {
        try
          {
            Thread.sleep(delay_amount);
          }
        catch (InterruptedException e)
          {
          }
      }

    //─────────────────────────────

    void draw_ball(int old_x, int x, int old_width, int char_width)
      {
        if (x < old_x)
          return;

        int x1 = old_x + old_width /2;
        int x2 = x + char_width/2;
        int mid_x = (x1 + x2) / 2;
        int mid_y = string_height;
        int radius = mid_x - x1;
        int y1;

        for (double r = Math.PI; r >= 0; r -= decrement)
          {
            g.setColor(Color.lightGray);
            g.fillArc(ball_x, ball_y, ball_size, ball_size, 0, 360);

            x1 = mid_x + (int) (Math.cos(r) * radius);
            y1 = mid_y - (int) (Math.sin(r) * radius);

            g.setColor(Color.red);
            g.fillArc(x1, y1, ball_size, ball_size, 0, 360);

            ball_x = x1;
            ball_y = y1;

            delay();
          }
      }

    //─────────────────────────────
```

```
    public void run()
      {
        int current_character = 0;
        int x = 0;
        int old_x = 0;
        int char_width = font_metrics.charWidth(char_array[0]);

        while (true)
          {
            g.setColor(Color.red);

            int old_width = char_width;
            char_width =
font_metrics.charWidth(char_array[current_character]);

            draw_ball(old_x, x, old_width, char_width);
            old_x = x;

            x += char_width;

            if (++current_character == message_length)
              {
                current_character = 0;
                x = 0;
              }

            delay();
          }
      }

    //————————————————————————

    public void paint(Graphics gc)
      {
        showStatus("Bouncing Ball:  running");
        g.setColor(Color.black);
        g.drawString(message, 0, string_height+point_size);
      }
  }
```

BREAKING APART BOUNCING BALL

As discussed, the **Bouncing Ball** applet bounces a ball from one character in a string to the next. To bounce the ball from one character to the next, the applet needs to know specifics about the characters in the string, such as their height and width. To determine font specifics, the applet uses a *FontMetrics* object to get the dimensions of the entire message, as well as the dimensions of individual characters, within the message:

```
FontMetrics font_metrics;
```

The applet stores the string dimensions within the *string_width* and *string_height* variables. Next, the applet must consider the window size relative to the string width and height. For example, ideally, the window should be twice as high as the message to provide enough space for the ball to bounce above the message. Also, as the ball bounces along its semi-circle path, the applet uses the *string_height* variable as the base of the semi-circle pattern:

```
int string_width;
int string_height;
```

As you can see, the applet stores the message within a *String* object. To bounce the ball from one character to the next, however, the applet must consider specific character widths. Therefore, the applet stores the message characters within an array of characters named *char_array*. Next, the applet defines the ball dimension as 10 pixels, and the delay amount the applet pauses when a ball rests on top of a character as one-half of a second (500 milliseconds):

```
String message = "JAMSA PRESS";
int point_size = 20;

int message_length;
char char_array[];

int ball_size = 10;
int delay_amount = 500;
```

If you recall your high school math, you may remember that you can express the measure of a circle using either radians or degrees. Trigonometric functions, such as the *sine* and *cosine* functions, typically work in terms of radians. As the ball moves across its semi-circle path, the applet decrements the number of radians the applet must move to complete its current path. As briefly discussed, the applet divides the bouncing ball's path of travel into a fixed number of divisions. Each division, therefore, corresponds to a fixed number of radians. The applet uses the *decrement* variable to hold the number of radians between each division of the semi-circle pattern. The applet uses the *decrement* variable within a *for* loop, which draws the ball as it travels its semi-circle pattern:

```
double decrement;
```

To move the ball, the applet needs a consistent frame of reference, such as the ball's center or one of the ball's outer edges. In the case of the **Bouncing Ball** applet, the applet tracks the top-left corner of the ball. The applet uses these variables in the *fillArc* function to draw the ball:

```
int ball_x = 0;
int ball_y = 0;
```

Initializing the Applet

To start, the applet first gets its graphics context:

```
g = getGraphics();
```

As discussed, the **Bouncing Ball** applet can get several parameters from user-based settings that reside within the HTML file. To retrieve the HTML-file settings, the applet uses the *getParameter* function:

```
String parameter;

parameter = getParameter("MESSAGE");
if (parameter != null)
  message = parameter;

parameter = getParameter("POINT_SIZE");
if (parameter != null)
  point_size = Integer.parseInt(parameter);

parameter = getParameter("BALL_SIZE");
if (parameter != null)
  ball_size = Integer.parseInt(parameter);

parameter = getParameter("DELAY");
if (parameter != null)
  delay_amount = Integer.parseInt(parameter);

int divisions = 10;
parameter = getParameter("DIVISIONS");
if (parameter != null)
  divisions = Integer.parseInt(parameter);
```

Notice that the applet stores the setting for the DIVISIONS parameter within a local variable. This is because the applet only uses the parameter long enough to determine the number of radians for each arc of the semi-circle pattern, and also to divide the delay amount into smaller delays that the applet will pause as the ball reaches each division along its path:

```
decrement = Math.PI / divisions;

delay_amount /= divisions;
```

As briefly discussed, for the applet to move the ball from one character to the next, the applet must have knowledge about the characters that make up the string. Therefore, the applet assigns the string's contents to an array of characters. Then, the applet selects the *Font* object it will use within the current graphics context. Based on the font selection, the applet determines the string's width and height, and then resizes the window:

```
message_length = message.length();
char_array = new char[message_length];
message.getChars(0, message_length, char_array, 0);

Font font = new Font("TimesRoman", Font.BOLD, point_size);
g.setFont(font);

font_metrics = g.getFontMetrics();

string_width = font_metrics.stringWidth(message);
string_height = font_metrics.getHeight();

resize(string_width, string_height*2);
```

Starting the Thread

As you will remember from previous chapters, the browser calls an applet's *start* function right after the *init* function finishes. Within the *start* function, the applet starts the thread that oversees moving the ball over its semi-circle path:

```
public void start()
   {
      (new Thread(this)).start();
   }
```

Drawing the Ball

The *draw_ball* function draws the ball that travels the semi-circle pattern, from letter to letter. The function accepts four parameters: the x-coordinate of the left-side of the previous character, the x-coordinate of the left-side of the current character, the character width of the previous character, and the character width of the current character. To start, the function erases the old ball first:

```
void draw_ball(int old_x, int x, int old_width, int char_width)
```

As briefly discussed, the applet first moves the ball across the letters from left to right. However, when the ball reaches the last character in the string, the applet wants to jump to the first character which you don't want. Therefore, the function first tests to see if the ball has reached the edge:

```
if (x < old_x)
  return;
```

Next, the function calculates the x-coordinate for the middle of the previous character. The function will use this coordinate information to erase the previous ball location. In a similar way, the applet will store the x-coordinate for the next middle character within the *x2* variable. By knowing the midpoint of the previous and next characters, the applet can calculate the semicircle path the ball will follow:

```
int x1 = old_x + old_width /2;
int x2 = x + char_width/2;
```

By knowing each letter's midpoint, the applet can calculate the mid-point of the semi-circle:

```
int mid_x = (x1 + x2) / 2;
int mid_y = string_height;
```

Likewise, using the mid-point values for the previous and next characters, the applet instantly knows the semi-circle's radius:

```
int radius = mid_x - x1;
```

The *for* loop starts at the left side of the semi-circle (mathematically at *pi*) and then moves in decrements that correspond to the equal divisions of the arc:

```
for (double r = Math.PI; r >= 0; r -= decrement)
```

Inside the *for* loop, the function first erases the old ball by redrawing the circle using the light gray background color:

```
g.setColor(Color.lightGray);
g.fillArc(ball_x, ball_y, ball_size, ball_size, 0, 360);
```

Then, the function calculates the ball's x and y coordinates for the new position. Using the trigonometric *cos* function (the cosine), the function calculates the amount to add to the x-coordinate. Similarly, using the *sin* function (the sine), the function calculates the amount to subtract from the y-coordinate:

```
x1 = mid_x + (int) (Math.cos(r) * radius);
y1 = mid_y - (int) (Math.sin(r) * radius);
```

The function then draws the ball red, saves the ball's new x-and-y coordinates, and pauses:

```
g.setColor(Color.red);
g.fillArc(x1, y1, ball_size, ball_size, 0, 360);

ball_x = x1;
ball_y = y1;

delay();
```

Running the Thread

Within the *run* function, the applet loops, infinitely bouncing the ball from one character to the next. Inside the loop, the function sets the current color to red, saves the old character width, and then gets the new character width:

```
g.setColor(Color.red);

int old_width = char_width;
char_width = font_metrics.charWidth(char_array[current_character]);
```

To draw the ball, the function uses the *draw_ball* function:

```
draw_ball(old_x, x, old_width, char_width);
```

The function then saves the old x-coordinate, which it will use the next time through the loop as the x-coordinate for the next character:

```
old_x = x;

x += char_width;
```

Next, if the applet is at the last character in the string, the applet moves back to the first character and starts the process again:

```
if (++current_character == message_length)
  {
     current_character = 0;
     x = 0;
  }
```

The paint Function

Within the *paint* function, the applet displays a status that tells the user that the applet is running and draws the string. Note that the function does not use the graphics context it receives as a parameter, but rather, the context that the applet previously saved within the global *g* variable: By using the original graphics context, the applet ensures the font and font metrics remain consistent.

```
public void paint(Graphics gc)
   {
     showStatus("Bouncing Ball:  running");
     g.setColor(Color.black);
     g.drawString(message, 0, string_height+point_size);
   }
```

ENHANCEMENTS YOU CAN MAKE TO BOUNCING BALL

To start, modify the applet so when the ball reaches the last character, it bounces backward from right to left. Next, change the color of the ball as it bounces from one character to the next.

PUTTING IT ALL TOGETHER

The **Bouncing Ball** applet shows you how to create a ball that bounces over characters whose sizes differ. In Chapter 18, you will enhance this program so that it makes a noise each time it bounces on one of the letters. Before you continue with Chapter 18, however, make sure that you understand the following key concepts:

- ☑ Using the *fillArc* function, your applet can draw a circle that is filled with a specific color.

- ☑ To move an object over a semi-circle path, you applet must use the mathematical value *pi*. The Java *Math* class defines the *pi* constant as *Math.PI*.

- ☑ To move a graphics object across the screen, draw the object at small intervals, erasing the old one before drawing the new one.

In the next chapter, you will learn how to change the color of the character and make noise as the ball bounces over the character.

CHAPTER 18

NOISY BOUNCING BALL
COPYING SCREEN AREAS AND COMBINING AUDIO

In Chapter 17, using the **Bouncing Ball** applet, you learned how to use the *Math* class trigonometric functions to display a ball that bounces across letters in a string. In this chapter, you will modify the **Bouncing Ball** applet to learn how to capture an area of the screen and display it somewhere else. In addition, you will change the applet so that it plays an audio clip every time the ball bounces on a letter. By the time you finish this chapter, you will understand the following key concepts:

- Using the *copyArea* function, your applet can copy a region of the screen to a different location.

- By knowing the pixel size of each letter in the string, the applet knows the size of the screen region to copy by using the *copyArea* function.

USING NOISY BOUNCING BALL

When you run the **Noisy Bouncing Ball** applet, your screen will display a window that contains a string of characters and a bouncing ball. As did the bouncing ball in Chapter 17's **Bouncing Ball** applet, the ball bounces from one letter to the next in a semi-circle pattern. As the ball bounces on the letter, the letter will change color, an audio clip will play, and the applet will display a copy of the screen area that contains the letter in the window's top-left corner, as shown in Figure 18.

Figure 18 The bouncing ball triggers a change to the current letter's color to display a copy of the letter.

THE HTML FILE

The **Noisy Bouncing Ball** applet supports several HTML-based parameters. The first parameter, MESSAGE, defines the character string upon which the ball bounces. The second parameter, POINT_SIZE, specifies the point size of the message within the applet window. Next, the BALL_SIZE parameter defines the diameter of the bouncing ball in pixels. The BALL_DELAY parameter specifies the amount of time it takes for the ball to bounce from one letter to another. The DIVISIONS parameter defines the number of times the ball is drawn as it bounces from one letter to the next. Lastly, the LETTER_DELAY parameter specifies the amount of time the applet pauses when the ball bounces on top of a letter:

```
<applet code=ball.class width=200 height=100>
<param name=message          value="Swedish Ice Cream">
<param name=point_size       value=100>
<param name=ball_size        value=20>
<param name=ball_delay       value=200>
<param name=divisions        value=8>
<param name=letter_delay value=500>
</applet>
```

LOOKING AT NOISY BOUNCING BALL

The **Noisy Bouncing Ball** applet enhances Chapter 17's **Bouncing Ball** applet by adding sound, a change in letter colors, and code to copy a region of the screen from one location to another. The following code implements the **Noisy Bouncing Ball** applet:

```
//*****************************************************************
// ball.java
//*****************************************************************

import java.applet.*;
import java.awt.*;

//*****************************************************************

public class ball extends Applet implements Runnable
  {
    Graphics g;

    FontMetrics font_metrics;
    AudioClip clip;

    int string_width;
    int string_height;

    String message = "JAMSA PRESS";
    int point_size = 20;

    int message_length;
    char char_array [];

    int ball_size = 10;
    int ball_delay = 300;
    int letter_delay = 500;

    double decrement;

    int ball_x = 0;
    int ball_y = 0;
```

```
//————————————————————————

public void init()
  {
    g = getGraphics();

    String parameter;

    parameter = getParameter("MESSAGE");
    if (parameter != null)
      message = parameter;

    parameter = getParameter("POINT_SIZE");
    if (parameter != null)
      point_size = Integer.parseInt(parameter);

    parameter = getParameter("BALL_SIZE");
    if (parameter != null)
      ball_size = Integer.parseInt(parameter);

    parameter = getParameter("BALL_DELAY");
    if (parameter != null)
      ball_delay = Integer.parseInt(parameter);

    parameter = getParameter("LETTER_DELAY");
    if (parameter != null)
      letter_delay = Integer.parseInt(parameter);

    int divisions = 10;
    parameter = getParameter("DIVISIONS");
    if (parameter != null)
      divisions = Integer.parseInt(parameter);

    decrement = Math.PI / divisions;

    ball_delay /= divisions;

    message_length = message.length();
    char_array = new char[message_length];
    message.getChars(0, message_length, char_array, 0);

    Font font = new Font("TimesRoman", Font.BOLD, point_size);
    g.setFont(font);

    font_metrics = g.getFontMetrics();

    string_width = font_metrics.stringWidth(message);
    string_height = font_metrics.getHeight();

    clip = getAudioClip(getCodeBase(), "sound.au");

    resize(string_width, string_height*2);
  }
```

```
//————————————————————

public void start()
  {
    (new Thread(this)).start();
  }

//————————————————————

void delay_for_ball ()
  {
    try
      {
        Thread.sleep(ball_delay);
      }
    catch (InterruptedException e)
      {
      }
  }

//————————————————————

void delay_between_letters()
  {
    try
      {
        Thread.sleep(letter_delay);
      }
    catch (InterruptedException e)
      {
      }
  }

//————————————————————

void draw_ball(int old_x, int x, int old_width, int char_width)
  {
    if (x < old_x)
      return;

    int x1 = old_x + old_width /2;
    int x2 = x + char_width/2;
    int mid_x = (x1 + x2) / 2;
    int mid_y = string_height;
    int radius = mid_x - x1;
    int y1;

    mid_x -= ball_size / 2;

    for (double r = Math.PI; r >= 0; r -= decrement)
      {
        g.setColor(Color.lightGray);
        g.fillArc(ball_x, ball_y, ball_size, ball_size, 0, 360);
```

```
                  x1 = mid_x + (int) (Math.cos(r) * radius);
                  y1 = mid_y - (int) (Math.sin(r) * radius);

                  g.setColor(Color.red);
                  g.fillArc(x1, y1, ball_size, ball_size, 0, 360);

                  ball_x = x1;
                  ball_y = y1;

                  delay_for_ball();
              }

          clip.play();
      }

//————————————————————————

void write_message()
    {
       g.setColor(Color.black);
       g.drawString(message, 0, string_height+point_size);
    }

//————————————————————————

void redraw_character(int x, int current_character, int old_width,
                      int char_width)

    {
       g.setColor(Color.red);
       g.drawChars(char_array, current_character, 1, x,
                   string_height+point_size);

       g.setColor(Color.lightGray);
       g.fillRect(0, 0, old_width, point_size);

       g.copyArea(x, string_height, char_width, point_size, -x,
                   -string_height);
    }

//————————————————————————

public void run()
    {
       int current_character = 0;
       int x = 0;
       int old_x = 0;
       int char_width =
           font_metrics.charWidth(char_array[current_character]);

       while (true)
         {
           write_message();

           g.setColor(Color.red);
```

```
            int old_width = char_width;
            char_width =
              font_metrics.charWidth(char_array[current_character]);

            draw_ball(old_x, x, old_width, char_width);
            redraw_character(x, current_character, old_width, char_width);
            old_x = x;

            x += char_width;

            if (++current_character == message_length)
              {
                current_character = 0;
                x = 0;
              }

            delay_between_letters();
          }
      }


    //————————————————————————————————

    public void paint(Graphics g)
      {
        showStatus("Bouncing Ball:  running");
        write_message();
      }
  }
```

BREAKING APART NOISY BOUNCING BALL

As discussed, the **Noisy Bouncing Ball** applet plays a sound each time the ball bounces on a character of the string. Therefore, the applet uses an *AudioClip* object:

```
    AudioClip clip;
```

The applet uses two delay variables that control the amount of time (in milliseconds) the applet uses to move the ball from one letter to the next, and the amount of time the applet pauses when the ball lands on a letter:

```
  int ball_delay = 300;
  int letter_delay = 500;
```

Initializing the Applet

Using HTML parameters, the user can override the default settings for the two delay variables just discussed:

```
  parameter = getParameter("BALL_DELAY");
  if (parameter != null)
    ball_delay = Integer.parseInt(parameter);
```

```
parameter = getParameter("LETTER_DELAY");
if (parameter != null)
  letter_delay = Integer.parseInt(parameter);
```

The *ball_delay* variable controls the amount of time the applet uses to move the ball from one letter to the next. As you will recall, the applet lets the user specify the number of times the applet should draw the ball as it moves across its semi-circle arc, from one letter to the next. The applet uses the *divisions* variable to track the number of times the ball is drawn. Therefore, to determine how long the applet pauses each time it draws the ball, the applet divides the total delay (from one letter to the next) by the number of images it must draw:

```
ball_delay /= divisions;
```

As discussed, each time the ball lands on top of a letter, the applet generates a sound. Using the *getAudioClip* function, the applet loads the corresponding sound file:

```
clip = getAudioClip(getCodeBase(), "sound.au");
```

The delay Functions

Unlike Chapter 17's **Bouncing Ball** applet that used one delay function, this applet uses two. The first function, *delay_for_ball*, specifies the amount of time, in milliseconds, the applet delays each time it draws the ball:

```
void delay_for_ball ()
  {
    try
      {
        Thread.sleep(ball_delay);
      }
    catch (InterruptedException e)
      {
      }
  }
```

The second delay function, *delay_between_letters*, specifies the amount of time, in milliseconds, the applet delays when the ball lands on top of a letter:

```
void delay_between_letters()
  {
    try
      {
        Thread.sleep(letter_delay);
      }
    catch (InterruptedException e)
      {
      }
  }
```

Drawing the Ball

In Chapter 17's **Bouncing Ball** applet, the ball did not land at the exact middle of each letter. Instead, rather than using the midpoint of the ball for positioning, the applet used the left side of the ball. In this applet, to draw the ball at the exact middle of the letter, the applet determines the ball's midpoint:

```
mid_x -= ball_size / 2;
```

After the ball gets to the end of its semi-circle path, and is sitting on top of a letter, the applet uses the *clip.play* method to play the audio clip:

```
clip.play();
```

Redrawing the Character that the Ball Hits

As briefly discussed, when the ball hits a character, the applet redraws the character in red, and then copies the character's screen area to the top-left corner of the applet window. To perform this processing, the applet uses the *redraw_character* function. As you can see, the function uses four parameters: the first parameter specifies the x-coordinate of the left side of the character to redraw, the second parameter contains the current-character index within the *character* array, the third parameter specifies the width of the old character, and the fourth is the width of the current character:

```
void redraw_character(int x, int current_character, int old_width,
                      int char_width)
```

To start, the applet redraws the current character in red:

```
g.setColor(Color.red);
g.drawChars(char_array, current_character, 1, x, string_height+point_size);
```

Then, the applet fills the top-left corner of the applet window with a light gray color to erase the previous character the applet copied there:

```
g.setColor(Color.lightGray);
g.fillRect(0, 0, old_width, point_size);
```

Lastly, using the *copyArea* function, the applet copies the current letter's screen region to the upper-left corner of the applet window:

```
g.copyArea(x, string_height, char_width, point_size, -x, -string_height);
```

As you can see, the *copyArea* function uses six parameters: the first four parameters define the x-and-y coordinates and the width-and-height of the screen area. The fifth and sixth parameters specify the number of pixels in the x-and-y direction to move the area. In this case, to move the region area to the coordinates (0, 0), the function call uses the negative of the x-and-y coordinates, which are stored in the *x* and the *string_height* variables.

Running the Thread

Inside the applet's *while* loop, the applet first writes a message to the screen. The applet must continually rewrite the message because the previous letter (the one the ball landed on last) is red. To ensure the letter is black, the applet rewrites the message:

```
write_message();
```

Next, after drawing the ball, the applet redraws the current character and copies the character to the top-left corner of the window:

```
redraw_character(x, current_character, old_width, char_width);
```

Lastly, the applet uses the *delay_between_letters* function to briefly suspend the applet's processing:

```
delay_between_letters();
```

The paint Function

Because the applet uses the *while* loop (in the *run* function) to write the message on the screen, the *paint* function differs slightly from the one you examined in Chapter 17's **Bouncing Ball** applet:

```
public void paint(Graphics g)
   {
      showStatus("Bouncing Ball:  running");
      write_message();
   }
```

ENHANCEMENTS YOU CAN MAKE TO NOISY BOUNCING BALL

To modify the **Noisy Bouncing Ball** applet, you might first use a random color to draw the current character. To do so, you can use the *Color* object RGB constructor to create a unique color, depending on the current letter. See Chapter 4 for a description of how you create a *Color* object using RGB values. Next, change the screen area the applet copies so that the applet does not copy the ball at the top of the letter. Lastly, you might draw different images as the ball hits a letter, instead of copying the area of the letter.

PUTTING IT ALL TOGETHER

The **Noisy Bouncing Ball** applet shows you how to copy the contents of an area of the screen to a different screen location. In Chapter 19, you will learn how to enhance the **Bouncing Image** demo applet provided in the Java Developer's Kit to display images against a background. Before you continue with Chapter 19, however, make sure you understand the following key concepts:

☑ Using the *copyArea* function, your applet can copy the contents of one region on your screen to another screen location.

☑ By copying a screen region to another location and then overwriting the copied region, you can quickly move a region on your screen.

CHAPTER 19

BOUNCING HEADS WITH BACKGROUND
MODIFYING THE JDK DEMO TO BOUNCE ON A BACKGROUND IMAGE

The Java Developers Kit (JDK) is an excellent source for programming examples. For example, the JDK **Bouncing Heads** demo bounces an image of a spinning head within the applet window. In this chapter, the **Bouncing Heads with Background** applet modifies the JDK demo to include a background image. As the images of the head move, the applet must restore the portion of the background the head previously covered. By the time you finish this chapter, you will understand the following key concepts:

◆ To display the spinning head, the demo program stores a sequence of images in an array.

◆ To display multiple occurrences of the spinning head, the applet creates multiple instances of the *BounceItem* thread, each of which repeatedly displays the array of images.

◆ To modify the demo program to support a background image, you must change the *paint* function.

USING BOUNCING HEADS WITH BACKGROUND

When you run the **Bouncing Heads with Background** applet, you will see a window with the bouncing heads that move randomly over a background image, as shown in Figure 19.

Figure 19 Displaying bouncing head images on top of a background image.

The HTML File

Use the following HTML file to run the **Bouncing Heads with Background** applet:

```
<applet code=bounce.class width=600 height=400> </applet>
```

Looking at Bouncing Heads with Background

If you have not already done so, you should examine the Bouncing Heads demo provided with the Java Developer's Kit. This applet modifies the **Bouncing Heads** demo by adding a background and a title. The following code implements the **Bouncing Heads with Background** applet:

```java
//*******************************************************************
// bounce.java
//*******************************************************************

import java.util.Hashtable;
import java.applet.*;
import java.io.*;
import java.awt.*;
import java.net.*;


//*******************************************************************

class BounceImage
  {
    static float inelasticity = .96f;
    static float Ax = 0.0f;
    static float Ay = 0.0002f;
    static float Ar = 0.9f;

    public float x = 0;
    public float y = 0;
    public float old_x = 0;
    public float old_y = 0;
    public float Vx = 0.1f;
    public float Vy = 0.05f;
    public float Vr = 0.005f + (float)Math.random() * 0.001f;
    public float findex = 0f;

    public int width;
    public int height;
    public int index;

    bounce parent;

    static boolean imagesReadIn = false;

    //-----------------------------------------------
```

```java
    public BounceImage(bounce parent)
      {
        this.parent = parent;

        width = 100;
        height = 100;
      }

    //———————————————————————————————

    public void move(float x1, float y1)
      {
        x = x1;
        y = y1;
      }

    //———————————————————————————————

    public void paint(Graphics g)
      {
        int i = index;

        if (parent.bounceimages[i] == null)
          i = 0;

        Graphics g2;
        g2 = g.create();
        g2.clipRect((int) old_x, (int) old_y, width, height);
        g2.drawImage(parent.background, 0, 0, parent.image_size.width,
                    parent.image_size.height, null);

        g.drawImage(parent.bounceimages[i], (int) x, (int) y, null);

        old_x = x;
        old_y = y;
      }

    //———————————————————————————————

    public void step(long deltaT)
      {
        boolean collision_x = false;
        boolean collision_y = false;

        float jitter = (float)Math.random() * .01f - .005f;

        x += Vx * deltaT + (Ax / 2.0) * deltaT * deltaT;
        y += Vy * deltaT + (Ay / 2.0) * deltaT * deltaT;
```

```
            if (x <= 0.0f)
              {
                x = 0.0f;
                Vx = -Vx * inelasticity + jitter;
                collision_x = true;
              }

        Dimension d = parent.image_size;

        if (x + width >= d.width)
          {
            x = d.width - width;
            Vx = -Vx * inelasticity + jitter;
            collision_x = true;
          }

        if (y <= 0)
          {
            y = 0;
            Vy = -Vy * inelasticity + jitter;
            collision_y = true;
          }

        if (y + height >= d.height)
          {
            y = d.height - height;
            Vx *= inelasticity;
            Vy = -Vy * inelasticity + jitter;
            collision_y = true;
          }

        move(x, y);
        Vy = Vy + Ay * deltaT;
        Vx = Vx + Ax * deltaT;

        findex += Vr * deltaT;
        if (collision_x || collision_y)
          Vr *= Ar;

        while (findex <= 0.0)
          findex += parent.bounceimages.length;

        index = ((int) findex) % parent.bounceimages.length;
      }
  }

//****************************************************************

public class bounce extends Applet implements Runnable
  {
    static Graphics g;
    static Image background;

    boolean images_initialized = false;
    boolean done_loading_image = false;
```

```java
      BounceImage images[];
      Image bounceimages[];

      boolean time_to_die;
      Dimension image_size;
      AudioClip music;

      //————————————————————————

      public void init()
        {
          g = getGraphics();

          background = getImage(getCodeBase(), "piano.gif");

          image_size = size();

          image_size.height -= 100;

          Image offScrImage = createImage(image_size.width,
                                          image_size.height);
          Graphics offScrGC = offScrImage.getGraphics();
          offScrGC.drawImage(background, 0, 0, image_size.width,
                             image_size.height, this);
        }

      //————————————————————————

      public boolean imageUpdate(Image img, int infoflags, int x, int y,
                                 int width, int height)
        {
          if (infoflags == ALLBITS)
            {
              done_loading_image = true;
              showStatus("");
              repaint();
              (new Thread(this)).start();
              return false;
            }
          else
            return true;
        }

      //————————————————————————

      void makeImages(int nimages)
        {
          bounceimages = new Image[8];
          for (int i = 1 ; i <= 8 ; i++)
            bounceimages[i-1] = getImage(getCodeBase (),
                                 "images/happy/t" + i + ".gif");
```

```
        images = new BounceImage[nimages];
        for (int i = 0; i < nimages; i++)
          {
          BounceImage img = images[i] = new BounceImage(this);
          img.move (1 + img.width*.8f*(i%3) + (i/3)*.3f*img.width,
                    img.height*.3f + (i%3)*.3f*img.height);
          }

        music = getAudioClip(getCodeBase(), "bounce.au");
      }

  //————————————————————————————

  public void run()
    {
      long lasttime;

      try
        {
          if (images == null)
            {
              System.out.println("Making images ...");
              makeImages(4);
            }

          if (music != null)
            music.loop();

          lasttime = System.currentTimeMillis();
          while (!time_to_die)
            {
              int i;
              long now = System.currentTimeMillis();
              long deltaT = now - lasttime;
              boolean active = false;
              Dimension d = image_size;

              for (i = 0; i < images.length; i++)
                {
                  BounceImage img = images[i];

                  img.step(deltaT);

                  if (img.Vy > .05 || -img.Vy > .05 ||
                      img.y + img.width < d.height - 10)
                    {
                      active = true;
                    }
                }
              if (!active && images.length != 0)
                {
                  for (i = 0; i < images.length; i++)
                    {
                      BounceImage img = images[i];
```

```
                              img.Vx = (float)Math.random() / 4.0f - 0.125f;
                              img.Vy = -(float)Math.random() / 4.0f - 0.2f;
                              img.Vr = 0.05f - (float)Math.random() * 0.1f;
                          }
                      }
                  paint_images();
                  lasttime = now;
                  try
                      {
                        Thread.sleep (100);
                      }
                  catch (InterruptedException e)
                      {
                        return;
                      }
                }
            }
        finally
          {
            if (music != null)
              music.stop ();
          }
    }

//——————————————————————

public void start()
    {
      time_to_die = false;
    }

//——————————————————————

public void stop()
    {
      time_to_die = true;
      music.stop();
    }

//——————————————————————

public void paint_images()
    {
      if (images != null)
        for (int i = 0; i < images.length; i++)
          if (images[i] != null)
            images[i].paint(g);
    }

//——————————————————————
```

```
    public void paint(Graphics g)
      {
        if (!done_loading_image)
          showStatus("Bounce:  loading image");

        else
          {
            g.drawImage(background, 0, 0, image_size.width,
                        image_size.height, this);

            paint_images();

            Font f = new Font("TimesRoman", Font.BOLD, 30);

            g.setFont(f);
            g.setColor(Color.blue);
            g.drawString("Joe's Sports Bar...Where heads roll!",
                        0, image_size.height+50);
          }
      }
  }
```

BREAKING APART BOUNCING HEADS WITH BACKGROUND

Rather than examining all of the code contained in the JDK **Bouncing Heads** demo, this section examines only those items the **Bouncing Heads with Background** applet adds to the previous applet. To start, the applet uses two classes: the *BounceImage* class and the *bounce* class. As you will learn, the *bounce* class replaces the *BounceItem* class defined in the original JDK demo program. The *BounceImage* class is very similar to the class defined in the JDK demo. There is one instance of the *bounce* class which is the applet. For each spinning head the applet displays, the applet uses an instance of the *BounceImage* class.

The BounceImage Class

So it can restore the background image as the images of the heads move across the screen, the applet tracks (for each instance of *BounceImage*) the image's old location. To track the location, the applet adds the following coordinate member-variables to the *BounceImage* class:

```
public float old_x = 0;
public float old_y = 0;
```

Next, because the *Applet* class is now called *bounce* (as opposed to *BounceItem*), the applet must change the *parent* member-variable's type. The *parent* variable points to the one instance of the *bounce* class, which is the actual applet:

```
bounce parent;
```

The original JDK **Bouncing Heads** applet plays a sound each time two of the spinning heads collide. So it can focus on the background-image processing, this applet eliminates the sounds.

Because the applet must restore the background image as the heads move, you must modify the *paint* function. The class stores the x-and-y coordinates for the area it needs to restore in the *old_x* and *old_y* variables. After the class restores the background and draws the current image (using the new x-and-y coordinates), it saves the new coordinates in *old_x* and *old_y* variables so it can use them to later redraw the background when the head moves from its current location:

```java
public void paint(Graphics g)
  {
    int i = index;

    if (parent.bounceimages[i] == null)
      i = 0;

    Graphics g2;
    g2 = g.create();
    g2.clipRect((int) old_x, (int) old_y, width, height);
    g2.drawImage(parent.background, 0, 0, parent.image_size.width,
              parent.image_size.height, null);

    g.drawImage(parent.bounceimages[i], (int) x, (int) y, null);

    old_x = x;
    old_y = y;
  }
```

Notice that the background image is actually a member variable of the *bounce* class. In this way, the applet can reference the background image here (because *background* is a public and static variable).

As discussed, this applet removes all references to the *play* function to eliminate the sounds the applet played when two spinning heads collide.

The bounce Applet Class

As discussed, the *bounce* class replaces the *BounceItem* class from the original demo program. The *bounce* class is your applet. To start, the *bounce* class needs variables to hold the graphics context, the background image, and the *done_loading_image* variable, which the *imageUpdate* function sets to *true* after the background image has finished loading. The class uses the *image_size* variable to hold the dimensions of the background window, which lets instances of the *BounceImage* class use the variable to determine the edges of the background area. Because the applet does not play sounds when the heads collide, the class removes the *sounds* variable:

```java
static Graphics g;
static Image background;

boolean done_loading_image = false;

Dimension image_size;
```

Within the *init* function, the applet now gets the graphics context and loads the background image. Because the applet must leave room at the bottom of the applet window for the title, the applet initializes the *image_size* variable to the size of the applet window, and then subtracts 100 from the height. In this way, the heads do not bounce into the title and stay within the image. When the applet loads the image in the *paint* function, it uses the *image_size* dimensions to load the image:

```
public void init()
  {
    g = getGraphics();

    background = getImage(getCodeBase(), "piano.gif");
    image_size = size();

    image_size.height -= 100;

    Image offScrImage = createImage(image_size.width, image_size.height);
    Graphics offScrGC = offScrImage.getGraphics();
    offScrGC.drawImage(background, 0, 0, image_size.width,
                       image_size.height, this);
  }
```

The *imageUpdate* function, as described in earlier chapters, is called by the thread, which loads the image (from the *drawImage* function call within the *init* function):

```
public boolean imageUpdate(Image img, int infoflags, int x, int y,
                           int width, int height)
  {
    if (infoflags == ALLBITS)
      {
        done_loading_image = true;
        showStatus("");
        repaint();
        (new Thread(this)).start();
        return false;
      }
    else
      return true;
  }
```

Because you can only start the heads bouncing after the image has finished loading, the applet starts the thread in the *imageUpdate* function.

The *makeImages* function builds the array of images that represent the spinning head. In this case, the image files reside in a directory named **happy** and are called t1.gif through t8.gif. The original JDK demo used the *sounds* array to hold the sounds the applet played when the heads hit the edges of the screen. Since this applet does not use those sounds, the applet removes the array from the *makeImages* function:

```
void makeImages(int nimages)
  {
    bounceimages = new Image[8];
    for (int i = 1 ; i <= 8 ; i++)
      bounceimages[i-1] = getImage (getCodeBase (), "images/happy/t" + i +
                                    ".gif");

    images = new BounceImage[nimages];
    for (int i = 0; i < nimages; i++)
```

```
        {
            BounceImage img = images[i] = new BounceImage(this);
            img.move(1 + img.width*.8f*(i%3) + (i/3)*.3f*img.width,
                img.height*.3f + (i%3)*.3f*img.height);
        }

    music = getAudioClip(getCodeBase(), "bounce.au");
}
```

As you can see, this function loads eight images of the same head (each image rotated a little more to create the spinning animation effect). The images, in this case, reside in a subdirectory named **images/happy**. Within the subdirectory, the image files are named t1.gif to t8.gif. Then, the function creates four *BounceImage* objects, each of which spins the images.

Note: *Only one sequence of heads (one array) is used in all four bouncing heads.*

The applet also removes the *sounds* variable from the *run* function, and replaces the call to *repaint* with a call to *paint_images,* which paints the head images on the background.

Unlike the original JDK demo program, the *start* function does not have the code to start the thread. As discussed, the applet waits to start the thread until after it has loaded the background image. See the *imageUpdate* function for the code that starts the thread.

The *paint_images* function contains code the original JDK demo program placed in the *paint* function. The reason this applet uses the *paint_images* function is because it must redraw in the *run* function without reloading the background image:

```
public void paint_images()
  {
    if (images != null)
      for (int i = 0; i < images.length; i++)
        if (images[i] != null)
          images[i].paint(g);
  }
```

Finally, as you will see, the *paint* function first checks whether the background image has finished loading. If the image has not loaded, the function displays a status-bar message that tells the user the applet is loading the image. When the background image is loaded, the *paint* function draws the background, the head images, and the title at the bottom of the window:

```
public void paint(Graphics g)
  {
    if (!done_loading_image)
      showStatus("Bounce:  loading image");
    else
      {
        g.drawImage(background, 0, 0, image_size.width, image_size.height,
            this);
```

```
      paint_images();

      Font f = new Font("TimesRoman", Font.BOLD, 30);

      g.setFont(f);
      g.setColor(Color.blue);
      g.drawString("Joe's Sports Bar...Where heads roll!",
                   0, image_size.height+50);
   }
}
```

ENHANCEMENTS YOU CAN MAKE TO BOUNCING HEADS WITH BACKGROUND

To start, you must create you own GIF files to use for the bouncing images. To create the GIFs, simply shoot and scan photographs. Next, change the window so that the title is at the top instead of the bottom. Make sure that the heads still bounce within the background image.

PUTTING IT ALL TOGETHER

This program modifies the **Bouncing Heads** demo provided by the Java Developers Kit to display the heads on a background image. To display the background, the applet restores the background image each time a bouncing image moves. In Chapter 20, you will modify this program to support two or more different spinning images instead of using just one, as shown here. Before you continue with Chapter 20, however, make sure you understand the following key concepts:

☑ To create the spinning object animation, the program stores a sequence of images in an array.

☑ For each spinning head, the program creates a *BounceImage* instance that controls the head's animation.

☑ By modifying the original *BounceImage* class *paint* function, the applet restores the background image as the head moves.

CHAPTER 20

MULTIPLE BOUNCING HEADS
COORDINATING MULTIPLE MOVING OBJECTS

In Chapter 19, you modified the Java Developer's Kit **Bouncing Heads** demo applet to include a background image. Although Chapter 19's **Bouncing Heads with Background** applet let you display multiple spinning heads, each head used the same set of pictures. In this chapter, you will improve upon the applet again, this time by letting the applet support a second sequence of images. By the time you finish this chapter, you will understand the following key concepts:

♦ To add another spinning object, you will need eight more rotated images.

♦ To store the images for two different spinning objects, the applet uses a two-dimensional array.

♦ By changing the *BounceImage* constructor function, you can specify an index to the two-dimensional array of animation images that controls which images a *BouceImage* object will display.

USING MULTIPLE BOUNCING HEADS

When you run the **Multiple Bouncing Heads** applet, you will see a window with two different bouncing heads that appear on top of a background image, as shown in Figure 20.

Figure 20 Displaying two different spinning objects on a background image.

THE HTML FILE

Use the following HTML file to run the **Multiple Bouncing Heads** applet:

```
<applet code=bounce.class width=576 height=460> </applet>
```

LOOKING AT MULTIPLE BOUNCING HEADS

As discussed, this applet further expands the Java Developer's Kit **Bouncing Heads** JDK demo by letting the applet display two different spinning images. The following code implements the **Multiple Bouncing Heads** applet:

```java
//*****************************************************************
// bounce.java
//*****************************************************************

import java.util.Hashtable;
import java.applet.*;
import java.io.*;
import java.awt.*;
import java.net.*;


//*****************************************************************

class BounceImage
   {
      static float inelasticity = .96f;
      static float Ax = 0.0f;
      static float Ay = 0.0002f;
      static float Ar = 0.9f;

      public float x = 0;
      public float y = 0;
      public float old_x = 0;
      public float old_y = 0;
      public float Vx = 0.1f;
      public float Vy = 0.05f;
      public float Vr = 0.005f + (float)Math.random() * 0.001f;
      public float findex = 0f;

      public int width;
      public int height;
      public int index;

      bounce parent;
      int bounce_index;

      static boolean imagesReadIn = false;

      //————————————————————————————

      public BounceImage(bounce parent, int index)
```

```
    {
      this.parent = parent;
      bounce_index = index;

      width  = 100;
      height = 100;
    }

  //———————————————————————————

  public void move(float x1, float y1)
    {
      x = x1;
      y = y1;
    }

  //———————————————————————————

  public void paint(Graphics g)
    {
      int i = index;

      if (parent.bounceimages[bounce_index][i] == null)
        i = 0;

      Graphics g2;
      g2 = g.create();
      g2.clipRect((int) old_x, (int) old_y, width, height);
      g2.drawImage(parent.background, 0, 0, parent.image_size.width,
                   parent.image_size.height, null);

      g.drawImage(parent.bounceimages[bounce_index][i],
                  (int) x, (int) y, null);

      old_x = x;
      old_y = y;
    }

  //———————————————————————————

  public void step(long deltaT)
    {
      boolean collision_x = false;
      boolean collision_y = false;

      float jitter = (float)Math.random() * .01f - .005f;

      x += Vx * deltaT + (Ax / 2.0) * deltaT * deltaT;
      y += Vy * deltaT + (Ay / 2.0) * deltaT * deltaT;

      if (x <= 0.0f)
        {
          x = 0.0f;
          Vx = -Vx * inelasticity + jitter;
```

```
                 collision_x = true;
             }

         Dimension d = parent.image_size;

         if (x + width >= d.width)
            {
              x = d.width - width;
              Vx = -Vx * inelasticity + jitter;
              collision_x = true;
            }

         if (y <= 0)
            {
              y = 0;
              Vy = -Vy * inelasticity + jitter;
              collision_y = true;
            }

         if (y + height >= d.height)
            {
              y = d.height - height;
              Vx *= inelasticity;
              Vy = -Vy * inelasticity + jitter;
              collision_y = true;
            }

         move(x, y);
         Vy = Vy + Ay * deltaT;
         Vx = Vx + Ax * deltaT;

         findex += Vr * deltaT;
         if (collision_x || collision_y)
           Vr *= Ar;

         while (findex <= 0.0)
           findex += parent.bounceimages[bounce_index].length;

         index = ((int)findex) %
      parent.bounceimages[bounce_index].length;
       }
  }

//******************************************************************

public class bounce extends Applet implements Runnable
  {
    static Graphics g;
    static Image background;

    boolean images_initialized = false;
    boolean done_loading_image = false;
```

```
      BounceImage images[];
      Image bounceimages[][];

      boolean time_to_die;
      Dimension image_size;
      AudioClip music;

   //————————————————————————

   public void init()
     {
        g = getGraphics ();

        background = getImage(getCodeBase(), "piano.gif");

        image_size = size();

        image_size.height -= 60;

        Image offScrImage = createImage(image_size.width,
                                        image_size.height);
        Graphics offScrGC = offScrImage.getGraphics();
        offScrGC.drawImage(background, 0, 0, image_size.width,
                        image_size.height, this);
     }

   //————————————————————————

   public boolean imageUpdate(Image img, int infoflags, int x, int y,
                              int width, int height)
     {
        if (infoflags == ALLBITS)
          {
             done_loading_image = true;
             showStatus("");
             repaint();
             (new Thread(this)).start();
             return false;
          }
        else
          return true;
     }

   //————————————————————————

   void makeImages()
     {
        bounceimages = new Image[2][];

        bounceimages[0] = new Image[8];
        for (int i = 1 ; i <= 8 ; i++)
          bounceimages[0][i-1] = getImage(getCodeBase(),
                                          "images/happy/t" + i + ".gif");
```

```java
        bounceimages[1] = new Image[8];
        for (int i = 1 ; i <= 8 ; i++)
          bounceimages[1][i-1] = getImage(getCodeBase(),
                                          "images/steph/t" + i+ ".gif");


        images = new BounceImage[2];
        for (int i = 0; i < 2; i++)
          {
            BounceImage img = images[i] = new BounceImage(this, i);
            img.move(1 + img.width*.8f*(i%3) + (i/3)*.3f*img.width,
                     img.height*.3f + (i%3)*.3f*img.height);
          }

        music = getAudioClip(getCodeBase(), "bounce.au");
      }

    //————————————————————————————————

    public void run()
      {
        long lasttime;

        try
          {
            if (images == null)
              {
                System.out.println("Making images ...");
                makeImages();
              }

            if (music != null)
              music.loop();

            lasttime = System.currentTimeMillis();
            while (!time_to_die)
              {
                int i;
                long now = System.currentTimeMillis ();
                long deltaT = now - lasttime;
                boolean active = false;
                Dimension d = image_size;

                for (i = 0; i < images.length; i++)
                  {
                    BounceImage img = images[i];

                    img.step(deltaT);

                    if (img.Vy > .05 || -img.Vy > .05 ||
                        img.y + img.width < d.height - 10)
                      {
                        active = true;
                      }
                  }
```

```
                    if (!active && images.length != 0)
                      {
                        for (i = 0; i < images.length; i++)
                          {
                            BounceImage img = images[i];

                            img.Vx = (float)Math.random() / 4.0f - 0.125f;
                            img.Vy = -(float)Math.random() / 4.0f - 0.2f;
                            img.Vr = 0.05f - (float) Math.random() * 0.1f;
                          }
                      }
                  paint_images();
                  lasttime = now;
                  try
                    {
                      Thread.sleep(100);
                    }
                  catch (InterruptedException e)
                    {
                      return;
                    }
                }
            }
        finally
          {
            if (music != null)
              music.stop();
          }
      }

  //————————————————————————————

  public void start()
    {
      time_to_die = false;
    }

  //————————————————————————————

  public void stop()
    {
      time_to_die = true;
      music.stop();
    }

  //————————————————————————————

  public void paint_images()
    {
      if (images != null)
        for (int i = 0; i < images.length; i++)
          if (images[i] != null)
            images[i].paint (g);
    }
```

```
//————————————————————————

public void paint(Graphics g)
   {
     if (!done_loading_image)
       showStatus("Bounce:  loading image");

     else
       {
         g.drawImage(background, 0, 0, image_size.width,
                     image_size.height, this);

         paint_images();

         Font f = new Font("TimesRoman", Font.BOLD, 30);

         g.setFont(f);
         g.setColor(Color.blue);
         g.drawString("Joe's Sports Bar...Where heads roll!",
                      0, image_size.height+50);
       }
   }
}
```

BREAKING APART MULTIPLE BOUNCING HEADS

As before, this section only examines the code changes you must make to the previous applet.

The BounceImage Class

To hold two different sets of images, the applet changes the *bounce* class *bounceimages* array to a two-dimensional array. Each *BounceImage* object, therefore, uses the *bounce_index* member variable to specify which of the two images the object will display:

```
int bounce_index;
```

The constructor accepts one more argument, and that is the index into *bounceimages*. You have to store this index into the *bounce_index* variable:

```
public BounceImage(bounce parent, int index)
   {
     this.parent = parent;
     bounce_index = index;

     width  = 65;
     height = 72;
   }
```

Wherever the *bounceimages* array of the *bounce* class is used, you have to modify it to include another index since it is now two-dimensional. The index, of course, is the *bounce_index* variable.

When you draw the current image to the window, you have to specify which sequence of images to use. Since you have stored the index into the array that holds these sequences, you have to modify the *paint* function to use this array in the *drawImage* function call, which draws the head on top of the background:

```
g.drawImage(parent.bounceimages[bounce_index][i], (int) x, (int) y, null);
```

If you examine the bottom of the *step* function, you will find that it also uses the *bounceimages* array, as shown here:

```
while (findex <= 0.0)
  findex += parent.bounceimages[bounce_index].length;

index = ((int)findex) % parent.bounceimages[bounce_index].length;
```

The bounce Applet Class

Within the *bounce* class, the applet first changes the *bounceimages* array to a two-dimensional array so that it can hold two different sets of images:

```
Image bounceimages[][];
```

Within the *makeImages* functions, the applet modifies the code so the function will load both sets of head images. Because this applet creates only two spinning heads, it does not pass a parameter to the *makeImages* function that specifies the number of objects to create, as did the original demo applet:

```
void makeImages()
```

When you initialize a two-dimensional array in Java, you must first initialize the first index by using the *new* keyword. The following statement, for example, creates a two-dimensional array:

```
bounceimages = new Image[2][];
```

Then, you can allocate space for the array elements using the new operator. The following statements allocate array space for eight images, and then assign the images to the array by using the *getImage* function:

```
bounceimages[0] = new Image[8];
for (int i = 1 ; i <= 8 ; i++)
  bounceimages[0][i-1] = getImage(getCodeBase(), "images/happy/t" + i +
                                  ".gif");

bounceimages[1] = new Image[8];
for (int i = 1 ; i <= 8 ; i++)
  bounceimages[1][i-1] = getImage(getCodeBase(), "images/steph/t" + i +
                                  ".gif");
```

In this case, the function loads the images from two subdirectories: one named **images/happy**, and the second named **images/steph**. The image files that reside in each subdirectory are named t1.gif through t8.gif.

Next, the applet creates an array to hold the *BounceImage* objects:

```
images = new BounceImage[2];
```

To create the *BounceImage* objects, the applet uses the *new* operator, and passes to the *BounceImage* constructor function the *array-index* value of the images the object is to display.

The rest of the function is similar to the same function in the previous chapter.

ENHANCEMENTS YOU CAN MAKE TO MULTIPLE BOUNCING HEADS

To further enhance the **Multiple Bouncing Heads** applet, add a third and possibly a fourth set of images. To do so, you simply extend the array size and create additional *BounceImage* objects that will manage each image's display.

PUTTING IT ALL TOGETHER

The **Multiple Bouncing Heads** applet lets you enhance Chapter 19's **Bouncing Heads with Background** applet by letting you display two different spinning heads. In Chapter 21, you will make your final enhancements to the **Bouncing Heads** applet by letting the applet get its image information from HTML parameters. Before you continue with Chapter 21, however, make sure you understand the following key concepts:

☑ To initialize a two-dimensional array in Java, you perform two steps. First, use the *new* operator to allocate the outer-dimension. Then, for each of the outer-dimension array entries, you use the *new* operator to allocate the second dimension.

☑ For a *BounceImage* object to access the images from within the two-dimensional array, the applet simply passes the desired array-index value to the object's constructor function.

CHAPTER 21

MODIFIABLE BOUNCING HEADS USING HTML PARAMETERS

In Chapter 20, you used the **Multiple Bouncing Heads** applet to modify the Java Developer's Kit **Bouncing Heads** demo applet to include a background and two different spinning heads. In this chapter, you will further expand the applet so that it interacts with the HTML file to get the number of heads to bounce, and the sequence of images to use for each head. In short, this chapter shows you how to build a generic applet that end users can instantly put to use to bounce any type of image, not just a spinning head. A bookstore, for example, might spin images of their best-selling books. Likewise, a sporting-goods store might spin images of their latest footballs and basketballs. By the time you finish this chapter, you will understand the following key concepts:

- By placing specifics about the number of objects to display and the images to use for each object within an HTML file, you build a truly generic applet.

- To access the HTML parameters, you use the *getParameter* function previously discussed.

USING MODIFIABLE BOUNCING HEADS

When you run the **Modifiable Bouncing Heads** applet, you will see a window with multiple bouncing heads, each one using a different sequence of images on top of an image, and a title at the bottom, as shown in Figure 21.

Figure 21 *The spinning objects and images specified within an HTML file.*

THE HTML FILE

The HTML file for the **Modifiable Bouncing Heads** applet contains multiple parameters. The first parameter, ITEMS, specifies the number of objects the applet will bounce. Each subsequent parameter specifies, for each object, the name of the directory that contains the sequence of images to use for the bouncing head animation.

```
<applet code=bounce.class width=540 height=360>
<param name=ITEMS  value=2>
<param name=ITEM_1 value="STEPH">
<param name=ITEM_2 value="HAPPY">
</applet>
```

LOOKING AT MODIFIABLE BOUNCING HEADS

The **Modifiable Bouncing Heads** program further enhances the Java Developer's Kit **Bouncing Heads** JDK demo by letting the user specify (within an HTML file) the number of objects to bounce and the subdirectory that contains each object's images. The following code implements the **Modifiable Bouncing Heads** applet:

```java
//*****************************************************************
// bounce.java
//*****************************************************************

import java.util.Hashtable;
import java.applet.*;
import java.io.*;
import java.awt.*;
import java.net.*;


//*****************************************************************

class BounceImage
  {
    static float inelasticity = .96f;
    static float Ax = 0.0f;
    static float Ay = 0.0002f;
    static float Ar = 0.9f;

    public float x = 0;
    public float y = 0;
    public float old_x = 0;
    public float old_y = 0;
    public float Vx = 0.1f;
    public float Vy = 0.05f;
    public float Vr = 0.005f + (float)Math.random() * 0.001f;
    public float findex = 0f;

    public int width;
    public int height;
    public int index;

    bounce parent;
    int bounce_index;
```

```
        static boolean imagesReadIn = false;

    //————————————————————————————

    public BounceImage(bounce parent, int index)
      {
        this.parent = parent;
        bounce_index = index;

        width  = 100;
        height = 100;
      }

    //————————————————————————————

    public void move(float x1, float y1)
      {
        x = x1;
        y = y1;
      }

    //————————————————————————————

    public void paint(Graphics g)
      {
        int i = index;

        if (parent.bounceimages[bounce_index][i] == null)
          i = 0;

        Graphics g2;
        g2 = g.create();
        g2.clipRect((int) old_x, (int) old_y, width, height);
        g2.drawImage(parent.background, 0, 0, parent.image_size.width,
                    parent.image_size.height, null);

        g.drawImage(parent.bounceimages[bounce_index][i],
                    (int) x, (int) y, null);

        old_x = x;
        old_y = y;
      }

    //————————————————————————————

    public void step(long deltaT)
      {
        boolean collision_x = false;
        boolean collision_y = false;

        float jitter = (float)Math.random() * .01f - .005f;

        x += Vx * deltaT + (Ax / 2.0) * deltaT * deltaT;
        y += Vy * deltaT + (Ay / 2.0) * deltaT * deltaT;
```

```
            if (x <= 0.0f)
              {
                x = 0.0f;
                Vx = -Vx * inelasticity + jitter;
                collision_x = true;
              }

            Dimension d = parent.image_size;

            if (x + width >= d.width)
              {
                x = d.width - width;
                Vx = -Vx * inelasticity + jitter;
                collision_x = true;
              }

            if (y <= 0)
              {
                y = 0;
                Vy = -Vy * inelasticity + jitter;
                collision_y = true;
              }

            if (y + height >= d.height)
              {
                y = d.height - height;
                Vx *= inelasticity;
                Vy = -Vy * inelasticity + jitter;
                collision_y = true;
              }

            move(x, y);
            Vy = Vy + Ay * deltaT;
            Vx = Vx + Ax * deltaT;

            findex += Vr * deltaT;
            if (collision_x || collision_y)
              Vr *= Ar;

            while (findex <= 0.0)
              findex += parent.bounceimages[bounce_index].length;

            index = ((int) findex) % parent.bounceimages[bounce_index].length;
        }
    }

//******************************************************************

public class bounce extends Applet implements Runnable
    {
    static Graphics g;
    static Image background;
```

```java
    boolean images_initialized = false;
    boolean done_loading_image = false;

    BounceImage images[];
    Image bounceimages[][];

    boolean time_to_die;
    Dimension image_size;
    AudioClip music;

    //————————————————————————

    public void init()
      {
        g = getGraphics();
        background = getImage (getCodeBase(), "piano.gif");
        image_size = size();
        image_size.height -= 60;

        Image offScrImage = createImage(image_size.width,
                                        image_size.height);
        Graphics offScrGC = offScrImage.getGraphics();
        offScrGC.drawImage(background, 0, 0, image_size.width,
                           image_size.height, this);
      }

    //————————————————————————

    public boolean imageUpdate(Image img, int infoflags, int x, int y,
                               int width, int height)
      {
        if (infoflags == ALLBITS)
          {
          done_loading_image = true;
          showStatus("");
          repaint();
          (new Thread(this)).start();
          return false;
          }
        else
          return true;
      }

    //————————————————————————

    void makeImages()
      {
        String parameter;

        int items = 1;
        parameter = getParameter("ITEMS");
        if (parameter != null)
          items = Integer.parseInt(parameter);
```

```java
            bounceimages = new Image[items][];

        for (int item = 0; item < items; item++)
          {
            bounceimages[item] = new Image[8];
            String dir_name = getParameter("ITEM_" + (item+1));
            for (int i = 1 ; i <= 8 ; i++)
              bounceimages[item][i-1] = getImage(getCodeBase(),
                          "images/" + dir_name + "/t" + i + ".gif");
          }

        images = new BounceImage[items];
        for (int i = 0; i < items; i++)
          {
            BounceImage img = images[i] = new BounceImage(this, i);
            img.move(1 + img.width*.8f*(i%3) + (i/3)*.3f*img.width,
                    img.height*.3f + (i%3)*.3f*img.height);
          }

        music = getAudioClip(getCodeBase(), "bounce.au");
      }

//————————————————————————————

public void run()
  {
    long lasttime;

    try
      {
        if (images == null)
          {
            System.out.println("Making images ...");
            makeImages();
          }

        if (music != null)
          music.loop();

        lasttime = System.currentTimeMillis();
        while (!time_to_die)
          {
            int i;
            long now = System.currentTimeMillis();
            long deltaT = now - lasttime;
            boolean active = false;
            Dimension d = image_size;

            for (i = 0; i < images.length; i++)
              {
                BounceImage img = images[i];

                img.step(deltaT);
```

```
                       if (img.Vy > .05 || -img.Vy > .05 ||
                           img.y + img.width < d.height - 10)
                      {
                         active = true;
                      }
                }
            if (!active && images.length != 0)
              {
                for (i = 0; i < images.length; i++)
                    {
                       BounceImage img = images[i];

                       img.Vx = (float)Math.random() / 4.0f - 0.125f;
                       img.Vy = -(float)Math.random() / 4.0f - 0.2f;
                       img.Vr = 0.05f - (float)Math.random() * 0.1f;
                    }
              }
            paint_images();
            lasttime = now;
            try
              {
                 Thread.sleep(100);
              }
            catch (InterruptedException e)
              {
                 return;
              }
          }
      }
    finally
      {
        if (music != null)
           music.stop();
      }
  }

//————————————————————————

public void start()
  {
    time_to_die = false;
  }

//————————————————————————

public void stop()
  {
    time_to_die = true;
    music.stop();
  }

//————————————————————————
```

```
public void paint_images()
  {
    if (images != null)
      for (int i = 0; i < images.length; i++)
        if (images[i] != null)
          images[i].paint(g);
  }


//————————————————————


public void paint(Graphics g)
  {
    if (!done_loading_image)
      showStatus("Bounce:  loading image");

    else
      {
        g.drawImage(background, 0, 0, image_size.width,
                    image_size.height, this);

        paint_images();

        Font font = new Font("TimesRoman", Font.BOLD, 30);
        g.setFont(font);
        g.setColor(Color.blue);
        g.drawString("Joe's Sports Bar...Where heads roll!",
                     0, image_size.height+50);
      }
  }
}
```

BREAKING APART MODIFIABLE BOUNCING HEADS

As before, this section will examine only those sections of the program you must change from the applet presented in Chapter 20.

The BounceImage Class

There are no changes to this class because the way each head bounces has not changed. The number of bouncing heads (instances of *BounceImage* classes) will change based upon the user's HTML settings.

The bounce Applet Class

Within the *bounce* class, the only function you must change is *makeImages*. As you may recall, the *makeImages* function is where the applet fills the arrays with the images for each bouncing head. As you will see, the function includes calls to the *getParameter* function to get the user settings from the HTML file.

To start, the applet checks the HTML file to get the number of items the user wants the applet to bounce:

```
String parameter;

int items = 1;
```

```
parameter = getParameter("ITEMS");
if (parameter != null)
  items = Integer.parseInt(parameter);
```

As you can see, the applet stores the number of items in the *items* variable. Using the *items* variable, the applet allocates space for the two-dimensional array that will hold the object images:

```
bounceimages = new Image[items][];
```

For each item the user wants to bounce, the applet must allocate space for 8 images. Then, the applet examines the HTML file to get the directory names for each directory where the images reside. Using the *getImage* function, the applet loads the images into the array. As you can see, the applet uses a *for* statement to perform the necessary processing for each object:

```
for (int item = 0; item < items; item++)
  {
     bounceimages[item] = new Image[8];
     String dir_name = getParameter("ITEM_" + (item+1));
     for (int i = 1 ; i <= 8 ; i++)
        bounceimages[item][i-1] = getImage(getCodeBase(),
                                  "images/" + dir_name + "/t" + i +
                                  ".gif");
  }
```

Next, the applet allocates the array that will contain the *BounceImage* objects:

```
images = new BounceImage[items];
```

For each *BounceImage* object, the applet calls the constructor with an index value that specifies which set of images (within the *bounceimages* array) the object will display. In addition, the function moves each image to its starting location:

```
for (int i = 0; i < items; i++)
  {
     BounceImage img = images[i] = new BounceImage(this, i);
     img.move(1 + img.width*.8f*(i%3) + (i/3)*.3f*img.width,
              img.height*.3f + (i%3)*.3f*img.height);
  }
```

Lastly, the applet loads the audio clip that plays as the objects bounce around:

```
music = getAudioClip(getCodeBase(), "bounce.au");
```

That's all there is to it! The rest of the applet functions determine the number of spinning objects by getting the *length* attribute of the *images* array. For example, in the *paint_images* function (which paints each image on the screen), the code uses *images.length* within a *for* loop:

```
public void paint_images()
  {
    if (images != null)
```

```
        for (int i = 0; i < images.length; i++)
          if (images [i] != null)
            images[i].paint(g);
    }
```

ENHANCEMENTS YOU CAN MAKE TO MULTIPLE BOUNCING HEADS

The last several chapters have made extensive modifications to the original JDK **Bouncing Heads** applet. Rather than spending more time with this code, take some time now to create some images that the program can access using the HTML parameters.

PUTTING IT ALL TOGETHER

The **Modifiable Bouncing Heads** applet shows you how to build a generic applet that end users can quickly enhance using HTML. In Chapter 22, you will use other *Graphics* class functions to draw pictures that you combine with a background image. Before you continue with Chapter 22, however, make sure you understand the following key concepts:

☑ Whenever possible, your applets should make extensive use of HTML parameters. In this way, end users can easily enhance your applet.

☑ You can never make an applet too easy for an end user to enhance. The more features you give them, the more they will want.

CHAPTER 22

FLOWER SHOP
USING THE *RANDOM* AND *TRANSLATE* FUNCTIONS

As you perform graphics operations, you will often display different objects at random positions on the screen. To provide your applets with a way to generate the random positions, the Java *Math* class provides the *random* function that generates random numbers. Likewise, if your applet performs animation, you need to move objects across the screen. Graphics programmers refer to the process of moving an object as *translation* (you translate the object's origin). In this chapter, you will learn how to use the *Math* class *random* function and the *Graphics* class *translate* function to create an applet that displays flowers at random locations. As you will see, the applet draws the simple flower images on top of a background image that contains a real picture of flowers. By combining (even simple) animated art with a photograph, you can generate cool graphics. By the time you finish this chapter, you will understand the following key concepts:

- ◆ You can use the *random* function of the *Math* class to generate random numbers.

- ◆ If you have items that you are drawing around the origin, you can use the *translate* function of the *Graphics* class to place these items wherever you want.

USING FLOWER SHOP

When you run the **Flower Shop** applet, you will see a window filled with a flower photograph within which simple flower graphics pop up at random locations. Eventually, the applet displays a billboard showing the name of the flower shop, as shown in Figure 22. If you resize the window, the billboard's size will change depending on the window's new width and height.

Figure 22 *Combining simple graphics with a background photograph.*

THE HTML FILE

This HTML file for the **Flower Shop** applet contains two parameters: the DELAY parameter specifies the amount of time the applet waits between drawing flowers, and the FLOWERS parameter specifies the number of flowers the applet draws before it displays the shop's billboard:

```
<applet code=flowers.class width=330 height=170>
<param name=delay    value=200>
<param name=flowers value=20>
</applet>
```

LOOKING AT FLOWER SHOP

The **Flower Shop** applet shows you how to display graphics-based objects at random locations, and how to resize an applet's output should the user change the window size. The following code implements the **Flower Shop** applet:

```
//************************************************************
// flowers.java
//************************************************************

import java.applet.*;
import java.awt.*;


//************************************************************

public class flowers extends Applet implements Runnable
   {
     Graphics g;

     Image background;
     boolean done_loading_image = false;

     int width;
     int height;
     int delay_amount = 100;

     int flower_width = 10;
     int flower_height = 20;
     int number_of_flowers = 20;


     //————————————————————————————————

     public void init()
       {
         g = getGraphics();

         String parameter;

         parameter = getParameter("DELAY");
         if (parameter != null)
           delay_amount = Integer.parseInt(parameter);
```

```java
      parameter = getParameter("FLOWERS");
      if (parameter != null)
        number_of_flowers = Integer.parseInt(parameter);

      get_defaults();

      background = getImage(getCodeBase(), "flowers.gif");
      Image offScrImage = createImage(width, height);
      Graphics offScrGC = offScrImage.getGraphics();
      offScrGC.drawImage(background, 0, 0, width, height, this);
    }

//—————————————————————————————

void get_defaults()
  {
    width = size().width;
    height = size().height;
  }

//—————————————————————————————

public boolean imageUpdate(Image img, int infoflags, int x, int y,
                           int width, int height)
  {
    if (infoflags == ALLBITS)
      {
        if (!done_loading_image)
          {
            done_loading_image = true;
            showStatus("");
            repaint();
            (new Thread(this)).start();
          }
        return false;
      }
    else
      return true;
  }

//—————————————————————————————

public void run()
  {
    int counter = 0;

    repaint();
    while (true)
      {
        add_flower();
```

```
          if (++counter == number_of_flowers)
            {
              counter = 0;
              draw_shop_name();
              delay(delay_amount * 5);
              repaint();
            }
          else
            delay(delay_amount);
      }
  }

//————————————————————

void draw_flower(Graphics g)
  {
    g.setColor(Color.red);
    g.drawArc(0, 0, flower_width*2, flower_height*2, 270, 135);
    g.setColor(Color.yellow);
    g.fillOval(flower_width, 0, flower_width, flower_height);
  }

//————————————————————

void add_flower()
  {
    Graphics g2 = g.create();
    g2.translate((int) (Math.random() * width),
                 (int) (Math.random() * height));
    draw_flower(g2);
  }

//————————————————————

void draw_shop_name()
  {
    g.setColor(Color.green);
    g.fillRect(width/4, height/4, width/2, height/2);
    g.setColor(Color.red);
    g.drawRect(width/4, height/4, width/2, height/2);

    Font font = new Font("TimesRoman", Font.BOLD, height/10);
    g.setFont(font);
    g.setColor(Color.black);
    g.drawString("Betty's", (width*3)/8, (height*3)/8);
    g.drawString("Flower", (width*3)/8, height/2);
    g.drawString("Shop", (width*3)/8, (height*5)/8);
  }

//————————————————————
```

```
      void delay(int delay_amount)
        {
          try
            {
              Thread.sleep(delay_amount);
            }
          catch (InterruptedException e)
            {
            }
        }


      //————————————————————————————————

      public void paint(Graphics g)
        {
          if (!done_loading_image)
            showStatus("Bounce:  loading image");
          else
            {
              get_defaults();
              g.drawImage(background, 0, 0, width, height, this);
            }
        }
    }
```

BREAKING APART FLOWER SHOP

As discussed, the **Flower Shop** applet uses the *Math* and *Graphics* classes. Therefore, the applet imports the following packages:

```
import java.applet.*;
import java.awt.*;
```

The *flowers* class is an applet that *extends* the *Applet* class. In addition, the applet will run as a thread, so it *implements* the *Runnable* interface:

```
public class flowers extends Applet implements Runnable
```

Class Variables

Within the class-member variables, the applet declares variables to store a graphics context, a background image, and a *boolean* variable that tells the applet when the background image has finished loading:

```
Graphics g;

Image background;
boolean done_loading_image = false;
```

In addition, the applet declares variables to store the width and the height of the window. Using these variables, the applet can make sure that it does not create flowers outside the window. Also, the applet uses these two variables to scale the shop's billboard in relation to the window:

```
int width;
int height;
```

As briefly discussed, the applet delays for a brief period after drawing a flower in the applet window. If the HTML file contains a DELAY parameter, the applet will use the value specified. Otherwise, the applet will delay for one-tenth of a second (100 milliseconds):

```
int delay_amount = 100;
```

Next, the applet uses two variables to specify the height and width of the flowers the applet draws within the applet window:

```
int flower_width = 10;
int flower_height = 20;
```

Lastly, the applet uses the *number_of_flowers* variable to determine how many flowers it displays on the screen before drawing the shop's billboard. If the HTML file contains a value, the applet will use the HTML setting. Otherwise, the applet will draw 20 flowers before it displays the billboard:

```
int number_of_flowers = 20;
```

Initializing the Applet

To start, the applet uses the *getGraphics* function to define the graphics context:

```
g = getGraphics();
```

Next, the applet uses the *getParameter* function to determine if the user has specified settings for the delay interval or the number of flowers within the applet's HTML file:

```
String parameter;

parameter = getParameter("DELAY");
if (parameter != null)
  delay_amount = Integer.parseInt(parameter);

parameter = getParameter("FLOWERS");
if (parameter != null)
  number_of_flowers = Integer.parseInt(parameter);
```

Lastly, the applet determines the width and height for the applet window, and loads the background image:

```
get_defaults();

background = getImage(getCodeBase(), "flowers.gif");
Image offScrImage = createImage(width, height);
```

```
Graphics offScrGC = offScrImage.getGraphics();
offScrGC.drawImage(background, 0, 0, width, height, this);
```

To get the applet window's default width and height, the applet uses the *Applet* class *size* function, which returns a *Dimension* object that contains two variables: *width* and *height*. As you can see, the applet assigns the default values to the *width* and *height* member variables:

```
void get_defaults()
   {
      width = size().width;
      height = size().height;
   }
```

As you have seen in previous chapters, the *imageUpdate* function lets the applet keep track of whether or not the background image has finished loading. As you can see, when the background image is finally loaded, the applet clears the status bar, repaints the screen, and starts the thread that will draw the random flowers:

```
public boolean imageUpdate(Image img, int infoflags, int x, int y,
                           int width, int height)
   {
     if (infoflags == ALLBITS)
       {
         if (!done_loading_image)
           {
               done_loading_image = true;
               showStatus("");
               repaint();
               (new Thread(this)).start();
           }
         return false;
       }
     else
       return true;
   }
```

Running the Thread

As discussed, the applet uses a *Thread* object to draw the flowers at random locations on the screen. Within the *run* function, the applet uses the *counter* variable to keep track of the number of flowers it has drawn:

```
int counter = 0;
```

Next, the function starts an infinite loop that keeps adding flowers to the screen until the maximum number has been reached. Then, the function draws the name of the shop, waits five times the normal delay, clears the screen, and starts drawing flowers again.

```
while (true)
   {
      add_flower();
```

```
        if (++counter == number_of_flowers)
          {
             counter = 0;
             draw_shop_name();
             delay(delay_amount * 5);
             repaint();
          }
        else
          delay(delay_amount);
   }
```

Drawing Flowers

To draw the flowers on the screen, the applet uses the *draw_flower* function. For simplicity, the function draws a flower stem and an oval for the flower. By modifying this function, you can draw a more realistic flower, or you could display actual images of flowers. The coordinates of the flower are (0, 0), which is normally the top-left corner of the window. The function accepts as a parameter the graphics context it uses to draw the flower:

```
void draw_flower(Graphics g)
  {
    g.setColor(Color.red);
    g.drawArc(0, 0, flower_width*2, flower_height*2, 270, 135);
    g.setColor(Color.yellow);
    g.fillOval(flower_width, 0, flower_width, flower_height);
  }
```

To add a flower to the screen, the applet calls the *draw_flower* function just discussed. However, if the applet only called that function and did nothing else, every flower would appear at the same spot (and you would only see one flower). To disperse the flowers around the screen, the applet uses the *translate* function, which moves the origin of the graphics context to a different position on the window.

The *translate* function accepts two parameters: the x-and-y coordinates of the new origin location. The x-and-y coordinates are in relation to the current origin. Therefore, if you were to translate the original graphics context, you would need to keep track of the previous flower so you would know where the origin had been moved. To get around such extra processing, you can instead create a copy of the graphics context and then translate the copy's origin.

To display the flowers at random locations across the screen, the applet uses the *random* function to determine the screen coordinates. The *random* function returns a value in the range 0.0 to 1.0. To get a random x-coordinate, the applet multiplies the random value by the width of the window. Likewise, to get a random y-coordinate, the applet multiplies the random value by the height of the window:

```
void add_flower()
  {
    Graphics g2 = g.create();
    g2.translate((int) (Math.random() * width), (int) (Math.random() *
                  height));
    draw_flower(g2);
  }
```

The Shop Name Billboard

To draw the billboard, the applet first draws a rectangle that is half the window's width and height. The color of this rectangle is green with red trim around the edge:

```
void draw_shop_name()
  {
    g.setColor(Color.green);
    g.fillRect(width/4, height/4, width/2, height/2);
    g.setColor(Color.red);
    g.drawRect(width/4, height/4, width/2, height/2);
```

To display the text on the sign, the applet uses a font size that is one-tenth of the sign's height. By using a point size that is dependent on the sign height, the applet can draw a string that gets bigger or smaller, depending on the window height:

```
    Font font = new Font("TimesRoman", Font.BOLD, height/10);
    g.setFont(font);
    g.setColor(Color.black);
    g.drawString("Betty's", (width*3)/8, (height*3)/8);
    g.drawString("Flower" , (width*3)/8,  height/2);
    g.drawString("Shop" , (width*3)/8, (height*5)/8);
  }
```

The Rest of the Program

The applet's *delay* function is pretty much the same as the *delay* functions you have seen in previous chapters. As you can see, the function uses a parameter to specify its delay amount:

```
void delay(int delay_amount)
  {
    try
      {
        Thread.sleep(delay_amount);
      }
    catch (InterruptedException e)
      {
      }
  }
```

The applet's *paint* function waits for the background image to load, and then gets the window's default width and height and paints the background image on the screen. While the image is still loading, the function displays the loading message on the status bar:

```
public void paint(Graphics g)
  {
    if (!done_loading_image)
      showStatus("Bounce:  loading image");
    else
      {
        get_defaults();
        g.drawImage(background, 0, 0, width, height, this);
      }
  }
```

ENHANCEMENTS YOU CAN MAKE TO FLOWER SHOP

As briefly discussed, by changing the *draw_flower* function, you can create realistic flower images or even display actual photographs of flowers. Next, you might display a picture of the shop's logo or sign in place of the billboard image.

PUTTING IT ALL TOGETHER

The **Flower Shop** applet shows you how to combine simple graphics with a real background image. In addition, the applet shows you how to place objects at random screen locations by translating the window's origin. In Chapter 23, you will revisit the **Free Samples** applet, this time to jitter the blinking star. Before you continue with Chapter 23, however, make sure you understand the following key concepts:

- ☑ The *Math* class *random* function returns a value in the range 0.0 to 1.0.

- ☑ By multiplying the random value by the width of a window, you create a random x-coordinate.

- ☑ By multiplying the random value by the height of a window, you create a random y-coordinate.

- ☑ Using the *Graphics* class *translate* function, you can move the origin for objects you plan to draw on the applet window.

CHAPTER 23

MOVING FREE SAMPLES
JITTERING THE BLINKING STAR

In Chapter 8, you created the **Free Samples** applet that flashed a star on the screen to capture the user's attention. In this chapter, you will learn how to jitter (shake) an image on the screen. By shaking the object, you will draw the user's attention immediately to the object. By the time you finish this chapter, you will understand the following key concepts:

- To make an object jitter, you repeatedly redraw the object, each time changing the object's coordinates slightly.

- If your object consists of several connected lines, you can use the *drawPolygon* function to draw the object.

USING MOVING FREE SAMPLES

When you run the **Moving Free Samples** applet, you will see a window with a star that jitters, as shown in Figure 23. If the user resizes the window, the applet will resize the star and the text the star contains.

Figure 23 *A snapshot of the jittering star.*

THE HTML FILE

This HTML file for the **Moving Free Samples** applet contains the DELAY parameter, which specifies the amount of time, in milliseconds, the applet pauses before redrawing the image.

```
<applet code=star.class width=200 height=200>
<param name=delay value=100>
</applet>
```

LOOKING AT MOVING FREE SAMPLES

The **Moving Free Samples** applet displays a jittering star that contains the message "Free Samples." If the user resizes the applet window, the applet will resize the star and the text it contains. The following code implements the **Moving Free Samples** applet:

```
//*****************************************************************
// star.java
//*****************************************************************

import java.applet.*;
import java.awt.*;

//*****************************************************************

public class star extends Applet implements Runnable
  {
    int x = 0;
    int y = 0;

    boolean blink = true;

    int delay_amount = 100;

    //————————————————————————

    public void init()
      {
        x = size().width  / 8;
        y = size().height / 8;

        String parameter = getParameter("DELAY");
        if (parameter != null)
          delay_amount = Integer.parseInt(parameter);
      }

    //————————————————————————

    public void start()
      {
        (new Thread(this)).start();
      }

    //————————————————————————
```

```java
    public void run()
      {
        while (true)
          {
            repaint();
            delay();
          }
      }

//————————————————————————

void delay()
  {
    try
      {
        Thread.sleep(delay_amount);
      }
    catch (InterruptedException e)
      {
      }
  }

//————————————————————————

public void paint(Graphics _g)
  {
    Graphics g = _g.create();

    if (blink)
      {
        g.setColor(Color.red);
        blink = false;
      }
    else
      {
        g.setColor(Color.blue);
        blink = true;
      }

    int width  = (size().width  * 3) / 4;
    int height = (size().height * 3) / 4;

    g.translate(x, y);

    Font font = new Font("TimesRoman", Font.BOLD, height/10);
    g.setFont(font);

    FontMetrics font_metrics = g.getFontMetrics();

    g.drawString("Free", (width-font_metrics.stringWidth ("Free")) / 2,
                 height/2 - height/20);

    g.drawString("Samples", (width-font_metrics.stringWidth
                 ("Samples")) / 2, height/2 + height/20);
```

```
            int xpoints[] = new int[9];
            int ypoints[] = new int[9];

            xpoints[0] =  width/2;        ypoints[0] = (height*9)/10;
            xpoints[1] = (width*3)/8;     ypoints[1] = (height*5)/8;
            xpoints[2] =  width/10;       ypoints[2] =  height/2;
            xpoints[3] = (width*3)/ 8;    ypoints[3] = (height*3)/8;
            xpoints[4] =  width/2;        ypoints[4] =  height/10;
            xpoints[5] = (width*5)/ 8;    ypoints[5] = (height*3)/ 8;
            xpoints[6] = (width*9)/10;    ypoints[6] =  height/2;
            xpoints[7] = (width*5)/ 8;    ypoints[7] = (height*5)/8;
            xpoints[8] =  width/2;        ypoints[8] = (height*9)/10;

            g.drawPolygon(xpoints, ypoints, 9);

            x += (int) (Math.random() * 7) - 3;
            y += (int) (Math.random() * 7) - 3;

            if (x < 0)
              x = 0;

            if (y < 0)
              y = 0;

            if (x > width/4)
              x = width/4;

            if (y > height/4)
              y = height/4;
        }
    }
```

BREAKING APART MOVING FREE SAMPLES

Like most of the applets this book presents, the **Moving Free Samples** applet imports the *applet* and *awt* packages:

```
import java.applet.*;
import java.awt.*;
```

Likewise, the applet inherits from the *Applet* class and runs as a thread:

```
public class star extends Applet implements Runnable
```

Class Variables

To start, the applet must keep track of the star's x-and-y coordinates:

```
int x = 0;
int y = 0;
```

The applet uses the *blink* variable to control whether it draws the star in red or blue. If the blink variable is true, the applet draws the star in red; otherwise, the applet uses blue:

```
boolean blink = true;
```

The amount of time to delay between blinks is initialized to a tenth of a second. This value will be obtained from the HTML file, if specified:

```
int delay_amount = 100;
```

Initializing the Applet

The size of the star will be three-fourths of the width and height, so, to center the star, initialize the x-and-y coordinates of the top-left corner of the star to one-eighth of the width and height:

```
x = size().width / 8;
y = size().height / 8;
```

Get the DELAY parameter, which will be the number of milliseconds to wait between blinks:

```
String parameter = getParameter("DELAY");
if (parameter != null)
  delay_amount = Integer.parseInt(parameter);
```

Start the thread running in the the same way that you have seen in previous applets:

```
public void start()
  {
    (new Thread(this)).start();
  }
```

Running the Thread

To run the thread, you just have to repaint the star and then wait the amount of time specified in the HTML file. You have to place these two functions in an infinite loop to continue running the thread for the life of the applet:

```
public void run()
  {
    while (true)
      {
        repaint();
        delay();
      }
  }
```

Drawing the Star

You have to create a new graphics context that you will use in the *paint* function because you will use the *translate* function, which resets the origin. If you do not create a new graphics context, you will have to keep track of where the origin is in relation to the actual origin of the window. You have to give the parameter a different variable name from the one you will use in the function:

```
public void paint(Graphics _g)
```

Then you have to create the local graphics context:

```
Graphics g = _g.create();
```

Set the color of the star depending on the *blink* boolean variable:

```
if (blink)
  {
     g.setColor(Color.red);
     blink = false;
  }
else
  {
     g.setColor(Color.blue);
     blink = true;
  }
```

The applet sets the star's width and height to three-fourths the size of the window. If the user resizes the window, the applet can resize the star and its text:

```
int width  = (size().width * 3)/4;
int height = (size().height * 3)/4;
```

Next, the applet translates the star's origin to the x-and-y coordinates first specified in the *init* function. If you examine the *paint* function, you will find that the *paint* function also changes the star's origin (it has to give the star the jitter effect). However, by resetting the star's origin here, the star never moves too far from its original starting point:

```
g.translate(x, y);
```

The applet then selects the font it will use to draw the "Free Samples" message on the screen. To center the message, the applet uses a *FontMetrics* object to determine specifics about the current font:

```
Font font = new Font("TimesRoman", Font.BOLD, height/10);
g.setFont(font);

FontMetrics font_metrics = g.getFontMetrics();
```

Next, the applet centers the strings horizontally by subtracting the width of the string from the width of the window and dividing by two. To center the strings vertically, the applet places the first string one-twentieth of the height above the center, and the second string one-twentieth of the height below the center:

```
g.drawString("Free", (width-fm.stringWidth ("Free"))/2,
             height/2-height/20);
```

```
g.drawString("Samples", (width-fm.stringWidth ("Samples")) / 2,
             height/2 + height/20);
```

The applet creates the star by connecting lines that form a polygon. As you can see, the applet stores the star's x-and-y coordinates in two integer arrays. The star's coordinates start at the bottom of the star and go clockwise. The endpoint must be the same as the first point:

```
int xpoints[] = new int[9];
int ypoints[] = new int[9];

xpoints[0] =  width/2;        ypoints[0] = (height*9)/10;
xpoints[1] = (width*3)/8;     ypoints[1] = (height*5)/ 8;
xpoints[2] =  width/10;       ypoints[2] =  height/2;
xpoints[3] = (width*3)/ 8;    ypoints[3] = (height*3)/8;
xpoints[4] =  width/2;        ypoints[4] =  height/10;
xpoints[5] = (width*5)/8;     ypoints[5] = (height*3)/8;
xpoints[6] = (width*9)/10;    ypoints[6] =  height/2;
xpoints[7] = (width*5)/8;     ypoints[7] = (height*5)/8;
xpoints[8] =  width/2;        ypoints[8] = (height*9)/10;
```

Because the star's lines connect to form a polygon, the applet can use the *drawPolygon* function to draw the lines. This function accepts three parameters: the x-coordinates, the y-coordinates, and the number of points in these arrays:

```
g.drawPolygon(xpoints, ypoints, 9);
```

To jitter the star, the applet moves the star's origin slightly and then redraws the star. In fact, the applet moves the origin by less than 2 pixels. To get random numbers between -2 and 2, the application performs the following processing. First, the applet calls the *random* function, which returns a value greater than 0.0 and less than 1.0. The applet multiplies the random number by 7 and converts the result to an integer (to get a value between 0 and 7). Next, the applet subtracts 3 from the result, producing a value greater than -3 and less than +3. The applet then converts that value to an integer, whose value is from -2 to +2:

```
x += (int) (Math.random() * 7) - 3;
y += (int) (Math.random() * 7) - 3;
```

Lastly, the applet ensures that the star's x-and-y coordinates do not become less than 0 or greater than one-fourth of the window's width and height (because the star is three-fourths of the window's width and height):

```
if (x < 0)
  x = 0;

if (y < 0)
  y = 0;

if (x > width/4)
  x = width/4;

if (y > height/4)
  y = height/4;
```

ENHANCEMENTS YOU CAN MAKE TO MOVING FREE SAMPLES

To change the **Moving Free Samples** applet, modify the star's shape to use a five-point star. Next, change the star's movement to follow the edge of the screen instead of jittering randomly. Lastly, rather than drawing the star's image, change the applet to jitter a photograph or another image.

PUTTING IT ALL TOGETHER

The **Moving Free Samples** applet shows you how to make an object jitter within a window. You might, for example, use this applet to jitter a corporate logo. In Chapter 24, you will learn how to move select objects to a random location. Before you continue with Chapter 24, however, make sure you understand the following key concepts:

- ☑ To jitter an object, simply redraw the object repeatedly at small random offsets from the object's current coordinates.
- ☑ By basing an object's font size on the window size, your applet can scale the font should the user change the window size.

CHAPTER 24

FISHES
IMAGES THAT RESPOND TO A MOUSE-BUTTON RELEASE

In several of this book's previous chapters, you have created applets that respond to a user's mouse click. In most cases, the applet simply needs to know the mouse (x-and-y) coordinates when the user clicks the button. In the **Fishes** applet, you will learn how to get the mouse coordinates of the location where the user released the mouse button. In short, this applet moves fish images away from the location at which the user released the mouse button. By the time you finish this chapter, you will understand the following key concepts:

◆ To determine the mouse coordinates at which the user released the mouse button, your program must implement the *mouseUp* function.

◆ To get the dimensions (width and height) of an image, your applet must wait until the image is loaded. Then, the applet can use the *getWidth* and *getHeight* functions.

USING FISHES

When you run the **Fishes** applet, you will see a window with a school of fish, as shown in Figure 24. When you release the mouse button when the mouse pointer is on top of a fish, the applet will move the fish (to a random position) to get away from the mouse pointer.

Figure 24 Fishes that respond to mouse clicks.

The HTML File

Use the following HTML file to run the **Fishes** applet:

```
<applet code=fishes.class width=600 height=400> </applet>
```

Looking at Fishes

The **Fishes** applet displays a school of fish which will flee when the user releases the mouse button. The following code implements the **Fishes** applet:

```java
//*****************************************************************
// fishes.java
//*****************************************************************

import java.applet.*;
import java.awt.*;

//*****************************************************************

class Coordinate
  {
    public int x;
    public int y;

    public Coordinate(int x, int y)
      {
        this.x = x;
        this.y = y;
      }
  }

//*****************************************************************

public class fishes extends Applet
  {
    final int TOTAL_FISHES = 9;

    Graphics g;
    Image background;
    Image fish_gif[];
    Coordinate coordinate[];
    Dimension fish_size[];

    boolean done_loading_image = false;
    boolean done_loading_all_images = false;

    FontMetrics fm;
```

```
    int loading_fish = 0;

    int width;
    int height;

    //————————————————————————

    public void init()
      {
        g = getGraphics();

        Font f = new Font("TimesRoman", Font.BOLD, 15);
        g.setFont(f);

        fm = g.getFontMetrics();

        background = getImage(getCodeBase(), "fishback.gif");

        width = size().width;
        height = size().height;

        fish_gif = new Image[TOTAL_FISHES];
        for (int i = 0; i < TOTAL_FISHES; i++)
          fish_gif[i] = getImage(getCodeBase(), "fish" + (i+1) + ".gif");

        get_coordinates();

        repaint();

        Image offScrImage = createImage(width, height);
        Graphics offScrGC = offScrImage.getGraphics();
        offScrGC.drawImage(background, 0, 0, this);

        while (!done_loading_image)
          ;

        fish_size = new Dimension[TOTAL_FISHES];
        for (int i = 0; i < TOTAL_FISHES; i++)
          {
            loading_fish = i;
            done_loading_image = false;
            offScrGC.drawImage(fish_gif[i], 0, 0, this);
            while (!done_loading_image)
              ;
            fish_size[i] = new Dimension(fish_gif[i].getWidth(null),
                                         fish_gif[i].getHeight(null));
          }

        done_loading_all_images = true;
      }

    //————————————————————————
```

```java
void get_coordinates()
  {
  coordinate = new Coordinate[TOTAL_FISHES];
  coordinate[0] = new Coordinate(118, 102);
  coordinate[1] = new Coordinate(243,  27);
  coordinate[2] = new Coordinate(361, 103);
  coordinate[3] = new Coordinate(496, 150);
  coordinate[4] = new Coordinate(500,  28);
  coordinate[5] = new Coordinate( 49, 238);
  coordinate[6] = new Coordinate(171, 220);
  coordinate[7] = new Coordinate(305, 252);
  coordinate[8] = new Coordinate(474, 260);
  }

//————————————————————————

public boolean mouseUp(Event evt, int x, int y)
  {
    System.out.println("Parameters (" + x + "," + y + ")");
    System.out.println("Event arg  (" + evt.x + "," + evt.y +")");
    System.out.println("<" + evt + ">\n" + Event.MOUSE_UP);

    for (int i = 0; i < TOTAL_FISHES; i++)
      {
        if (x > coordinate[i].x &&
            x < coordinate[i].x + fish_size[i].width &&
            y > coordinate[i].y &&
            y < coordinate[i].y + fish_size[i].height)
          {
            move_fish(i);
          }
      }

    return true;
  }

//————————————————————————

void move_fish(int index)
  {
    int old_x = coordinate[index].x;
    int old_y = coordinate[index].y;
    int new_x = (int) (Math.random() * (background.getWidth(this)
                                - fish_size[index].width));
    int new_y = (int) (Math.random() * (background.getHeight(this)
                                - fish_size[index].height));
    int dx = new_x - old_x;
    int dy = new_y - old_y;
    int end = Math.max(Math.abs(dx), Math.abs(dy));

    for (int i = 0; i < end; i++)
      {
        int x = old_x + dx * i / end;
        int y = old_y + dy * i / end;
```

```java
        Graphics g2;
        g2 = g.create();

        g2.clipRect(coordinate[index].x, coordinate[index].y,
                    fish_size[index].width,
                    fish_size[index].height);
        g2.drawImage(background, 0, 0, null);

        coordinate[index].x = x;
        coordinate[index].y = y;

        g.drawImage (fish_gif[index], coordinate[index].x,
                     coordinate[index].y, this);
      }

    repaint();
  }

//————————————————————————

public boolean imageUpdate(Image img, int infoflags, int x, int y,
                           int width, int height)
  {
    if (infoflags == ALLBITS)
      {
        done_loading_image = true;
        showStatus("");
        repaint();
        return false;
      }
    else
      return true;
  }

//————————————————————————

public void paint(Graphics g)
  {
    if (!done_loading_all_images)
      showStatus("Fishtank:  loading image " + loading_fish);

    else
      {
        g.drawImage(background, 0, 0, this);

        for (int i = 0; i < TOTAL_FISHES; i++)
          g.drawImage(fish_gif[i], coordinate[i].x, coordinate[i].y,
                      this);
      }
  }
}
```

Breaking Apart Fishes

Within the **Fishes** applet, the code uses *Coordinate* class objects to keep track of the fish locations:

```
class Coordinate
  {
    public int x;
    public int y;

    public Coordinate(int x, int y)
      {
        this.x = x;
        this.y = y;
      }
  }
```

Because the **Fishes** applet does not run as a thread, you do not have to define it as *implements Runnable*. Instead, the applet simply extends the *Applet* class, as shown here:

```
public class fishes extends Applet
```

The school of fish within the **Fishes** applet consists of 9 fish. The applet uses the *final* keyword to define TOTAL_FISHES as a constant:

```
final int TOTAL_FISHES = 9;
```

To display the background and fish images, the applet requires a graphics context and variables to hold the background and fish images, as well as an array of x-and-y coordinate values that track the location of each fish:

```
Graphics g;
Image background;
Image fish_gif[];
Coordinate coordinate[];
```

Because the fish are different sizes, the applet uses an array of *Dimension* objects. Each *Dimension* object contains two attributes: *width* and *height:*

```
Dimension fish_size[];
```

Before the applet displays the fish, the applet waits for all the images to load. Therefore, the applet uses two variables: the first, *done_loading_image*, tracks when a specific image has been loaded; the second, *done_loading_all_images*, tracks when the applet has loaded the background and each of the fish images:

```
boolean done_loading_image = false;
boolean done_loading_all_images = false;
```

As the applet loads the fish images, the *loading_fish* variable contains the index of the current fish. The only time the applet uses this variable is when it loads the fish images:

```
int loading_fish = 0;
```

Initializing the Applet

To start, the applet loads each image before it starts running. The applet must load each fish so the applet can get the dimensions of the fish images. Before the applet loads the fish images, the applet waits for the background image to finish loading. When the background image is loaded, the variable *done_loading_image* is set to *true* by the *imageUpdate* function (which, as you know, is called by the thread that the *drawImage* function started):

```
while (!done_loading_image)
  ;
```

After the background image loads, the applet creates the *fish_size* array, and starts a loop which loads each fish image. Within the loop, the applet sets the *loading_fish* variable to the current image and then uses the variable within the status bar message the *paint* function displays to give the user an indication of the applet's processing. Next, the applet loads the image. After the image is loaded, the applet creates a new *Dimension* object within the *fish_size* array, and assigns the object the correct width and height for the current fish:

```
fish_size = new Dimension[TOTAL_FISHES];
for (int i = 0; i < TOTAL_FISHES; i++)
  {
    loading_fish = i;
    done_loading_image = false;
    offScrGC.drawImage(fish_gif[i], 0, 0, this);
    while (!done_loading_image)
      ;
    fish_size[i] = new Dimension(fish_gif[i].getWidth(null),
                                 fish_gif[i].getHeight(null));
  }
```

After the applet has loaded all the images, the applet sets the *done_loading_all_images* variable to *true* so that the *paint* function will know that it can draw the images on the applet window:

```
done_loading_all_images = true;
```

New Functions in this Applet

This applet contains two new functions which you have not seen yet. The first function, *mouseUp,* traps the user's release of the mouse button. The second, *move_fish,* moves the selected fish to a random position inside the applet window. The *mouseUp* function is similar to the *mouseDown* function that you have used in previous applets. It accepts three parameters: the event information, and the x-and- y-coordinates where the user released the mouse:

```
public boolean mouseUp(Event evt, int x, int y)
```

You can use the *x* and *y* member variables of the *evt* event object to get the x and y coordinates where the mouse button was released. These coordinates contain the same value as the parameters *x* and *y*. To see the values of these variables, use the following output statements that will print to the console:

```
System.out.println("Parameters (" + x + "," + y + ")");
System.out.println("Event arg  (" + evt.x + "," + evt.y +")");
System.out.println("<" + evt + ">\n" + Event.MOUSE_UP);
```

The output of these debug statements are as follows:

```
Parameters (529,200)

Event arg  (529,200)

<java.awt.Event[id=502,x=529,y=200,target=fishes[0,0,640x400,layout=java.awt.FlowLayout]]>

502
```

The first line of the debug output displays the values of the *x* and *y* parameters Java passed to the *mouseUp* function. The second line displays the values of the *x* and *y* member variables of the *Event* object passed as a parameter. The third line (continued on the fourth line) contains the *String* representation of the *evt* object. The fifth line has the value of the *MOUSE_UP* attribute of the *Event* class, which is 502. Notice that the *id* attribute of *evt* (in the third line) is also 502. This is because the event was the mouse-up event. The rest of the line contains information stored in the *evt* argument that you might find useful in your programming.

Knowing the x-and-y coordinates where the user released the mouse, the applet can simply loop through the fish array to determine whether or not the user released the mouse button when the mouse pointer was on top of a fish. After the applet determines which fish the user released the mouse button on, the applet moves the fish to a random location by calling the *move_fish* function and passing it the index of the fish:

```
for (int i = 0; i < TOTAL_FISHES; i++)
  {
    if (x > coordinate[i].x &&
        x < coordinate[i].x + fish_size[i].width &&
        y > coordinate[i].y &&
        y < coordinate[i].y + fish_size[i].height)
      {
        move_fish(i);
      }
  }
```

Finally, the *mouseUp* function returns *true* to tell Java that it handled this mouse event:

```
return true;
```

The *move_fish* function accepts the index of the fish to move as a parameter:

```
void move_fish(int index)
```

To start, the function stores the fish's current x-and-y coordinates so it can redraw the background image after it moves the fish:

```
int old_x = coordinate[index].x;
int old_y = coordinate[index].y;
```

Next, the function calculates the new x-and-y coordinates for the fish. To do so, the function first makes sure that the random x-and-y coordinates reside within the width and the height of the background image. Second, because the applet knows the size of each fish, the function sets the new x-and-y coordinates to the width and the height of the background minus the dimensions of the fish:

```
int new_x = (int) (Math.random() * (background.getWidth(this)
                             - fish_size[index].width));
int new_y = (int) (Math.random() * (background.getHeight(this)
                             - fish_size[index].height));
```

To determine how far to move the fish, the function subtracts the old location from the new location:

```
int dx = new_x - old_x;
int dy = new_y - old_y;
```

Next, the applet determines whether the horizontal or the vertical distance is greater, and stores that value in the *end* variable:

```
int end = Math.max(Math.abs(dx), Math.abs(dy));
```

The applet uses the *end* variable within a *for* loop, which steps through each pixel in the direction that was greater:

```
for (int i = 0; i < end; i++)
```

To determine the x-coordinate for each iteration through the loop, the function multiplies the total distance to move by the percentage that the fish has moved so far. The function calculates this percentage by dividing the loop counter with the end value. The function repeats this processing to determine the y-coordinate:

```
int x = old_x + dx * i / end;
int y = old_y + dy * i / end;
```

Before the applet draws the fish, the applet has to erase the current area by redrawing the background in that rectangle used by the fish image. Because the applet has to specify a clip rectangle, the applet creates a second copy of the graphics context:

```
Graphics g2;
g2 = g.create();

g2.clipRect(coordinate[index].x, coordinate[index].y,
fish_size[index].width,
            fish_size[index].height);
g2.drawImage(background, 0, 0, null);
```

Then, the applet saves the new x-and-y coordinates as the fish's current coordinates and redraws the fish image at its new position:

```
coordinate[index].x = x;
coordinate[index].y = y;

g.drawImage (fish_gif[index], coordinate[index].x, coordinate[index].y,
this);
```

Finally, the function repaints the whole window using the *repaint* function:

```
repaint();
```

Enhancements You Can Make to Fishes

To start, you might play a sound clip while the fish moves to its new location (ideally, a tune from the movie, *Jaws!*). The **Fishes** applet presented here moves multiple fish if the user releases the mouse in an area shared by all of them. Modify the program so that you only move the top fish.

Putting It All Together

The **Fishes** applet shows you how to capture the mouse-up event that occurs when the user releases the mouse button. In addition, by sending messages to the system console, you may have learned the power of debug-write statements in helping you locate errors within your applet, or to help you better understand your applet's processing. In Chapter 25, you will modify the **Fishes** applet to let the user move a fish to a specific location by clicking on it first and then dragging the mouse to the desired location. When you release the mouse button, the selected fish will move to the mouse-pointer location. Before you continue with Chapter 25, however, make sure you understand the following key concepts:

- ☑ Using the *mouseUp* function, your applets can capture the user's release of the mouse button.

- ☑ When Java calls the *mouseUp* function, it passes an *Event* parameter that contains information about the mouse event, such as the event id, and the x-and-y coordinates when the event occurred.

- ☑ Using the *getWidth* and *getHeight* functions, your applet can determine the size of an image.

Chapter 25

Moving the Fishes
Moving a Fish to a User-Specified Location

In Chapter 24, within the **Fishes** applet, you used the *mouseUp* function to capture the user's release of the mouse button. As you will recall, when you moved the mouse pointer on top of a fish and released the mouse button, the **Fishes** applet moved the fish away from the mouse to a random position. In the **Moving the Fishes** applet, you will use the *handleEvent* function to capture and respond to mouse events. Specifically, the applet will let the user select a fish and drag the mouse to a specific location. When the user releases the mouse button, the applet will move the selected fish to the corresponding location. This chapter continues your examination of mouse functions. By the time you finish this chapter, you will understand the following key concepts:

◆ Using the *handleEvent* function, you can respond to any events that Java sends to the applet.

◆ To determine the event, your applet simply examines the parameter Java passes to the *handleEvent* function.

Using Moving the Fishes

When you run the **Moving the Fishes** applet, you will see a window filled with a school of fish, as shown in Figure 25. To move a fish, click your mouse on the fish to select it. Next, drag your mouse to the location you desire. When you release your mouse button, the applet will move the fish to the specified location.

Figure 25 *Fishes that the user can move using the mouse.*

THE HTML FILE

Use the following HTML file to run the **Moving the Fishes** applet:

```
<applet code=fishes.class width=600 height=400> </applet>
```

LOOKING AT MOVING THE FISHES

As discussed, the **Moving the Fishes** applet lets the user click on a fish to select the fish. Next, the user can drag their mouse to the location at which they want to place the fish. When the user releases their mouse button, the applet will move the fish to the desired location. The following code implements the **Moving the Fishes** applet:

```java
//********************************************************************
// fishes.java
//********************************************************************

import java.applet.*;
import java.awt.*;

//********************************************************************

class Coordinate
   {
     public int x;
     public int y;

     public Coordinate(int x, int y)
       {
         this.x = x;
         this.y = y;
       }
   }

   //********************************************************************

public class fishes extends Applet
   {
     final int TOTAL_FISHES = 9;

     Graphics g;
     Image background;
     Image fish_gif[];

     boolean done_loading_image = false;
     boolean done_loading_all_images = false;

     Coordinate coordinate[];
     Dimension fish_size[];
     FontMetrics font_metrics;
```

```java
    int current_item = 0;

    int new_x;
    int new_y;

    int loading_fish = 0;

    //————————————————————————

    public void init()
      {
        g = getGraphics();

        Font font = new Font("TimesRoman", Font.BOLD, 15);
        g.setFont(font);

        font_metrics = g.getFontMetrics();

        background = getImage(getCodeBase(), "fishback.gif");

        int width  = size().width;
        int height = size().height;

        fish_gif = new Image[TOTAL_FISHES];
        for (int i = 0; i < TOTAL_FISHES; i++)
          fish_gif [i] = getImage (getCodeBase(), "fish" + (i+1) + ".gif");

        get_coordinates();

        repaint();

        Image offScrImage = createImage(width, height);
        Graphics offScrGC = offScrImage.getGraphics();
        offScrGC.drawImage(background, 0, 0, this);

        while (!done_loading_image)
          ;

        fish_size = new Dimension[TOTAL_FISHES];
        for (int i = 0; i < TOTAL_FISHES; i++)
          {
            loading_fish = i;
            done_loading_image = false;
            offScrGC.drawImage(fish_gif[i], 0, 0, this);
            while (!done_loading_image)
              ;
            fish_size[i] = new Dimension(fish_gif[i].getWidth(null),
                                        fish_gif[i].getHeight(null));
          }

        done_loading_all_images = true;
      }

    //————————————————————————
```

```java
void get_coordinates()
  {
    coordinate = new Coordinate[TOTAL_FISHES];

    coordinate[0] = new Coordinate(118, 102);
    coordinate[1] = new Coordinate(243,  27);
    coordinate[2] = new Coordinate(361, 103);
    coordinate[3] = new Coordinate(496, 150);
    coordinate[4] = new Coordinate(500,  28);
    coordinate[5] = new Coordinate( 49, 238);
    coordinate[6] = new Coordinate(171, 220);
    coordinate[7] = new Coordinate(305, 252);
    coordinate[8] = new Coordinate(474, 260);
  }

//————————————————————————————

public boolean handleEvent(Event evt)
  {
    switch (evt.id)
      {
        case Event.MOUSE_DOWN:
          for (int i = 0; i < TOTAL_FISHES; i++)
            {
              if (evt.x > coordinate[i].x &&
                  evt.x < coordinate[i].x + fish_size[i].width &&
                  evt.y > coordinate[i].y &&
                  evt.y < coordinate[i].y + fish_size[i].height)
                {
                  current_item = i + 1;
                  break;
                }
            }

          return true;

        case Event.MOUSE_UP:
          new_x = evt.x - fish_size[current_item-1].width/2;
          new_y = evt.y - fish_size[current_item-1].height/2;

          if (new_x < 0)
            new_x = 0;

          if (new_y < 0)
            new_y = 0;

          if (current_item != 0)
            move_fish(current_item - 1);

          current_item = 0;
          return true;
      }
```

```
        return false;
    }

    //————————————————————

    void move_fish(int index)
    {
        int old_x = coordinate[index].x;
        int old_y = coordinate[index].y;
        int dx = new_x - old_x;
        int dy = new_y - old_y;
        int end = Math.max(Math.abs(dx), Math.abs(dy));

        for (int i = 0; i < end; i++)
        {
            int x = old_x + dx * i / end;
            int y = old_y + dy * i / end;

            Graphics g2;
            g2 = g.create();

            g2.clipRect(coordinate[index].x, coordinate[index].y,
                        fish_size[index].width,
                        fish_size[index].height);
            g2.drawImage(background, 0, 0, null);

            coordinate[index].x = x;
            coordinate[index].y = y;

            g.drawImage (fish_gif[index], coordinate[index].x,
                        coordinate[index].y, this);
        }

        repaint();
    }


    //————————————————————

    public boolean imageUpdate(Image img, int infoflags, int x, int y,
                                int width, int height)
    {
        if (infoflags == ALLBITS)
        {
            done_loading_image = true;
            showStatus("");
            repaint();
            return false;
        }
        else
            return true;
    }

    //————————————————————
```

```
public void paint(Graphics g)
   {
     if (!done_loading_all_images)
        showStatus("Fishtank:  loading image " + loading_fish);

     else
        {
        g.drawImage(background, 0, 0, this);

        for (int i = 0; i < TOTAL_FISHES; i++)
           g.drawImage(fish_gif[i], coordinate[i].x, coordinate[i].y,
                    this);
        }
     }
}
```

BREAKING APART MOVING THE FISHES

This applet has many of the same features as the previous applet. Therefore, this section will discuss the code that is different between the applets. To start, the applet replaces the *mouseUp* function with the *handleEvent* function, which this section will discuss in detail. Also, the *move_fish* function contains minor changes that this section will also discuss.

As briefly mentioned, the **Moving the Fishes** applet uses the *handleEvent* function to handle all events, such as mouse operations. The function accepts one argument—the event that caused Java to call this function:

```
public boolean handleEvent(Event evt)
```

As you can see, the parameter to the *handleEvent* function is an *Event* class object. Using the object's *id* member variable, your applet can determine which event occurred. The easiest way for your applet to test the *id* member variable is to use a *switch* statement within which your applet tests for only those events it requires:

```
switch (evt.id)
```

For the **Moving the Fishes** applet, the first event the applet must process is the mouse-down event. As it turns out, the *Event* class defines several constants that correspond to common events, such as the MOUSE_DOWN constant:

```
case Event.MOUSE_DOWN:
```

When the user clicks the mouse, the applet must search the coordinates for each fish to determine which fish (if any) the user selected. When the applet finds the selected fish, it sets the *current_item* variable to a value one greater than the index. (Remember, the first index value is 0 and the applet considers a *current_item* of 0 to mean no item is selected):

```
for (int i = 0; i < TOTAL_FISHES; i++)
   {
     if (evt.x > coordinate[i].x &&
        evt.x < coordinate[i].x + fish_size[i].width &&
        evt.y > coordinate[i].y &&
        evt.y < coordinate[i].y + fish_size[i].height)
```

JAVA PROGRAMMER'S LIBRARY

```
            {
                current_item = i + 1;
                break;
            }
        }
```

At the end of the *case* statement, the applet returns the *true* value to Java to indicate that the applet has handled this event:

```
    return true;
```

Just as the MOUSE_DOWN event lets your program detect when the user has pressed the mouse button, the MOUSE_UP event lets you detect the user's release of the mouse button:

```
    case Event.MOUSE_UP:
```

When the user releases the mouse button, the applet moves the selected fish to the specified location. Actually, the applet centers the fish at the location. Therefore, the applet must calculate the top-left coordinates by subtracting half the width and height of the fish from the x and y coordinates:

```
    new_x = evt.x - fish_size[current_item-1].width/2;
    new_y = evt.y - fish_size[current_item-1].height/2;
```

Next, the applet must make sure that the new coordinate is not less than the origin (0, 0):

```
    if (new_x < 0)
      new_x = 0;

    if (new_y < 0)
      new_y = 0;
```

Assuming the user has selected a fish, the applet moves the fish by calling the *move_fish* function. As you can see, the applet subtracts the value one from the *current_item* variable to pass the *move_fish* function the actual index of the selected fish:

```
    if (current_item != 0)
      move_fish(current_item - 1);
```

Next, the applet resets the *current_item* variable to zero, since it has processed the request to move the current fish:

```
    current_item = 0;
```

Finally, the applet returns the *true* value to Java to indicate that it has processed the mouse-up event:

```
    return true;
```

For this applet, if the event is not a mouse-down or a mouse-up event, the applet returns the *false* value to Java to indicate that the applet did not process the event:

```
    return false;
```

The only difference in the *move_fish* function from the previous **Fishes** applet is that the function does not have to calculate the new coordinates, because the event handler assigns the coordinates to the *new_x* and the *new_y* variables.

ENHANCEMENTS YOU CAN MAKE TO MOVING THE FISHES

To start, modify the program so that it handles the mouse-move event. To do so, simply compare the *Event id* to the *Event.MOUSE_MOVE* constant. Also, you might include code that displays a message telling the user to select a fish, should the user drag the mouse without first selecting the fish they want to move.

PUTTING IT ALL TOGETHER

The **Moving the Fishes** applet has focused on how your applet can handle events. In Chapter 26, you will continue to expand this applet by learning how you can click on and drag a fish object. Before you continue with Chapter 26, however, make sure you understand the following key concepts:

- ☑ Within your applets, you can use the *handleEvent* function to respond to any events that Java sends to the applet.

- ☑ To determine the current event, your applet tests the *id* member variable of the *Event* object Java passes to the *handleEvent* function.

- ☑ If your applet handles the event, your applet should return the *true* value to Java. If, however, your applet does not handle the event, your applet should return the *false* value to Java.

CHAPTER 26

DRAG-AND-DROP FISH
USING THE MOUSE TO DRAG-AND-DROP ITEMS

In Chapter 25, you used the **Moving the Fishes** applet to respond to mouse events. Specifically, the applet let you click on a fish to select a fish, and then drag your mouse to the location at which you wanted the fish to move. When you released the mouse button, the applet moved the selected fish as you desired. In this applet, you will learn how to drag-and-drop an object to a new position. By the time you finish this chapter, you will understand the following key concepts:

◆ Using the *mouseDrag* function, your applet can determine when the user is dragging the mouse (moving the mouse with the mouse-select button held down).

◆ Using the *handleEvent* function, your applet can capture the mouse-drag event by testing for the *Event.MOUSE_DRAG* constant.

USING DRAG-AND-DROP FISH

When you run the **Drag-and-Drop Fish** applet, you will see a window filled with a school of fish, as shown in Figure 26. When you click your mouse on a fish and drag the mouse, the selected fish will follow the mouse pointer until you release the mouse button.

Figure 26 Fish you can move using drag-and-drop mouse operations.

The HTML File

Use the following HTML file to run the **Drag-and-Drop Fish** applet:

```
<applet code=fishes.class width=600 height=400> </applet>
```

Looking at Drag-and-Drop Fish

As discussed, the **Drag-and-Drop Fish** applet lets you select a fish by clicking on the fish with your mouse, and then lets you drag-and-drop the fish at a new location. The following code implements Drag-and Drop Fish:

```java
//*******************************************************************
// fishes.java
//*******************************************************************

import java.applet.*;
import java.awt.*;

//*******************************************************************

class Coordinate
   {
     public int x;
     public int y;

     public Coordinate(int x, int y)
        {
          this.x = x;
          this.y = y;
        }
   }

//*******************************************************************

public class fishes extends Applet
   {
     final int TOTAL_FISHES = 9;

     Graphics g;
     Image background;
     Image fish_gif[];

     boolean done_loading_image = false;
     boolean done_loading_all_images = false;

     Coordinate coordinate[];
     Dimension fish_size[];
     FontMetrics font_metrics;

     int current_fish = 0;
```

```java
    int new_x;
    int new_y;

    int loading_fish = 0;

    //——————————————————————————

    public void init()
      {
        g = getGraphics();

        Font font = new Font("TimesRoman", Font.BOLD, 15);
        g.setFont(font);

        font_metrics = g.getFontMetrics();

        background = getImage(getCodeBase(), "fishback.gif");

        int width  = size().width;
        int height = size().height;

        fish_gif = new Image[TOTAL_FISHES];
        for (int i = 0; i < TOTAL_FISHES; i++)
          fish_gif[i] = getImage(getCodeBase(), "fish" + (i+1) + ".gif");

        get_coordinates();

        repaint();

        Image offScrImage = createImage(width, height);
        Graphics offScrGC = offScrImage.getGraphics();
        offScrGC.drawImage(background, 0, 0, this);

        while (!done_loading_image)
          ;

        fish_size = new Dimension[TOTAL_FISHES];
        for (int i = 0; i < TOTAL_FISHES; i++)
          {
            loading_fish = i;
            done_loading_image = false;
            offScrGC.drawImage(fish_gif[i], 0, 0, this);
            while (!done_loading_image)
              ;
            fish_size[i] = new Dimension(fish_gif[i].getWidth(null),
                                         fish_gif[i].getHeight(null));
          }

        done_loading_all_images = true;
      }

    //——————————————————————————
```

```
void get_coordinates()
  {
    coordinate = new Coordinate[TOTAL_FISHES];

    coordinate[0] = new Coordinate(118, 102);
    coordinate[1] = new Coordinate(243,  27);
    coordinate[2] = new Coordinate(361, 103);
    coordinate[3] = new Coordinate(496, 150);
    coordinate[4] = new Coordinate(500,  28);
    coordinate[5] = new Coordinate( 49, 238);
    coordinate[6] = new Coordinate(171, 220);
    coordinate[7] = new Coordinate(305, 252);
    coordinate[8] = new Coordinate(474, 260);
  }

//————————————————————————

void draw_fishes()
  {
    for (int i = 0; i < TOTAL_FISHES; i++)
      g.drawImage(fish_gif[i],
                  coordinate[i].x,
                  coordinate[i].y,
                  this);
  }

//————————————————————————

public boolean mouseDrag(Event evt, int x, int y)
  {
    if (current_fish != 0)
      {
        new_x = x - fish_size[current_fish-1].width/2;
        new_y = y - fish_size[current_fish-1].height/2;

        if (new_x < 0)
          new_x = 0;

        if (new_y < 0)
          new_y = 0;

        move_fish(current_fish - 1);
      }

    return true;
  }

//————————————————————————

public boolean mouseUp(Event evt, int x, int y)
  {
    current_fish = 0;
    return true;
  }

//————————————————————————
```

```java
    public boolean mouseDown(Event evt, int x, int y)
      {
        for (int i = 0; i < TOTAL_FISHES; i++)
          {
          if (x > coordinate[i].x &&
              x < coordinate[i].x + fish_size[i].width &&
              y > coordinate[i].y &&
              y < coordinate[i].y + fish_size[i].height)
            {
              current_fish = i + 1;
            }
          }

        return true;
      }

//————————————————————————

void move_fish(int index)
  {
    int old_x = coordinate [index].x;
    int old_y = coordinate [index].y;
    int dx     = new_x - old_x;
    int dy     = new_y - old_y;
    int end    = Math.max(Math.abs(dx), Math.abs(dy));

    for (int i = 0; i < end; i++)
      {
        int x = old_x + dx * i / end;
        int y = old_y + dy * i / end;

        Graphics g2;
        g2 = g.create();

        g2.clipRect(coordinate [index].x, coordinate [index].y,
                    fish_size[index].width,
                    fish_size[index].height);
        g2.drawImage(background, 0, 0, null);

        coordinate[index].x = x;
        coordinate[index].y = y;

        g.drawImage(fish_gif[index], coordinate[index].x,
                    coordinate[index].y, this);
      }

    draw_fishes();
  }

//————————————————————————
```

```
      public boolean imageUpdate(Image img, int infoflags, int x, int y,
                                  int width, int height)
        {
          if (infoflags == ALLBITS)
            {
              done_loading_image = true;
              showStatus("");
              repaint();
              return false;
            }
          else
            return true;
        }


      //————————————————————————————


      public void paint(Graphics g)
        {
          if (!done_loading_all_images)
            showStatus("Fishtank:  loading image " + loading_fish);
          else
            {
              g.drawImage(background, 0, 0, this);
              draw_fishes();
            }
        }
    }
```

BREAKING APART DRAG-AND-DROP FISH

This applet has many of the same features as the **Moving the Fishes** applet you created in Chapter 25. Therefore, this section will only discuss the sections of the code that differ between the two applets.

Because the applet must redraw all the fish each time it repaints the screen and when the user drags a fish, the applet will call the *draw_fishes* function to draw all the fish at their coordinates, instead of drawing the fish in the *paint* function as was done in the previous applet:

```
void draw_fishes()
  {
    for (int i = 0; i < TOTAL_FISHES; i++)
      g.drawImage(fish_gif[i], coordinate[i].x, coordinate[i].y, this);
  }
```

To select the fish to move, the user will click on the fish. When the mouse button is clicked, the *mouseDown* function is called. In this function, you have to figure out which fish has been selected:

```
public boolean mouseDown(Event evt, int x, int y)
  {
    for (int i = 0; i < TOTAL_FISHES; i++)
      {
        if (x > coordinate[i].x &&
            x < coordinate[i].x + fish_size[i].width &&
```

```
                    y > coordinate[i].y &&
                    y < coordinate[i].y + fish_size[i].height)
              {
                    current_fish = i + 1;
              }
          }

      return true;
  }
```

After the user presses the mouse button to select the fish, the user can drag the fish. To support mouse-drag operations, the applet uses the *mouseDrag* function to capture mouse-drag events. The *mouseDrag* function, like the *mouseUp*, *mouseDown*, and *mouseMove* functions, accepts three parameters: the mouse-drag event and the current mouse x-and-y coordinates:

```
public boolean mouseDrag(Event evt, int x, int y)
```

Within the *mouseDrag* function, the applet uses the *current_fish* variable to ensure the user has selected the fish to drag:

```
if (current_fish != 0)
```

If the user is dragging a fish, the applet assumes that the mouse pointer is at the center of the fish image, and calculates the top-left corner of the image by subtracting one-half of the image width and height current coordinates. In this way, the applet can center the fish image at the location the user desires:

```
new_x = x - fish_size[current_fish-1].width/2;
new_y = y - fish_size[current_fish-1].height/2;
```

As the applet prepares to move the fish, it must ensure that the fish coordinates do not become less than the origin:

```
if (new_x < 0)
   new_x = 0;

if (new_y < 0)
   new_y = 0;
```

To move the fish, the applet calls the *move_fish* function:

```
move_fish(current_fish - 1);
```

As usual, the function must return the *true* value to Java to indicate that it has handled the event:

```
return true;
```

If you want to use the *handleEvent* function instead of having a separate function for each mouse event, use the *Event.MOUSE_DRAG* constant to check against the *id* member variable of the *Event* parameter.

When the user releases the mouse button, the applet simply resets the *current_fish* variable to zero, indicating that no fish is currently selected (the user just dropped the previously selected fish). Also, the *mouseUp* function returns the *true* value to Java to indicate that the function handled the mouse event:

```
public boolean mouseUp(Event evt, int x, int y)
   {
      current_fish = 0;
      return true;
   }
```

Within the *move_fish* function, the applet replaces the *repaint* function call with a call to the *draw_fishes* function. The reason the applet uses the *draw_fishes* function is that whenever a user moves a fish, the fish may move on top of a second fish and erase it. The other fish get erased because, when the applet erases the current fish, it redraws the background image where there may have been another fish. By calling the *draw_fishes* function each time the user moves a fish, the applet ensures the screen contents remain correct.

ENHANCEMENTS YOU CAN MAKE TO DRAG-AND-DROP FISH

When you drag and drop a fish on top of another fish, move the fish that was there to a new position. This is useful when you cannot have items which use the same space. Create an array which holds properties for the fishes; for instance, whether they can be moved or not. If they cannot be moved, then the *mouseDown* function will have to be modified so it does not set the variable holding the fish to be moved.

PUTTING IT ALL TOGETHER

The **Drag-and-Drop Fish** applet shows you how to capture mouse-drag events. As your Java applets become more complex, they should behave more like the application programs users run on their systems. Because most Windows-, UNIX, and Mac-based programs support drag-and-drop operations, so too should Java applets. In Chapter 27, you will finish your enhancements to the **Fishes** applets when you create a fish tank where the fish move by themselves without user interaction. Before you continue with Chapter 27, however, make sure you understand the following key concepts:

☑ Using the *mouseDrag* function, your applet can capture mouse-drag operations.

☑ If you prefer to capture events using the *handleEvent* function, you can capture a mouse-drag operation by testing the *Event* class *id* variable for the value *Event.MOUSE_DRAG*.

CHAPTER 27

FISH TANK
FISHES THAT MOVE RANDOMLY

The **Fish Tank** applet lets you combine several of the concepts and functions presented in the last three chapters. Specifically, the **Fish Tank** applet displays a school of fish where each fish moves independently of the other fish. In other words, the applet displays a tank of fish where the fish can move at random speeds and in random directions. Although the **Fish Tank** applet chooses to move fish objects, you can use the concepts this applet presents to move any type of objects on the screen independent of other objects. By the time you finish this chapter, you will understand the following key concepts:

- Using an array of entries that corresponds to the fish, an applet can assign each fish its own speed.

- Using a second (direction) array, the applet can keep track of the direction each fish is currently swimming.

- When a fish hits the edge of the tank, the fish should swim in the opposite direction.

USING FISH TANK

When you run the **Fish Tank** applet, you will see a window filled with a school of fish, as shown in Figure 27. The fish in the tank start at random positions and move at random speeds.

Figure 27 *Fish that move on their own accord within a Fish Tank.*

THE HTML FILE

Use the following HTML to run the **Fish Tank** applet:

```
<applet code=fishes.class width=600 height=400> </applet>
```

LOOKING AT FISH TANK

The **Fish Tank** applet presents a tank full of fish, each of which moves independently of the others. In other words, each fish moves in its own direction and at its own speed. The following code implements the **Fish Tank** applet:

```java
//**********************************************************************
// fishes.java
//**********************************************************************

import java.applet.*;
import java.awt.*;

//**********************************************************************

class Coordinate
  {
    public int x;
    public int y;

    public Coordinate(int x, int y)
      {
        this.x = x;
        this.y = y;
      }
  }

//**********************************************************************

public class fishes extends Applet implements Runnable
  {
    final int TOTAL_FISHES = 9;

    Graphics g;
    Image background;
    Image fish_gif[];
    Coordinate coordinate[];
    Dimension fish_size[];
    int speed[];

    boolean done_loading_image = false;
    boolean done_loading_all_images = false;

    Thread my_thread;

    int new_x;
    int new_y;
```

```java
    int width;
    int height;

    int loading_fish = 0;

    //—————————————————————————————————

    public void init()
      {
        g = getGraphics();

        background = getImage(getCodeBase(), "fishback.gif");

        width = size().width;
        height = size().height;

        fish_gif = new Image[TOTAL_FISHES];
        for (int i = 0; i < TOTAL_FISHES; i++)
          fish_gif[i] = getImage(getCodeBase(), "fish" + (i+1) + ".gif");

        repaint();

        Image offScrImage = createImage(width, height);
        Graphics offScrGC = offScrImage.getGraphics();
        offScrGC.drawImage(background, 0, 0, this);

        while (!done_loading_image)
          ;

        fish_size = new Dimension[TOTAL_FISHES];
        for (int i = 0; i < TOTAL_FISHES; i++)
          {
            loading_fish = i;
            done_loading_image = false;
            offScrGC.drawImage(fish_gif[i], 0, 0, this);
            while (!done_loading_image)
              ;
            fish_size[i] = new Dimension(fish_gif[i].getWidth(null),
                                         fish_gif[i].getHeight(null));
          }

        get_coordinates();

        done_loading_all_images = true;
      }

    //—————————————————————————————————

    public void start()
      {
        if (my_thread == null)
          {
            my_thread = new Thread(this);
            my_thread.start();
```

```
      }
   }

//————————————

void get_coordinates()
   {
     coordinate = new Coordinate[TOTAL_FISHES];
     for (int i = 0; i < TOTAL_FISHES; i++)
       coordinate[i] = new Coordinate
                         ((int) (Math.random() * (width -
                          fish_size[i].width)),
                          (int) (Math.random() * (height -
                          fish_size[i].height)));

     speed = new int[TOTAL_FISHES];
     for (int i = 0; i < TOTAL_FISHES; i++)
       {
         speed[i] = (int) (Math.random() * 41) - 20;
         if (speed[i] == 0)
           speed[i] = 1;
       }
   }

//————————————

public void delay ()
   {
     try
       {
         Thread.sleep(1000);
       }
     catch (InterruptedException e)
       {
       }
   }

//————————————

void draw_fishes()
   {
     for (int i = 0; i < TOTAL_FISHES; i++)
       g.drawImage(fish_gif[i], coordinate[i].x, coordinate[i].y, this);
   }

//————————————

void move_fish(int index)
   {
     Graphics g2;
     g2 = g.create();

     g2.clipRect(coordinate [index].x, coordinate [index].y,
                fish_size[index].width, fish_size[index].height);
```

```
                g2.drawImage(background, 0, 0, null);

          coordinate[index].x = new_x;
          coordinate[index].y = new_y;

          g.drawImage(fish_gif[index], coordinate[index].x,
                    coordinate[index].y, this);
      }

    //————————————————————————

    public void run()
      {
        while (true)
          {
            for (int i = 0; i < TOTAL_FISHES; i++)
              {
                new_x = coordinate[i].x + speed[i];
                new_y = coordinate[i].y;

                if (new_x < 0)
                  {
                    new_x = 0;
                    speed[i] *= -1;
                  }

                if (new_x > width-fish_size[i].width)
                  {
                    new_x = width - fish_size[i].width;
                    speed[i] *= -1;
                  }

                move_fish(i);
              }

            draw_fishes();
            delay();
          }
      }

    //————————————————————————

    public boolean imageUpdate(Image img, int infoflags, int x, int y,
                               int width, int height)
      {
        if (infoflags == ALLBITS)
          {
            done_loading_image = true;
            showStatus("");
            resize(background.getWidth(this),
                   background.getHeight(this) + 50);

            repaint();
```

```
            return false;
        }
    else
        return true;
    }

    //————————————————————————————

    public void paint(Graphics g)
    {
        if (!done_loading_all_images)
            showStatus("Fishtank:  loading image " + loading_fish);
        else
            {
                g.drawImage(background, 0, 0, this);
                draw_fishes();
                g.setColor(Color.blue);
                Font font = new Font("TimesRoman", Font.BOLD, 35);
                g.setFont(font);
                g.drawString("Joe's Aquariums and Supplies", 20, height+40);
            }
    }
}
```

BREAKING APART FISH TANK

To start, the **Fish Tank** applet uses the *Coordinate* class that you have seen in a few of the previous applets. Next, because the **Fish Tank** applet runs as a thread, you implement the *Runnable* interface:

```
public class fishes extends Applet implements Runnable
```

For the **Fish Tank** applet, the number of fish in the school is 9:

```
final int TOTAL_FISHES = 9;
```

If you examine the loops that appear throughout the applet, you will find that several of the loops are based on the TOTAL_FISHES constant. Next, the applet declares several variables to store the graphics context, the background image, images for the fishes, their coordinates, their dimensions, and their speeds:

```
Graphics g;
Image background;

Image fish_gif[];
Coordinate coordinate[];
Dimension fish_size[];
int speed[];
```

The applet does not begin its processing until the background image and each of the fish images has been loaded. The applet uses the following variables to determine when the current image is loaded and when all images are loaded:

```
boolean done_loading_image = false;
boolean done_loading_all_images = false;
```

As discussed, the applet will run as a thread. The applet does not start the thread until all of the images are loaded:

```
Thread my_thread;
```

As the applet moves a fish, the applet stores the new coordinates for the current fish in the *new_x* and *new_y* variables, which the *move_fish* function uses to move the fish:

```
int new_x;
int new_y;
```

Finally, the applet stores the width and the height of the background image, so it can tell when a fish hits the left or the right edge of the window and should change direction:

```
int width;
int height;
```

Initializing the Applet

To start, the applet must get the graphics context, load the background image as well as each of the fish images. The applet uses the *imageUpdate* function to determine if the current image has been loaded:

```
g = getGraphics();

background = getImage(getCodeBase(), "fishback.gif");

width  = size().width;
height = size().height;

fish_gif = new Image[TOTAL_FISHES];
for (int i = 0; i < TOTAL_FISHES; i++)
  fish_gif[i] = getImage(getCodeBase(), "fish" + (i+1) + ".gif");

repaint();

Image offScrImage = createImage(width, height);
Graphics offScrGC = offScrImage.getGraphics();
offScrGC.drawImage(background, 0, 0, this);
```

Next, the applet must load each fish image, and after the image is loaded, determine the image dimensions. When all fish images have been loaded, the applet assigns random starting locations for each fish:

```
while (!done_loading_image)
  ;

fish_size = new Dimension[TOTAL_FISHES];
for (int i = 0; i < TOTAL_FISHES; i++)
  {
```

```
        loading_fish = i;
        done_loading_image = false;
        offScrGC.drawImage(fish_gif[i], 0, 0, this);
        while (!done_loading_image)
          ;
        fish_size[i] = new Dimension(fish_gif[i].getWidth(null),
                                     fish_gif[i].getHeight(null));

    }

  get_coordinates();

  done_loading_all_images = true;
```

Getting the Coordinates

As discussed, the applet initially assigns random locations to each fish. To calculate the random coordinates, the applet uses the *Math* class *random* function:

```
void get_coordinates()
  {
    coordinate = new Coordinate[TOTAL_FISHES];
    for (int i = 0; i < TOTAL_FISHES; i++)
      coordinate[i] = new Coordinate
              ((int) (Math.random() * (width -fish_size[i].width)),
               (int) (Math.random() * (height-fish_size[i].height)));
```

Next, the applet calculates and assigns a random speed for each fish. The applet will let each fish move a maximum of 20 pixels left or right (per movement). To get a value in this range, the applet multiplies the random number by 41 and then subtracts the value 20 (to get a number between -20 and 20). The applet determines each fish's direction of movement based on whether its speed is positive or negative. Positive speeds make the fish move to the right (because the applet can add the speed to the x-coordinate). Likewise, negative speeds make the fish move to the left:

```
  speed = new int[TOTAL_FISHES];
  for (int i = 0; i < TOTAL_FISHES; i++)
    {
      speed[i] = (int) (Math.random() * 41) - 20;
      if (speed[i] == 0)
        speed[i] = 1;
    }
```

Drawing All the Fishes

The applet creates the *draw_fishes* function that draws all the fish. The applet uses this function because it must draw all the fishes within the *paint* function, and also within the *run* function:

```
void draw_fishes()
  {
    for (int i = 0; i < TOTAL_FISHES; i++)
      g.drawImage(fish_gif[i], coordinate[i].x, coordinate[i].y, this);
  }
```

Moving Each Fish

To move a fish, the applet calls the *move_fish* function. As you can see, the function accepts the array index that corresponds to the current fish:

```
void move_fish(int index)
```

To erase the old position of the fish, the applet creates a clip rectangle within which it redraws the background image piece that the fish previously covered:

```
Graphics g2;
g2 = g.create();

g2.clipRect(coordinate [index].x, coordinate [index].y,
          fish_size[index].width, fish_size[index].height);
g2.drawImage(background, 0, 0, null);
```

Then, the applet saves the new fish coordinates and draws the fish there:

```
coordinate[index].x = new_x;
coordinate[index].y = new_y;

g.drawImage(fish_gif[index], coordinate[index].x, coordinate[index].y,
          this);
```

Running the Thread

As you will remember, when the thread starts, its *run* function is called. As ususal, the *run* function contains an infinite loop that runs forever (or until the applet terminates). For the **Fish Tank** applet, the *run* function's loop contains the code to move the fishes, one fish at a time:

```
public void run()
  {
    while (true)
      {
        for (int i = 0; i < TOTAL_FISHES; i++)
          {
```

To determine the new coordinates for a fish, the function adds the fish's *speed* value to its previous *coordinate* values. Notice that the y-coordinate remains constant:

```
new_x = coordinate[i].x + speed[i];
new_y = coordinate[i].y;
```

If the fish hits the left edge, the applet changes the fish's speed to positive so the fish can move toward the right edge:

```
if (new_x < 0)
  {
    new_x = 0;
    speed[i] *= -1;
  }
```

Likewise, if the fish hits the right edge, the applet changes the fish's speed to negative so it can move toward the left edge:

```
if (new_x > width-fish_size[i].width)
  {
    new_x = width - fish_size[i].width;
    speed[i] *= -1;
  }
```

After the function determines the new fish coordinates and speed, it calls the *move_fish* function to actually move the fish:

```
move_fish(i);
```

After the applet has moved all the fish, the applet redraws each fish, just in case one or more fish got erased as other fish moved past. After redrawing the fish, the applet delays for one second:

```
draw_fishes();
delay();
```

Enhancements You Can Make to Fish Tank

As briefly discussed, the current **Fish Tank** applet does not let the fish move up and down. To start, change the applet so the fish move vertically as well as horizontally. The fish's direction of vertical movement should not change only when the fish reach the top or bottom; rather, the direction should change constantly. Next, this applet does not flip the fish when they turn around to swim the other way. Create two images for each fish, one where the fish is facing the right, and another where the fish is facing the left. Keep track of which direction the fish are moving and draw the appropriate image. When the fish hit the edge, draw the flip image.

Putting It All Together

The **Fish Tank** applet shows you how to manage multiple independent objects on your screen. As you saw, the **Fish Tank** applet lets fish move in random directions and in random speeds. To track different attributes, the applet simply allocates an array within which it can store the corresponding settings. In Chapter 28, you will create an image magnifier that lets you zoom in on an image. Before you continue with Chapter 28, however, make sure you understand the following key concepts:

- ☑ To track different characteristics for multiple screen objects, such as each object's direction or speed, you should create an array for each characteristic, within which you store the settings for each object.

- ☑ To provide realistic animations, each screen object should be independent.

CHAPTER 28

MAGNIFY
SCALING A PORTION OF THE IMAGE

In this chapter, you will examine the **Magnify** applet that lets you use the mouse pointer as a magnifying glass to zoom in on the background image. Using the **Magnify** applet, a car dealership might let you zoom in on different parts of the car, such as its chrome rims or high-tech dashboard. Likewise, students who are viewing a frog dissection across the Web could zoom in on different parts of the frog. As you examine the **Magnify** applet, you may find yourself quite impressed by what a powerful Java applet you can create using a small amount of code. By the time you finish this chapter, you will understand the following key concepts:

- To magnify the background image, your applet creates a small window, which the user can move with their mouse.

- To respond to mouse operations, the **Magnify** applet uses the *mouseMove* function.

- To magnify the image within the small window, the applet defines a clip rectangle and draws the image larger within the rectangle.

USING MAGNIFY

When you run the **Magnify** applet, you will see a window that contains an image of a baseball game at Yankee Stadium. As shown in Figure 28.1 and Figure 28.2, when you move the mouse, the applet will display a small window within which it will magnify part of the image.

Figure 28.1 Magnifying a baseball game in Yankee Stadium.

Figure 28.2 *As you move the mouse, the applet moves the magnification window.*

The HTML File

Use the following HTML file to run the **Magnify** applet:

```
<applet code=magnify.class width=640 height=400> </applet>
```

Looking at Magnify

The **Magnify** applet lets you magnify (or zoom in on) a square portion of an image. The window's magnification level is two, which means that the applet doubles the image within the magnify window. Since the size of the magnify window is 100x100 pixels, the portion inside it that you will magnify must be 50x50 pixels. To center the magnify portion so that the applet always magnifies the 50x50 portion that is in the middle of the 100x100 window, the applet uses the x-and-y coordinates (25, 25) relative to the top-left of the magnify window. In this way, the image is between (25, 25) and (75, 75) inside the 100x100 window.

If the applet were to draw the background image so that the top-left of the image is at the origin, the applet could not magnify the top 25 pixel lines and the left 25 pixel lines of the image. The **Magnify** applet, therefore, always positions the image so that the top-left corner is at the (50, 50) mark of the applet window, one-half of the box width and height. The following code implements the **Magnify** applet:

```
//******************************************************************
// magnify.java
//******************************************************************

import java.applet.*;
import java.awt.*;

//******************************************************************
```

```java
public class magnify extends Applet
  {
    Graphics g;

    Image background;
    int width;
    int height;
    boolean done_loading_image = false;

    int box_x = 0;
    int box_y = 0;
    int box_width = 100;
    int box_height = 100;

    //————————————————————

    public void init()
      {
        g = getGraphics();

        background = getImage(getCodeBase(), "yankee.gif");

        Image offscreen_image = createImage(640, 400);
        Graphics offscreen_GC = offscreen_image.getGraphics();
        offscreen_GC.drawImage(background, 0, 0, this);
      }

    //————————————————————

    public boolean mouseMove(Event evt, int x, int y)
      {
        erase_box();

        box_x = x;
        box_y = y;

        if (box_x > width)
          box_x = width;

        if (box_y > height)
          box_y = height;

        draw_box();

        return true;
      }

    //————————————————————

    void draw_box()
      {
        Graphics g2;
        g2 = g.create();
```

```java
      g2.clipRect(box_x, box_y, box_width, box_height);

      g2.drawImage(background, -box_x+box_width/2, -box_y+box_height/2,
                  width*2, height*2, null);

      g.setColor(Color.red);
      g.drawRect(box_x, box_y, box_width-1, box_height-1);
  }

//————————————————————

void erase_box()
  {
    Graphics g2;
    g2 = g.create();

    g2.clipRect(box_x, box_y, box_width, box_height);

    g2.drawImage(background, box_width/2, box_height/2, null);

    if (box_x < box_width/2)
      {
        g.setColor(Color.lightGray);
        g.fillRect(0, 0, box_width/2, height+box_height);
      }

    if (box_y < box_height/2)
      {
        g.setColor(Color.lightGray);
        g.fillRect(0, 0, width+box_width, box_height/2);
      }

    if (box_x > (width-box_width/2))
      {
        g.setColor(Color.lightGray);
        g.fillRect(width+box_width/2, 0, box_width/2,
                  height+box_height);
      }

    if (box_y > (height-box_height))
      {
        g.setColor(Color.lightGray);
        g.fillRect(0, height+box_height/2, width+box_width,
                  box_height/2);
      }
  }

//————————————————————

public boolean imageUpdate(Image img, int infoflags, int x, int y,
                          int w, int h)
  {
    if (infoflags == ALLBITS)
```

237

```
                {
                  width = background.getWidth(this);
                  height = background.getHeight(this);

                  resize(width+box_width, height+box_height);

                  done_loading_image = true;
                  repaint();

                  return false;
                }
              else
                return true;
          }

          //─────────────────────────────────

          public void paint(Graphics _g)
            {
              if (!done_loading_image)
                showStatus("Magnify:  loading image");

              else
                {
                showStatus("Magnify:  done");
                g.drawImage(background, box_width/2, box_height/2, this);
                draw_box();
                }
            }
        }
```

BREAKING APART MAGNIFY

To start, the applet declares variables to store the graphics context, the background image, and the image width and height, as well as a flag that tells the applet when the image has been loaded:

```
Graphics g;
Image background;
int width;
int height;
boolean done_loading_image = false;
```

Next, the applet declares variables which define the x-and-y coordinates of the magnify box, as well as the box size in pixels (100x100):

```
int box_x = 0;
int box_y = 0;
int box_width = 100;
int box_height = 100;
```

Initializing the Applet

Within its initialization function, *init*, the **Magnify** applet gets the applet's graphics context and the background image, and loads the image off screen since it is not loaded when the applet calls *getImage*:

```
public void init()
  {
     g = getGraphics();

     background = getImage(getCodeBase(), "yankee.gif");

     Image offscreen_image = createImage(640, 400);
     Graphics offscreen_GC = offscreen_image.getGraphics();
     offscreen_GC.drawImage(background, 0, 0, this);
  }
```

Handling Mouse Movements

As the user moves the mouse, the **Magnify** applet moves the magnify box. To zoom in on a specific part of the image, you simply aim the mouse at the content you want to magnify. Within the *mouseMove* function, the x-and-y coordinates the function receives are at the top-left corner of the magnify window:

```
public boolean mouseMove(Event evt, int x, int y)
```

Before the applet can move the magnify box and display a new image, the applet must erase the previous magnify box. To erase the box, the applet calls the *erase_box* function:

```
erase_box();
```

Next, the function stores the new x-and-y coordinates so it can use them the next time to erase the box that the applet will draw next:

```
box_x = x;
box_y = y;
```

If you examine Figure 28.1, you may note that the band that surrounds the image is half the size of the magnify box's width and height. Therefore, when the magnify box is at the bottom-right edge of the image, its coordinates will be the width and height of the image. To prevent the box from going past these coordinates, the function compares the box location to the window's width and height:

```
if (box_x > width)
  box_x = width;

if (box_y > height)
  box_y = height;
```

Using the x-and-y coordinates of the top-left corner of the box, the function calls the *draw_box* function to draw the magnify box and to magnify its contents:

```
draw_box();
```

239

Lastly, the function returns the *true* value to Java to indicate that the function has handled the mouse event:

```
return true;
```

Drawing the Magnify Box

To magnify the image, the applet creates a clip rectangle. Rather than chancing that the clip rectangle causes problems to the graphics context, the applet creates a copy of the graphics context. Next, the applet applies the clip rectangle to the graphics-context copy. As you can see, the clip rectangle corresponds to the x-and-y coordinates of the magnify box, as well as to the box's width and height:

```
void draw_box()
   {
      Graphics g2;
      g2 = g.create();

      g2.clipRect(box_x, box_y, box_width, box_height);
```

Here comes the tricky part. To double the 50x50 box centered inside the magnify box, the applet can give the *drawImage* function the negative x-and-y coordinate as the image origin. The coordinates that the applet wants to use are such that if you were to double the image starting at those coordinates, you would double the 50x50 box inside the magnify box.

If the image was drawn at the origin and you negated the magnify box's x-and-y coordinates, you would double the portion of the image which starts at the top-left corner of the magnify box. Since the image is actually offset by half the width and height of the magnify box, you should add that amount to the x-and-y coordinates of the location at which you want to draw the double image:

```
g2.drawImage(background, -box_x + box_width/2, -box_y + box_height/2,
             width * 2, height * 2, null);
```

Finally, you can draw a red box around the magnify portion so it is easy to find:

```
g.setColor(Color.red);
g.drawRect(box_x, box_y, box_width-1, box_height-1);
```

Erasing the Old Magnify Box

To erase the old magnify box, you can create a clip rectangle and redraw the background in its normal size:

```
void erase_box()
   {
      Graphics g2;
      g2 = g.create();

      g2.clipRect(box_x, box_y, box_width, box_height);

      g2.drawImage(background, box_width/2, box_height/2, null);
```

However, since the background is offset slightly from the origin, this code will not erase the light-gray band that surrounds the image. Therefore, the applet must check where the magnify box was, and then redraw the band that is in the light gray color. Remember that the bands are slightly larger than the width and the height of the image. For instance, the height of the top band is half of the magnify box, and the width is the width of the image plus half the magnify box on both sides, which makes it a whole width of the magnify box:

```
if (box_x < box_width/2)
  {
     g.setColor(Color.lightGray);
     g.fillRect(0, 0, box_width/2, height+box_height);
  }

if (box_y < box_height/2)
  {
     g.setColor(Color.lightGray);
     g.fillRect(0, 0, width+box_width, box_height/2);
  }

if (box_x > (width-box_width/2))
  {
     g.setColor(Color.lightGray);
     g.fillRect(width+box_width/2, 0, box_width/2, height+box_height);
  }

if (box_y > (height-box_height))
  {
     g.setColor(Color.lightGray);
     g.fillRect(0, height+box_height/2, width+box_width, box_height/2);
  }
```

Updating the Image

The *imageUpdate* function is basically the same as the one you have seen in previous applets. The only difference is that you have to resize the window to add room for the bands around the image:

```
public boolean imageUpdate(Image img, int infoflags, int x, int y, int w,
int h)
  {
     if (infoflags == ALLBITS)
       {
          width = background.getWidth(this);
          height = background.getHeight(this);
          resize(width+box_width, height+box_height);

          done_loading_image = true;
          repaint();

          return false;
       }
     else
       return true;
  }
```

The paint Function

The *paint* function waits until the image has been loaded off screen, draws the image so that it is offset half the size of the magnify box, and then draws the magnify box:

```
public void paint(Graphics _g)
  {
    if (!done_loading_image)
      showStatus("Magnify:  loading image");
    else
      {
        showStatus("Magnify:  done");
        g.drawImage(background, box_width/2, box_height/2, this);
        draw_box();
      }
  }
```

ENHANCEMENTS YOU CAN MAKE TO MAGNIFY

To start, change the program so that the magnify box never contains the bands. You will have to change the offset that you used for the top-left of the background image, and the coordinates passed to *drawImage* in the *draw_box* function. Also, change the program so that it triples the magnification.

PUTTING IT ALL TOGETHER

The **Magnify** applet shows you how to magnify (or zoom in on) a small piece of an image. Using the **Magnify** applet, for example, users who have trouble reading their screen contents can zoom in on text. In Chapter 29, you will look at ways to eliminate some of the screen flicker that occurs as you move the magnify box across the screen. Before you continue with Chapter 29, however, make sure you understand the following key concepts:

☑ To move the magnify box as the user moves their mouse, the applet must capture the *mouseMove* function.

☑ To control graphics operations, the **Magnify** applet makes extensive use of clip rectangles.

☑ To magnify the contents of the magnify box, the applet simply defines a clip rectangle whose size corresponds to the box, and within which the applet displays the larger image.

CHAPTER 29

IMPROVED MAGNIFY
TAKING OUT SOME OF THE FLICKER

In Chapter 28, you created the **Magnify** applet, which lets you zoom in on or magnify an image. Unfortunately, every time you moved the magnify window, the applet first redrew the background image to erase the previous magnify box, and then redrew the window to display the new magnify box. The net result of the image-redraw operations was screen flickering. In this chapter, you will use the **Improved Magnify** applet to eliminate some of this flicker. By the time you finish this chapter, you will understand the following key concepts:

- ◆ Rather than redrawing the entire background image, the applet can determine the parts of the background image that need to be restored.

- ◆ To prevent the magnify box from magnifying the band that surrounds the image, the applet simply needs to move the box offset.

USING IMPROVED MAGNIFY

When you run the **Improved Magnify** applet, you will see a window that contains an image of a baseball game at Yankee Stadium, and the magnify box, as shown in Figure 29.1. Again, as you move the mouse, the magnify box will follow, magnifying the image's contents.

Figure 29.1 An image of a baseball game within the magnify window.

THE HTML FILE

Use the following HTML file to run the **Improved Magnify** applet:

```
<applet code=magnify.class width=640 height=400> </applet>
```

LOOKING AT IMPROVED MAGNIFY

The **Improved Magnify** applet lets you magnify a square portion of an image. By reducing the number of image redraw operations, the applet reduces screen flicker. In Chapter 28, the **Magnify** applet displayed a band around the image. This band, however, was a little large because it appeared in the magnify window. The **Improved Magnify** applet will show you how to reduce the band so that when the magnify box is at the edge of the image, the box magnifies the image edge. As you will learn, the applet reduces the band to one-fourth of the magnify-box width on the left and right side, and one-fourth of the magnify-box height on the top and bottom. The following code implements the **Improved Magnify** applet:

```java
//***************************************************************
// magnify.java
//***************************************************************

import java.applet.*;
import java.awt.*;


//***************************************************************

public class magnify extends Applet
  {
    Graphics g;

    Image offscreen_image;
    Image background;
    int width;
    int height;
    boolean done_loading_image = false;

    int box_x = 0;
    int box_y = 0;
    int box_width = 100;
    int box_height = 100;

    //————————————————————

    public void init()
      {
        g = getGraphics();

        background = getImage(getCodeBase(), "yankee.gif");

        offscreen_image = createImage(640, 400);
        Graphics offscreen_GC = offscreen_image.getGraphics();
        offscreen_GC.drawImage(background, 0, 0, this);

    //————————————————————
```

```
    public boolean mouseMove(Event evt, int x, int y)
      {
        erase_box(box_x, box_y, x, y);

        box_x = x;
        box_y = y;

        if (box_x > (width - box_width/2))
          box_x = width - box_width/2;

        if (box_y > (height - box_height/2))
          box_y = height - box_width/2;

        draw_box();

        return true;
      }

    //————————————————————————

    void draw_box()
      {
        Graphics g2;
        g2 = g.create();

        g2.clipRect(box_x, box_y, box_width, box_height);

        g2.drawImage(background, -box_x, -box_y, width*2, height*2, null);

        g.setColor(Color.red);
        g.drawRect(box_x, box_y, box_width-1, box_height-1);
      }

    //————————————————————————

    void erase_box(int old_x, int old_y, int new_x, int new_y)
      {
        Graphics g2;
        g2 = g.create();

        if (new_x <= old_x && new_y <= old_y)
          {
            g2.clipRect(new_x, new_y+box_height,
                        box_width+old_x-new_x, old_y-new_y);
            g2.drawImage(offscreen_image, 0, 0, null);
            g2 = g.create();
            g2.clipRect(new_x+box_width, new_y,
                        old_x-new_x, box_height+old_y-new_y);
            g2.drawImage(offscreen_image, 0, 0, null);
          }
        else if (new_x > old_x && new_y <= old_y)
          {
            g2.clipRect(old_x, new_y+box_height,
                        box_width+new_x-old_x, old_y-new_y);
```

```
                    g2.drawImage(offscreen_image, 0, 0, null);
                    g2 = g.create();
                    g2.clipRect(old_x, new_y,
                              new_x-old_x, box_height+old_y-new_y);
                    g2.drawImage(offscreen_image, 0, 0, null);
                }
            else if (new_x > old_x && new_y > old_y)
              {
                g2.clipRect(old_x, old_y,
                          box_width+new_x-old_x, new_y-old_y);
                g2.drawImage(offscreen_image, 0, 0, null);
                g2 = g.create();
                g2.clipRect(old_x, old_y,
                          new_x-old_x, box_height+new_y-old_y);
                g2.drawImage(offscreen_image, 0, 0, null);
              }
            else // if (new_x <= old_x && new_y > old_y)
              {
                g2.clipRect(new_x, old_y,
                          box_width+old_x-new_x, new_y-old_y);
                g2.drawImage(offscreen_image, 0, 0, null);
                g2 = g.create();
                g2.clipRect(new_x+box_width, old_y,
                          old_x-new_x, box_height+new_y-old_y);
                g2.drawImage(offscreen_image, 0, 0, null);
              }
      }

   //—————————————————————————————


   public boolean imageUpdate(Image img, int infoflags, int x, int y,
                              int w, int h)
     {
       if (infoflags == ALLBITS)
         {
           width = background.getWidth(this);
           height = background.getHeight(this);

           resize(width+box_width/2, height+box_height/2);

           offscreen_image = createImage(width  + box_width /2,
                                         height + box_height/2);

           Graphics offscreen_GC = offscreen_image.getGraphics();
           offscreen_GC.setColor(Color.lightGray);
           offscreen_GC.fillRect(0, 0, width  + box_width /2,
                            height + box_height/2);
           offscreen_GC.drawImage (background, box_width/4, box_height/4,
                                   this);

           done_loading_image = true;
           repaint();

           return false;
         }
```

```
        else
          return true;
    }


    //————————————————————————

    public void paint(Graphics _g)
      {
        if (!done_loading_image)
          showStatus("Magnify:  loading image");

        else
          {
            showStatus("Magnify:  done");
            g.drawImage(background, box_width/4, box_height/4, this);
            draw_box();
          }
      }
  }
```

BREAKING APART IMPROVED MAGNIFY

Much of the **Improved Magnify** applet is similar to code you examined for the **Magnify** applet in Chapter 28. Therefore, this section only examines the code that differs between the two applets.

Within the class variable declarations, the **Improved Magnify** applet declares an off-screen image that will contain the image with the band around it. The applet will use this image for restoring the background image when the magnify window moves:

```
    Image offscreen_image;
```

Moving the Mouse

When calling the *erase_box* function, the applet must pass it the x-and-y coordinates of the current magnify box, and the new x-and-y coordinates for the new magnify window:

```
    erase_box(box_x, box_y, x, y);
```

As discussed, the band around the image is now one-fourth the size of the magnify box width and height. So, when that magnify box is at the bottom-right corner of the image, its coordinates will be the width and height of the image minus one-half the box's width and height. As you can see, the *erase_box* function includes the following code to make sure the applet does not go past those coordinates:

```
    if (box_x > (width - box_width/2))
        box_x = width - box_width/2;

    if (box_y > (height - box_height/2))
        box_y = height - box_width/2;
```

Drawing the Magnify Box

Because the applet placed the top-left corner of the image at one-fourth of the magnify box, the magnify box will contain the top-left corner of the image when it is at the origin. This means that to double the image, you do not have to add anything to the negative of the box's x-and-y coordinates:

```
g2.drawImage(background, -box_x, -box_y, width*2, height*2, null);
```

Erasing the Old Magnify Box

To erase the old magnify box, the applet has to replace the portions of the image that become visible when the magnify window moves. The magnify window will move up and left, or up and right, or down and right, or down and left. For each of these cases, there is a different portion of the image that the applet must replace. To start, the applet must copy the graphics context:

```
void erase_box(int old_x, int old_y, int new_x, int new_y)
  {
     Graphics g2;
     g2 = g.create();
```

If the user moves the magnify box up and left, as shown in Figure 29.2, the applet must restore the background image below and to the right of the new position of the magnify box. To redraw the image, the applet first defines the clip rectangle for the area beneath the magnify box. Next, the applet can draw an off-screen image within that rectangle. Then, before it defines a new clip rectangle for the area to the right side of the magnify box, the applet creates another copy of the graphics context. After defining the second clip rectangle, the applet again draws the image within that rectangle.

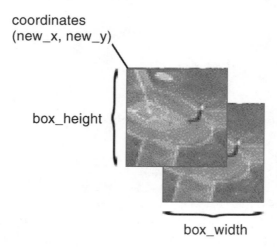

coordinates
(new_x, new_y)

box_height

box_width

Figure 29.2 The old magnify window with a new magnify window to the left and above.

The applet calculates the clip rectangle for the area beneath the magnify box by taking *new_x* as the x-coordinate, and taking *new_y* and adding *box_height* to it to get the y-coordinate. The width is the *box_width* plus the distance between the *old_x* and the *new_x*. The height is the distance between the *old_y* and the *new_y*.

To calculate the clip rectangle for the right side, the applet takes the *new_x* and adds to it the *box_width* to get the x-coordinate, and the *new_y* as the y-coordinate. The width is the distance between the *old_x* and the *new_x*. The height is the *box_height* plus the distance between the *old_y* and the *new_y*:

```
    if (new_x <= old_x && new_y <= old_y)
      {
        g2.clipRect(new_x, new_y+box_height, box_width+old_x-new_x,
                  old_y-new_y);
        g2.drawImage(offscreen_image, 0, 0, null);
        g2 = g.create();
        g2.clipRect(new_x+box_width, new_y, old_x-new_x,
                  box_height+old_y-new_y);
        g2.drawImage(offscreen_image, 0, 0, null);
      }
```

Then, the applet checks whether the magnify box was moved to the right and above the old position. The calculations of the clip rectangles are similar to the procedure described above:

```
    else if (new_x > old_x && new_y <= old_y)
      {
        g2.clipRect(old_x, new_y+box_height,
        box_width+new_x-old_x, old_y-new_y);
        g2.drawImage(offscreen_image, 0, 0, null);
        g2 = g.create();
        g2.clipRect(old_x, new_y, new_x-old_x, box_height+old_y-new_y);
        g2.drawImage(offscreen_image, 0, 0, null);
      }
```

Next, the applet checks whether the magnify window was moved to the right and below the old position. The calculations of the clip rectangles are similar to the procedure described above:

```
    else if (new_x > old_x && new_y > old_y)
      {
        g2.clipRect(old_x, old_y, box_width+new_x-old_x, new_y-old_y);
        g2.drawImage(offscreen_image, 0, 0, null);
        g2 = g.create();
        g2.clipRect(old_x, old_y, new_x-old_x, box_height+new_y-old_y);
        g2.drawImage(offscreen_image, 0, 0, null);
      }
```

Finally, the applet checks whether the magnify window was moved to the left and below the old position. The calculations of the clip rectangles are similar to the procedure described above:

```
    else // if (new_x <= old_x && new_y > old_y)
      {
        g2.clipRect(new_x, old_y, box_width+old_x-new_x, new_y-old_y);
        g2.drawImage(offscreen_image, 0, 0, null);
        g2 = g.create();
        g2.clipRect(new_x+box_width, old_y, old_x-new_x,
                  box_height+new_y-old_y);
        g2.drawImage(offscreen_image, 0, 0, null);
      }
```

Updating the Image

After all the bits of the image have been loaded, the applet resizes the window to add a band that is one-fourth of the magnify box's width and height on each side, which adds a total of one-half the width horizontally, and one-half the height vertically:

249

```
resize(width+box_width/2, height+box_height/2);
```

Then, the applet creates an off-screen image it uses to repaint the image when the magnify window moves. This image will also contain the band around the image, so it will be a duplicate of what is on the screen, minus the magnify window:

```
offscreen_image = createImage(width  + box_width /2,
                              height + box_height/2);

Graphics offscreen_GC = offscreen_image.getGraphics();
offscreen_GC.setColor(Color.lightGray);
offscreen_GC.fillRect(0, 0, width + box_width /2, height + box_height/2);
offscreen_GC.drawImage (background, box_width/4, box_height/4, this);
```

The paint Function

The only difference within the *paint* function is that the image is drawn at an offset of one-fourth the size of the magnify window from the origin:

```
public void paint(Graphics _g)
  {
    if (!done_loading_image)
      showStatus("Magnify:  loading image");
    else
      {
        showStatus("Magnify:  done");
        g.drawImage(background, box_width/4, box_height/4, this);
        draw_box();
      }
  }
```

ENHANCEMENTS YOU CAN MAKE TO IMPROVED MAGNIFY

To start, try to further eliminate some of the flicker still left in the program (such as when you place the magnify window around the band). Also, change the magnify window so it is not a square; for instance, make the width wider than the height.

PUTTING IT ALL TOGETHER

The **Improved Magnify** applet shows you how to remove some of the screen flicker when you move objects across the screen. As you create other animations, you will constantly seek ways to eliminate screen flicker. For such applets, remember the steps you performed within this applet. In Chapter 30, you will create a **Digital Clock** applet. Before you continue with Chapter 30, however, make sure you understand the following key concepts:

☑ As opposed to redrawing the entire background image, as an applet updates other screen objects, the applet can determine which part of the image it needs to redraw.

☑ By working with off-screen images, your applets can reduce screen flicker.

Chapter 30

Digital Clock
Drawing a Running Clock on the Screen

The next several chapters will show you ways you can use the Java *Graphics* class to create clock applications. To start, the **Digital Clock** applet will show you how to create a digital clock that runs continuously. To obtain the current time, the applet uses the Java *Date* class. In addition to looking at the *Graphics* and *Date* classes, this applet introduces you to the *stop* function, which Java calls automatically when your applet ends, and the *update* function, which your applet can use to control screen updates. By the time you finish this chapter, you will understand the following key concepts:

- To get the current date-and-time, your applets should use the *Date* object.

- When your applet calls the *repaint* function, Java will automatically call the *update* function (if it exists) instead of the *paint* function.

- When an applet is closed, Java automatically calls the *stop* function, if the function exists.

Using Digital Clock

When you run the **Digital Clock** applet, you will see a window with a digital clock that updates every second, as shown in Figure 30.

Figure 30 A digital clock that updates every second.

The HTML File

Use the following HTML file to run the **Digital Clock** applet:

```
<applet code=clock.class width=100 height=13> </applet>
```

LOOKING AT DIGITAL CLOCK

As discussed, the **Digital Clock** applet displays a digital clock within a window that updates the time it displays every second. The following code implements the **Digital Clock** applet:

```
//****************************************************************
// clock.java
//****************************************************************

import java.applet.*;
import java.awt.*;
import java.util.Date;


//****************************************************************

public class clock extends Applet implements Runnable
  {
     Graphics g;
     Font font;
     FontMetrics font_metrics;
     Thread my_thread;

     int width;
     int height;
     Date current_time;

     //────────────────────────────────────

     public void init()
       {
          g = getGraphics();

          current_time = new Date();

          set_defaults();
       }

     //────────────────────────────────────

     void set_defaults()
       {
          width  = size().width;
          height = size().height;

          if (width > height*6)
            width = height*6;
          else
            height = width/6;

          font = new Font("TimesRoman", Font.BOLD, height*3/2);
          g.setFont(font);
          font_metrics = g.getFontMetrics();
       }

     //────────────────────────────────────
```

```
   public void start()
     {
       if (my_thread == null)
         {
           my_thread = new Thread(this);
           my_thread.start();
         }
     }

//─────────────────────────────

   public void stop()
     {
       my_thread.stop();
       my_thread = null;
     }

//─────────────────────────────

   public void run()
     {
       while (my_thread != null)
         {
           repaint();

           try
             {
               Thread.sleep(1000);
             }
           catch (InterruptedException e)
             {
             }
         }
     }

//─────────────────────────────

   public void update(Graphics g)
     {
       g.setColor(Color.lightGray);
       g.fillRect(0, 0, width, height);

       current_time = new Date();

       int hours   = current_time.getHours();
       int minutes = current_time.getMinutes();
       int seconds = current_time.getSeconds();

       String time;

       if (hours < 10)
         time = "0" + hours;
       else
         time = "" + hours;
```

```
          if (minutes < 10)
            time += ":0" + minutes;
          else
            time += ":" + minutes;

          if (seconds < 10)
            time += ":0" + seconds;
          else
            time += ":" + seconds;

          g.setColor(Color.black);

          g.setFont(f);
          g.drawString(time, 0, height);
        }

    //———————————————————————————

    public void paint(Graphics g)
      {
        set_defaults();
        update(g);
      }
  }
```

BREAKING APART DIGITAL CLOCK

As you can see, the **Digital Clock** applet imports three packages. First, it imports the *applet* package because it is an applet. Next, it uses the *awt* package to access the *Graphics* class. Lastly, **Digital Clock** uses the *util.Date* package to access the *Date* class:

```
import java.applet.*;
import java.awt.*;
import java.util.Date;
```

Next, the applet declares variables to store the graphics context, the font and font metrics it uses to display the clock, the thread that continuously runs to update the clock, the width and height of the applet window, and a variable to hold the *Date* object, which contains the current time:

```
Graphics g;
Font font;
FontMetrics font_metrics;
Thread my_thread;

int width;
int height;
Date current_time;
```

Initializing the Applet

Within the *init* function, the applet simply stores its graphics context, creates the *Date* object that will store the current date-and-time, and then calls the *set_default* function, which performs more assignments, as discussed next:

```
public void init()
   {
      g = getGraphics();

      current_time = new Date();

      set_defaults();
   }
```

Setting the Default Variables

As just discussed, the *init* function calls *set_defaults* to determine the window size, font, and font metrics. The function calculates the width and height of the clock by using the ratio 6:1 for the width to the height. The function approximates this ratio based on the Times-Roman font:

```
void set_defaults()
   {
      width  = size().width;
      height = size().height;

      if (width > height*6)
        width = height*6;
      else
      height = width/6;

      font = new Font("TimesRoman", Font.BOLD, height*3/2);
      g.setFont(font);
      font_metrics = g.getFontMetrics();
   }
```

Stopping the Thread

As you know, Java calls the *start* function when your applet begins. In a similar way, Java calls the *stop* function as your applet ends. Within the *stop* function, you might, for example, stop any threads the applet has running. You have not seen the *stop* function in previous applets. For example, the *stop* function within the **Digital Clock** applet stops the thread that updates the clock:

```
public void stop()
   {
     my_thread.stop();
     my_thread = null;
   }
```

By stopping threads within the *stop* function, your applets will shut down in a smoother process. In other words, if you have one thread that is playing music and a second that is spinning an object, you can stop both threads using the *stop* function.

Running the Thread

The **Digital Clock** applet uses one thread that continuously updates the clock. As you can see, within the *run* function, the applet enters a loop so that it repeatedly calls the *repaint* function (which calls the *update* function to display the clock) and then delays one second (hence the clock's one-second updates):

```
public void run()
  {
    while (my_thread != null)
      {
        repaint();

        try
          {
            Thread.sleep(1000);
          }
        catch (InterruptedException e)
          {
          }
      }
  }
```

Updating the Applet

As it turns out, if your applet defines an *update* function, Java will call the function each time the applet calls *repaint*. If the *update* function does not exist, Java calls the *paint* function instead. The *update* function, like the *paint* function, gets the graphics context as the parameter:

```
public void update(Graphics g)
```

To start, the function first clears the old time from the screen:

```
g.setColor(Color.lightGray);
g.fillRect(0, 0, width, height);
```

Next, the function creates a *Date* object, which it uses to store the current time. When you create the object by calling the constructor with no arguments, the constructor initializes the object to the current date and time:

```
current_time = new Date();
```

The function then uses the *Date* class functions to get the current time:

```
int hours   = current_time.getHours();
int minutes = current_time.getMinutes();
int seconds = current_time.getSeconds();
```

To display the current time, the function creates a *String* object, whose characters correspond to the current hours, minutes, and seconds, which are separated by colons, as shown here:

```
String time;

if (hours < 10)
  time = "0" + hours;
else
  time = "" + hours;

if (minutes < 10)
```

```
    time += ":0" + minutes;
  else
    time += ":" + minutes;

  if (seconds < 10)
    time += ":0" + seconds;
  else
    time += ":" + seconds;
```

Lastly, the function sets the foreground color to black, sets the current font, and then draws the time string at the top-left corner of the window. Remember that you must specify the baseline coordinates when drawing a string. So, you can use zero for the x-coordinate, but you have to use the height of the font for the y-coordinate:

```
  g.setColor(Color.black);

  g.setFont(font);
  g.drawString(time, 0, height);
```

The paint Function

The *paint* function simply gets the default settings and then updates the screen. Only Java calls the *paint* function, and only when the whole screen needs to be repainted (for instance, when the window is resized). Otherwise, the *update* function oversees the window updates:

```
public void paint(Graphics g)
  {
     set_defaults();
     update(g);
  }
```

Enhancements You Can Make To Digital Clock

The 6:1 ratio the applet uses for the font is not exact. So, erasing the time may leave one scan-line at the bottom. So, modify the *update* function to properly erase the previous time. Next, change the font to see how that affects the applet's width and height ratios.

Putting It All Together

The **Digital Clock** applet shows you how to create a digital clock that continuously updates on the screen. In addition, the applet introduced you to the *update* and *stop* functions. In Chapter 31, you will create an analog (round clock with a big and little hand). Before you continue with Chapter 31, however, make sure you understand the following key concepts:

- ☑ To determine the current date-and-time, your applets can use a *Date* object.

- ☑ If your applet defines an *update* function, the *repaint* will use *update* instead of the *paint* function. Java, however, will call the *paint* function whenever your entire screen needs to be updated.

- ☑ When an applet is closed, Java automatically calls the *stop* function, if the applet has defined one.

CHAPTER 31

ROUND CLOCK
DRAWING A RUNNING ROUND CLOCK ON THE SCREEN

In Chapter 30, using the **Digital Clock** applet, you learned how to use the *Date* class to get the current date-and-time, and also how to display the time by using a digital clock. In this chapter, you will learn how to convert the time values to a form you can display using a traditional round clock. As you will learn, much of the code within the **Round Clock** applet is similar to the code you examined in Chapter 30. However, if you enjoy graphics programming, you will find the code that translates the current time into big-hand and little-hand clock positions interesting. By the time you finish this chapter, you will understand the following key concepts:

◆ To determine the position of the clock's big hand and little hand, you can use the *Math* class trigonometric functions (such as sine and cosine).

◆ By adding a *set* function to the *Coordinate* class, you simplify the process of changing an object's coordinates.

USING ROUND CLOCK

When you run the **Round Clock** applet, you will see a window with a round (traditional) clock, as shown in Figure 31. The shortest line corresponds to the hour hand, the longest line to the minute hand, and the line in between to the second hand.

Figure 31 A traditional round clock.

THE HTML FILE

Use the following HTML file to run the **Round Clock** applet:

```
<applet code=clock.class width=150 height=150> </applet>
```

LOOKING AT ROUND CLOCK

Like the **Digital Clock** applet, the **Round Clock** applet uses a *Date* object to determine the current date-and-time. Next, the program translates the current time into hours, minutes, and seconds, displaying the correct hand locations on the clock. The following code implements the **Round Clock** applet:

```java
//*********************************************************************
// clock.java
//*********************************************************************

import java.applet.*;
import java.awt.*;
import java.util.Date;

//*********************************************************************

class Coordinate
   {
     public int x;
     public int y;

     //───────────────────────────────

     public void set(int x, int y)
        {
          this.x = x;
          this.y = y;
        }

     //───────────────────────────────

     public Coordinate(int x, int y)
        {
          set(x, y);
        }
   }

   //*********************************************************************

public class clock extends Applet implements Runnable
   {
     Graphics g;
     FontMetrics font_metrics;
     Thread my_thread;

     static final double pi   = Math.PI;
     static final double _2pi = 2 * pi;
```

```
       int width;
       int height;

       Date current_time;

       Coordinate center;

       int radius = 80;
       int inside_radius;
       int h_len;
       int m_len;
       int s_len;

   //————————————————————————

   public void init()
      {
        g = getGraphics();

        center = new Coordinate(100, 100);
        current_time = new Date();

        set_defaults();
      }

   //————————————————————————

   void set_defaults()
      {
        width  = size().width;
        height = size().height;

        if (width < height)
          height = width;
        else
          width = height;

        center.set(width/2, height/2);
        radius = (width * 8) / 20;

        h_len = (radius * 5) / 10;
        m_len = (radius * 7) / 10;
        s_len = (radius * 6) / 10;

        inside_radius = (radius * 8) / 10;

        Font font = new Font("TimesRoman", Font.BOLD, width/8);
        g.setFont(font);

        font_metrics = g.getFontMetrics();
      }

   //————————————————————————
```

```
public void start()
  {
    if (my_thread == null)
      {
        my_thread = new Thread(this);
        my_thread.start();
      }
  }

//————————————————————

public void stop()
  {
    my_thread.stop();
    my_thread = null;
  }

//————————————————————

public void run()
  {
    while (my_thread != null)
      {
        repaint();

        try
          {
            Thread.sleep(1000);
          }
        catch (InterruptedException e)
          {
          }
      }
  }

//————————————————————

public void update(Graphics g)
  {
    g.setColor(Color.yellow);
    g.fillOval(center.x - inside_radius, center.y - inside_radius,
               inside_radius * 2, inside_radius * 2);

    current_time = new Date();

    int hours   = current_time.getHours();
    int minutes = current_time.getMinutes();
    int seconds = current_time.getSeconds();

    g.setColor(Color.black);
    draw_hands(hours, minutes, seconds);
  }

//————————————————————
```

```java
    void draw_hands(int h, int m, int s)
      {
        int x = center.x;
        int y = center.y;

        double hour_value = h + m/60.0 + s/3600.0;
        hour_value *= _2pi / 12.0;

        g.drawLine (x, y, (int) (x + h_len * Math.sin(hour_value)),
                    (int) (y - h_len * Math.cos(hour_value)));

        double minute_value = m + s/60.0;
        minute_value *= _2pi / 60.0;

        g.drawLine (x, y, (int) (x + m_len * Math.sin(minute_value)),
                    (int) (y - m_len * Math.cos(minute_value)));

        double second_value = s * _2pi / 60.0;

        g.drawLine (x, y, (int) (x + s_len * Math.sin(second_value)),
                    (int) (y - s_len * Math.cos(second_value)));
      }

    //————————————————————

    void draw_string(String string, int x, int y)
      {
        int string_width = font_metrics.stringWidth(string);
        int string_height = font_metrics.getAscent();

        g.drawString(string, x - string_width/2, y + string_height/2);
      }

    //————————————————————

    public void paint(Graphics g)
      {
        set_defaults();

        g.setColor(Color.black);
        g.fillRect(0, 0, size().width, size().height);

        g.setColor(Color.lightGray);
        g.fillOval(0, 0, width, height);

        g.setColor(Color.black);
        for (int i = 1; i <= 12; i++)
          draw_string ("" + i, (int) (center.x + radius * Math.sin(_2pi *
                       i/12)),
                       (int) (center.y - radius * Math.cos(_2pi * i/12)));
      }
  }
```

BREAKING APART ROUND CLOCK

As discussed, much of the code in the **Round Clock** applet is very similar to the code you examined for the **Digital Clock** applet in Chapter 30. Therefore, this section will focus only on the code that differs. To start, the applet adds a *set* function to the *Coordinate* class, which makes it easy to reset the coordinate values:

```
public void set(int x, int y)
  {
    this.x = x;
    this.y = y;
  }
```

Next, because the applet will be drawing images on a circle, the applet defines constants for the radian values *pi* and *_2pi*. Because you can't start a variable name with a digit (*2pi*), the applet precedes the variable name with an underscore (*_2pi*). The applet declares the constants as *static* and *final*, which means that they are only created once for this class, and that their values will never change:

```
static final double pi   = Math.PI;
static final double _2pi = 2 * pi;
```

Next, the applet creates a coordinate object to store the location of the clock's center, from which the applet draws the hands of the clock:

```
Coordinate center;
```

The applet then declares variables to store the outer and inner radius of the clock, where the numbers will reside, and the length of each of the clock's hands:

```
int radius = 80;
int inside_radius;
int h_len;
int m_len;
int s_len;
```

Initializing the Applet

The only change to the *init* function you examined in Chapter 30 is the statement that defines the default coordinates for the center of the clock. (Note that, depending on the size of the applet window, the *set_defaults* function may change the center of the window):

```
center = new Coordinate(100, 100);
```

Setting the Default Variables

Depending on the size of the window, the applet changes the size of the numbers that appear on the clock's face, the center of the clock, and the length of the hour, minute, and second hands:

```
void set_default()
  {
    width  = size().width;
    height = size().height;

    if (width < height)
      height = width;
    else
      width = height;

    center.set(width/2, height/2);
    radius = (width * 8) / 20;
    inside_radius = (radius * 8) / 10;

    h_len = (radius * 5) / 10;
    m_len = (radius * 7) / 10;
    s_len = (radius * 6) / 10;
```

Finally, based on the size of the window, the applet selects a font size and gets the font metrics. Notice that the size of the font is dependent on the width of the clock:

```
Font font = new Font("TimesRoman", Font.BOLD, width/8);
g.setFont(font);

font_metrics = g.getFontMetrics();
```

The *start*, *stop*, and *run* functions are the same as in the previous **Digital Clock** applet.

Updating the Applet

The *update* function assumes that the non-changing parts of the clock (such as the numbers) have already been drawn. To start, the function erases the old hands, gets the time values for the new hands, and calls *draw_hands* to display them:

```
public void update(Graphics g)
```

To erase the old hands that appear on the clock's yellow face, the function sets the color to yellow and then fills the region:

```
g.setColor(Color.yellow);
g.fillOval(center.x - inside_radius, center.y - inside_radius,
           inside_radius * 2,
           inside_radius * 2);
```

Next, the applet creates a new *Date* object and uses its member functions to get the current time:

```
current_time = new Date();

int hours   = current_time.getHours();
int minutes = current_time.getMinutes();
int seconds = current_time.getSeconds();
```

Finally, the function calls the *draw_hands* function to display the clock hands:

```
g.setColor(Color.black);
draw_hands(hours, minutes, seconds);
```

Drawing the Clock Hands

The *draw_hands* function receives the hours, minutes, and seconds as its arguments:

```
void draw_hands(int h, int m, int s)
```

As discussed, the applet draws the clock's hands from the center of the clock, whose coordinates are stored in the center variable:

```
int x = center.x;
int y = center.y;
```

To draw the hands of the clock, the function must determine the angle at which to draw the lines. To calculate the angle for the current hour, however, the applet uses the *hour* value plus fractions of the minutes and seconds:

```
double hour_value = h + m/60.0 + s/3600.0;
hour_value *= _2pi / 12.0;
```

To determine the x-coordinate offset of the end-point of the hour hand, the function calculates the sine of the hour radians, and then multiplies the result by the length of the hour hand. Next, the function adds the offset value to the x-coordinate that corresponds to the center of the clock. To get the y-coordinate, the processing is the same except that the function uses the cosine function, and then subtracts from the y-coordinate of the center:

```
g.drawLine (x, y, (int) (x + h_len * Math.sin(hour_value)),
            (int) (y - h_len * Math.cos(hour_value)));
```

The applet performs similar processing to determine the locations for the minute and second hands:

```
double minute_value = m + s/60.0;
minute_value *= _2pi / 60.0;

g.drawLine (x, y, (int) (x + m_len * Math.sin(minute_value)),
            (int) (y - m_len * Math.cos(minute_value)));

double second_value = s * _2pi / 60.0;

g.drawLine (x, y, (int) (x + s_len * Math.sin(second_value)),
            (int) (y - s_len * Math.cos(second_value)));
```

Drawing the Strings for the Clock

To display the hours on the face of the clock, the applet calls the *draw_string* function with each value. The *draw_string* function, in turn, calculates the size of the string and centers it around the given x-and-y coordinates:

```
void draw_string(String string, int x, int y)
  {
     int string_width = font_metrics.stringWidth(string);
     int string_height = font_metrics.getAscent();

     g.drawString(string, x - string_width/2, y + string_height/2);
  }
```

The paint Function

As you learned in Chapter 30, if your applet provides an *update* function, the only time the *paint* function is called is when the whole window must be repainted. Within the *paint* function, the applet must initialize the entire clock face. To start, the applet calls the *set_defaults* function to set the default values based on the size of the window:

```
set_defaults();
```

Next, the applet clears the entire window by overwriting the window's contents with a large black rectangle:

```
g.setColor(Color.black);
g.fillRect(0, 0, size().width, size().height);
```

After clearing the window, the applet draws a light-gray circle, which includes the area for the clock's numbers:

```
g.setColor(Color.lightGray);
g.fillOval(0, 0, width, height);
```

Lastly, the function displays the clock's twelve numbers:

```
g.setColor(Color.black);
for (int i = 1; i <= 12; i++)
draw_string ("" + i, (int) (center.x + radius * Math.sin(_2pi * i/12)),
             (int) (center.y - radius * Math.cos(_2pi * i/12)));
```

The function calculates each number's x-and-y coordinates, using the same principles used in the *draw_hands* function.

ENHANCEMENTS YOU CAN MAKE TO ROUND CLOCK

The current hour and minute hands used by the **Round Clock** applet need improvement. To start, make the hour and minute hands thicker, so they are easier to distinguish from the second hand. Next, change the clock face to display Roman numerals.

PUTTING IT ALL TOGETHER

The **Round Clock** applet shows you how to use the *Math* class *trigonometric* functions to create a traditional round clock with numbers and hands. In Chapter 32, you will jump from applets that display the current time within a clock to an applet that displays the current date within a calendar. Before you continue with Chapter 32, however, make sure you understand the following key concepts:

☑ Using the *Math* class *trigonometric* functions, you can translate the current time to positions that correspond to a clock's hour, minute, and second hands.

☑ By adding a *set* method to the *Coordinate* class, you make it easier for an applet to update the coordinate values.

CHAPTER 32

CALENDAR
CREATING AN ONLINE CALENDAR

In Chapters 31 and 32, you created applets that used the *Date* class objects to create clock programs. In this chapter, you will use the *Date* class objects to create an online Calendar. The **Calendar** applet will show you how to create and use interactive buttons. Specifically, the user can click their mouse on the buttons to change the current month. By the time you finish this chapter, you will understand the following key concepts:

- The *Date* object contains all the information you need to create a calendar. By passing parameters to the *Date* class constructor, your applet can get information about a specific month.

- You can calculate the number of days for any given month and year.

- Using the *getDay* function, your applet can determine on what day of the week a month starts.

- Using the *Panel* class, you can add buttons to the calendar that let the user display the next or previous month.

USING CALENDAR

When you run the **Calendar** applet, you will see a window with a calendar, as shown in Figure 32. By clicking your mouse on the forward and backward buttons, you can display the next or previous month's calendar.

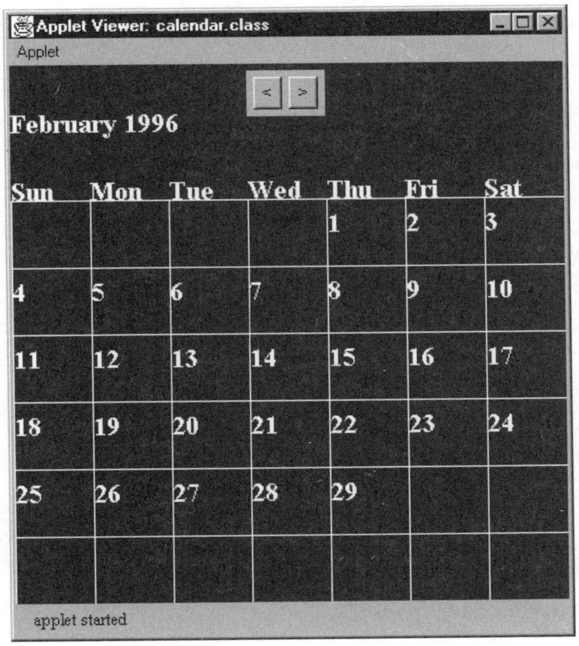

Figure 32 A calendar with buttons to change months.

THE HTML FILE

Use the following HTML file to run the **Calendar** applet:

```
<applet code=calendar.class width=400 height=400> </applet>
```

LOOKING AT CALENDAR

As discussed, the **Calendar** applet displays an online calendar with buttons that let the user scroll through the months of the year. As you will learn, using the Java *Date* class, the applet can get the information it needs to know about any month. The following code implements the **Calendar** applet:

```
//******************************************************************
// calendar.java
//******************************************************************

import java.applet.*;
import java.awt.*;
import java.util.Date;


//******************************************************************

public class calendar extends Applet
   {
     Graphics g;
     Font f;
     FontMetrics fm;

     Date current_date;
     Date month_to_show;
     int width;
     int height;
     int year;
     int month;

     //————————————————————————————

     public void init()
       {
         g = getGraphics();

         current_date = new Date();
         year = current_date.getYear();
         month = current_date.getMonth();
         month_to_show = new Date(year, month, 1);

         Panel p = new Panel();
         add("North", p);
         p.add(new Button("<"));
         p.add(new Button(">"));
       }

     //————————————————————————————
```

```
    public boolean action(Event evt, Object arg)
      {
        if (arg.equals("<"))
          {
            if (--month < 0)
              {
                month = 11;
                year--;
              }
          }
        else
          {
            if (++month > 11)
              {
                month = 1;
                year++;
              }
          }

        month_to_show = new Date(year, month, 1);
        repaint();

        return true;
      }

    //————————————————————————

    String day_of_week(int day)
      {
        switch (day)
          {
            case 0 :  return ("Sun");
            case 1 :  return ("Mon");
            case 2 :  return ("Tue");
            case 3 :  return ("Wed");
            case 4 :  return ("Thu");
            case 5 :  return ("Fri");
            default:  return ("Sat");
          }
      }

    //————————————————————————

    String month_name(int month)
      {
        switch (month)
          {
            case 0 :  return ("January");
            case 1 :  return ("February");
            case 2 :  return ("March");
            case 3 :  return ("April");
            case 4 :  return ("May");
            case 5 :  return ("June");
            case 6 :  return ("July");
```

```java
        case 7 :   return ("August");
        case 8 :   return ("September");
        case 9 :   return ("October");
        case 10:   return ("November");
        default:   return ("December");
      }
  }

//————————————————————

int number_of_days(int month, int year)
  {
    switch (month+1)
      {
        case 1:
        case 3:
        case 5:
        case 7:
        case 8:
        case 10:
        case 12:
          return (31);

        case 4:
        case 6:
        case 9:
        case 11:
          return (30);

        default:
          if (year%4 != 0)
            return (28);
          else if (year%100 != 0)
            return (29);
          else if (year%400 != 0)
            return (28);
          else
            return (29);
      }
  }

//————————————————————

public void paint(Graphics g)
  {
    width  = size().width;
    height = size().height;

    if (width < height)
      height = width;
    else
      width = height;
```

```
      g.setColor(Color.blue);
      g.fillRect(0, 0, size().width, size().height);

      g.setColor(Color.white);

      for (int i = 2; i < 9; i++)              // horizontal lines
        {
          int y = (height * i) / 8;
          g.drawLine(0, y, width-1, y);
        }

      int y = height / 4;
      for (int i = 0; i < 8; i++)              // vertical lines
        {
          int x = (width * i) / 7;
          g.drawLine(x, y, x, height-1);
        }

      font = new Font("TimesRoman", Font.BOLD, height/20);
      g.setFont(font);
      font_metrics = g.getFontMetrics();

      g.drawString(month_name (month_to_show.getMonth()) + " " +
                   (1900 + month_to_show.getYear()), 0,
                   height/8);

      y = height / 4;
      for (int i = 0; i < 7; i++)
        g.drawString(day_of_week(i), (width * i) / 7, y);

      int first = month_to_show.getDay();
      int last = number_of_days(month_to_show.getMonth(),
                                month_to_show.getYear());

      int day = first;

      y = (height * 5) / 16;
      for (int i = 1; i <= last; i++)
        {
          g.drawString("" + i, (width * day) / 7, y);
          if (++day > 6)
            {
              day = 0;
              y += height / 8;
            }
        }
    }
  }
```

BREAKING APART CALENDAR

The **Calendar** applet uses three packages: the *java.applet* package because it extends the *Applet* class; the *java.awt* package, because it performs graphics; and the *java.util.Date* package, because it uses a *Date* object:

```
import java.applet.*;
import java.awt.*;
import java.util.Date;
```

The applet declares variables to hold the current date, the month to show on the window, and the width and the height of the window. You also need integer values for the year and the month currently showing on the window so that you can perform calculations on them, depending on the options selected by the user:

```
Date current_date;
Date month_to_show;
int width;
int height;
int year;
int month;
```

Initializing the Applet

Within the *init* function, the applet, as always, gets the graphics context:

```
g = getGraphics();
```

Then, the applet creates a *Date* object that contains the current date and breaks the date into the year and the month. The applet also assigns the month value to the *month_to_show* variable, which specifies the first month the applet will display:

```
current_date = new Date();
year = current_date.getYear();
month = current_date.getMonth();
month_to_show = new Date(year, month, 1);
```

As discussed, the applet displays forward- and backward-facing buttons that let the user select the next or previous month for display. To display the buttons, the applet creates a *Panel* object and displays the *Panel* on the window. Then, the applet adds two buttons to the panel. By using the "North" option, when adding the *Panel* to the window, the buttons will appear at the top of the window:

```
Panel p = new Panel();
add("North", p);
p.add(new Button("<"));
p.add(new Button(">"));
```

Action on Buttons

When the user clicks their mouse on a button, Java will call the applet's *action* function, which in turn, handles the button event. The *action* function receives two parameters: the event and an object. The event will correspond to the button click, and the object will specify the button that the user clicked:

```
public boolean action(Event evt, Object arg)
```

By using the *Object* class *equals* function, the function can use the button labels to determine which button the user clicked. In this case, based on the button selected, the function will simply increment or decrement the *month* variable, which will contain a value in the range 0 (January) to 11 (December), not 1 to 12. As you can see, if the month becomes less than zero, the applet resets the value to 11 (for December) and decrements the year. Likewise, if the month moves past December, the function resets the month to 0 (for January), and increments the year:

```
if (arg.equals("<"))
  {
    if (—month < 0)
      {
        month = 11;
        year—;
      }
  }
else
  {
    if (++month > 11)
      {
        month = 1;
        year++;
      }
  }
```

Next, the applet creates a *Date* object and assigns it the month and year selected. As you can see, the applet specifies the first day of the month. Then, the function repaints the window to display the selected month:

```
month_to_show = new Date(year, month, 1);
repaint();
```

Return *true*, which means that you processed this event:

```
return true;
```

The paint Function

The real meat of the **Calendar** applet occurs in the *paint* function. To start, the function gets the window's width and height so it can recalculate the width and the height of the calendar to the largest possible size:

```
width  = size().width;
height = size().height;

if (width < height)
  height = width;
else
  width = height;
```

After the function determines the calendar size, it fills the entire window with blue and sets the color to white to display the calendar's letters:

```
g.setColor(Color.blue);
g.fillRect(0, 0, size().width, size().height);

g.setColor(Color.white);
```

The applet uses the following *for* statement to draw the calendar's horizontal gridlines:

```
for (int i = 2; i < 9; i++)              // horizontal lines
  {
     int y = (height * i) / 8;
     g.drawLine(0, y, width-1, y);
  }
```

In a similar way, the applet uses the following statements to draw the vertical lines that separate the seven days of the week:

```
int y = height / 4;
for (int i = 0; i < 8; i++)              // vertical lines
  {
     int x = (width * i) / 7;
     g.drawLine(x, y, x, height-1);
  }
```

Next, the applet sizes the font it will use for the calendar's lettering. The point size the function uses depends on the height of the calendar:

```
font = new Font("TimesRoman", Font.BOLD, height/20);
g.setFont(font);
font_metrics = g.getFontMetrics();
```

The applet then calls the *month_name* function to get the name of the current month. Using the *drawString* function, the applet displays the month's name:

```
g.drawString(month_name (month_to_show.getMonth()) + " " +
          (1900 + month_to_show.getYear()), 0, height/8);
```

Next, the applet draws the names of the days of the week. The applet uses a y-coordinate that is above the first week, and an x-coordinate that is to the left of the day box. With each iteration of the loop, the applet steps one-seventh of the calendar width:

```
y = height / 4;
for (int i = 0; i < 7; i++)
  g.drawString(day_of_week(i), (width * i) / 7, y);
```

Since the applet has initialized the *month_to_show* variable to the first of the month, it can use the *getDay* function to determine the corresponding day of the week (that's how the applet can determine on which day of the week the month starts). Using the *number_of_days* function, the applet can determine the last day of the month:

```
int first = month_to_show.getDay();
int last = number_of_days(month_to_show.getMonth(),
month_to_show.getYear());
```

The applet uses the following *for* loop to assign the dates to the calendar:

```
int day = first;

y = (height * 5) / 16;
for (int i = 1; i <= last; i++)
   {
      g.drawString("" + i, (width * day) / 7, y);
      if (++day > 6)
         {
            day = 0;
            y += height / 8;
         }
   }
```

ENHANCEMENTS YOU CAN MAKE TO CALENDAR

To start, modify the **Calendar** applet to highlight holidays. Then, using Julian dates as your starting point, change the calendar to display the number of days that remain in the year from any given date.

PUTTING IT ALL TOGETHER

The **Calendar** applet shows you how to create an interactive applet that responds to user mouse operations. In addition, the applet shows you the ins and outs of the Java *Date* class. In Chapter 33, you will again visit a clock applet. This time, however, you will create an LED clock the user can scale. Before you continue with Chapter 33, however, make sure you understand the following key concepts:

☑ Using the *Date* class, an applet can determine information about any given date, such as its day of the week.

☑ To determine the day of the week for a specific date, use the *getDay* function.

☑ Using the *Panel* class, your applet can quickly add buttons to a window. When the user clicks their mouse on a button, Java will call the applet's *action* function.

Chapter 33

LED Clock
Creating a Scaleable LED Clock

In Chapters 30 and 31 you first created a **Digital Clock** applet, and then a traditional **Round Clock** applet. In this chapter, you will create an LED Clock that the user can scale by resizing the applet window. As you will learn, the applet draws the clock by building the numbers using vectors (lines), which it really creates using the *Graphics* class *fillPolygon* function. To simplify your programming, the applet builds an *LED* class. By the time you finish this chapter, you will understand the following key concepts:

- By creating an *LED* class, your program can create an LED clock by passing an *LED* object five parameters: a string that contains the current time, the x-and-y coordinates at which you want the clock drawn, and the clock width and height.

- The *LED* object will scale its display to fit within a specified area.

- The *LED* class uses the *fillPolygon* function to draw each LED digit. Therefore, the object can scale the digits if the clock window is resized.

Using LED Clock

When you run the **LED Clock** applet, you will see a window with a digital clock displayed using the LED font, as shown in Figure 33.1. When you resize the window, the font will also resize to fit inside the window, as shown in Figure 33.2.

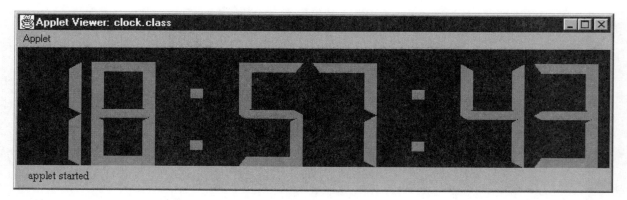

Figure 33.1 *An LED clock.*

Take a close look at the digits that make up the LED clock. If you look closely, you may realize the parts of the digits are actually filled polygons. As you will learn, the **LED Clock** applet builds the digits by connecting filled polygons.

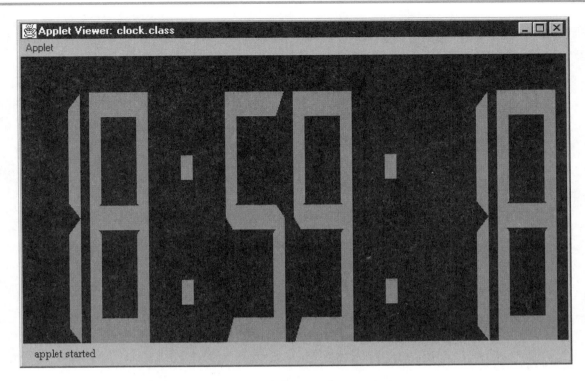

Figure 33.2 *The same LED clock shown in Figure 33.1, but in a larger window.*

THE HTML FILE

Use the following HTML file to run the **LED Clock** applet:

```
<applet code=clock.class width=300 height=60> </applet>
```

LOOKING AT LED CLOCK

The **LED Clock** applet contains two classes. Because both of the classes are long, they are stored in separate files.

The clock Applet Class

As you will find, the code is very similar to the **Digital Clock** applet you examined in Chapter 30. In this case, however, instead of using the system fonts to draw the clock string on the window, the applet uses the *LED* class. The following code implements the **LED Clock** applet:

```
//****************************************************************
// clock.java
//****************************************************************

import java.applet.*;
import java.awt.*;
import java.util.Date;


//****************************************************************
```

```java
public class clock extends Applet implements Runnable
  {
    Graphics g;
    LED led;

    Thread my_thread;

    int width;
    int height;
    Date current_time;

    //————————————————————————

    public void init()
      {
        g = getGraphics();

        led = new LED(g);

        current_time = new Date();

        set_defaults();
      }

    //————————————————————————

    void set_defaults()
      {
        width  = size().width;
        height = size().height;
      }

    //————————————————————————

    public void start()
      {
        if (my_thread == null)
          {
            my_thread = new Thread(this);
            my_thread.start();
          }
      }

    //————————————————————————

    public void stop()
      {
        my_thread.stop();
        my_thread = null;
      }

    //————————————————————————
```

```
    public void run()
      {
        while (my_thread != null)
          {
            repaint();

            try
              {
                Thread.sleep(1000);
              }
            catch (InterruptedException e)
              {
              }
          }
      }


    //————————————————————————————


    public void update(Graphics _g)
      {
        g.setColor(Color.black);
        g.fillRect(0, 0, width, height);

        current_time = new Date();

        int hours   = current_time.getHours();
        int minutes = current_time.getMinutes();
        int seconds = current_time.getSeconds();

        String time;

        if (hours < 10)
          time = "0" + hours;
        else
          time = "" + hours;

        if (minutes < 10)
          time += ":0" + minutes;
        else
          time += ":" + minutes;

        if (seconds < 10)
          time += ":0" + seconds;
        else
          time += ":" + seconds;

        g.setColor(Color.green);

        led.draw_string(time, 0, height, width, height);
      }

    //————————————————————————————
```

```
        public void paint(Graphics g)
          {
            set_defaults();
            update(g);
          }
    }
```

The LED Class

The code for the *LED* class is by far the more interesting code presented in this chapter. The code defines the *LED* class and creates the ten digits in LED format, as well as a colon that the clock uses to separate the hours from minutes and minutes from seconds. The following code implements the *LED* class:

```java
//*******************************************************************
// LED.java
//*******************************************************************

import java.awt.*;

//*******************************************************************

public class LED
  {
    private Graphics g;

    private int x_points[];
    private int y_points[];

    private int dx = 5;
    private int dy = 10;

    private int digits[][] =
      {
        {1, 1, 1, 1, 1, 1, 0},      // 0
        {0, 0, 0, 0, 1, 1, 0},      // 1
        {1, 0, 1, 1, 0, 1, 1},      // 2
        {1, 0, 0, 1, 1, 1, 1},      // 3
        {0, 1, 0, 0, 1, 1, 1},      // 4
        {1, 1, 0, 1, 1, 0, 1},      // 5
        {1, 1, 1, 1, 1, 0, 1},      // 6
        {1, 0, 0, 0, 1, 1, 0},      // 7
        {1, 1, 1, 1, 1, 1, 1},      // 8
        {1, 1, 0, 1, 1, 1, 1},      // 9
      };

    //——————————————————————————————

    public LED(Graphics g)
      {
        this.g = g;

        x_points = new int[6];
        y_points = new int[6];
      }
```

```
    //─────────────────────────

    public void draw_string(String string, int x, int y, int w, int h)
      {
        int string_length = string.length();
        char char_array[] = new char[string_length];
        string.getChars(0, string_length, char_array, 0);

        w /= string_length;

        int char_width  = (w * 7) / 8;
        int char_height = (h * 7) / 8;

        for (int i = 0; i < string_length; i++)
          {
            draw_char(char_array[i], x, y, char_width, char_height);
            x += w;
          }
      }


    //─────────────────────────

    private void draw_char(char c, int x, int y, int w, int h)
      {
        switch (c)
          {
            case ":":
              g.fillRect(x+2*w/dx, y-(h  )/4, w/dx, h/dy);
              g.fillRect(x+2*w/dx, y-(h*3)/4, w/dx, h/dy);
              break;

            default:
              int index = Character.digit(c, 10);
              for (int i = 0; i < 7; i++)
                if (digits[index][i] == 1)
                  switch (i)
                    {
                        case 0:  top    (x  , y-h  , w   , h/dy); break;
                        case 1:  left   (x  , y-h/2, w/dx, h/ 2); break;
                        case 2:  left   (x  , y    , w/dx, h/ 2); break;
                        case 3:  bottom (x  , y    , w   , h/dy); break;
                        case 4:  right  (x+w, y    , w/dx, h/ 2); break;
                        case 5:  right  (x+w, y-h/2, w/dx, h/ 2); break;
                        case 6:  middle (x  , y-h/2, w   , h/dy); break;
                    }
              break;
          }
      }

    //─────────────────────────
```

```
    private void top(int x, int y, int w, int h)
      {
        x_points[0] = x          ;  y_points[0] = y  ;
        x_points[1] = x+w        ;  y_points[1] = y  ;
        x_points[2] = x+(w*7)/8;  y_points[2] = y+h;
        x_points[3] = x+(w   )/8;  y_points[3] = y+h;

        g.fillPolygon(x_points, y_points, 4);
      }

    //————————————————————————

    private void middle(int x, int y, int w, int h)
      {
        x_points[0] = x          ;  y_points[0] = y     ;
        x_points[1] = x+(w   )/8 ;  y_points[1] = y-h/2;
        x_points[2] = x+(w*7)/8 ;  y_points[2] = y-h/2;
        x_points[3] = x+w        ;  y_points[3] = y     ;
        x_points[4] = x+(w*7)/8 ;  y_points[4] = y+h/2;
        x_points[5] = x+(w   )/8 ;  y_points[5] = y+h/2;

        g.fillPolygon(x_points, y_points, 6);
      }

    //————————————————————————

    private void bottom(int x, int y, int w, int h)
      {
        x_points[0] = x          ;  y_points[0] = y  ;
        x_points[1] = x+w        ;  y_points[1] = y  ;
        x_points[2] = x+(w*7)/8;  y_points[2] = y-h;
        x_points[3] = x+(w   )/8;  y_points[3] = y-h;

        g.fillPolygon(x_points, y_points, 4);
      }

    //————————————————————————

    private void left(int x, int y, int w, int h)
      {
        x_points[0] = x  ;  y_points[0] = y          ;
        x_points[1] = x  ;  y_points[1] = y-h        ;
        x_points[2] = x+w;  y_points[2] = y-(h*7)/8;
        x_points[3] = x+w;  y_points[3] = y-(h   )/8;

        g.fillPolygon(x_points, y_points, 4);
      }

    //————————————————————————
```

```
    private void right(int x, int y, int w, int h)
      {
        x_points[0] = x  ;   y_points[0] = y          ;
        x_points[1] = x  ;   y_points[1] = y-h        ;
        x_points[2] = x-w;   y_points[2] = y-(h*7)/8;
        x_points[3] = x-w;   y_points[3] = y-(h  )/8;

        g.fillPolygon(x_points, y_points, 4);
      }
  }
```

BREAKING APART LED CLOCK

As discussed, the **LED Clock** applet is very similar to the **Digital Clock** applet you examined in Chapter 30. Therefore, this section will only examine the parts of the code that differ. To start, the applet replaces the *Font* object and the *FontMetrics* object with one *LED* object:

```
LED led;
```

Within the *init* function, the applet initializes this *LED* object by passing the applet's graphics context to it:

```
led = new LED(g);
```

Within the *set_defaults* function, you do not use a proportional width and height because the *LED* class will resize the digits to fit inside of any area. Also, you do not have to create a font and get the font metrics. Therefore, the *set_defaults* function is very simple, and is as follows:

```
void set_defaults()
  {
    width  = size().width;
    height = size().height;
  }
```

The *update* function contains the only other changes in this applet. To start, the function clears the screen using a black background instead of light-gray:

```
g.setColor(Color.black);
g.fillRect(0, 0, width, height);
```

After the function formats the current time into a *String*, it sets the color to green (to produce a nice LED effect), and then calls the *draw_string* function of the *LED* object to display the time:

```
g.setColor(Color.green);

led.draw_string(time, 0, height, width, height);
```

The LED Class

The *LED* class imports one package—the *java.awt* package, which contains the *Graphics* class:

```
import java.awt.*;
```

Class Variables

The *LED* class declares its member variables as *private* to prevent another object from accessing them directly. Likewise, some of the *LED* class functions are also private.

To start, the *LED* class declares a variable that will hold its graphics context. When an applet creates an *LED* class object, the applet will pass the corresponding graphics context to the *LED* class constructor function. The constructor function, in turn, will assign the context to the *private* member variable *g* shown here:

```
private Graphics g;
```

Each LED character consists of multiple lines. Actually, the *LED* class draws each digit segment by using a filled polygon. The *LED* class stores each character's x-and-y coordinates in two arrays:

```
private int x_points[];
private int y_points[];
```

Later, when the class needs to draw a digit, the class uses the x-and-y coordinates to specify a polygon region the class fills using the *fillPoly* function. Each vertical LED will be one-fifth of the width of the character, and each horizontal LED will be one-tenth of the height of the character:

```
private int dx = 5;
private int dy = 10;
```

Next, the class must define which LEDs to use for each digit. To define the LEDs, the class uses a two-dimensional array, for which the first dimension is an index into the array specifying which digit you need. The second dimension contains seven items, each one for a specific LED. The order of the LEDs are as follows: top, left-top, left-bottom, bottom, right-bottom, right-top, and middle. A 1 means you want to draw it, a 0 means you do not want to draw it. By connecting the LED points and filling the area with the green color, the class creates the LED digit:

```
private int digits[][] =
  {
    {1, 1, 1, 1, 1, 1, 0},     // 0
    {0, 0, 0, 0, 1, 1, 0},     // 1
    {1, 0, 1, 1, 0, 1, 1},     // 2
    {1, 0, 0, 1, 1, 1, 1},     // 3
    {0, 1, 0, 0, 1, 1, 1},     // 4
    {1, 1, 0, 1, 1, 0, 1},     // 5
    {1, 1, 1, 1, 1, 0, 1},     // 6
    {1, 0, 0, 0, 1, 1, 0},     // 7
    {1, 1, 1, 1, 1, 1, 1},     // 8
    {1, 1, 0, 1, 1, 1, 1},     // 9
  };
```

The Constructor

The *LED* class constructor function is quite simple. The function accepts one parameter—the graphics context. As you can see, the constructor assigns the parameter to the local graphics context, and then allocates space for the arrays of x and y coordinates:

```
public LED(Graphics g)
  {
    this.g = g;

    x_points = new int[6];
    y_points = new int[6];
  }
```

Drawing the String

The *draw_string* function is a public function that displays a string using the LED font. As you can see, the function accepts five parameters: the string to display, the x-and-y coordinates of the bottom-left corner of the display area, and the width and height of the display area. The function assumes that the color has already been set by the calling object:

```
public void draw_string(String string, int x, int y, int w, int h)
```

To start, the *draw_string* function breaks the string apart into an array of individual characters:

```
int string_length = string.length();
char char_array[] = new char[string_length];
string.getChars(0, string_length, char_array, 0);
```

The function then divides the width by the number of characters in the string to determine the width available for each character:

```
w /= string_length;
```

Next, the function uses seven-eighths of the width and height for each character. This will leave one-eighth for spacing so the characters do not run into each other:

```
int char_width  = (w * 7) / 8;
int char_height = (h * 7) / 8;
```

Finally, to draw each character, the function calls the *draw_char* function for each character within a *for* loop. As you can see, the *for* loop increments the x-coordinate with each iteration to position the next character:

```
for (int i = 0; i < string_length; i++)
  {
    draw_char(char_array[i], x, y, char_width, char_height);
    x += w;
  }
```

Drawing Each Character

The *draw_char* function is a private function that can only be called by functions inside the *LED* class. The function uses five parameters: the character to draw, the character's x-and-y coordinates, and the character's width and height. As you will recall, the calling function has taken care of the spacing between characters, so the *draw_char* function can use the entire area for the character:

```
private void draw_char(char c, int x, int y, int w, int h)
```

To start, using a *switch* statement, the function checks whether the character is a colon or a digit. The function uses a *switch* statement (as opposed to an *if* statement) to make it easier for you to support other characters in the future:

```
switch (c)
```

If the current character is a colon, the function draws two small rectangles. The first rectangle is centered in the top half of the character space. Likewise, the second rectangle is centered in the bottom half:

```
case ":":
  g.fillRect(x+2*w/dx, y-(h  )/4, w/dx, h/dy);
  g.fillRect(x+2*w/dx, y-(h*3)/4, w/dx, h/dy);
  break;
```

If it is not a colon, it must be a digit. Therefore, the function must first convert the character into an integer by using the *Character* class *digit* member function. Because the function is working with digital numbers, it uses the base-10 conversion:

```
default:
  int index = Character.digit(c, 10);
```

Next, the function loops through the digit's LED settings to determine which parts of the LED it needs to draw:

```
for (int i = 0; i < 7; i++)
  if (digits[index][i] == 1)
    switch (i)
      {
        case 0:  top    (x  , y-h  , w   , h/dy); break;
        case 1:  left   (x  , y-h/2, w/dx, h/ 2); break;
        case 2:  left   (x  , y    , w/dx, h/ 2); break;
        case 3:  bottom (x  , y    , w   , h/dy); break;
        case 4:  right  (x+w, y    , w/dx, h/ 2); break;
        case 5:  right  (x+w, y-h/2, w/dx, h/ 2); break;
        case 6:  middle (x  , y-h/2, w   , h/dy); break;
      }
  break;
```

Drawing the LEDs

To draw an LED digit, the class uses five functions. The first is the top-horizontal LED. Here, you create a trapezoid that uses the entire width at the top, and at the bottom indents the width by an eighth on both sides:

```
private void top(int x, int y, int w, int h)
{
    x_points[0] = x         ;  y_points[0] = y  ;
    x_points[1] = x+w       ;  y_points[1] = y  ;
    x_points[2] = x+(w*7)/8;  y_points[2] = y+h;
    x_points[3] = x+(w  )/8;  y_points[3] = y+h;

    g.fillPolygon(x_points, y_points, 4);
}
```

The middle LED uses six points. The top and bottom of the polygon indent one-eighth of the width, and the middle is outdented to use the entire width:

```
private void middle(int x, int y, int w, int h)
{
    x_points[0] = x           ;  y_points[0] = y     ;
    x_points[1] = x+(w  )/8 ;  y_points[1] = y-h/2;
    x_points[2] = x+(w*7)/8 ;  y_points[2] = y-h/2;
    x_points[3] = x+w         ;  y_points[3] = y     ;
    x_points[4] = x+(w*7)/8 ;  y_points[4] = y+h/2;
    x_points[5] = x+(w  )/8 ;  y_points[5] = y+h/2;

    g.fillPolygon(x_points, y_points, 6);
}
```

The function draws the bottom LED in a manner similar to the *top* function:

```
private void bottom(int x, int y, int w, int h)
{
    x_points[0] = x         ;  y_points[0] = y  ;
    x_points[1] = x+w       ;  y_points[1] = y  ;
    x_points[2] = x+(w*7)/8;  y_points[2] = y-h;
    x_points[3] = x+(w  )/8;  y_points[3] = y-h;

    g.fillPolygon(x_points, y_points, 4);
}
```

There are two left pieces: the left-top and left-bottom. The calling function specifies the x-and-y coordinates and the width and height, so the function does not have to worry about whether it is drawing the left-top or the left-bottom:

```
private void left(int x, int y, int w, int h)
{
    x_points[0] = x ;  y_points[0] = y         ;
    x_points[1] = x ;  y_points[1] = y-h        ;
    x_points[2] = x+w;  y_points[2] = y-(h*7)/8;
    x_points[3] = x+w;  y_points[3] = y-(h  )/8;

    g.fillPolygon(x_points, y_points, 4);
}
```

In a similar way, there are also two right pieces: the right-top and right-bottom. As it did in the *left* function, the calling function specifies the x-and-y coordinates and the width and height, so the function does not have to worry about whether it is drawing the right-top or the right-bottom:

```
private void right(int x, int y, int w, int h)
  {
    x_points[0] = x  ;  y_points[0] = y        ;
    x_points[1] = x  ;  y_points[1] = y-h      ;
    x_points[2] = x-w;  y_points[2] = y-(h*7)/8;
    x_points[3] = x-w;  y_points[3] = y-(h  )/8;

    g.fillPolygon(x_points, y_points, 4);
  }
```

ENHANCEMENTS YOU CAN MAKE TO LED CLOCK

Currently, the *LED* class only supports the digits 0 through 9 and the colon. Therefore, your first step to enhance this program is to add more characters to the class. Next, change the class to support different colors.

PUTTING IT ALL TOGETHER

The **LED Clock** applet shows you how to create screen objects that an applet can scale easily. In addition, the applet presents ways to use the *fillPolygon* function. In Chapter 34, you will examine a second font type: bitmap fonts. Specifically, after you define the font for 256 characters, you will use the font to create a digital clock the user can size by simply resizing the window. Before you continue with Chapter 34, however, make sure you understand the following key concepts:

☑ By defining an *LED* class, you provide a powerful way for applets to scale text.

☑ The *fillPolygon* function provides a very convenient way to draw shapes your applet may later scale.

CHAPTER 34

BITMAP FONT CLOCK
CREATING A BITMAP OBJECT

In several of the previous chapters, you have created clock applets. By now, you should feel very comfortable working with the Java *Date* class to determine the current system date-and-time, and then with displaying the time using different formats. In this chapter, you will again create a clock applet. However, this chapter's goal is to show you how to create and work with a bitmap-font object. By the time you finish this chapter, you will understand the following key concepts:

◆ You can create a bitmap-font object you can scale to fit within a specific area.

◆ The bitmap font this chapter presents contains an 8x8 bitmap for each of the 256 characters supported by an IBM-PC and PC-compatible computer.

USING BITMAP FONT CLOCK

When you run the **Bitmap Font Clock** applet, you will see a window with a digital clock displayed. As you can see in Figure 34.1, the clock uses a bitmap font. When you resize the window, the applet will resize the font to fit inside the window, as shown in Figure 34.2.

Figure 34.1 A bitmap font clock.

Figure 34.2 *The same bitmap font clock as shown in Figure 34.1, this time in a smaller window.*

THE HTML FILE

Use the following HTML file to run the **Bitmap Clock** applet:

```
<applet code=clock.class width=300 height=120> </applet>
```

LOOKING AT BITMAP CLOCK

As was the case in Chapter 33, the **Bitmap Clock** applet contains two classes. Because both classes are fairly long, the classes reside in two separate files.

The clock Applet Class

The code for the **Bitmap Clock** applet is very similar to the **LED Clock** applet you examined in Chapter 34, except, instead of using the *LED* class to draw the clock string, the **Bitmap Clock** applet uses the *font_8x8* class, which is the bitmap-font class. The following code implements the **Bitmap Clock** applet:

```
//*******************************************************************
// clock.java
//*******************************************************************

import java.applet.*;
import java.awt.*;
import java.util.Date;

//*******************************************************************

public class clock extends Applet implements Runnable
  {
    Graphics g;
    font_8x8 font;

    Thread my_thread;

    int width;
    int height;
    Date current_time;

    //——————————————————————————
```

```
    public void init()
      {
        g = getGraphics();

        font = new font_8x8(g);

        current_time = new Date();

        set_defaults();
      }
//——————————————————

void set_defaults()
      {
        width  = size().width;
        height = size().height;
      }
//——————————————————

public void start()
      {
        if (my_thread == null)
          {
            my_thread = new Thread(this);
            my_thread.start();
          }
      }
//——————————————————

public void stop()
      {
        my_thread.stop();
        my_thread = null;
      }
//——————————————————

public void run()
      {
        while (my_thread != null)
          {
          repaint();

          try
            {
              Thread.sleep(1000);
            }
          catch (InterruptedException e)
            {
            }
          }
      }
//——————————————————
```

```
    public void update(Graphics _g)
      {
        g.setColor(Color.black);
        g.fillRect(0, 0, width, height);

        current_time = new Date();

        int hours   = current_time.getHours();
        int minutes = current_time.getMinutes();
        int seconds = current_time.getSeconds();

        String time;
        boolean am;

        if (hours < 12)
          am = true;
        else
          {
            am = false;
            if (hours > 12)
              hours -= 12;
          }

        if (hours < 10)
          time = "0" + hours;
        else
          time = "" + hours;

        if (minutes < 10)
          time += ":0" + minutes;
        else
          time += ":" + minutes;

        if (seconds < 10)
          time += ":0" + seconds;
        else
          time += ":" + seconds;

        if (am)
          time += "am";
        else
          time += "pm";

        g.setColor(Color.green);

        font.draw_string("The time is:", 0, height/2,
                         width, height/2);
        font.draw_string(time, 0, height, width, height/2);
      }

//————————————————————————————————
```

```
      public void paint(Graphics g)
        {
          set_defaults();
          update(g);
        }
    }
```

The Bitmap-Font Class

The bitmap-font class implements a class named *font_8x8* that contains the code to define each letter in an 8x8 bitmap. The font contains the 256 characters used on an IBM-PC and PC-compatible computer. The following code implements the *font_8x8* class:

```
//****************************************************************
// font_8x8.java
//****************************************************************

import java.awt.*;

//****************************************************************

public class font_8x8
  {
    private Graphics g;

    static final int table[][] =
      {
        {0x00, 0x00, 0x00, 0x00, 0x00, 0x00, 0x00, 0x00},
        {0x7e, 0x81, 0xa5, 0x81, 0xbd, 0x99, 0x81, 0x7e},
        {0x7e, 0xff, 0xdb, 0xff, 0xc3, 0xe7, 0xff, 0x7e},
        {0x6c, 0xfe, 0xfe, 0xfe, 0x7c, 0x38, 0x10, 0x00},
        {0x10, 0x38, 0x7c, 0xfe, 0x7c, 0x38, 0x10, 0x00},
        {0x38, 0x7c, 0x38, 0xfe, 0xfe, 0x7c, 0x38, 0x7c},
        {0x10, 0x10, 0x38, 0x7c, 0xfe, 0x7c, 0x38, 0x7c},
        {0x00, 0x00, 0x18, 0x3c, 0x3c, 0x18, 0x00, 0x00},
        {0xff, 0xff, 0xe7, 0xc3, 0xc3, 0xe7, 0xff, 0xff},
        {0x00, 0x3c, 0x66, 0x42, 0x42, 0x66, 0x3c, 0x00},
        {0xff, 0xc3, 0x99, 0xbd, 0xbd, 0x99, 0xc3, 0xff},
        {0x0f, 0x07, 0x0f, 0x7d, 0xcc, 0xcc, 0xcc, 0x78},
        {0x3c, 0x66, 0x66, 0x66, 0x3c, 0x18, 0x7e, 0x18},
        {0x3f, 0x33, 0x3f, 0x30, 0x30, 0x70, 0xf0, 0xe0},
        {0x7f, 0x63, 0x7f, 0x63, 0x63, 0x67, 0xe6, 0xc0},
        {0x99, 0x5a, 0x3c, 0xe7, 0xe7, 0x3c, 0x5a, 0x99},
        {0x80, 0xe0, 0xf8, 0xfe, 0xf8, 0xe0, 0x80, 0x00},
        {0x02, 0x0e, 0x3e, 0xfe, 0x3e, 0x0e, 0x02, 0x00},
        {0x18, 0x3c, 0x7e, 0x18, 0x18, 0x7e, 0x3c, 0x18},
        {0x66, 0x66, 0x66, 0x66, 0x66, 0x00, 0x66, 0x00},
        {0x7f, 0xdb, 0xdb, 0x7b, 0x1b, 0x1b, 0x1b, 0x00},
```

```
        {0x3e, 0x63, 0x38, 0x6c, 0x6c, 0x38, 0xcc, 0x78},
        {0x00, 0x00, 0x00, 0x00, 0x7e, 0x7e, 0x7e, 0x00},
        {0x18, 0x3c, 0x7e, 0x18, 0x7e, 0x3c, 0x18, 0xff},
        {0x18, 0x3c, 0x7e, 0x18, 0x18, 0x18, 0x18, 0x00},
        {0x18, 0x18, 0x18, 0x18, 0x7e, 0x3c, 0x18, 0x00},
        {0x00, 0x18, 0x0c, 0xfe, 0x0c, 0x18, 0x00, 0x00},
        {0x00, 0x30, 0x60, 0xfe, 0x60, 0x30, 0x00, 0x00},
        {0x00, 0x00, 0xc0, 0xc0, 0xc0, 0xfe, 0x00, 0x00},
        {0x00, 0x24, 0x66, 0xff, 0x66, 0x24, 0x00, 0x00},
        {0x00, 0x18, 0x3c, 0x7e, 0xff, 0xff, 0x00, 0x00},
        {0x00, 0xff, 0xff, 0x7e, 0x3c, 0x18, 0x00, 0x00},
        {0x00, 0x00, 0x00, 0x00, 0x00, 0x00, 0x00, 0x00},
        {0x30, 0x78, 0x78, 0x30, 0x30, 0x00, 0x30, 0x00},
        {0x6c, 0x6c, 0x6c, 0x00, 0x00, 0x00, 0x00, 0x00},
        {0x6c, 0x6c, 0xfe, 0x6c, 0xfe, 0x6c, 0x6c, 0x00},
        {0x30, 0x7c, 0xc0, 0x78, 0x0c, 0xf8, 0x30, 0x00},
        {0x00, 0xc6, 0xcc, 0x18, 0x30, 0x66, 0xc6, 0x00},
        {0x38, 0x6c, 0x38, 0x76, 0xdc, 0xcc, 0x76, 0x00},
        {0x60, 0x60, 0xc0, 0x00, 0x00, 0x00, 0x00, 0x00},
        {0x18, 0x30, 0x60, 0x60, 0x60, 0x30, 0x18, 0x00},
        {0x60, 0x30, 0x18, 0x18, 0x18, 0x30, 0x60, 0x00},
        {0x00, 0x66, 0x3c, 0xff, 0x3c, 0x66, 0x00, 0x00},
        {0x00, 0x30, 0x30, 0xfc, 0x30, 0x30, 0x00, 0x00},
        {0x00, 0x00, 0x00, 0x00, 0x00, 0x30, 0x30, 0x60},
        {0x00, 0x00, 0x00, 0xfc, 0x00, 0x00, 0x00, 0x00},
        {0x00, 0x00, 0x00, 0x00, 0x00, 0x30, 0x30, 0x00},
        {0x06, 0x0c, 0x18, 0x30, 0x60, 0xc0, 0x80, 0x00},
        {0x7c, 0xc6, 0xce, 0xde, 0xf6, 0xe6, 0x7c, 0x00},
        {0x30, 0x70, 0x30, 0x30, 0x30, 0x30, 0xfc, 0x00},
        {0x78, 0xcc, 0x0c, 0x38, 0x60, 0xcc, 0xfc, 0x00},
        {0x78, 0xcc, 0x0c, 0x38, 0x0c, 0xcc, 0x78, 0x00},
        {0x1c, 0x3c, 0x6c, 0xcc, 0xfe, 0x0c, 0x1e, 0x00},
        {0xfc, 0xc0, 0xf8, 0x0c, 0x0c, 0xcc, 0x78, 0x00},
        {0x38, 0x60, 0xc0, 0xf8, 0xcc, 0xcc, 0x78, 0x00},
        {0xfc, 0xcc, 0x0c, 0x18, 0x30, 0x30, 0x30, 0x00},
        {0x78, 0xcc, 0xcc, 0x78, 0xcc, 0xcc, 0x78, 0x00},
        {0x78, 0xcc, 0xcc, 0x7c, 0x0c, 0x18, 0x70, 0x00},
        {0x00, 0x30, 0x30, 0x00, 0x00, 0x30, 0x30, 0x00},
        {0x00, 0x30, 0x30, 0x00, 0x00, 0x30, 0x30, 0x60},
        {0x18, 0x30, 0x60, 0xc0, 0x60, 0x30, 0x18, 0x00},
        {0x00, 0x00, 0xfc, 0x00, 0x00, 0xfc, 0x00, 0x00},
        {0x60, 0x30, 0x18, 0x0c, 0x18, 0x30, 0x60, 0x00},
        {0x78, 0xcc, 0x0c, 0x18, 0x30, 0x00, 0x30, 0x00},
        {0x7c, 0xc6, 0xde, 0xde, 0xde, 0xc0, 0x78, 0x00},
        {0x30, 0x78, 0xcc, 0xcc, 0xfc, 0xcc, 0xcc, 0x00},
        {0xfc, 0x66, 0x66, 0x7c, 0x66, 0x66, 0xfc, 0x00},
        {0x3c, 0x66, 0xc0, 0xc0, 0xc0, 0x66, 0x3c, 0x00},
        {0xf8, 0x6c, 0x66, 0x66, 0x66, 0x6c, 0xf8, 0x00},
        {0xfe, 0x62, 0x68, 0x78, 0x68, 0x62, 0xfe, 0x00},
        {0xfe, 0x62, 0x68, 0x78, 0x68, 0x60, 0xf0, 0x00},
        {0x3c, 0x66, 0xc0, 0xc0, 0xce, 0x66, 0x3e, 0x00},
        {0xcc, 0xcc, 0xcc, 0xfc, 0xcc, 0xcc, 0xcc, 0x00},
        {0x78, 0x30, 0x30, 0x30, 0x30, 0x30, 0x78, 0x00},
        {0x1e, 0x0c, 0x0c, 0x0c, 0xcc, 0xcc, 0x78, 0x00},
```

```
{0xe6, 0x66, 0x6c, 0x78, 0x6c, 0x66, 0xe6, 0x00},
{0xf0, 0x60, 0x60, 0x60, 0x62, 0x66, 0xfe, 0x00},
{0xc6, 0xee, 0xfe, 0xfe, 0xd6, 0xc6, 0xc6, 0x00},
{0xc6, 0xe6, 0xf6, 0xde, 0xce, 0xc6, 0xc6, 0x00},
{0x38, 0x6c, 0xc6, 0xc6, 0xc6, 0x6c, 0x38, 0x00},
{0xfc, 0x66, 0x66, 0x7c, 0x60, 0x60, 0xf0, 0x00},
{0x78, 0xcc, 0xcc, 0xcc, 0xdc, 0x78, 0x1c, 0x00},
{0xfc, 0x66, 0x66, 0x7c, 0x6c, 0x66, 0xe6, 0x00},
{0x78, 0xcc, 0xe0, 0x70, 0x1c, 0xcc, 0x78, 0x00},
{0xfc, 0xb4, 0x30, 0x30, 0x30, 0x30, 0x78, 0x00},
{0xcc, 0xcc, 0xcc, 0xcc, 0xcc, 0xcc, 0xfc, 0x00},
{0xcc, 0xcc, 0xcc, 0xcc, 0xcc, 0x78, 0x30, 0x00},
{0xc6, 0xc6, 0xc6, 0xd6, 0xfe, 0xee, 0xc6, 0x00},
{0xc6, 0xc6, 0x6c, 0x38, 0x38, 0x6c, 0xc6, 0x00},
{0xcc, 0xcc, 0xcc, 0x78, 0x30, 0x30, 0x78, 0x00},
{0xfe, 0xc6, 0x8c, 0x18, 0x32, 0x66, 0xfe, 0x00},
{0x78, 0x60, 0x60, 0x60, 0x60, 0x60, 0x78, 0x00},
{0xc0, 0x60, 0x30, 0x18, 0x0c, 0x06, 0x02, 0x00},
{0x78, 0x18, 0x18, 0x18, 0x18, 0x18, 0x78, 0x00},
{0x10, 0x38, 0x6c, 0xc6, 0x00, 0x00, 0x00, 0x00},
{0x00, 0x00, 0x00, 0x00, 0x00, 0x00, 0x00, 0xff},
{0x30, 0x30, 0x18, 0x00, 0x00, 0x00, 0x00, 0x00},
{0x00, 0x00, 0x78, 0x0c, 0x7c, 0xcc, 0x76, 0x00},
{0xe0, 0x60, 0x60, 0x7c, 0x66, 0x66, 0xdc, 0x00},
{0x00, 0x00, 0x78, 0xcc, 0xc0, 0xcc, 0x78, 0x00},
{0x1c, 0x0c, 0x0c, 0x7c, 0xcc, 0xcc, 0x76, 0x00},
{0x00, 0x00, 0x78, 0xcc, 0xfc, 0xc0, 0x78, 0x00},
{0x38, 0x6c, 0x60, 0xf0, 0x60, 0x60, 0xf0, 0x00},
{0x00, 0x00, 0x76, 0xcc, 0xcc, 0x7c, 0x0c, 0xf8},
{0xe0, 0x60, 0x6c, 0x76, 0x66, 0x66, 0xe6, 0x00},
{0x30, 0x00, 0x70, 0x30, 0x30, 0x30, 0x78, 0x00},
{0x0c, 0x00, 0x0c, 0x0c, 0x0c, 0xcc, 0xcc, 0x78},
{0xe0, 0x60, 0x66, 0x6c, 0x78, 0x6c, 0xe6, 0x00},
{0x70, 0x30, 0x30, 0x30, 0x30, 0x30, 0x78, 0x00},
{0x00, 0x00, 0xcc, 0xfe, 0xfe, 0xd6, 0xc6, 0x00},
{0x00, 0x00, 0xf8, 0xcc, 0xcc, 0xcc, 0xcc, 0x00},
{0x00, 0x00, 0x78, 0xcc, 0xcc, 0xcc, 0x78, 0x00},
{0x00, 0x00, 0xdc, 0x66, 0x66, 0x7c, 0x60, 0xf0},
{0x00, 0x00, 0x76, 0xcc, 0xcc, 0x7c, 0x0c, 0x1e},
{0x00, 0x00, 0xdc, 0x76, 0x66, 0x60, 0xf0, 0x00},
{0x00, 0x00, 0x7c, 0xc0, 0x78, 0x0c, 0xf8, 0x00},
{0x10, 0x30, 0x7c, 0x30, 0x30, 0x34, 0x18, 0x00},
{0x00, 0x00, 0xcc, 0xcc, 0xcc, 0xcc, 0x76, 0x00},
{0x00, 0x00, 0xcc, 0xcc, 0xcc, 0x78, 0x30, 0x00},
{0x00, 0x00, 0xc6, 0xd6, 0xfe, 0xfe, 0x6c, 0x00},
{0x00, 0x00, 0xc6, 0x6c, 0x38, 0x6c, 0xc6, 0x00},
{0x00, 0x00, 0xcc, 0xcc, 0xcc, 0x7c, 0x0c, 0xf8},
{0x00, 0x00, 0xfc, 0x98, 0x30, 0x64, 0xfc, 0x00},
{0x1c, 0x30, 0x30, 0xe0, 0x30, 0x30, 0x1c, 0x00},
{0x18, 0x18, 0x18, 0x00, 0x18, 0x18, 0x18, 0x00},
{0xe0, 0x30, 0x30, 0x1c, 0x30, 0x30, 0xe0, 0x00},
{0x76, 0xdc, 0x00, 0x00, 0x00, 0x00, 0x00, 0x00},
{0x00, 0x10, 0x38, 0x6c, 0xc6, 0xc6, 0xfe, 0x00},
{0x78, 0xcc, 0xc0, 0xcc, 0x78, 0x18, 0x0c, 0x78},
```

```
        {0x00, 0xcc, 0x00, 0xcc, 0xcc, 0xcc, 0x7e, 0x00},
        {0x1c, 0x00, 0x78, 0xcc, 0xfc, 0xc0, 0x78, 0x00},
        {0x7e, 0xc3, 0x3c, 0x06, 0x3e, 0x66, 0x3f, 0x00},
        {0xcc, 0x00, 0x78, 0x0c, 0x7c, 0xcc, 0x7e, 0x00},
        {0xe0, 0x00, 0x78, 0x0c, 0x7c, 0xcc, 0x7e, 0x00},
        {0x30, 0x30, 0x78, 0x0c, 0x7c, 0xcc, 0x7e, 0x00},
        {0x00, 0x00, 0x78, 0xc0, 0xc0, 0x78, 0x0c, 0x38},
        {0x7e, 0xc3, 0x3c, 0x66, 0x7e, 0x60, 0x3c, 0x00},
        {0xcc, 0x00, 0x78, 0xcc, 0xfc, 0xc0, 0x78, 0x00},
        {0xe0, 0x00, 0x78, 0xcc, 0xfc, 0xc0, 0x78, 0x00},
        {0xcc, 0x00, 0x70, 0x30, 0x30, 0x30, 0x78, 0x00},
        {0x7c, 0xc6, 0x38, 0x18, 0x18, 0x18, 0x3c, 0x00},
        {0xe0, 0x00, 0x70, 0x30, 0x30, 0x30, 0x78, 0x00},
        {0xc6, 0x38, 0x6c, 0xc6, 0xfe, 0xc6, 0xc6, 0x00},
        {0x30, 0x30, 0x00, 0x78, 0xcc, 0xfc, 0xcc, 0x00},
        {0x1c, 0x00, 0xfc, 0x60, 0x78, 0x60, 0xfc, 0x00},
        {0x00, 0x00, 0x7f, 0x0c, 0x7f, 0xcc, 0x7f, 0x00},
        {0x3e, 0x6c, 0xcc, 0xfe, 0xcc, 0xcc, 0xce, 0x00},
        {0x78, 0xcc, 0x00, 0x78, 0xcc, 0xcc, 0x78, 0x00},
        {0x00, 0xcc, 0x00, 0x78, 0xcc, 0xcc, 0x78, 0x00},
        {0x00, 0xe0, 0x00, 0x78, 0xcc, 0xcc, 0x78, 0x00},
        {0x78, 0xcc, 0x00, 0xcc, 0xcc, 0xcc, 0x7e, 0x00},
        {0x00, 0xe0, 0x00, 0xcc, 0xcc, 0xcc, 0x7e, 0x00},
        {0x00, 0xcc, 0x00, 0xcc, 0xcc, 0x7c, 0x0c, 0xf8},
        {0xc3, 0x18, 0x3c, 0x66, 0x66, 0x3c, 0x18, 0x00},
        {0xcc, 0x00, 0xcc, 0xcc, 0xcc, 0xcc, 0x78, 0x00},
        {0x18, 0x18, 0x7e, 0xc0, 0xc0, 0x7e, 0x18, 0x18},
        {0x38, 0x6c, 0x64, 0xf0, 0x60, 0xe6, 0xfc, 0x00},
        {0xcc, 0xcc, 0x78, 0xfc, 0x30, 0xfc, 0x30, 0x30},
        {0xf8, 0xcc, 0xcc, 0xfa, 0xc6, 0xcf, 0xc6, 0xc7},
        {0x0e, 0x1b, 0x18, 0x3c, 0x18, 0x18, 0xd8, 0x70},
        {0x1c, 0x00, 0x78, 0x0c, 0x7c, 0xcc, 0x7e, 0x00},
        {0x38, 0x00, 0x70, 0x30, 0x30, 0x30, 0x78, 0x00},
        {0x00, 0x1c, 0x00, 0x78, 0xcc, 0xcc, 0x78, 0x00},
        {0x00, 0x1c, 0x00, 0xcc, 0xcc, 0xcc, 0x7e, 0x00},
        {0x00, 0xf8, 0x00, 0xf8, 0xcc, 0xcc, 0xcc, 0x00},
        {0xfc, 0x00, 0xcc, 0xec, 0xfc, 0xdc, 0xcc, 0x00},
        {0x3c, 0x6c, 0x6c, 0x3e, 0x00, 0x7e, 0x00, 0x00},
        {0x38, 0x6c, 0x6c, 0x38, 0x00, 0x7c, 0x00, 0x00},
        {0x30, 0x00, 0x30, 0x60, 0xc0, 0xcc, 0x78, 0x00},
        {0x00, 0x00, 0x00, 0xfc, 0xc0, 0xc0, 0x00, 0x00},
        {0x00, 0x00, 0x00, 0xfc, 0x0c, 0x0c, 0x00, 0x00},
        {0xc3, 0xc6, 0xcc, 0xde, 0x33, 0x66, 0xcc, 0x0f},
        {0xc3, 0xc6, 0xcc, 0xdb, 0x37, 0x6f, 0xcf, 0x03},
        {0x18, 0x18, 0x00, 0x18, 0x18, 0x18, 0x18, 0x00},
        {0x00, 0x33, 0x66, 0xcc, 0x66, 0x33, 0x00, 0x00},
        {0x00, 0xcc, 0x66, 0x33, 0x66, 0xcc, 0x00, 0x00},
        {0x22, 0x88, 0x22, 0x88, 0x22, 0x88, 0x22, 0x88},
        {0x55, 0xaa, 0x55, 0xaa, 0x55, 0xaa, 0x55, 0xaa},
        {0xdb, 0x77, 0xdb, 0xee, 0xdb, 0x77, 0xdb, 0xee},
        {0x18, 0x18, 0x18, 0x18, 0x18, 0x18, 0x18, 0x18},
        {0x18, 0x18, 0x18, 0x18, 0xf8, 0x18, 0x18, 0x18},
        {0x18, 0x18, 0xf8, 0x18, 0xf8, 0x18, 0x18, 0x18},
        {0x36, 0x36, 0x36, 0x36, 0xf6, 0x36, 0x36, 0x36},
```

```
{0x00, 0x00, 0x00, 0x00, 0xfe, 0x36, 0x36, 0x36},
{0x00, 0x00, 0xf8, 0x18, 0xf8, 0x18, 0x18, 0x18},
{0x36, 0x36, 0xf6, 0x06, 0xf6, 0x36, 0x36, 0x36},
{0x36, 0x36, 0x36, 0x36, 0x36, 0x36, 0x36, 0x36},
{0x00, 0x00, 0xfe, 0x06, 0xf6, 0x36, 0x36, 0x36},
{0x36, 0x36, 0xf6, 0x06, 0xfe, 0x00, 0x00, 0x00},
{0x36, 0x36, 0x36, 0x36, 0xfe, 0x00, 0x00, 0x00},
{0x18, 0x18, 0xf8, 0x18, 0xf8, 0x00, 0x00, 0x00},
{0x00, 0x00, 0x00, 0x00, 0xf8, 0x18, 0x18, 0x18},
{0x18, 0x18, 0x18, 0x18, 0x1f, 0x00, 0x00, 0x00},
{0x18, 0x18, 0x18, 0x18, 0xff, 0x00, 0x00, 0x00},
{0x00, 0x00, 0x00, 0x00, 0xff, 0x18, 0x18, 0x18},
{0x18, 0x18, 0x18, 0x18, 0x1f, 0x18, 0x18, 0x18},
{0x00, 0x00, 0x00, 0x00, 0xff, 0x00, 0x00, 0x00},
{0x18, 0x18, 0x18, 0x18, 0xff, 0x18, 0x18, 0x18},
{0x18, 0x18, 0x1f, 0x18, 0x1f, 0x18, 0x18, 0x18},
{0x36, 0x36, 0x36, 0x36, 0x37, 0x36, 0x36, 0x36},
{0x36, 0x36, 0x37, 0x30, 0x3f, 0x00, 0x00, 0x00},
{0x00, 0x00, 0x3f, 0x30, 0x37, 0x36, 0x36, 0x36},
{0x36, 0x36, 0xf7, 0x00, 0xff, 0x00, 0x00, 0x00},
{0x00, 0x00, 0xff, 0x00, 0xf7, 0x36, 0x36, 0x36},
{0x36, 0x36, 0x37, 0x30, 0x37, 0x36, 0x36, 0x36},
{0x00, 0x00, 0xff, 0x00, 0xff, 0x00, 0x00, 0x00},
{0x36, 0x36, 0xf7, 0x00, 0xf7, 0x36, 0x36, 0x36},
{0x18, 0x18, 0xff, 0x00, 0xff, 0x00, 0x00, 0x00},
{0x36, 0x36, 0x36, 0x36, 0xff, 0x00, 0x00, 0x00},
{0x00, 0x00, 0xff, 0x00, 0xff, 0x18, 0x18, 0x18},
{0x00, 0x00, 0x00, 0x00, 0xff, 0x36, 0x36, 0x36},
{0x36, 0x36, 0x36, 0x36, 0x3f, 0x00, 0x00, 0x00},
{0x18, 0x18, 0x1f, 0x18, 0x1f, 0x00, 0x00, 0x00},
{0x00, 0x00, 0x1f, 0x18, 0x1f, 0x18, 0x18, 0x18},
{0x00, 0x00, 0x00, 0x00, 0x3f, 0x36, 0x36, 0x36},
{0x36, 0x36, 0x36, 0x36, 0xff, 0x36, 0x36, 0x36},
{0x18, 0x18, 0xff, 0x18, 0xff, 0x18, 0x18, 0x18},
{0x18, 0x18, 0x18, 0x18, 0xf8, 0x00, 0x00, 0x00},
{0x00, 0x00, 0x00, 0x00, 0x1f, 0x18, 0x18, 0x18},
{0xff, 0xff, 0xff, 0xff, 0xff, 0xff, 0xff, 0xff},
{0x00, 0x00, 0x00, 0x00, 0xff, 0xff, 0xff, 0xff},
{0xf0, 0xf0, 0xf0, 0xf0, 0xf0, 0xf0, 0xf0, 0xf0},
{0x0f, 0x0f, 0x0f, 0x0f, 0x0f, 0x0f, 0x0f, 0x0f},
{0xff, 0xff, 0xff, 0xff, 0x00, 0x00, 0x00, 0x00},
{0x00, 0x00, 0x76, 0xdc, 0xc8, 0xdc, 0x76, 0x00},
{0x00, 0x78, 0xcc, 0xf8, 0xcc, 0xf8, 0xc0, 0xc0},
{0x00, 0xfc, 0xcc, 0xc0, 0xc0, 0xc0, 0xc0, 0x00},
{0x00, 0xfe, 0x6c, 0x6c, 0x6c, 0x6c, 0x6c, 0x00},
{0xfc, 0xcc, 0x60, 0x30, 0x60, 0xcc, 0xfc, 0x00},
{0x00, 0x00, 0x7e, 0xd8, 0xd8, 0xd8, 0x70, 0x00},
{0x00, 0x66, 0x66, 0x66, 0x66, 0x7c, 0x60, 0xc0},
{0x00, 0x76, 0xdc, 0x18, 0x18, 0x18, 0x18, 0x00},
{0xfc, 0x30, 0x78, 0xcc, 0xcc, 0x78, 0x30, 0xfc},
{0x38, 0x6c, 0xc6, 0xfe, 0xc6, 0x6c, 0x38, 0x00},
{0x38, 0x6c, 0xc6, 0xc6, 0x6c, 0x6c, 0xee, 0x00},
{0x1c, 0x30, 0x18, 0x7c, 0xcc, 0xcc, 0x78, 0x00},
{0x00, 0x00, 0x7e, 0xdb, 0xdb, 0x7e, 0x00, 0x00},
```

```
            {0x06, 0x0c, 0x7e, 0xdb, 0xdb, 0x7e, 0x60, 0xc0},
            {0x38, 0x60, 0xc0, 0xf8, 0xc0, 0x60, 0x38, 0x00},
            {0x78, 0xcc, 0xcc, 0xcc, 0xcc, 0xcc, 0xcc, 0x00},
            {0x00, 0xfc, 0x00, 0xfc, 0x00, 0xfc, 0x00, 0x00},
            {0x30, 0x30, 0xfc, 0x30, 0x30, 0x00, 0xfc, 0x00},
            {0x60, 0x30, 0x18, 0x30, 0x60, 0x00, 0xfc, 0x00},
            {0x18, 0x30, 0x60, 0x30, 0x18, 0x00, 0xfc, 0x00},
            {0x0e, 0x1b, 0x1b, 0x18, 0x18, 0x18, 0x18, 0x18},
            {0x18, 0x18, 0x18, 0x18, 0x18, 0xd8, 0xd8, 0x70},
            {0x30, 0x30, 0x00, 0xfc, 0x00, 0x30, 0x30, 0x00},
            {0x00, 0x76, 0xdc, 0x00, 0x76, 0xdc, 0x00, 0x00},
            {0x38, 0x6c, 0x6c, 0x38, 0x00, 0x00, 0x00, 0x00},
            {0x00, 0x00, 0x00, 0x18, 0x18, 0x00, 0x00, 0x00},
            {0x00, 0x00, 0x00, 0x00, 0x18, 0x00, 0x00, 0x00},
            {0x0f, 0x0c, 0x0c, 0x0c, 0xec, 0x6c, 0x3c, 0x1c},
            {0x78, 0x6c, 0x6c, 0x6c, 0x6c, 0x00, 0x00, 0x00},
            {0x70, 0x18, 0x30, 0x60, 0x78, 0x00, 0x00, 0x00},
            {0x00, 0x00, 0x3c, 0x3c, 0x3c, 0x3c, 0x00, 0x00},
            {0x00, 0x00, 0x00, 0x00, 0x00, 0x00, 0x00, 0x00},
        };

    //————————————————————————

    public font_8x8(Graphics g)
      {
        this.g = g;
      }

    //————————————————————————

    public void draw_string(String string, int x, int y, int w, int h)
      {
        int string_length = string.length();
        char char_array [] = new char[string_length];
        string.getChars(0, string_length, char_array, 0);

        w /= string_length;

        for (int i = 0; i < string_length; i++)
          {
            draw_char(char_array[i], x, y, w, h);
            x += w;
          }
      }

    //————————————————————————

    private void draw_char(char c, int x, int y, int w, int h)
      {
        int index = (int) c;

        for (int i = 0; i < 8; i++)
          {
```

```
            for (int j = 0; j < 8; j++)
              {
                int bit = table[index][i] >> j;
                if ((bit & 1) == 1)
                  g.fillRect(x+(7-j)*w/8, y-(8-i)*h/9, w/8+1,
                          h/9+1);
              }
          }
        }
    }
```

BREAKING APART BITMAP CLOCK

The **Bitmap Clock** applet is very similar to the **LED Clock** applet you examined in Chapter 33. Therefore, this section will only examine the parts of the code that differ.

To start, the **Bitmap Clock** applet replaces the *LED* object with the *font_8x8* object:

```
font_8x8 font;
```

Within the *init* function, the applet creates the *font_8x8* object and passes the applet's graphics context to the object's constructor function:

```
font = new font_8x8(g);
```

Next, the *update* function displays time based on am/pm instead of a 24-hour military time. In other words, if it is morning, the clock appends the "am" letters to the current time. Likewise, in the afternoon, the clock appends the "pm" letters. To determine whether it is morning or afternoon, the function examines the *hours* variable:

```
boolean am;

if (hours < 12)
  am = true;
else
  {
    am = false;
    if (hours > 12)
      hours -= 12;
  }
```

As you can see, depending on the time of day, the function appends either the "am" or "pm" characters to the current time. Next, to display the time, the function calls the *font* object *draw_string* function:

```
if (am)
  time += "am";
else
  time += "pm";

g.setColor(Color.green);

font.draw_string("The time is:", 0, height/2, width, height/2);
font.draw_string(time, 0, height, width, height/2);
```

The Bitmap-Font Class

Because the bitmap-font class displays graphics, it must import the *java.awt* package:

```
import java.awt.*;
```

Class Variables

This bitmap-font class has only two variables: the first is the graphics context, and the second is the two-dimensional array that contains the bits for 256 characters. The array, called *table*, is *static* and *final*, which means that there is only one copy of the table (regardless of the number of instances) and its values will not change.

The first dimension of the *table* array corresponds to the character. The second dimension contains a row of bits for this character. Each character has eight rows of bytes, and each byte has, of course, eight bits, hence the 8x8 in the class name. The array definition starts as follows:

```
static final int table[][] =
 {
    {0x00, 0x00, 0x00, 0x00, 0x00, 0x00, 0x00, 0x00},
    {0x7e, 0x81, 0xa5, 0x81, 0xbd, 0x99, 0x81, 0x7e},
    {0x7e, 0xff, 0xdb, 0xff, 0xc3, 0xe7, 0xff, 0x7e},
```

and ends as follows:

```
    {0x70, 0x18, 0x30, 0x60, 0x78, 0x00, 0x00, 0x00},
    {0x00, 0x00, 0x3c, 0x3c, 0x3c, 0x3c, 0x00, 0x00},
    {0x00, 0x00, 0x00, 0x00, 0x00, 0x00, 0x00, 0x00},
 };
```

In between are the rest of the 250 characters.

The Class Constructor

The constructor function for the bitmap-font is quite simple. It receives a graphics context as a parameter and stores it into the local graphics-context variable:

```
public font_8x8(Graphics g)
   {
      this.g = g;
   }
```

Drawing the String

The *draw_string* function performs the same function as in the *LED* class: it accepts the string to display, the x-and-y coordinates of the bottom-left of the area within which it displays the string, and the width and height of the area to use. The function assumes that the color has already been set by the calling object:

```
public void draw_string(String string, int x, int y, int w, int h)
```

To start, the function breaks apart the string into individual characters:

```
int string_length = string.length();
char char_array [] = new char[string_length];
string.getChars(0, string_length, char_array, 0);
```

Next, the function divides the width of the string with the number of characters to determine the width of each character:

```
w /= string_length;
```

Lastly, the function uses a *for* loop to draw each character by calling the *draw_char* function. After the function draws a character, it increments the x-coordinate to determine the location at which the next character will be drawn:

```
for (int i = 0; i < string_length; i++)
  {
    draw_char(char_array[i], x, y, w, h);
    x += w;
  }
```

Drawing Each Character

The *draw_char* function is a *private* function that accepts as parameters the character to draw, the x-and-y coordinates at which it will display the character, and the character's width and height:

```
private void draw_char(char c, int x, int y, int w, int h)
```

To determine the location of the character's font within the bitmap-font array, the function uses the character's ASCII value as an index:

```
int index = (int) c;
```

Then, the function loops through each row and each bit in the character table:

```
for (int i = 0; i < 8; i++)
  {
    for (int j = 0; j < 8; j++)
      {
```

If the current bit is set, the function fills a rectangle at the proper spot. If the bit is not set, the function leaves the corresponding rectangle blank. The function divides the height of the character by 9, even though there are only 8 rows, because the ninth row provides spacing:

```
int bit = table[index][i] >> j;
if ((bit & 1) == 1)
  g.fillRect(x+(7-j)*w/8, y-(8-i)*h/9, w/8+1, h/9+1);
```

ENHANCEMENTS YOU CAN MAKE TO BITMAP FONT CLOCK

Add a function that allows you to draw the mirror image of a character. Change each bit from filling a rectangle to a small circle. This will create a ticker-like font.

PUTTING IT ALL TOGETHER

The **Bitmap Font Clock** applet shows you how to manipluate bitmap objects. Although this applet uses the bitmap font to display a clock, you can use the bitmap font to display the text for any application. Your advantage in using the bitmap font is that you can easily scale the font on the fly. In Chapter 35, you will learn how to rotate two-dimensional graphics objects. Then, in Chapter 36, you will revisit the bitmap font, learning how to rotate the font text. Before you continue with Chapter 35, however, make sure you understand the following key concepts:

- ☑ By creating a bitmap-font class, you provide applets with an easy way to display scaleable text.

- ☑ The bitmap font presented in this chapter uses an 8x8 bitmap for the 256 characters used by the IBM-PC and PC-compatible computer.

- ☑ Bitmapped fonts are so named because they use a series of bits to define the font's appearance.

CHAPTER 35

ROTATE CLASS
ROTATING 2-D OBJECTS

As you use Java to create animations, you will eventually need to rotate an object on your screen. If you examine any books on graphics programming, you may be surprised to learn that it is actually quite easy to rotate a two-dimensional object. In fact, this chapter presents the code you need in order to rotate objects. What makes this chapter unique is that it shows you how to create a rotate class, with which you can rotate any object about a specific origin and at a specific angle of rotation. By the time you finish the chapter, you will understand the following key concepts:

◆ You can create another graphics class that will allow you to rotate 2-D objects.

◆ By using trigonometric functions, you can rotate objects around a specified origin.

USING ROTATE CLASS

When you run the **Rotate Class** applet, you will see a window that contains a few graphics objects, as shown in Figure 35.1.

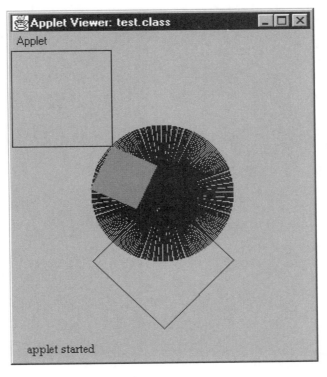

Figure 35.1 Graphics objects drawn using the rotate class.

THE HTML FILE

Use the following HTML file to run the **Rotate Class** applet:

```
<applet code=test.class width=300 height=300> </applet>
```

LOOKING AT THE ROTATE CLASS

The *test* applet contains two classes. The first is the applet, and the second is the rotate class.

The Applet

The **Rotate Class** applet contains code that uses the rotate class (*Graphics_R*) to display images to the screen. With respect to the drawing functions, *Graphics_r* is identical to the standard *Graphics* class in that they both use *drawLine*, *setColor*, *fillPolygon*, and so on. The difference between the two classes is that using the *Graphics_R* class, the applet can use the origin and angle methods to rotate about the origin. The following code implements the **Rotate Class** applet:

```
//******************************************************************
// test.java
//******************************************************************

import java.applet.*;
import java.awt.*;

//******************************************************************

public class test extends Applet
  {
    public void paint(Graphics g)
      {
        g.setColor(Color.black);

        Graphics_R g2 = new Graphics_R(g);

        g2.drawLine(  0,   0, 100,   0);
        g2.drawLine(100,   0, 100, 100);
        g2.drawLine(100, 100,   0, 100);
        g2.drawLine(  0, 100,   0,   0);

        g2.origin(150, 150);
        g2.angle(45.0);

        g2.drawLine(  0,   0, 100,   0);
        g2.drawLine(100,   0, 100, 100);
        g2.drawLine(100, 100,   0, 100);
        g2.drawLine(  0, 100,   0,   0);

        for (double x = 0.0; x < 360.0; x += 1.0)
          {
            g2.angle(x);
            g2.drawLine(0, 0, 50, 50);
          }
```

```
         g2.origin(100, 100);
         g2.angle(25.0);

         int x[] = new int[4];
         int y[] = new int[4];

         x[0] =  0;  y[0] =  0;
         x[1] = 50;  y[1] =  0;
         x[2] = 50;  y[2] = 50;
         x[3] =  0;  y[3] = 50;

         g2.setColor(Color.green);
         g2.fillPolygon(x, y, 4);
      }
   }
```

The Rotate Class

As briefly discussed, the rotate class *Graphics_R* contains functions that let you define an origin and an angle. Then subsequent graphics operations will be drawn at that angle from the origin specified. A few functions are implemented here to give you an idea of how to draw rotated graphics objects. With this existing class, you can draw lines and fill polygons. The following code implements the rotate class:

```
//******************************************************************
// Graphics_R.java
//******************************************************************

import java.awt.*;

//******************************************************************

public class Graphics_R
  {
    Graphics g;

    int ox = 0;
    int oy = 0;

    double radians = 0.0;
    double cos = 1.0;
    double sin = 0.0;

    //─────────────────────────────────

    public Graphics_R(Graphics g)
      {
        this.g = g.create();
      }

    //─────────────────────────────────
```

```
    public void origin(int x, int y)
      {
        ox = x;
        oy = y;
      }

    //————————————————————

    public void angle(double a)
      {
        radians = (a * 2 * Math.PI) / 360;

        cos = Math.cos(radians);
        sin = Math.sin(radians);
      }

    //————————————————————

    public void setColor(Color c)
      {
        g.setColor(c);
      }

    //————————————————————

    int rotate_x(int x, int y)
      {
        return ((int) (ox + x * cos - y * sin));
      }

    //————————————————————

    int rotate_y(int x, int y)
      {
        return ((int) (oy + y * cos + x * sin));
      }

    //————————————————————

    public void drawLine(int x1, int y1, int x2, int y2)
      {
        g.drawLine(rotate_x(x1, y1),
                   rotate_y(x1, y1),
                   rotate_x(x2, y2),
                   rotate_y(x2, y2));
      }

    //————————————————————

    public void fillPolygon(int x[], int y[], int n)
      {
        int new_x[] = new int[n];
        int new_y[] = new int[n];
```

```
        for (int i = 0; i < n; i++)
          {
          new_x[i] = rotate_x(x[i], y[i]);
          new_y[i] = rotate_y(x[i], y[i]);
          }

        g.fillPolygon(new_x, new_y, n);
      }
  }
```

BREAKING APART THE ROTATE CLASS

Since there are two classes for this program, this section will examine the applet first, followed by the rotate class.

The Applet

The rotate class contains only one function: the *paint* function. In this function, you will draw some objects, rotate them, and then draw some more objects:

```
public void paint(Graphics g)
```

First, the function creates a new graphics object based on the rotate class *Graphics_R*. As you can see, the *paint* function passes the current graphics context to the new rotate-class object. Next, *paint* sets the current color to black:

```
Graphics_R g2 = new Graphics_R(g);

g.setColor(Color.black);
```

Second, by drawing four separate lines with connecting end-points, *paint* draws a 100x100 box with no rotation:

```
g2.drawLine(  0,   0, 100,   0);
g2.drawLine(100,   0, 100, 100);
g2.drawLine(100, 100,   0, 100);
g2.drawLine(  0, 100,   0,   0);
```

Then, using the new *Graphics_R* class *origin* and *angle* methods, *paint* selects an origin of (150,150) and a rotation angle of 45 degrees:

```
g2.origin(150, 150);
g2.angle(45.0);
```

Next, the *paint* function will redraw the same 100x100 box just shown. This time, however, the box will show up with its origin at (150, 150) and rotated 45 degrees:

```
g2.drawLine(  0,   0, 100,   0);
g2.drawLine(100,   0, 100, 100);
g2.drawLine(100, 100,   0, 100);
g2.drawLine(  0, 100,   0,   0);
```

The *paint* function then uses a loop that changes the angle of rotation from 0 to 360 and draws a line for each angle. The loop creates the effect of an almost solid circle:

```
for (double x = 0.0; x < 360.0; x += 1.0)
  {
    g2.angle(x);
    g2.drawLine(0, 0, 60, 0);
  }
```

Then, *paint* resets the origin to (100, 100), and the rotatation angle to 25 degrees:

```
g2.origin(100, 100);
g2.angle(25.0);
```

Finally, *paint* creates a polygon with four points, sets the color to green, and draws the polygon. This polygon is simply a 50x50 box that will show up at (100, 100) rotated 25 degrees and filled with the green color:

```
int x[] = new int[4];
int y[] = new int[4];

x[0] =  0;   y[0] =  0;
x[1] = 50;   y[1] =  0;
x[2] = 50;   y[2] = 50;
x[3] =  0;   y[3] = 50;

g2.setColor(Color.green);
g2.fillPolygon(x, y, 4);
```

The Rotate Class

To start, the class declares a variable to hold its graphics context. The class will get the value for this graphics context from the parameter passed to the constructor by the object using this class:

```
Graphics g;
```

Next, the class declares variables that will hold the origin coordinates around which it will rotate objects:

```
int ox = 0;
int oy = 0;
```

The class then declares the variables it will use with the trigonometric functions to rotate lines and polygons:

```
double radians = 0.0;
double cos = 1.0;
double sin = 0.0;
```

The Constructor

The rotate class constructor is pretty simple. It receives, as a parameter, the graphics context of the applet using this class, and then creates a copy of it for use in this class:

```
public Graphics_R(Graphics g)
  {
    this.g = g.create();
  }
```

Setting the Origin and Angle

When you rotate anything, you must know the point about which you will rotate around, and at what angle to rotate. Therefore, the rotate class provides two functions: one to set the origin and the other to get the angle of rotation.

Setting the origin requires an x-coordinate and a y-coordinate. Save these values in the local variables *ox* and *oy*:

```
public void origin(int x, int y)
  {
    ox = x;
    oy = y;
  }
```

Setting an angle of rotation requires, of course, the angle. To start, the function must convert the angle into radians. Then, it must determine the sine and cosine values for this angle. It is better to calculate the angle's sine and cosine values here instead of when you rotate the object, because you might need to rotate many points with the same angle value:

```
public void angle(double a)
  {
    radians = (a * 2 * Math.PI) / 360;

    cos = Math.cos(radians);
    sin = Math.sin(radians);
  }
```

Rotating the X-and-Y Coordinates

This section examines the processing the rotate class performs to rotate lines and other objects. As you examine the following expressions, use the points and angles shown in Figure 35.2 to better understand the processing.

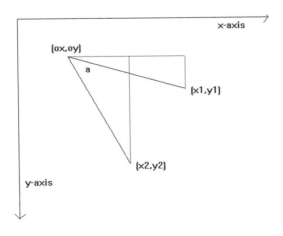

Figure 35.2 Rotating (x1,y1) to (x2,y2) around the origin (ox,oy).

309

Assume (x1,y1) is a relative point from (ox,oy), and you rotate it using angle *a*. To calculate the point (x2,y2), which is also relative to (ox,oy), you would use the following formula:

```
x2 = x1 * cos(a) - y1 * sin(a)


y2 = y1 * cos(a) + x1 * sin(a)
```

To get the actual coordinates for (x2,y2), you must add *ox* to the x-coordinate, and *oy* to the y-coordinate. The rotate class will use the following function to rotate the x-coordinate:

```
int rotate_x(int x, int y)
  {
    return ((int) (ox + x * cos - y * sin));
  }
```

Likewise, the class will use the function to rotate the y-coordinate:

```
int rotate_y(int x, int y)
  {
    return ((int) (oy + y * cos + x * sin));
  }
```

Drawing a Rotated Line

To draw a rotated line, you have to get the two points to connect. In this function, those points are (x1,y1) and (x2,y2). Using these coordinates, you can call the real *drawLine* function of the graphics context and pass it the rotated x-and-y coordinates:

```
public void drawLine(int x1, int y1, int x2, int y2)
  {
    g.drawLine(rotate_x(x1, y1),
               rotate_y(x1, y1),
               rotate_x(x2, y2),
               rotate_y(x2, y2));
  }
```

Filling a Rotated Polygon

To fill a rotated polygon, you need the array of x-coordinates, the array of y-coordinates, and the number of points the array contains. Using these parameters, you can create two arrays that will contain the rotated coordinates. Then, you can iterate through each point and rotate it. Finally, you can call the real *fillPolygon* function of the graphics context and pass to it the new (rotated) arrays and the number of points in the arrays:

```
public void fillPolygon(int x[], int y[], int n)
  {
    int new_x[] = new int[n];
    int new_y[] = new int[n];

    for (int i = 0; i < n; i++)
```

```
    {
    new_x[i] = rotate_x(x[i], y[i]);
    new_y[i] = rotate_y(x[i], y[i]);
    }

  g.fillPolygon(new_x, new_y, n);
}
```

ENHANCEMENTS YOU CAN MAKE TO ROTATE CLASS

To enhance the rotate class, add other graphics functions. To start, add *drawRect*, *fillRect*, and *drawPolygon* functions.

PUTTING IT ALL TOGETHER

The rotate class shows you how to create a class that lets you rotate 2-D objects. As you learned, by creating the rotate class, you can easily rotate existing objects by changing only a few lines of code in your applets. In Chapter 36, for example, you will use the rotate class to rotate the **Bitmap Clock** that you created in Chapter 34. Before you continue with Chapter 36, however, make sure you understand the following key concepts:

☑ By creating a rotate class, you simplify common 2-D graphics operations.

☑ For a rotate class to be successful, the class must be easy to use. In the case of the *Graphics_R* class presented here, the programmer could continue to use the graphics functions with which they are already familiar.

CHAPTER 36

ROTATED BITMAP CLOCK
ROTATING A BITMAP FONT

In Chapter 35, you learned how to rotate graphics objects using the *rotate* class. In Chapter 34, you learned how to create and use a bitmap font. In this chapter, you will combine these concepts to create a bitmap font that your applets can rotate. Using the rotated bitmap font, for example, you could display text along a window at a 90-degree angle. By the time you finish this chapter, you will understand the following key concepts:

- ◆ You can modify the bitmap-font class to use the rotate class.

- ◆ To display text using the rotated bitmap-font class, you specify the text, its origin, and an angle at which the class will draw the text.

USING ROTATED BITMAP CLOCK

When you run the **Rotated Bitmap Clock** applet, you will see a window with a rotated clock, as shown in Figure 36.

Figure 36 A rotated bitmap-font clock.

THE HTML FILE

Use the following HTML file to run the **Rotated Bitmap Clock** applet:

```
<applet code=clock.class width=400 height=400> </applet>
```

In this case, the HTML entries are very simple. Depending on your application, you may want to include HTML settings that specify the desired string as well as the angle of rotation.

LOOKING AT ROTATED BITMAP CLOCK

The **Rotated Bitmap Clock** applet uses three classes: the *Clock* applet, the bitmap-font class, and the *rotate* class.

The Rotated Bitmap Clock Applet

As you will find, the *clock* class is similar to the **Bitmap Font Clock** applet presented in Chapter 34. The main difference between the two is in the *update* function, where the class must now specify the origin and the angle for the rotation. The following code implements the *clock* applet:

```java
//*************************************************************
// clock.java
//*************************************************************

import java.applet.*;
import java.awt.*;
import java.util.Date;


//*************************************************************

public class clock extends Applet implements Runnable
  {
    Graphics g;
    font_8x8 font;

    Thread my_thread;

    int width;
    int height;
    Date current_time;

    //————————————————————————

    public void init()
      {
        g = getGraphics();

        font = new font_8x8(g);

        current_time = new Date();

        set_defaults();
      }

    //————————————————————————
```

```java
  void set_defaults ()
    {
      width  = size().width;
      height = size().height;
    }

//————————————————————————————

public void start()
  {
    if (my_thread == null)
      {
        my_thread = new Thread(this);
        my_thread.start();
      }
  }

//————————————————————————————

public void stop()
  {
    my_thread.stop();
    my_thread = null;
  }

//————————————————————————————

public void run()
  {
    while (my_thread != null)
      {
        repaint();

        try
          {
            Thread.sleep(1000);
          }
        catch (InterruptedException e)
          {
          }
      }
  }

//————————————————————————————

public void update(Graphics _g)
  {
    g.setColor(Color.black);
    g.fillRect(0, 0, width, height);

    current_time = new Date();

    int hours   = current_time.getHours();
    int minutes = current_time.getMinutes();
```

```
        int seconds = current_time.getSeconds();

    String time;
    boolean am;

    if (hours < 12)
      am = true;
    else
      {
        am = false;
        if (hours > 12)
          hours -= 12;
      }

    if (hours < 10)
      time = "0" + hours;
    else
      time = "" + hours;

    if (minutes < 10)
      time += ":0" + minutes;
    else
      time += ":" + minutes;

    if (seconds < 10)
      time += ":0" + seconds;
    else
      time += ":" + seconds;

    if (am)
      time += "am";
    else
      time += "pm";

    font.set_color(Color.green);

    font.origin(100, 100);
    font.angle(45.0);

    font.draw_string("The time is:", 0, 50, 300, 50);
    font.draw_string(time, 0, 100, 300, 50);
  }

//————————————————————————————————

public void paint(Graphics g)
  {
    set_defaults();
    update(g);
  }
}
```

The Bitmap-Font Class

The bitmap-font class presented here is similar to the class you examined in Chapter 34. The main difference between the two is that this class uses the *Graphics_R* object instead of the *Graphics* object to perform graphics. The following code implements the bitmap-font class. To save pages, we have removed the bitmap table. However, if you examine the source-code file that resides on the CD-ROM that accompanies this book, you will find the table:

```java
//******************************************************************
// font_8x8.java
//******************************************************************

import java.awt.*;

//******************************************************************

public class font_8x8
   {
     private Graphics_R g;

     //————————————————————————————————
     //                bitmap table removed - see chapter 34
     //————————————————————————————————

     public font_8x8(Graphics g)
       {
         this.g = new Graphics_R(g);
       }

     //————————————————————————————————

     public void set_color(Color c)
       {
         g.setColor(c);
       }

     //————————————————————————————————

     public void origin(int x, int y)
       {
         g.origin(x, y);
       }

     //————————————————————————————————

     public void angle(double a)
       {
         g.angle(a);
       }

     //————————————————————————————————

     public void draw_string(String string, int x, int y, int w, int h)
       {
         int string_length = string.length();
         char char_array[] = new char[string_length];
```

```
        string.getChars(0, string_length, char_array, 0);

        w /= string_length;

        for (int i = 0; i < string_length; i++)
          {
            draw_char(char_array[i], x, y, w, h);
            x += w;
          }
      }

    //————————————————————————————

    public void draw_char(char c, int x, int y, int w, int h)
      {
        int index = (int) c;

        for (int i = 0; i < 8; i++)
          {
          for (int j = 0; j < 8; j++)
            {
              int bit = table[index][i] >> j;
              if ((bit & 1) == 1)
                 g.fillRect(x+(7-j)*w/8, y-(8-i)*h/9, w/8+1, h/9+1);
            }
          }
      }
  }
```

The rotate Class

The *rotate* class presented here is similar to the one you examined in Chapter 35. The main difference between the two is that the *rotate* class presented here adds the *fillRect* function. The following code implements the *rotate* class:

```
//*****************************************************************
// Graphics_R.java
//*****************************************************************

import java.awt.*;

//*****************************************************************

public class Graphics_R
  {
    Graphics g;

    int ox = 0;
    int oy = 0;

    double radians = 0.0;
    double cos = 1.0;
    double sin = 0.0;

    //————————————————————————————
```

```java
public Graphics_R(Graphics g)
  {
    this.g = g.create();
  }

//————————————————————

public void origin(int x, int y)
  {
    ox = x;
    oy = y;
  }

//————————————————————

public void angle(double a)
  {
    radians = (a * 2 * Math.PI) / 360;

    cos = Math.cos(radians);
    sin = Math.sin(radians);
  }

//————————————————————

public void setColor(Color c)
  {
    g.setColor(c);
  }

//————————————————————

int rotate_x(int x, int y)
  {
    return ((int) (ox + x * cos - y * sin));
  }

//————————————————————

int rotate_y(int x, int y)
  {
    return ((int) (oy + y * cos + x * sin));
  }

//————————————————————

public void drawLine(int x1, int y1, int x2, int y2)
  {
    g.drawLine(rotate_x(x1, y1),
               rotate_y(x1, y1),
               rotate_x(x2, y2),
               rotate_y(x2, y2));
  }

//————————————————————
```

```
   public void fillPolygon(int x[], int y[], int n)
     {
       int new_x[] = new int[n];
       int new_y[] = new int[n];

       for (int i = 0; i < n; i++)
         {
           new_x[i] = rotate_x(x[i], y[i]);
           new_y[i] = rotate_y(x[i], y[i]);
         }

       g.fillPolygon(new_x, new_y, n);
     }


   //——————————————————————————

   public void fillRect(int x, int y, int w, int h)
     {
       int new_x[] = new int[4];
       int new_y[] = new int[4];

       new_x[0] = x  ;   new_y[0] = y  ;
       new_x[1] = x+w;   new_y[1] = y  ;
       new_x[2] = x+w;   new_y[2] = y+h;
       new_x[3] = x  ;   new_y[3] = y+h;

       fillPolygon(new_x, new_y, 4);
     }
 }
```

BREAKING APART ROTATED BITMAP CLOCK

The only difference between this applet and the **Bitmap Font Clock** applet you examined in Chapter 34 is at the tail end of the *update* function. In the applet in Chapter 34, the bitmap-font's *draw_string* function was called using the width and the height of the window. In this applet, however, you must first set the origin around which the graphics will rotate, and then set the angle of rotation. Then, you can draw the time strings at specific coordinates:

```
font.origin(100, 100);
font.angle(45.0);

font.draw_string("The time is:", 0, 50, 300, 50);
font.draw_string(time, 0, 100, 300, 50);
```

The Bitmap-Font Class

The bitmap-font class presented here is very similar to the class you examined in Chapter 34. In this class, however, instead of using a *Graphics* object for the graphics context, the class uses a *Graphics_R* object, which contains the rotate functions:

```
private Graphics_R g;
```

The *Graphics_R* class adds three functions to the *Graphics* class. The first function, *set_color*, sets the color for the bitmap font:

```
public void set_color(Color c)
   {
      g.setColor(c);
   }
```

The second function, *origin*, sets the x-and-y coordinates for an object's origin:

```
public void origin(int x, int y)
   {
      g.origin(x, y);
   }
```

The third function, *angle*, sets the font's angle of rotation:

```
public void angle(double a)
   {
      g.angle(a);
   }
```

The rotate Class

The *rotate* class presented here adds one function to those you examined in Chapter 35: the *fillRect* function. The class requires this function for the bitmap font.

As you can see, the *fillRect* function uses the local *fillPolygon* function to fill the arrays, as opposed to *g.fillPolygon*. Because the rotated rectangle can only be drawn as a polygon, not as a rectangle, the function creates the four points that define this rectangle, and then calls the local *fillPolygon* function, which, in turn, rotates the points and calls the real *fillPolygon* function:

```
public void fillRect(int x, int y, int w, int h)
   {
      int new_x[] = new int[4];
      int new_y[] = new int[4];

      new_x[0] = x   ;  new_y[0] = y   ;
      new_x[1] = x+w;   new_y[1] = y   ;
      new_x[2] = x+w;   new_y[2] = y+h;
      new_x[3] = x   ;  new_y[3] = y+h;

      fillPolygon(new_x, new_y, 4);
   }
```

ENHANCEMENTS YOU CAN MAKE TO ROTATED BITMAP FONT

As discussed, one of you advantages to using bitmap fonts is that you can scale them. Therefore, modify this program so it resizes the strings as the applet window is resized.

Putting It All Together

The **Rotated Bitmap Clock** applet shows how to combine multiple classes to build a complex program. Do not consider this chapter simply a programming exercise. As you create Java applets, there will be times when you need to display rotated text. Using the classes presented here, you can quickly display any text (not just a clock) rotated at any angle you require. In Chapter 37, you will examine recursion within Java as you look at a programming classic (the Tower of Hanoi) in a new light (visually, with the Java *Graphics* object). Before you continue with Chapter 37, however, make sure you understand the following key concepts:

- ☑ By combining the bitmap-font and *rotate* classes, you can create a bitmap-font you can rotate.

- ☑ When you use the rotated bitmap-font class, you specify the origin and an angle to use to draw a string's characters.

CHAPTER 37

TOWER OF HANOI
USING RECURSION WITH GRAPHICS IN JAVA

For years, programmers have written different algorithms to the classic programming problem presented by the Tower of Hanoi. To review the problem, the programmer is presented with two or more disks, which are stacked from largest to smallest on one tower. The programmer must move the disks to a second tower (using a temporary tower), again stacking the disks from largest to smallest. However, as the programmer moves the disks, the programmer must always place each disk onto a tower and can never place a larger disk on top of a smaller disk. In short, the programmer must find an algorithm that lets them shuffle the disks on the towers in such a way that they never put a larger disk on top of a smaller one. In this chapter, you will learn how to use *recursion* (where a Java function calls itself to solve a task). In addition, you will use the Java *Graphics* class to draw and move the disks that sit on the Tower of Hanoi. By the time you finish this chapter, you will understand the following key concepts:

- ◆ You can use the *Vector* class to hold a list of values.

- ◆ A recursive function is a function that calls itself to solve a specific task.

- ◆ The *Thread* class contains an *isAlive* function, which you can use to check if the thread is still running or if it has stopped.

USING TOWER OF HANOI

When you run the **Tower of Hanoi** applet, you will see a window with an image and three towers and disks, as shown in Figure 37.1. When you click on the screen, the program will start solving the problem by moving the disks, as shown in Figure 37.2. The best way to understand the solution to the **Tower of Hanoi** problem is to watch how the applet moves the disks from tower to tower.

Figure 37.1 The Tower of Hanoi initial screen.

Figure 37.2 *The Tower of Hanoi applet running.*

THE HTML FILE

The HTML file for the **Tower of Hanoi** applet contains two parameters: TOTAL, which contains the number of disks to use; and DELAY, which specifies the amount of time the applet waits (in milliseconds) between each move of a disk:

```
<applet code=hanoi.class width=320 height=200>
<param name=total value=5>
<param name=delay value=50>
</applet>
```

LOOKING AT TOWER OF HANOI

The **Tower of Hanoi** program contains two classes. The first class is the *hanoi* applet, and the second class is the *tower* object. The *hanoi* applet will create three instances of the *tower* object (one for each tower), which will hold the disks.

The hanoi Applet

The *hanoi* applet paints the background image and then tells each of the *tower* objects to paint themselves. When you click your mouse on the applet window, the *hanoi* applet starts the thread to solve the **Tower of Hanoi** problem. The following code implements the *hanoi* applet:

```
//*******************************************************************
// hanoi.java
//*******************************************************************
```

```java
import java.applet.*;
import java.awt.*;

//******************************************************************

public class hanoi extends Applet implements Runnable
  {
    Graphics g;

    static public Image background;

    static public int width;
    static public int height;

    static public int delay = 500;

    private boolean done_loading_image = false;

    private int total_disks = 5;

    private Thread my_thread;

    private boolean thread_started = false;

    tower t[];

    int from_tower = 0;
    int to_tower   = 2;

    //─────────────────────────────────────

    public void init()
      {
        g = getGraphics();

        String parameter;

        parameter = getParameter("TOTAL");
        if (parameter != null)
          total_disks = Integer.parseInt(parameter);

        parameter = getParameter("DELAY");
        if (parameter != null)
          delay = Integer.parseInt(parameter);

        width  = size().width;
        height = size().height;

        background = getImage(getCodeBase(), "egypt.gif");

        Image offScrImage = createImage(width, height);
        Graphics offScrGC = offScrImage.getGraphics();
        offScrGC.drawImage(background, 0, 0, this);
```

```java
        t = new tower[3];

      t[0] = new tower(g);
      t[1] = new tower(g);
      t[2] = new tower(g);

      for (int i = 0; i < total_disks; i++)
        t[0].add(i);
    }

  //————————————————————————

  public boolean imageUpdate(Image img, int infoflags, int x, int y,
                             int width, int height)
    {
      if (infoflags == ALLBITS)
        {
          done_loading_image = true;
          repaint();
          return false;
        }
      else
        return true;
    }

  //————————————————————————

  public void paint(Graphics g)
    {
      if (!done_loading_image)
        showStatus("Tower of Hanoi:  loading image");

      else
        {
          if (thread_started)
            if (my_thread.isAlive())
              showStatus("Tower of Hanoi:  Running");
            else
              showStatus("Tower of Hanoi:  Click again to restart");
          else
            showStatus("Tower of Hanoi:  Click to start");

          width  = size().width;
          height = size().height;

          g.drawImage(background, 0, 0, width, height, this);

          int x_inc = width / 10;

          t[0].paint(x_inc*1, x_inc*2, height);
          t[1].paint(x_inc*4, x_inc*2, height);
          t[2].paint(x_inc*7, x_inc*2, height);
        }
    }

  //————————————————————————
```

```
      public boolean mouseDown(Event evt, int x, int y)
        {
          if (!thread_started || !my_thread.isAlive())
            {
              my_thread = new Thread(this);
              my_thread.start();
              showStatus("Tower of Hanoi:  Running");
              thread_started = true;
            }

          return true;
        }

    //—————————————————————————

    public void run()
        {
          move_tower(total_disks, from_tower, to_tower, 1);

          int temp = to_tower;
          to_tower = from_tower;
          from_tower = temp;

          showStatus("Tower of Hanoi:  Click again to restart");
        }

    //—————————————————————————

    private void move_tower(int disks, int from, int to, int using)
        {
          if (height > 0)
            {
              move_tower(disks-1, from, using, to);
              move_disk(from, to);
              move_tower(disks-1, using, to, from);
            }
        }

    //—————————————————————————

    private void move_disk(int from, int to)
        {
          int disk = t[from].pop();
          t[to].push(disk, from);
        }
    }
```

The tower Class

The *tower* class keeps track of the disks for a specific tower. The class contains functions to add and remove disks. It also contains the functions to draw a disk as it moves up and down the tower, and to erase the disks as they move:

```
//******************************************************************
// tower.java
//******************************************************************

import java.awt.*;
import java.util.Vector;

//******************************************************************

public class tower
  {
    Graphics g;

    Vector v;

    int x;
    int y;
    int w;
    int d;

    //————————————————————————————

    tower(Graphics g)
      {
        this.g = g;

        v = new Vector();
      }

    //————————————————————————————

    public void add(int i)
      {
        Integer I = new Integer(i);

        v.addElement(I);
      }

    //————————————————————————————

    public int pop()
      {
        int disk = ((Integer) (v.lastElement())).intValue();
        int size = v.size();

        move_disk_up(size, disk);
        v.removeElementAt(size - 1);

        return(disk);
      }

    //————————————————————————————
```

```java
    public void push(int i, int from)
      {
        Integer I = new Integer(i);

        v.addElement(I);

        int size = v.size();

        move_disk_down(size, i);
      }

  //——————————————————————

    public void paint(int _x, int _w, int h)
      {
        x = _x;
        w = _w;
        y = h / 20;
        d = w / 20;

        draw_holders(g);

        int number_of_disks = v.size();
        if (number_of_disks == 0)
          return;

        for (int i = 0; i < number_of_disks; i++)
          {
            int j = ((Integer) (v.elementAt(i))).intValue();
            draw_disk(x+j*d, y*(18-i), w-2*j*d, y);
          }
      }

  //——————————————————————

  void draw_holders(Graphics g)
    {
      g.setColor(Color.green);
      g.fillRect(x, y*19, w, y/5);
      g.fillRect(x+w/2-w/20, y*2, w/10, y*17);
      g.setColor(Color.black);
    }

  //——————————————————————

  void delay()
    {
      try
        {
          Thread.sleep(hanoi.delay);
        }
      catch (InterruptedException e)
        {
        }
    }

  //——————————————————————
```

```java
void move_disk_up(int size, int disk)
  {
    erase_disk(x+disk*d, y*(19-size), w-2*disk*d, y);

    for (int i = y*(18-size); i >= y; i-=y)
      {
        draw_disk(x+disk*d, i, w-2*disk*d, y);
        delay();
        erase_disk(x+disk*d, i, w-2*disk*d, y);
      }
  }

//————————————————————————

void move_disk_down(int size, int disk)
  {
    for (int i = y; i < y*(19-size); i+=y)
      {
        draw_disk(x+disk*d, i, w-2*disk*d, y);
        delay();
        erase_disk(x+disk*d, i, w-2*disk*d, y);
      }

    draw_disk(x+disk*d, y*(19-size), w-2*disk*d, y);
  }

//————————————————————————

void draw_disk(int x, int y, int w, int h)
  {
    g.setColor(Color.black);
    g.fillRect(x, y, w-1, h-1);

    g.setColor(Color.white);
    g.drawRect(x, y, w-1, h-1);

    g.setColor(Color.black);
  }

//————————————————————————

void erase_disk(int x, int y, int w, int h)
  {
    Graphics g2;
    g2 = g.create();

    g2.clipRect(x, y, w, h);

    g2.drawImage(hanoi.background,
                 0, 0,
                 hanoi.width, hanoi.height,
                 null);
```

```
        draw_holders(g2);
    }
}
```

BREAKING APART TOWERS OF HANOI

This section will explain the two classes separately. First will be the *hanoi* applet, and then the *tower* class.

The hanoi Applet

Like most of the applets this book presents, the *hanoi* applet uses the *applet* and *awt* packages:

```
import java.applet.*;
import java.awt.*;
```

Class Variables

To start, the applet defines a variable to store the applet's graphics context:

```
Graphics g;
```

The applet declares four variables as *static* because it needs them only once for this class, and so the *tower* class can have access to them without using an instance of the *hanoi* class. These variables are the background image, the width and height of the window, and the time delay between redrawing the disks when they move:

```
static public Image background;
static public int width;
static public int height;
static public int delay = 500;
```

The applet then declares several *private* variables it uses to keep track of whether the image has finished loading, the total number of disks, the thread variable that corresponds to the thread that will solve the **Tower of Hanoi** problem, a variable to tell you when the thread is running, and an array of *tower* objects, which will keep track of the three towers:

```
private boolean done_loading_image = false;

private int total_disks = 5;

private Thread my_thread;
private boolean thread_running = false;

tower t[];
```

Finally, the applet declares two variables that tell it the *from-tower* (towers are numbered 0, 1, and 2) and the *to-tower* for disk-move operations. In other words, the applet might move a disk *from* tower 0 *to* tower 2:

```
int from_tower = 0;
int to_tower   = 2;
```

Initializing the Applet

Within the *init* function, the applet first gets the graphics context and the parameter values from the HTML file:

```
g = getGraphics();

String parameter;

parameter = getParameter("TOTAL");
if (parameter != null)
  total_disks = Integer.parseInt(parameter);

parameter = getParameter("DELAY");
if (parameter != null)
  delay = Integer.parseInt(parameter);
```

Next, the applet determines the width and height of the applet window, gets the background image, and starts drawing the image off screen. Using the *this* keyword as a parameter to the *drawImage* function, the applet gets the image-loading thread to call the applet's *imageUpdate* function as it loads the image:

```
width  = size().width;
height = size().height;

background = getImage(getCodeBase(), "x.gif");

Image offScrImage = createImage(width, height);
Graphics offScrGC = offScrImage.getGraphics();
offScrGC.drawImage(background, 0, 0, this);
```

Finally, the *init* function allocates space for three towers, initializes each tower with the applet's graphics context, and then adds all the disks on the first tower (tower 0) by using the tower's *add* function. The *add* function is discussed in detail in the "Adding a Disk to the Tower" section that explains the *tower* class:

```
t = new tower[3];

t[0] = new tower(g);
t[1] = new tower(g);
t[2] = new tower(g);

for (int i = 0; i < total_disks; i++)
  t[0].add(i);
```

The paint Function

If the image is not done loading, the *paint* function displays a status-bar message that tells the user it is still loading the image:

```
if (!done_loading_image)
  showStatus("Tower of Hanoi:  loading image");
```

After the image is loaded, the function changes the status message based on its current status. If the applet is running, the function displays the message "Running." If the thread was started, but is no longer alive, the function displays the message, "Click again to restart." If the thread has not yet been started, the applet displays, "Click to start," which directs the user to click on the applet window:

```
if (thread_started)
  if (my_thread.isAlive())
    showStatus("Tower of Hanoi:  Running");
  else
    showStatus("Tower of Hanoi:  Click again to restart");
else
  showStatus("Tower of Hanoi:  Click to start");
```

Next, the function gets the width and the height of the applet window, and uses them to draw the background image on the screen so the image fits in this area:

```
width  = size().width;
height = size().height;

g.drawImage(background, 0, 0, width, height, this);
```

Lastly, the function starts (and places) the first tower at 10% of the window's width, the second tower at 40% of the width, and the third tower at 70% of the width. The size of each tower is 20% of the width of the window:

```
int x_inc = width / 10;

t[0].paint(x_inc*1, x_inc*2, height);
t[1].paint(x_inc*4, x_inc*2, height);
t[2].paint(x_inc*7, x_inc*2, height);
```

Click the Mouse to Start the Thread

To start the *hanoi* applet, the user must click their mouse on the applet window. When the user clicks the mouse, Java calls the applet's *mouseDown* function. The function, in turn, runs the thread (if the thread has not been started, or it was started but is not alive anymore). The *Thread* object's *isAlive* function returns *true* if the thread is running, and *false* otherwise. Before running the thread, the function creates an instance of the *Thread* class, displays a status-bar message that the thread is running, and sets the *thread_started* variable to *true*:

```
public boolean mouseDown(Event evt, int x, int y)
  {
    if (!thread_started || !my_thread.isAlive())
      {
        my_thread = new Thread(this);
        my_thread.start();
        showStatus("Tower of Hanoi:  Running");
        thread_started = true;
      }

    return true;
  }
```

Running the Thread

As briefly discussed, a recursive function is a function that calls itself to perform a specific task. In this case, the *move_tower* function recursively calls itself to move all the disks from the *from_tower* to the *to_tower*, using the second tower as the temporary tower. The second tower is signified by the number "1," because the towers are numbered 0, 1, and 2. After all the disks have been moved, the function swaps the *from_tower* and the *to_tower* variables, and then updates the status message:

```java
public void run()
  {
     move_tower(total_disks, from_tower, to_tower, 1);

     int temp = to_tower;
     to_tower = from_tower;
     from_tower = temp;
     showStatus("Tower of Hanoi:  Click again to restart");
  }
```

Moving the Tower

The *move_tower* function is a recursive function that calls itself to move disks. If there are more than 0 disks to move, the function moves all but the last disk to the temporary tower. Then, the function moves the last disk to the destination tower (the *to* tower). Finally, the function moves the disks from the temporary tower to the destination tower:

```java
private void move_tower(int disks, int from, int to, int using)
  {
    if (height > 0)
      {
         move_tower(disks-1, from, using, to);
         move_disk(from, to);
         move_tower(disks-1, using, to, from);
      }
  }
```

Moving Each Disk

To move one disk, the function calls the *tower* class *pop* method to move it off the *from* tower. The function then calls the *tower* class *push* method to place the disk on the *to* tower, telling the *to* tower which disk and from which tower the disk came. The *pop* and *push* functions will be discussed in detail in the *tower* class explanation section:

```java
private void move_disk(int from, int to)
  {
    int disk = t[from].pop();
    t[to].push(disk);
  }
```

The tower Class

The *tower* class requires two packages: *java.awt* for graphics, and *java.util.Vector* to create a *Vector* object:

```
import java.awt.*;
import java.util.Vector;
```

The *tower* class does not inherit attributes from any other classes; it is a *base class* in and of itself:

```
public class tower
```

Class Variables

The *tower* class declares variables to hold the graphics context, a *Vector* object to hold the disks, the x-coordinate for this tower, the y increment to use for each disk, the width of the tower, and the amount to subtract from each side of the disk for the next smaller disk:

```
Graphics g;

Vector v;

int x;
int y;
int w;
int d;
```

The Constructor

The *tower* class constructor takes one argument—the graphics context to use for this object. The constructor also creates a *Vector* object to hold a list of disks:

```
tower(Graphics g)
  {
    this.g = g;

    v = new Vector();
  }
```

Adding a Disk to the Tower

Think of a *Vector* object as a list. Using the *addElement* method, you can add objects to the list. Likewise, using the *removeElement* method, you can remove an object from the list. In this case, you add or remove objects (disks) from a tower.

The *add* function adds a disk to the tower. To start, the function converts the integer that corresponds to a disk ID into the *Integer* object, and then adds it into the local *Vector* object. The function must convert the integer, because the *addElement* function of the *Vector* class only accepts a variable of the *Object* type, and the *Integer* class is inherited from the *Object* class:

Note: *The disks are numbered starting from 0.*

```
public void add(int i)
   {
      Integer I = new Integer(i);

      v.addElement(I);
   }
```

Popping a Disk off the Tower

The *pop* function pops a disk off the top of the tower's stack of disks. To start, the function uses the *Vector* class *lastElement* function to get the last element in the vector. The last element corresponds to the top element on the stack. After the function has the disk ID, it gets the size of the vector and passes it to the *move_disk_up* function, along with the disk ID (so that the function will know from where to start moving the disk up). Finally, the function uses the *Vector* class *removeElementAt* function to remove the last element and return the disk ID. The *removeElementAt* function needs the index of the element to remove. The elements are indexed starting from 0, so the last element is the size of the vector minus 1:

```
public int pop()
   {
      int disk = ((Integer) (v.lastElement())).intValue();
      int size = v.size();

      move_disk_up(size, disk);
      v.removeElementAt(size - 1);

      return(disk);
   }
```

Pushing a Disk on the Tower

The *push* function pushes a disk on top of the stack of disks already on the tower. The applet calls this function after it pops the disk off another tower. To start, the function converts the integer to an *Integer* object and adds it to the vector:

```
public void push(int i)
   {
      Integer I = new Integer(i);
      v.addElement(I);
```

Next, to draw the disk moving down on the tower, the applet gets the current size of the vector and passes it to the *move_disk_down* function, along with the disk ID (so that the function will know when to stop moving the disk down):

```
int size = v.size();

move_disk_down(size, i);
```

Painting the Tower

The *tower* class *paint* function paints the tower on the screen when given the x-coordinate, the width of the tower, and the height of the applet window:

```
public void paint(int _x, int _w, int h)
```

First, the function saves the x-coordinate and the width of the tower in member variables, so it can use them in the other member functions. Next, the function calculates the height of the disks (which in this case is one-twentieth of the height of the window) and stores it into the variable *y*. The function must also calculate the amount to subtract from each side of the disk to get the width of the next smaller disk. The function stores this amount in the variable *d*:

```
x = _x;
w = _w;
y = h / 20;
d = w / 20;
```

Then, the function draws tower holders that hold the disks:

```
draw_holders(g);
```

Next, the function must draw the disks. Each disk on the tower get its ID, which is an integer starting from 0 for the largest disk (and which increments for each successive smaller disk, meaning the largest disk is always disk 0). Since you have the disk ID, you can calculate how wide to make the disk. The largest disk is as wide as the tower, the next smaller disk subtracts the value held in the variable *d* from both the left and the right side, and so on. To get the x-coordinate, you have to take the x-coordinate of the tower and then add the disk ID times *d*.

The y-coordinate of the base of the tower is one-twentieth of the window height from the bottom. For example, if the height of the window is 100 pixels, the y-coordinate of the base will be 95. So, the y-coordinate of the bottom disk is 18 times *y*, or 90 in the example. The next disk's y-coordinate will be 17 times *y*, and so on. Inside the *for* loop, you can just subtract the loop index from 18, and then multiply by the variable *y* to get the y-coordinate of the disk.

The width of each disk will be the width of the tower minus the amount to subtract from both sides, which is 2 times the disk ID times *d*:

```
int number_of_disks = v.size();

for (int i = 0; i < number_of_disks; i++)
  {
    int j = ((Integer) (v.elementAt(i))).intValue();
    draw_disk(x+j*d, y*(18-i), w-2*j*d, y);
  }
```

Drawing the Holders

The class initially draws the holders within the *paint* function, and then again when you erase a disk (because you have to restore the portion of the holder that was hidden by the disk). Since the function might have to draw the holders with different graphics contexts, it accepts the context as a parameter, and uses it to draw the holder.

The holders are green. The height of the base is one-fifth the height of a disk, and the width of the base is the value of the variable *w*, which was set in the *paint* function. The x-coordinate is the value of the variable *x*, which was also set in the *paint* function, and the y-coordinate is 19 times the height of the disk, which is in the variable *y*. The variable *y* was set to one-twentieth of the height of the window.

The width of the vertical bar is one-tenth of the width of the tower. Its height is 17 times the height of a disk:

```
void draw_holders(Graphics g)
  {
    g.setColor(Color.green);
    g.fillRect(x, y*19, w, y/5);
    g.fillRect(x+w/2-w/20, y*2, w/10, y*17);
    g.setColor(Color.black);
  }
```

The delay Function

The class uses the *delay* function to pause between drawing the disk as it moves the disk up and down the holder. The amount of time to delay is in a variable in the *hanoi* class. Because the *hanoi* class declares this variable *static*, you can use it here without having access to an instance of the *hanoi* class:

```
void delay()
  {
    try
      {
        Thread.sleep(hanoi.delay);
      }
    catch (InterruptedException e)
      {
      }
  }
```

Moving a Disk up the Tower

The *move_disk_up* function moves a disk to the top of the holder. The function takes the number of disks on the tower and the disk ID of the top disk as parameters. To start, the function has to erase the disk where it sits, then loops through each disk position, drawing the disk, delaying for some time, and then erasing the disk, until the disk reaches the top of the tower:

```
void move_disk_up(int size, int disk)
  {
    erase_disk(x+disk*d, y*(19-size), w-2*disk*d, y);

    for (int i = y*(18-size); i >= y; i-=y)
      {
        draw_disk(x+disk*d, i, w-2*disk*d, y);
        delay();
        erase_disk(x+disk*d, i, w-2*disk*d, y);
      }
  }
```

Moving a Disk down the Tower

The *move_disk_down* function is similar to the *move_disk_up* function, except that it moves a disk down the tower. The function takes the number of disks in the tower (including the disk to move down) and the disk ID of the disk to move down as parameters.

To begin, the function loops through each disk position from the top of the tower to the tower location where the disk is supposed to be. For each iteration, the function draws the disk, delays a certain amount, and then erases the disk. When the function ends the loop, it must draw the disk in its final spot:

```java
void move_disk_down(int size, int disk)
  {
    for (int i = y; i < y*(19-size); i+=y)
      {
        draw_disk(x+disk*d, i, w-2*disk*d, y);
        delay();
        erase_disk(x+disk*d, i, w-2*disk*d, y);
      }

    draw_disk(x+disk*d, y*(19-size), w-2*disk*d, y);
  }
```

Drawing the Disk

The *draw_disk* function actually draws a disk. The function receives the x-and-y coordinates and the width and the height of the disk as its parameters. To draw the disk, the function first sets the color to black, and then fills a rectangle using its coordinate and size parameters. Then, the function resets the color to white and draws a border around the disk:

```java
void draw_disk(int x, int y, int w, int h)
  {
    g.setColor(Color.black);
    g.fillRect(x, y, w-1, h-1);

    g.setColor(Color.white);
    g.drawRect(x, y, w-1, h-1);
    g.setColor(Color.black);
  }
```

Erasing the Disk

To erase a disk, the *erase_disk* function has to draw the background image and the holder that the disk was hiding. The function receives four parameters: the x-and-y coordinates, and the width and height of the disk to erase. First, the function creates a copy of the graphics context. Then, using the copy, the function defines a clip rectangle and draws the background image and the holders. Because the *hanoi* applet declared the background, the image width, and the image height as static members, the function can access them here without having access to an instance of the *hanoi* class:

```
void erase_disk(int x, int y, int w, int h)
  {
      Graphics g2;
      g2 = g.create();

      g2.clipRect(x, y, w, h);

      g2.drawImage(hanoi.background, 0, 0, hanoi.width, hanoi.height,
                  null);

      draw_holders(g2);
  }
```

ENHANCEMENTS YOU CAN MAKE TO TOWER OF HANOI

Modify the program so it doesn't solve the problem automatically, but lets the user click on a disk and drag it to a tower. If the user gives up, let them click somewhere to automatically solve the problem.

PUTTING IT ALL TOGETHER

The **Tower of Hanoi** applet shows you how to solve a classic programming problem. In addition, the solution presented here shows you how you can share class variables by declaring the variables as *static*. In Chapter 38, you will create a Java client applet that communicates with a server program. Before you continue with Chapter 38, however, make sure you understand the following key concepts:

☑ You can use the *Vector* class to hold a list of values. The class contains various member functions that let you add and delete values, get the list size, and access values of elements at any position in the list.

☑ A recursive function is a function that calls itself to accomplish a specific task. The **Tower of Hanoi** program, for example, uses the recursive *move_tower* function.

☑ The *Thread* class *isAlive* function lets your applets test if a thread is still running or if it has stopped.

CHAPTER 38

CLIENT/SERVER
EXCHANGING MESSAGES ACROSS THE WEB

Across the Internet, all programs are based upon the concept of clients and servers. For example, when you browse the Web, your Web browser is a client program with which you connect to a Web site and ask for a home page. As you might guess, hundreds or even thousands of clients (users with browsers) can connect to a Web site at any given time. A server program is at the site to which you connect. In short, the server program waits for a user to connect, and then it provides a service. In the case of a Web server, it sends the browser the files it requests. In the case of an FTP server, it lets the client download programs. In this chapter, you will use Sun's network classes to build a client and a server that let you exchange messages. By the time you finish this chapter, you will understand the following key concepts:

- You can write Java programs that are not applets. You run these programs by using the Java interpreter program provided in the JDK.

- You can extend the *NetworkServer* class to create a server program.

- You can define a *NetworkClient* object to create a client program.

- Java client/server programs communicate through ports.

- There are various streams available that your programs can use to read and write data over the network.

USING CLIENT SERVER

You can run these programs on two different computers that communicate with each other via TCP/IP (your Winsock). If you want to test these programs by using only one machine, make sure that it is set up to support TCP/IP.

These programs are Java programs that are not applets. Unlike Java applets that you run using a browser or the appletviewer, you run Java programs by using the Java interpreter. To run the server program, for example, you type the following at a command prompt:

```
java server <ENTER>
```

To run the client program, you type the following at a command prompt:

```
java client <ENTER>
```

You must start the server program before you start the client. When the server program runs, it waits for a client to connect to it, and its console will look like that in Figure 38.1. When the client connects, the server asks for a login, gets the username, and returns "login successful" to the client. When the client logs off, the server displays a message to the screen. Then it waits for another connection. Figure 38.2 illustrates how the server's screen might appear after a client connects, logs in, and logs off.

When you run the client program, it connects to the server, waits for a login prompt, sends the username, waits for a response, and then logs off. The client's console, in this case, will look like the one in Figure 38.3.

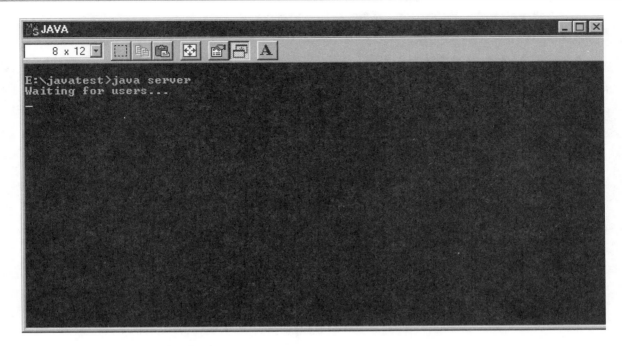

Figure 38.1 *The server waiting for clients.*

Figure 38.2 *The server connects a client, gets the username, and then the client logs off.*

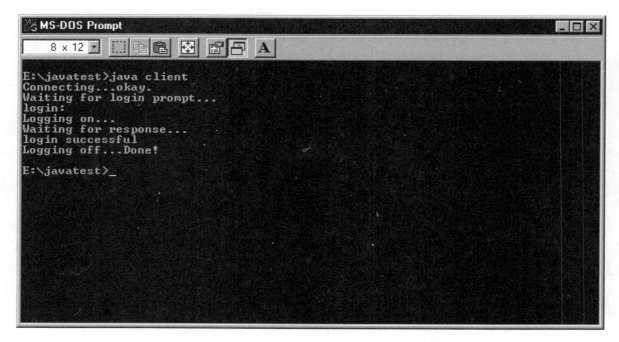

Figure 38.3 The client screen after it connects to the server, logs on, waits for a response, and then logs off.

THE HTML FILE

Because **Client/Server** is a standalone program and not an applet, there is no HTML file.

LOOKING AT CLIENT/SERVER

There are two programs in this chapter. The first program is the server, and the second program is the client.

The Server Program

As discussed, the server program waits for a client to connect. Next, the server sends the client a login prompt. After the client logs in, the server displays a staus message that states the login was successful. The server, in this case, then displays a message stating the user has been logged off and the server program waits for another connection. As you will learn, the *server* class extends the *NetworkServer* class and contains a *main* function, which the Java interpreter executes first:

```
//*****************************************************************
// server.java
//*****************************************************************


import java.io.*;
import sun.net.*;


//*****************************************************************
```

```
class server extends NetworkServer
  {
    //————————————————————————

    public static void main(String args [])
      {
        System.out.println("Waiting for users...");

        try
          (new server()).startServer(1111);
        catch (IOException e)
          System.out.println("Unable to start server");
      }


    //————————————————————————

    public void serviceRequest()
      {
        DataInputStream net_input = new DataInputStream(clientInput);
        String username;

        System.out.println("Connecting client...");

        clientOutput.println("login:");
        clientOutput.flush();

        try
          {
            if ((username = net_input.readLine()) == null)
              {
                System.out.println("readLine returned null");
                return;
              }
          }
        catch (IOException e)
          {
            System.out.println("Error in readLine");
            return;
          }

        System.out.println("Username: " + username);

        clientOutput.println("login successful");
        clientOutput.flush();

        System.out.println(username + " has logged off");
      }
  }
```

The Client Program

Like the *server* class, the *client* class is a standalone program with a *main* function. Since the *main* function calls the other functions in this class, and uses the member variables, the program declares them all as *static*. So you can see that these classes can be extended, or they can be used as objects within classes. The *client* class does not extend the *NetworkClient* class as the *server* class extended the *NetworkServer* class. In the next chapter, you will extend both the *server* and the *client* classes. The following code implements the client:

```java
//******************************************************************
// client.java
//******************************************************************

import java.io.*;
import sun.net.*;


//******************************************************************

class client
  {
    static NetworkClient    net;
    static DataInputStream  net_input;
    static PrintStream      net_output;


    //——————————————————————————————


    public static void main(String args [])
      {
        System.out.print("Connecting...");
        System.out.flush();

        try
          net = new NetworkClient("sam", 1111);
        catch (IOException e)
          {
            System.out.println("Error creating NetworkClient");
            return;
          }

        if (net.serverIsOpen())
          System.out.println("okay.");
        else
          {
            System.out.println("error.");
            System.out.println("Could not connect to host");
            return;
          }

        net_input  = new DataInputStream(net.serverInput);
        net_output = net.serverOutput;

        System.out.println("Waiting for login prompt...");
        System.out.println("Server says <" + get_net_input() + ">");

        System.out.println("Logging on...");
        net_output.println("a_client");

        System.out.println("Waiting for response...");
        System.out.println("Server says <" + get_net_input() + ">");
```

```
        System.out.print("Logging off...");
        System.out.flush();
        close_server();
        System.out.println("Done!");
    }

    //————————————————————————————————

    static String get_net_input()
      {
        String string;

        try
           string = net_input.readLine();
        catch (IOException e)
           string = "";

        return string;
      }

    //————————————————————————————————

    static void close_server()
      {
        try
          net.closeServer();
        catch (Exception e)
          System.out.println("Unable to close server");
      }
  }
```

BREAKING APART CLIENT/SERVER

In this section, you will examine the client and server programs in detail. First, you will examine the server program, and then you will examine the client program.

The Server Program

The server program imports two packages: the *java.io* package, and the *sun.net* package. The *sun.net* package, which contains the *NetworkServer* and the *NetworkClient* classes, is provided with the JDK, but is not considered a standard Java package. The classes provided in this package are <u>very</u> useful. In fact, this package was a part of the standard library in the alpha stage of Java, and many developers used the classes provided in the package. Because early Java programmers all over the world have written programs that contain these classes, it is important that you understand these classes. Later in the book, you will see programs based on the network classes which belong in the standard packages of the released JDK:

```
import java.io.*;
import sun.net.*;
```

The *server* class extends the *NetworkServer* class. However, there are no class variables that you need to define, because you will do all the work in one function, the *serviceRequest* function:

```
class server extends NetworkServer
```

The main Function

Since the server program is a standalone program, you have to define a *main* function. You must declare the *main* function as *public* and *static* and *void*. The function accepts command-line arguments in an array of *String* objects passed as a parameter. In this program, you do not need to receive any command-line arguments:

```
public static void main(String args [])
```

Since this program does not have a window, it displays all its output on the console. As it starts, the program displays a status message that it is waiting for users:

```
System.out.println("Waiting for users...");
```

Next, the function starts a new thread of the *server* class, and calls the object's *startServer* function with a parameter containing the port number to use for network communications. When two computers communicate across the net, the programs need a way to send messages to one another — that's where the port number comes in. In short, the port number tells TCP/IP to which server to send incoming messages. Each server must have a unique port number. By sending messages to a port number, you ensure the message gets to the correct server. The *startServer* function, in turn, spawns a thread that waits for a client connection. When it detects a connection, it calls the *serviceRequest* function, which the program must define. The *startServer* function throws an exception of the *IOException* type if an error occurs:

```
try
  (new server()).startServer(1111);
 catch (IOException e)
  System.out.println("Unable to start server");
```

The serviceRequest Function

In this program, the *serviceRequest* function is where all the server work is performed. The *serviceRequest* function is called by the *startServer* function, which you called in the *main* function. You have to declare this function *public* because the base class declaration, which you can't override, declares this function to be public. Also, this function does not return a value:

```
public void serviceRequest()
```

Within the *server* class, there are two member variables that you can use. The first is the *clientInput* object, which is of the type *InputStream*, and the second is the *clientOutput* object, which is of the *PrintStream* type. The *InputStream* class is defined in the *java.io* package, and it is an input stream of bytes. The *PrintStream* class is also defined in the *java.io* package, and it is an output stream of bytes.

As you will see, the program defines a variable, called *net_input*, of the *DataInputStream* type which gives it the capability of reading a line terminated by a newline character. The programs use the *clientInput* variable to create a new *DataInputStream*:

```
DataInputStream net_input = new DataInputStream(clientInput);
```

Next, the program defines a string that will contain the username for the connected client:

```
String username;
```

When this function executes, it displays a status message that states a user has connected:

```
System.out.println("Connecting client...");
```

After a client connects, the server sends a "login" message by using the *println* function, which sends a newline character at the end of the string. On many systems, if you send a string with a newline character at the end, the output is flushed automatically. However, just in case some systems do not automatically flush the output to the port, the server calls the *flush* function:

```
clientOutput.println("login:");
clientOutput.flush();
```

After asking for a login, the server waits for a line from the client, and this line should contain a username. To read a line from the client, the server uses the *readLine* function. This function will read all characters up to a newline character, and then return the line as a *String* object. If a null is returned, or an exception is thrown, the server displays an appropriate message to the console. Otherwise, the server displays the username it received:

```
try
  {
    if ((username = net_input.readLine()) == null)
      {
        System.out.println("readLine returned null");
        return;
      }
  }
catch (IOException e)
  {
    System.out.println("Error in readLine");
    return;
  }

System.out.println("Username: " + username);
```

After the server receives a username, it sends a message to the client that the login was successful (again, you might want to flush the output). Then, because the server is exiting the function, the client will be disconnected. So, the server displays a message that the client has logged off:

```
clientOutput.println("login successful");
clientOutput.flush();

System.out.println(username + " has logged off");
```

The Client Program

The *client* class imports the same two packages as the *server* class:

```
import java.io.*;
import sun.net.*;
```

Class Variables

Within the *client* class, you declare the variables that will create a network-client class, get network input, and send network output:

```
static NetworkClient   net;
static DataInputStream net_input;
static PrintStream     net_output;
```

The main Function

As was the case for the *Server* program, the *main* function for the client must be *public, static,* and *void.* As did the server, the client accepts command-line arguments in an array of *String* objects passed as a parameter:

```
public static void main(String args [])
```

The first thing the client does is to print a message to the screen telling the user that it is attempting to connect to the server. The function uses the *print* function (which does not add a newline character at the end) instead of the *println* function to display the message. Then, the function calls *flush* to make sure that the string gets flushed out to the console. Many systems do not flush a string to the screen until a newline character is printed. On some systems, the newline character is the LF (line-feed) character, and on other systems, it is the CR/LF (carriage-return, line-feed) pair of characters:

```
System.out.print("Connecting...");
System.out.flush();
```

Next, the function creates a new network-client object, with the first parameter being the host name of the computer that you want to connect to. In this example, the host name used was "sam," but you should change it to the computer where the server program that was described earlier is running. For instance, if the server program is running on the "jamsa.com" computer, you would replace "sam" with "jamsa.com," and the client should be able to find it as long as both computers are connected to the Internet, are on the same network, or are running on the same computer, and the host name specified is the name of the computer.

The second parameter to the *NetworkClient* constructor is the port number. You have to use the same port number as the one used in the server program. In this example, you will use port number 1111. Remember that the server program described earlier also used this same port number.

The *NetworkClient* constructor throws the *IOException* object, should an error occur. One of the reasons that an error would be thrown is if it was unable to locate the specified host name:

```
try
   net = new NetworkClient("sam", 1111);
catch (IOException e)
   {
      System.out.println("Error creating NetworkClient");
      return;
   }
```

If the function successfully creates a *NetworkClient* object, it checks to see if the server is open. If the server is open, the function prints "okay" and continues; if it is not open, the function prints an error message, and ends:

```
if (net.serverIsOpen())
  System.out.println("okay.");
else
  {
    System.out.println("error.");
    System.out.println("Could not connect to host");
    return;
  }
```

After the client establishes a connection, it creates the network input and output variables. There are two member variables of the *NetworkClient* class that the client uses, and they are *serverInput*, which is of the *InputStream* type, and *serverOutput*, which is of the *PrintStream* type. Since it is easier to use the *readLine* function than to read one character at a time, the function uses the input stream to create a *DataInputStream* object, and calls it *net_input*. Likewise, the function calls the output stream *net_output*. After the function creates streams, it waits for a login prompt from the server by calling the local *get_net_input* function, which is described in the next section:

```
net_input  = new DataInputStream(net.serverInput);
net_output = net.serverOutput;

System.out.println("Waiting for login prompt...");
System.out.println("Server says <" + get_net_input() + ">");
```

At this point, you could verify the input received from the server, but since this is just a sample application, you can assume you received the correct input, and continue on to sending a login name. In this example, you can use "a_client" as the login name:

```
System.out.println("Logging on...");
net_output.println("a_client");
```

The function then waits again for another response from the server that acknowledges the login:

```
System.out.println("Waiting for response...");
System.out.println("Server says <" + get_net_input() + ">");
```

Next, the client logs off by calling the local *close_server* function:

```
System.out.print("Logging off...");
System.out.flush();
close_server();
System.out.println("Done!");
```

Getting Network Input

To make network input a little easier, you can create a function that returns a whole line read from the network as a *String* object. Then, since you will call this function from the *main* function, which is static, you have to make this function static also:

```
static String get_net_input()
```

Next, you can create a *String* object that you will use as the function's return value. Then, try to read a line from the network input, and if an exception was thrown, set the return value to an empty string. Lastly, return the string:

```
String string;

try
  string = net_input.readLine();
catch (IOException e)
  string = "";

return string;
```

Closing the Server

Because you call it from the *main* function, the *close_server* function also has to be declared *static*:

```
static void close_server()
```

The *closeServer* member function of the *NetworkClient* class throws an exception (that your program must catch) if it cannot close the connection:

```
try
  net.closeServer();
catch (Exception e)
  System.out.println("Unable to close server");
```

And that's all there is to client/server communications!

ENHANCEMENTS YOU CAN MAKE TO CLIENT/SERVER

Modify the server so it only accepts certain usernames. Modify the client so that it gets the host name, the port number, and the username as parameters passed on the command line.

PUTTING IT ALL TOGETHER

The programs in this chapter demonstrate how to write client/server programs that communicate with each other across the Net. In Chapter 39, you will create client and server programs that let multiple users chat. Before you continue with Chapter 39, however, make sure you understand the following key concepts:

- ☑ You can write Java programs that are not applets. You run these programs by using the Java interpreter program provided in the JDK.

- ☑ You can extend the *NetworkServer* class to create a server program.

- ☑ You can define a *NetworkClient* object to create a client program.

- ☑ Client/Server programs communicate with one another using ports. Each server program must have a unique port number.

- ☑ To read and write data over the network, your applets can take advantage of several different streams.

CHAPTER 39

MULTIPLE CLIENTS
CONNECTING MULTIPLE CLIENTS TO ONE SERVER AND SENDING MESSAGES

In Chapter 38, you created simple server and client programs that connect to each other over the Internet and communicate with each other. In this chapter, you will learn how to connect multiple clients to the same server. In this case, if multiple clients connect to the server, each client can send messages to the server. The server, in turn, will display each client's messages to its console. The clients, however, do not see the messages. In other words, the programs presented here only support the one-way chat. The clients can chat to the server, but the server can't chat back. By the time you finish this chapter, you will understand the following key concepts:

◆ Each time a client connects to the server, the server creates a new thread, which runs the *serviceRequest* function of the *NetworkServer* object.

◆ You can create a class that inherits attributes of the *NetworkClient* object.

◆ To access values passed to the *main* function, you use the *String* argument passed to the program.

◆ To call the base class constructor, you use the *super* function.

USING MULTIPLE CLIENTS

As you did in Chapter 38, this chapter helps you create both client and server programs. The server program must be running when you run the client program. As was the case in Chapter 38, the programs this chapter presents are standalone programs. To run the server program using the Java interpreter, type the following command:

```
java server <ENTER>
```

To run each client program, type the following at a command prompt, where <host> is the name of the host computer, and <username> is the username for this client:

```
java client <host> <username> <ENTER>
```

When you run the server program, it waits for clients to connect to it. The server's console will look like the one shown in Figure 39.1. When a client connects, the server gets the username and displays it on the console, as shown in Figure 39.2. When the client sends messages to the server, they are displayed on the server screen, as shown in Figure 39.3. When another client connects and sends messages, they are also displayed. Messages from multiple clients are displayed on the screen, each message preceded by the username of the client that sent the message, as shown in Figure 39.4. When the clients log off, the server is notified and it displays the appropriate output on the console, as shown in Figure 39.5.

When you run the client program and connect to the server, the server sends you a message that you are connected and that you can type "EXIT" to exit the program. You can then type any messages that you want, and the server will display them on the server's console. When you type "EXIT," the client will disconnect from the server. The whole session for client "one" is shown in Figure 39.6, and the session for client "two" is shown in Figure 39.7.

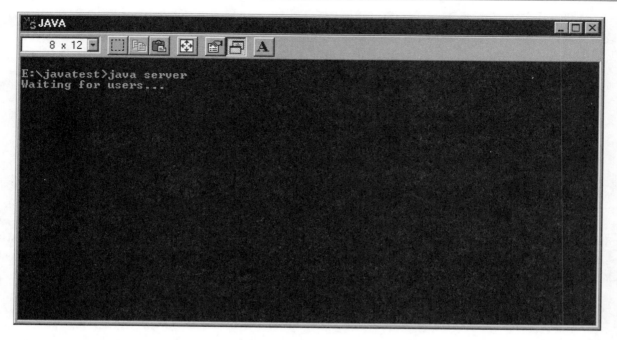

Figure 39.1 *The server waiting for clients.*

Figure 39.2 *The server screen after client "one" connects.*

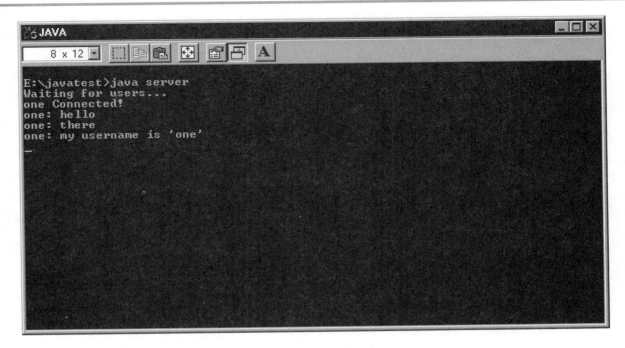

Figure 39.3 *The server screen with message from client "one" displayed.*

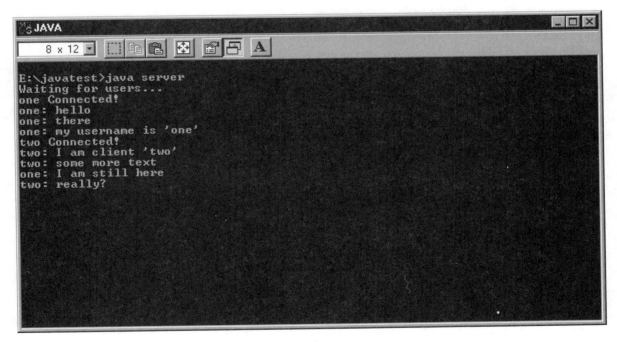

Figure 39.4 *The server screen with messages from multiple clients.*

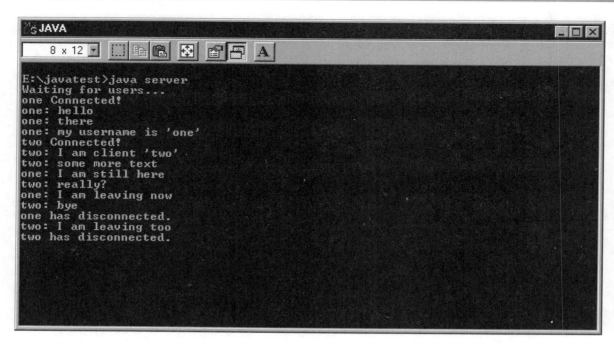

Figure 39.5 *The server screen after the clients log off.*

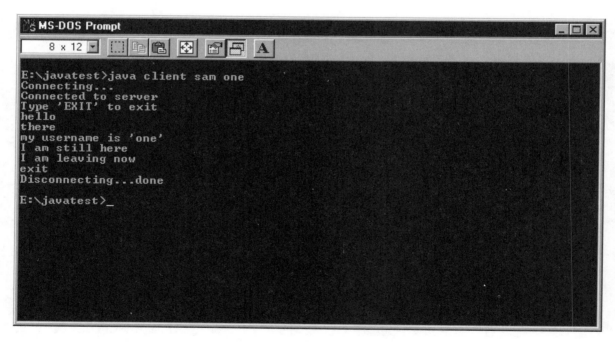

Figure 39.6 *The screen for client "one," containing the whole session.*

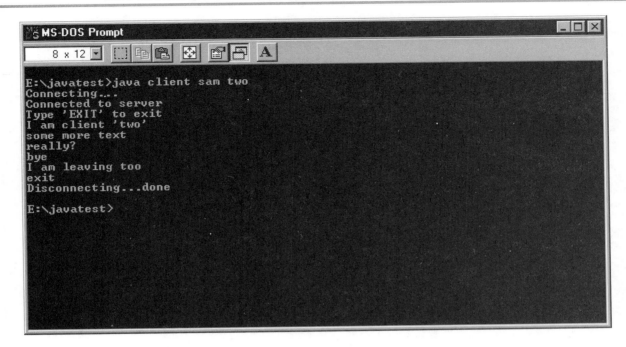

Figure 39.7 The screen for client "two" containing the whole session.

THE HTML FILE

Because **Multiple Clients** is a standalone program and not an applet, there is no HTML file.

THE PROGRAMS

This chapter presents the server program first, and then the client program.

The Server Program

As did the server program in Chapter 38, the *server* class extends the *NetworkServer* class and contains a *main* function, which the Java interpreter executes first. The following code implements the server:

```
//*************************************************************
// server.java
//*************************************************************

import java.io.*;
import sun.net.*;


//*************************************************************

class server extends NetworkServer
  {
    DataInputStream net_input;
    PrintStream net_output;


    //—————————————————————————
```

```java
      public static void main(String args[])
        {
          new server();
        }

    //————————————————————————

    public server()
      {
        try
          startServer(1111);
        catch (Exception e)
          {
            System.out.println("Unable to start server");
            return;
          }

        System.out.println("Waiting for users...");
      }

    //————————————————————————

    public void serviceRequest()
      {
        net_input = new DataInputStream(clientInput);
        net_output = System.out;

        String user = read_net_input();
        System.out.println(user + " Connected!");

        while (true)
          {
            String string;

            if ((string = read_net_input()) == null)
              break;

            write_net_output(user + ": " + string);
          }

        System.out.println(user + " has disconnected.");
      }

    //————————————————————————

    String read_net_input()
      {
        try
          return net_input.readLine();
        catch (IOException e)
          return null;
      }

    //————————————————————————
```

```
    void write_net_output(String string)
      {
        net_output.println(string);
        net_output.flush();
      }
  }
```

The Client Program

In Chapter 38, you did not extend the *NetworkClient* class. In this chapter, however, you will extend the *NetworkClient* class, and, as before, the program contains a *main* function that the Java interpreter executes first. The following code implements the client:

```
//****************************************************************
// client.java
//****************************************************************

import java.io.*;
import sun.net.*;


//****************************************************************

class client extends NetworkClient
  {
    DataInputStream net_input;
    PrintStream     net_output;


    //──────────────────────────────


    public static void main(String args[])
      {
        if (args.length < 2)
          {
            System.out.println("To run, type:\n");
            System.out.println("\tjava client <host> <username>");
            return;
          }

        System.out.println("Connecting...");

        try
          new client(args[0], args[1]);
        catch (Exception e)
          {
            System.out.println("Unable to create NetworkClient");
            return;
          }
      }

    //──────────────────────────────
```

```
    client(String host, String username) throws IOException
      {
        super(host, 1111);

        if (serverIsOpen ())
          {
            System.out.println("Connected to server");
            net_input = new DataInputStream(System.in);
            net_output = serverOutput;

            net_output.println(username);

            chat();
          }
        else
          System.out.println("Error - Could not connect to host");
      }

//————————————————————

void chat()
  {
    String string;

    System.out.println("Type 'EXIT' to exit");

    while (true)
      {
        string = read_net_input();

        if (string.equalsIgnoreCase("EXIT"))
          break;

        write_net_output(string);
      }

    System.out.print("Disconnecting...");
    close_server();
    System.out.println("done");
  }

//————————————————————

String read_net_input()
  {
    try
      return net_input.readLine();
    catch (IOException e)
      return null;
  }

//————————————————————
```

```
    void write_net_output(String string)
      {
        net_output.println(string);
        net_output.flush();
      }

    //————————————————————————

    void close_server()
      {
        try
          closeServer();
        catch (Exception e)
          System.out.println("Unable to close server");
      }
}
```

BREAKING APART MULTIPLE CLIENTS

In this section, you will examine the client and server programs in detail. First, you will examine the server program, and then you will examine the client program.

The Server Program

As did the server in Chapter 38, this server program imports two packages: the *java.io* package, and the *sun.net* package:

```
import java.io.*;
import sun.net.*;
```

The server class also extends the *NetworkServer* class, which contains the function that will wait for a client to connect. The program calls the *startServer* function from the server constructor:

```
class server extends NetworkServer
```

Class Variables

There are two variables that you will use in the server class. The first variable, *net_input*, gets input from the client, and the second variable, *net_output*, sends output to the console. You can set the output variable to send output over the network back to the client, as you saw in the previous chapter, or to the console, as you will do in this program:

```
    DataInputStream net_input;
    PrintStream net_output;
```

The main Function

The first function the Java interpreter executes is *main*. This function simply creates a new *server* object. The function leaves all the "details" to be handled in the constructor of the *server* object:

```
public static void main(String args[])
  {
    new server();
  }
```

The Server Constructor

The *server* constructor function actually starts the server. To start the server, the function calls the *startServer* function, and passes it the server's port number. After spawning the thread that will wait for client connections, the *startServer* function returns. At this point, the server displays a message to the console that the server is waiting for users. Notice that if the server was unable to start, an exception is thrown. If an exception is thrown, you should print an appropriate message, and return:

```
public server()
  {
    try
      startServer(1111);
    catch (Exception e)
      {
        System.out.println("Unable to start server");
        return;
      }

    System.out.println("Waiting for users...");
  }
```

The serviceRequest Function

When a client connects to the server, the server spawns (creates and starts) a thread which calls the *serviceRequest* function:

```
public void serviceRequest()
```

The *serviceRequest* function first sets up the input and output variables. In this case, the input will come from the client, and the Server must read the input a line at a time. So, the function takes the *clientInput* class variable provided by *NetworkServer* and uses it to create a *DataInputStream*. To send the output to the console, the function sets the *net_output* variable to the *out* member variable of the *System* class:

```
net_input = new DataInputStream(clientInput);
net_output = System.out;
```

As before, the server uses *read_net_input* to read the username from the network. After the user logs in, the server displays the username to the console:

```
String user = read_net_input();
System.out.println(user + " Connected!");
```

Next, the server continues to read and display messages from the client until it gets a null which tells it that the client has disconnected. For each line that the server reads, it writes the line using the *write_net_output* function, which will use the *net_output* variable:

```
while (true)
  {
    String string;

    if ((string = read_net_input()) == null)
      break;

    write_net_output(user + ": " + string);
  }
```

When the client disconnects, the server prints a message to the console:

```
System.out.println(user + " has disconnected.");
```

Reading Network Input

The server reads a line from the network by calling the *readLine* function of the *net_input* object. If an exception is thrown, the function returns a null string. If there is no exception, the function returns the string it has read:

```
String read_net_input()
  {
    try
      return net_input.readLine();
    catch (IOException e)
      return null;
  }
```

Writing Network Output

The *write_net_output* function can write a string to either the console or network based on the *net_output* object. In this program, the server used the function to display messages to the console. However, by changing the *net_output* object, the server could send messages across the Net. Make sure that you flush the output after writing the string:

```
void write_net_output(String string)
  {
    net_output.println(string);
    net_output.flush();
  }
```

The Client Program

The *client* class has to import the same 2 packages as the *server* class:

```
import java.io.*;
import sun.net.*;
```

As opposed to the previous chapter where you used *NetworkClient* as an object, here you will extend the *NetworkClient* class:

```
class client extends NetworkClient
```

Class Variables

Just as in the server program, there are two variables that you will use in this class. You will use the first variable, *net_input*, to get input from the user, and the second variable, *net_output*, to send output to the network:

```
DataInputStream net_input;
PrintStream      net_output;
```

The main Function

Because the client program is a standalone program, its execution starts in the *main* function. The client program accepts two command-line arguments: the *host name* and the *username*. The *main* function can access these arguments using the array of *String* arguments:

```
public static void main(String args[])
```

In this case, the program should receive a port number and username as command-line arguments. If the program gets less than two arguments, it displays a message to the user that explains how to run the program, and then exits. To get the length (number of entries) of an array, the function uses the *length* member variable:

```
if (args.length < 2)
  {
    System.out.println("To run, type:\n");
    System.out.println("\tjava client <host> <username>");
    return;
  }
```

Next, the *main* function tries to connect to the network by creating a *client* object. The *client* class is inherited from the *NetworkClient* class, and the *NetworkClient* class throws an exception. The function has to catch this exception. To get the arguments passed to the program, use index 0 for the first argument, index 1 for the second argument, and so on.

```
System.out.println("Connecting...");

try
  new client(args[0], args[1]);
catch (Exception e)
  {
    System.out.println("Unable to create NetworkClient");
    return;
  }
```

The Client Constructor

The base class *NetworkClient* throws an exception, so the derived class, *client*, either has to catch it, or rethrow. However, the derived class cannot catch the exception because the call to the constructor of a base class has to be the first line in the method, even before any *try* statements. Therefore, the *client* constructor has to rethrow the exception. To specify that this method throws an exception, you have to place a *throws* keyword following the parameters, followed by the type of the object that it throws:

```
client(String host, String username) throws IOException
```

If a constructor function has to call the base-class constructor, the call has to be the first statement in the constructor. To call the base-class constructor, use the *super* keyword. The base-class is *NetworkClient*, and its constructor takes two arguments: the *host computer name* and the *port number*:

```
super(host, 1111);
```

Next, the function checks to see if the base-class constructor has established a connection to the server by calling the *serverIsOpen* function:

```
if (serverIsOpen ())
```

If the server is open, the function sets the input variable *net_input* to *System.in*, which is keyboard input, and sets the *net_output* variable to *serverOutput*, which is a member variable of *NetworkClient* that lets you send output to the server. Then, the function sends the username to the server, and finally, it calls the *chat* function:

```
System.out.println("Connected to server");
net_input = new DataInputStream(System.in);
net_output = serverOutput;

net_output.println(username);

chat();
```

If the client could not connect to the server, it displays a message to the console:

```
else
  System.out.println("Error - Could not connect to host");
```

The chat Function

The *chat* function lets the client talk to the server. The function sends any lines that you type to the server. To start, the function diplays a message to the user saying that they can type "EXIT" to exit the program. Then, the function enters a loop reading user messages and sending them to the server until the user types "EXIT." The function then closes the connection to the server:

```
void chat()
  {
    String string;

    System.out.println("Type 'EXIT' to exit");

    while (true)
      {
        string = read_net_input();

        if (string.equalsIgnoreCase("EXIT"))
          break;

        write_net_output(string);
      }
```

```
    System.out.print("Disconnecting...");
    close_server();
    System.out.println("done");
}
```

Reading Input

A client program can use the *read_net_input* function to read keyboard input or a message from across the Net based on the *net_input* variable. This client program sets the *net_input* object to the keyboard, but it could have been set to read from the network and you still would not have to modify this function:

```
String read_net_input()
  {
    try
      return net_input.readLine();
    catch (IOException e)
      return null;
  }
```

When you set the *read_net_input* function to read from the network, the function reads incoming messages from the server.

Writing Output

To send messages to the server, the client uses the *net_output* object. In this case, the client sends string messages to the server by using the *println* function. As a precaution against systems that don't immediately send data to a port when they encounter a newline character, the function calls the *flush* function to force the output to the port:

```
void write_net_output(String string)
  {
    net_output.println(string);
    net_output.flush();
  }
```

Closing the Server

To close the connection to the Server, the function calls the base-class *closeServer* member function. The *closeServer* function throws an exception the function must catch:

```
void close_server()
  {
    try
      closeServer();
    catch (Exception e)
      System.out.println("Unable to close server");
  }
```

ENHANCEMENTS YOU CAN MAKE TO MULTIPLE CLIENTS

To start, modify the server to send a verification of the login to the client, and have the client wait for the verification before continuing. Also, verify the logout and have the server send back the amount of time that the client was connected. The client should wait for the time and print it on the console before exiting. Lastly, modify the server so each client sees the messages the other clients type.

PUTTING IT ALL TOGETHER

The **Multiple Clients** applet demonstrates how to write a server program that will respond to multiple clients, and how a client inherits the *NetworkClient* class. As you learned, each time a client connects to a server, the server simply spawns a thread to service the client. Therefore, whether the server is handling one client or one-hundred clients, its code does not change. In Chapter 40, you will create a **Graphical Client/Server** applet that combines graphics and network operations. Before you continue with Chapter 40, however, make sure you understand the following key concepts:

☑ For every client that connects to the server, the server creates a new thread, which runs the *serviceRequest* function of the *NetworkServer* object.

☑ You can create a client that inherits from the *NetworkClient* object.

☑ To access arguments passed to the program, you use the *String* argument passed to the *main* function.

☑ To call the base-class constructor, you have to call the *super* function.

CHAPTER 40

GRAPHICAL CLIENT/SERVER
COMBINING GRAPHICS WITH NETWORKING

In Chapter 39, you created a server that can communicate with multiple clients. Because each of the previous programs are standalone programs and not applets, you have to run the programs from the system prompt, using the Java interpreter. In each case, the programs displayed their output to a text-based screen. In this chapter, you will learn how to add graphics to a standalone networking program. By the time you finish this chapter, you will understand the following key concepts:

◆ You can use the *Frame* and *Panel* classes to create a window in a standalone Java program.

◆ By capturing and sending one character at a time to the server, you have total control over your screen output.

◆ To exit a standalone program, you call the *System.exit* function.

◆ You can use the *keyDown* function to capture keystrokes in a graphics window.

USING GRAPHICAL CLIENT/SERVER

As was the case in Chapters 38 and 39, this chapter presents a server program and a client program. The server program must be running when you run the client program. To run the server program, you can type the following command to start the Java interpretter:

```
java server <ENTER>
```

To run each client program, type the following command where <host> is the name of the host computer, and <username> is the username for this client:

```
java client <host> <username> <ENTER>
```

When you run the server program, it waits for clients to connect to it. When a client connects, the server gets the client username and displays it on the console. As the client sends each character to the server, the server displays the characters on its screen. When another client connects and sends characters, those characters are also displayed. The server displays characters from multiple clients on its screen, each character preceded by the username of the client that sent it. When a client disconnects, the server is notified and it in turn displays the appropriate output on the console. The server's console output after a session with two clients is shown in Figure 40.1.

When you run the client program, the Java interpreter will display a graphics screen. As you type characters, the client will send the characters to the server who, in turn, will echo them back. The client program will append each echoed character to a string and then will display the string on a red bar on the graphics screen. When the client receives the twenty-first character, it will reset the string to contain only the one character. To exit the client program, hit the ESCAPE key.

The graphics screen output of the first client is shown in Figure 40.2, and its console output is shown in Figure 40.3. The graphics screen output of the second client is shown in Figure 40.4, and its console output is shown in Figure 40.5.

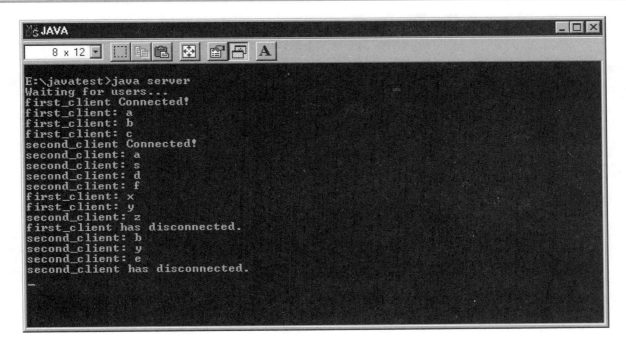

Figure 40.1 The server console.

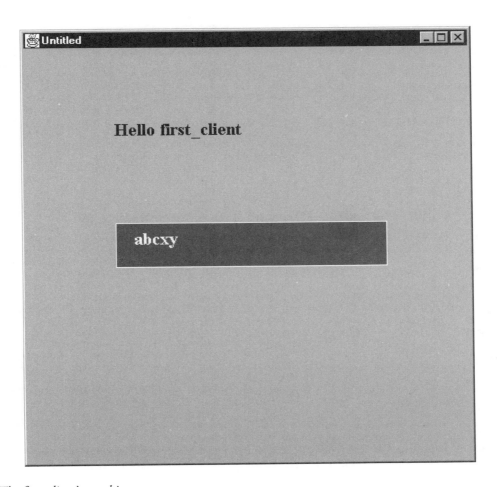

Figure 40.2 The first client's graphics screen.

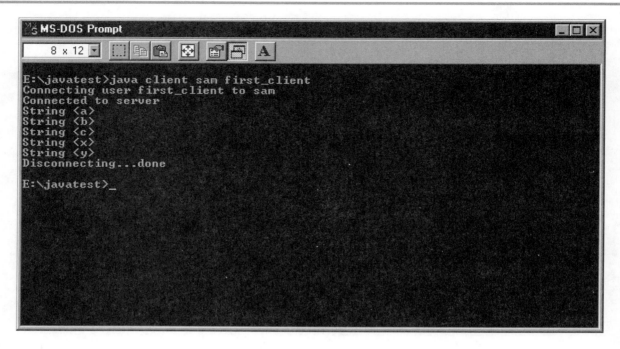

Figure 40.3 The first client's console.

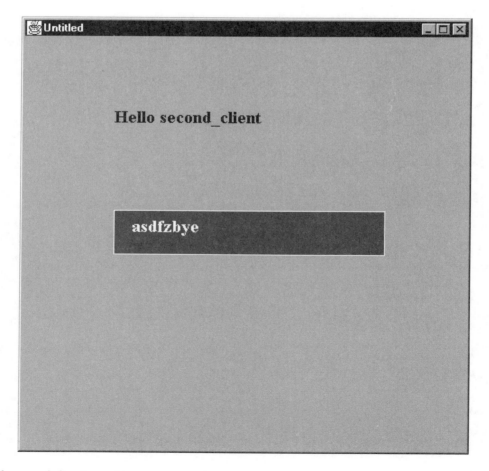

Figure 40.4 The second client's graphics screen.

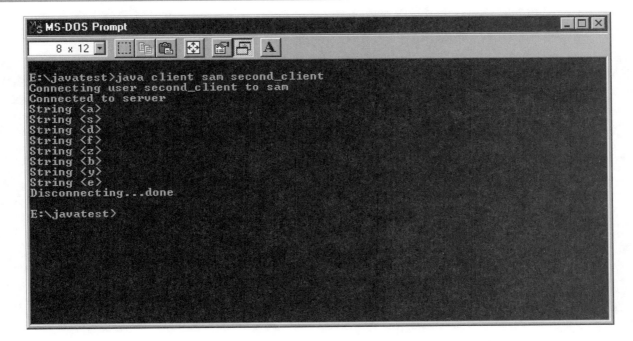

Figure 40.5 *The second client's console.*

LOOKING AT GRAPHICAL CLIENT/SERVER

This chapter first presents the server program, followed by the client that now uses the graphical interface.

The Server Program

This server program is very similar to the server program you examined in Chapter 39. However, this program receives one character at a time and echoes each one back to the client that sent it. The following code implements the server:

```
//**********************************************************************
// server.java
//**********************************************************************


import java.io.*;
import sun.net.*;


//**********************************************************************

class server extends NetworkServer
  {
    DataInputStream net_input;
    PrintStream net_output;

    //——————————————————————

    public static void main(String args[])
      {
        new server();
      }

    //——————————————————————
```

```java
    public server()
      {
        try
          startServer(1111);
        catch (Exception e)
          {
            System.out.println("Unable to start server");
            return;
          }

        System.out.println("Waiting for users...");
      }

    //—————————————————————————

    public void serviceRequest()
      {
        net_input = new DataInputStream(clientInput);
        net_output = clientOutput;

        String user = read_net_input();
        System.out.println(user + " Connected!");

        while (true)
          {
            String string;

            if ((string = read_net_input()) == null)
              break;

            System.out.println(user + ": " + string);
            write_net_output(string);
          }

        System.out.println(user + " has disconnected.");
      }

    //—————————————————————————

    String read_net_input()
      {
        try
          return net_input.readLine();
        catch (IOException e)
          return null;
      }

    //—————————————————————————

    void write_net_output(String string)
      {
        net_output.println(string);
        net_output.flush();
      }
}
```

The Client Program

The client program contains three classes: the *client* class, the *network* class, and the *writer* class. The *client* class is the main class of this program, and it contains the *main* function which is executed first by the Java interpreter when you run this program. The class extends the *Frame* class which will contain a *network* panel that you will add to create the graphical user interface.

The *network* class extends the *Panel* class which you will use to display graphics, and contains all the networking input/output functions. The user input function is also in this class.

The *writer* class is a thread that starts in the *network* class. As each character comes across the network, this thread reads it, appends it to a string, and repaints the *network* class to display the string on the graphics screen. The following code implements the client:

```
//*****************************************************************
// client.java
//*****************************************************************

import java.awt.*;
import java.io.*;
import sun.net.*;

//*****************************************************************

public class client extends Frame
  {
    public static void main(String args[])
      {
        if (args.length < 2)
          {
            System.out.println("To run, type:\n");
            System.out.println("\tjava client <host> <username>");
            return;
          }

        new client(args[0], args[1]);
      }


      //————————————————————————

    public client(String host, String username)
      {
        add("Center", new network(host, username));
        resize(500, 500);
        show();
      }
  }

//*****************************************************************

class network extends Panel
  {
    NetworkClient network_client;
    DataInputStream net_input;
```

```java
    PrintStream net_output;

    String username;
    boolean connected = false;
    writer w;

    //————————————————————————————

    public network(String host, String username)
      {
        this.username = username;

        if (connect(host, username))
          {
            connected = true;
            w = new writer(this);
            w.start();
          }
        else
          {
            System.out.println("Unable to connect");
            return;
          }
      }

    //————————————————————————————

    boolean connect(String host, String username)
      {
        System.out.println("Connecting user " + username +
                            " to " + host);

        try
          network_client = new NetworkClient(host, 1111);
        catch (Exception e)
          {
            System.out.println("Error...could not connect to host <" +
                                e + ">");
            return false;
          }

        if (network_client.serverIsOpen ())
          {
            System.out.println("Connected to server");
            net_input = new DataInputStream
                                (network_client.serverInput);
            net_output = network_client.serverOutput;

            write_net_output(username);

            return true;
          }
        else
          {
```

```java
            System.out.println("Server is NOT open");
            return false;
        }
    }

    //————————————————————————

String read_net_input()
    {
      try
        return net_input.readLine();
      catch (IOException e)
        return null;
    }

    //————————————————————————

void write_net_output(String string)
    {
      net_output.println(string);
      net_output.flush();
    }

    //————————————————————————

void close_server()
    {
      try
        network_client.closeServer();
      catch (Exception e)
        System.out.println("Unable to close server");
    }

    //————————————————————————

public boolean keyDown(Event evt, int key)
    {
      if (key == 27)
        {
          if (connected)
            {
                System.out.print("Disconnecting...");
                close_server();
                System.out.println("done");
            }

          System.exit (0);
        }

      else if (connected)
        write_net_output("" + (char) key);

      return true;
    }
```

```java
    //————————————————————————————

    public void paint(Graphics g)
      {
        Font font = new Font("TimesRoman", Font.BOLD, 20);
        g.setFont(font);
        g.drawString("Hello " + username, 100, 100);

        g.setColor(Color.red);
        g.fillRect(100, 200, 300, 50);
        g.setColor(Color.white);
        g.drawRect(100, 200, 300, 50);
        g.drawString(w.net_line, 120, 225);
      }
  }

//*******************************************************************

class writer extends Thread
  {
    String net_line = "";

    network n;

    //————————————————————————————

    public writer(network n)
      {
        this.n = n;
      }

    //————————————————————————————

    public void run()
      {
        while (true)
          {
            String character = n.read_net_input();
            net_line = net_line + character;

            if (net_line.length () > 20)
              net_line = character;

            n.repaint();
            System.out.println("String <" + character + ">");
          }
      }
  }
```

BREAKING APART GRAPHICAL CLIENT/SERVER

This section will first examine the server program, and then the client program.

The Server Program

The server program is very similar to the server program you examined in Chapter 39. The only differences are in the *serviceRequest* function. In this server, the *net_output* variable is set to the *clientOutput* member variable of the *NetworkServer* class:

```
net_output = clientOutput;
```

By assigning the *net-output* variable to *clientOutput*, the server can echo each character the client sends to it back to the client by calling the *write_net_output* function defined in this class. Before the server echoes the character, it displays the character to its screen preceded by the username of the client that sent it, so you can follow what is going on if you are looking at the server console:

```
System.out.println(user + ": " + string);
write_net_output(string);
```

The Client Program

The client program imports three packages: *java.awt* to perform graphics, *java.io* for networking input/output streams, and *sun.net* to use the *NetworkClient* class:

```
import java.awt.*;
import java.io.*;
import sun.net.*;
```

The client Class

The *client* class is the main class of the client program. Because this program is a standalone program which normally displays output to a console screen, you must use the *Frame* class to create a frame for the graphics window. In this case, the *client* class extends the *Frame* class:

```
public class client extends Frame
```

As you have learned, the first function in a standalone program that executes is *main*. In this case, *main* takes two arguments: the host computer name, and the username for this client. If *main* receives less than two arguments, it prints a message to the console to instruct the user how to run the program. If *main* has two or more arguments, it creates a new *client* class with the first two arguments:

```
public static void main(String args[])
   {
    if (args.length < 2)
      {
       System.out.println("To run, type:\n");
       System.out.println("\tjava client <host> <username>");
       return;
```

```
        }

    new client(args[0], args[1]);
    }
```

The constructor of the *client* class accepts a host computer name and the username as parameters. To start, the function creates an instance of the *network* class, which inherits the *Panel* class, and adds it to the center of the frame. Then, the function resizes the frame, and shows the frame on the screen:

```
public client(String host, String username)
    {
    add("Center", new network(host, username));
    resize(500, 500);
    show();
    }
```

The network Class

The *network* class is the "work horse" for the client program. To start, because it displays output on the graphics window, it extends the *Panel* class, and then overrides the *paint* class to display output:

```
class network extends Panel
```

Next, the function declares variables for the network client, the network input stream, and the network output stream. It also declares variables to store the username, a variable which tells it whether the client is connected to the server or not, and a *writer* thread object, which will wait for characters from the network and write them on the screen:

```
NetworkClient network_client;
DataInputStream net_input;
PrintStream net_output;

String username;
boolean connected = false;
writer w;
```

The Constructor

The *network* class constructor accepts the host computer name and the username as parameters:

```
public network(String host, String username)
```

To start, the function stores the parameters into their respective member variables:

```
this.host = host;
this.username = username;
```

Next, the function tries to connect to the server program somewhere on the network. The function uses the host computer name to find the server, and the username to log in. If the client connects, the function sets the *connected* variable to *true*, creates a new *writer* object, and then starts it. The function passes the current *network* object to the *writer* object so it can call the *paint* function of this class. If the client is unable to connect to the server, the function prints a message to the console:

```
if (connect(host, username))
  {
    connected = true;
    w = new writer(this);
    w.start();
  }
else
  {
    System.out.println("Unable to connect");
    return;
  }
```

Connecting to the Server

To connect to the server, you need the host computer name and the username. The *connect* function tries to establish the connection, and then returns a boolean value which indicates whether or not it was able to connect to the server:

```
boolean connect(String host, String username)
```

To start, the function displays a "Connecting" message and then tries to create a new *NetworkClient* object, passing to the object the desired host computer name and the port number. The *NetworkClient* object constructor will throw an exception if it is unable to connect to the server. Should the exception occur, the function displays an error message and returns *false*.

```
System.out.println("Connecting user " + username +
                   " to " + host);

try
  network_client = new NetworkClient(host, 1111);
catch (Exception e)
  {
    System.out.println("Error...could not connect to host <" +
                       e + ">");
    return false;
  }
```

If the connection to the server is open, the function prints a message that the client is connected, and then creates the network input and output objects. Then, the function sends the username to the server, and returns a *true*, meaning that you successfully connected to the server:

```
if (network_client.serverIsOpen ())
  {
    System.out.println("Connected to server");
    net_input = new DataInputStream
                        (network_client.serverInput);
    net_output = network_client.serverOutput;
```

```
    write_net_output(username);

    return true;
}
```

If the connection to the server is not open, the function prints a message and returns a *false*:

```
else
  {
    System.out.println("Server is NOT open");
    return false;
  }
```

Getting Keyboard Input

When a program runs within a graphics window, it needs a way to get user input. To capture keystrokes in a graphics window, you can use the *keyDown* function. This function receives as parameters the event and the key that was hit:

```
public boolean keyDown(Event evt, int key)
```

If the key pressed is an ESCAPE key, the function checks to see if the client is connected. If the client is connected, the function closes the server and disconnects. Then, the function uses the *System* class *exit* function to exit the program. A parameter value of 0 signifies a successful exit status:

```
if (key == 27)
  {
    if (connected)
      {
        System.out.print("Disconnecting...");
        close_server();
        System.out.println("done");
      }

    System.exit (0);
  }
```

If the user presses any other key, the function converts the key to a string and sends it to the server. To convert the key to a string, the function simply appends a null string:

```
else if (connected)
  write_net_output("" + (char) key);
```

Finally, the function returns *true* to Java to indicate that you processed the keyboard event:

```
return true;
```

The paint Function

Every time Java needs to repaint the screen, it calls the *paint* function. First, this function greets the user by printing "Hello" followed by the username. Then, the function creates a red box with a white outline. Lastly, the function prints the current string inside the box by using the white color. The current string is stored in the *net_line* member variable of the *writer* object:

```java
public void paint(Graphics g)
  {
    Font font = new Font("TimesRoman", Font.BOLD, 20);
    g.setFont(font);
    g.drawString("Hello " + username, 100, 100);

    g.setColor(Color.red);
    g.fillRect(100, 200, 300, 50);
    g.setColor(Color.white);
    g.drawRect(100, 200, 300, 50);
    g.drawString(w.net_line, 120, 225);
  }
```

The writer Class

As discussed, the *writer* class creates a thread that continually gets characters from the server and displays them in the frame. Because the *writer* object will run as a thread, it extends the *Thread* class:

```java
class writer extends Thread
```

There are two *writer* class member variables: the *net_line* variable is a string that holds the current line (which has been typed by the user), and the *network* object that created this instance of the *writer* class:

```java
String net_line = "";

network n;
```

The *writer* class constructor accepts a reference to the calling object, and stores it into the member variable:

```java
public writer(network n)
  {
    this.n = n;
  }
```

The thread's *run* function is a loop that will run forever, or until the program exits. The loop reads a character by using the *network* object *read_net_input* member function, and appends the character at the end of the current line. If the length becomes greater than 20, the function sets the line to the current character, which will remove the rest of the characters. The function then repaints the *network* object and prints the character to the console:

```java
public void run()
  {
    while (true)
      {
        String character = n.read_net_input();
```

```
        net_line = net_line + character;

        if (net_line.length () > 20)
          net_line = character;

        n.repaint ();
        System.out.println("String <" + character + ">");
      }
    }
```

Enhancements You Can Make to Graphical Client/Server

Modify the program so you can print multiple lines on the graphics screen, and scroll lines as new input is displayed. Next, change the program to ask for the username when the program runs, instead of specifying it as an argument to the program.

Putting It All Together

The **Graphical Client/Server** applet demonstrates how to use graphical windows with a standalone networking program. In Chapter 41, you will continue to enhance the client/server programs. Specifically, the **Two Way Chat** applet will let two users communicate through a server. Before you continue with Chapter 41, however, make sure you understand the following key concepts:

☑ Using the *Frame* and *Panel* classes, you can create a window in a standalone Java program.

☑ To exit a standalone program, you call the *System.exit* function.

☑ Using the *keyDown* function, your applet can capture keystrokes in a graphics window.

Chapter 41

Two-Way Chat
Two Clients Communicating through a Server

For the past several chapters, you have been building an applet that lets client programs communicate with a server. In each case, the communication was only between a client and the server. Two clients, for example, could not communicate. In this chapter, you will create a **Two-Way Chat** program that lets two clients communicate by way of a common server. By the time you finish this chapter, you will understand the following key concepts:

◆ In the server, you keep track of the clients using an array.

◆ Using the *String* class *substring* function, you can extract a substring from a string.

◆ To create a chat, the server sends the characters it receives from one client to the second client.

Using Two-Way Chat

The **Two-Way Chat** program uses a client and server. The server program must be running when you run the client program. To run the server program, type the following command to start the Java interpreter:

```
java server <ENTER>
```

To run each client program, type the following command, where <host> is the name of the host computer, and <username> is the username for this client:

```
java client <host> <username> <ENTER>
```

When you run the server program, it waits for exactly two clients to connect to it. When a client connects, the server gets the username and displays it on the console, and sends the client a "WAIT" message. When both clients have connected, the server sends a "GO" message to each of them. As each client sends a character, the server displays it on the server screen, preceded by the username of the client that sent it. Then, the server sends the character to the other client. When a client disconnects, the server is notified, and it displays the appropriate output on the console. When both clients disconnect, the server program exits. The server's console output after a session with two clients is shown in Figure 41.1.

When you run the client program, the Java interpreter will display a graphics screen with two boxes: the red box will contain the characters typed at that screen, and the green box will contain the characters typed at the other client, and other messages sent by the server. When it first connects, the client will receive a "WAIT" message. When both clients have connected, they will receive a "GO" message from the server. At this point, users can type characters on either client. As characters are typed on a client, they are displayed on its red box, and sent to the server. The server will display the characters it receives to its console and will send them to the other client. On the other client, the characters will be displayed in the green box. To exit the client programs, users hit the <ESCAPE> key.

The graphics screen output of the first client is shown in Figure 41.2, and its console output is shown in Figure 41.3. The graphics screen output of the second client is shown in Figure 41.4, and its console output is shown in Figure 41.5.

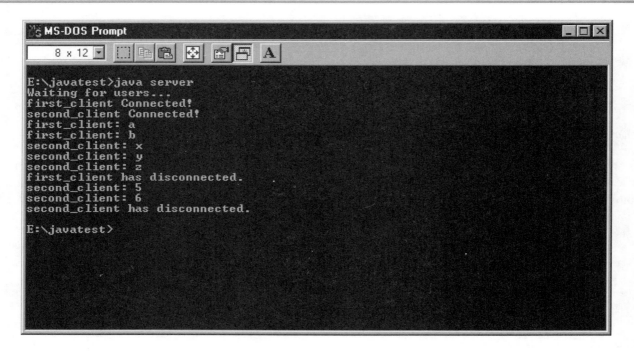

Figure 41.1 The server console.

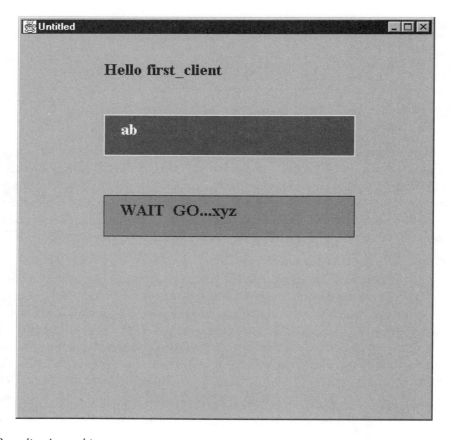

Figure 41.2 The first client's graphics screen.

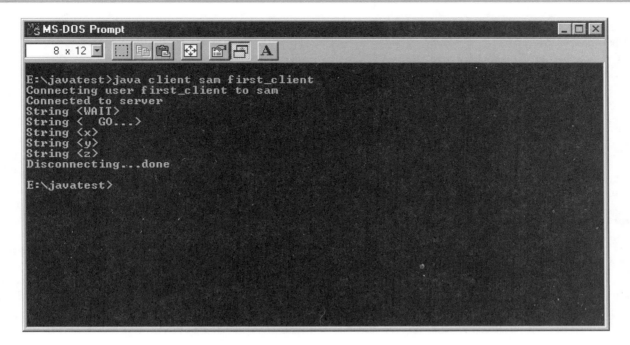

Figure 41.3 The first client's console.

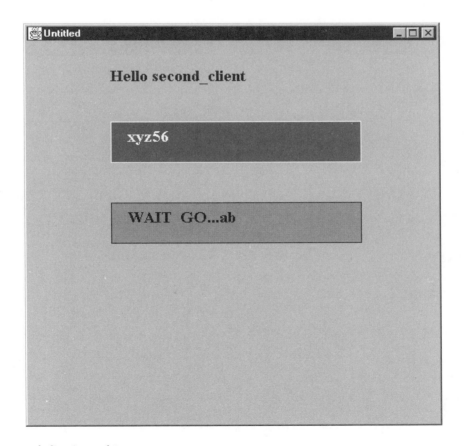

Figure 41.4 The second client's graphics screen.

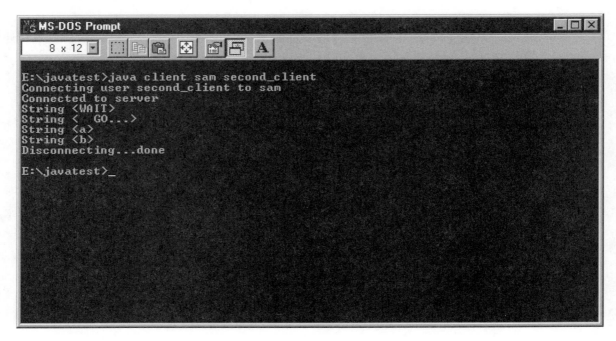

Figure 41.5 *The second client's console.*

LOOKING AT TWO-WAY CHAT

The **Two-Way Chat** program uses a client and a server. The following sections will examine the server first, and then the client.

The Server Program

The server program contains a lot of code from the previous chapter. In addition, it contains a new class called *reader*, which is a thread. It also keeps track of two clients, and allows them to chat by sending characters received from one client to the other client. When both clients disconnect, the server exits. The following code implements the server:

```java
//****************************************************************
// server.java
//****************************************************************

import java.io.*;
import sun.net.*;


//****************************************************************

class server extends NetworkServer
  {
    String user[];
    DataInputStream net_input[];
    PrintStream net_output[];

    static int client_counter = 0;

    //————————————————————————
```

```java
public static void main(String args[])
  {
    new server();
  }

//————————————————————————

public server()
  {
    user = new String[2];
    net_input = new DataInputStream[2];
    net_output = new PrintStream[2];

    try
      startServer(1111);
    catch (Exception e)
      {
        System.out.println ("Unable to start server");
        return;
      }

    System.out.println("Waiting for users...");
  }

//————————————————————————

public void serviceRequest()
  {
    DataInputStream input = new DataInputStream(clientInput);
    PrintStream output = clientOutput;

    if (client_counter >= 2)
      {
        write_net_output(output, "There are already two clients");
        return;
      }

    net_input[client_counter] = input;
    net_output[client_counter] = output;
    user[client_counter] = read_net_input(input);

    System.out.println(user[client_counter] + " Connected!");

    (new reader(this, client_counter)).start();
    int c = client_counter++;
    while (user[c] != null)
      try
        Thread.sleep(5000);
      catch (InterruptedException e)
        ;
  }

//————————————————————————
```

```
    String read_net_input(DataInputStream input)
      {
        try
          return input.readLine();
        catch (IOException e)
          return null;
      }

    //————————————————————————

    void write_net_output(PrintStream output, String string)
      {
        output.println(string);
        output.flush();
      }
  }

//******************************************************************

class reader extends Thread
  {
    server s;
    int index;

    //————————————————————————

    public reader(server s, int index)
      {
        this.s = s;
        this.index = index;
      }

    //————————————————————————

    public void run()
      {
        setPriority(MIN_PRIORITY);

        s.write_net_output(s.net_output [index], "WAIT");
        while (s.client_counter < 2)
          ;

        s.write_net_output(s.net_output [index], "  GO...");

        while (true)
          {
            String string = s.read_net_input(s.net_input [index]);

            if (string == null)
              break;

            System.out.println(s.user[index] + ": " + string);
            s.write_net_output(s.net_output[(index+1)%2], string);
          }
```

```
        System.out.println(s.user[index] + " has disconnected.");
        s.user[index] = null;

        if (—s.client_counter == 0)
          System.exit(0);
    }
  }
```

The Client Program

The client program is very similar to the client program in the previous chapter. However, it adds a green box on the screen to keep track of characters sent by the other client. The following code implements the client:

```java
//****************************************************************
// client.java
//****************************************************************

import java.awt.*;
import java.io.*;
import sun.net.*;


//****************************************************************

public class client extends Frame
  {
    public static void main(String args[])
      {
        if (args.length < 2)
          {
            System.out.println("To run, type:\n");
            System.out.println("\tjava client <host> <username>");
            return;
          }

        new client(args [0], args [1]);
      }

    //————————————————————————————

    public client(String host, String username)
      {
        add("Center", new network(host, username));
        resize(500, 500);
        show();
      }
  }

//****************************************************************

class network extends Panel
  {
    NetworkClient network_client;
    DataInputStream net_input;
```

```java
    PrintStream net_output;

    String username;
    boolean connected = false;
    writer w;

    String typed_line = "";

    //————————————————————————

    public network(String host, String username)
      {
        this.username = username;

        if (connect(host, username))
          {
            connected = true;
            w = new writer(this);
            w.start();
          }
        else
          {
            System.out.println("Unable to connect");
            return;
          }
      }


    //————————————————————————

    boolean connect(String host, String username)
      {
        System.out.println("Connecting user " + username +
                           " to " + host);

        try
          network_client = new NetworkClient(host, 1111);
        catch (Exception e)
          {
            System.out.println("Error...could not connect to host <" +
                               e + ">");
            return false;
          }

        if (network_client.serverIsOpen())
          {
            System.out.println("Connected to server");
            net_input = new DataInputStream
                                (network_client.serverInput);
            net_output = network_client.serverOutput;

            write_net_output(username);

            return true;
          }
```

```
        else
          {
            System.out.println("Server is NOT open");
            return false;
          }
      }


//————————————————————————————


String read_net_input()
    {
      try
        return net_input.readLine();
      catch (IOException e)
        return null;
    }


//————————————————————————————


void write_net_output(String string)
    {
      net_output.println(string);
      net_output.flush();
    }


//————————————————————————————


void close_server()
    {
      try
        network_client.closeServer();
      catch (Exception e)
        System.out.println("Unable to close server");
    }


//————————————————————————————


public boolean keyDown(Event evt, int key)
    {
      if (key == 27)
        {
          if (connected)
            {
              System.out.print("Disconnecting...");
              close_server();
              System.out.println("done");
            }

          System.exit(0);
        }
```

```
                  else if (connected)
                    {
                      typed_line = typed_line + (char) key;
                      if (typed_line.length () > 20)
                        typed_line = typed_line.substring(1);
                      write_net_output("" + (char) key);
                      repaint();
                    }

                return true;
              }

        //————————————————————————————

        public void paint(Graphics g)
          {
            Font f = new Font("TimesRoman", Font.BOLD, 20);
            g.setFont(f);
            g.drawString("Hello " + username, 100, 50);

            g.setColor(Color.red);
            g.fillRect(100, 100, 300, 50);
            g.setColor(Color.white);
            g.drawRect(100, 100, 300, 50);
            g.drawString(typed_line, 120, 125);

            g.setColor(Color.green);
            g.fillRect(100, 200, 300, 50);
            g.setColor(Color.black);
            g.drawRect(100, 200, 300, 50);
            g.drawString(w.net_line, 120, 225);
          }
      }

//********************************************************************

class writer extends Thread
  {
    String net_line = "";

    network n;

    //————————————————————————————

    public writer(network n)
      {
        this.n = n;
      }

    //————————————————————————————
```

```
    public void run()
      {
        while (true)
          {
            String character = n.read_net_input();
            net_line = net_line + character;

            if (net_line.length () > 20)
              net_line = net_line.substring(1);

            n.repaint();
            System.out.println("String <" + character + ">");
          }
      }
  }
```

BREAKING APART TWO-WAY CHAT

In this section, you will examine the server and client programs in detail. First, you will examine the server program, and then you will examine the client program.

The Server Program

To start, the server declares several array variables. The class variables for the username, network input, and network output have to be arrays because the server must keep track of two clients. The server uses a counter that tells it how many clients it currently has. This counter is static so each thread does not create its own copy:

```
String user[];
DataInputStream net_input[];
PrintStream net_output[];

static int client_counter = 0;
```

With the *server* class constructor, the function allocates space for the arrays:

```
user = new String[2];
net_input = new DataInputStream[2];
net_output = new PrintStream[2];
```

Next, the *serviceRequest* function must now be aware of which client has just connected. If the server already has two clients, it displays a message and returns:

```
public void serviceRequest()
  {
    DataInputStream input = new DataInputStream(clientInput);
    PrintStream output = clientOutput;

    if (client_counter >= 2)
      {
        write_net_output(output, "There are already two clients");
        return;
      }
```

The function then fills the arrays with information about the current client: the network input, the network output, and the username. Then, the function displays the username of the client that connected to the console:

```
net_input[client_counter] = input;
net_output[client_counter] = output;
user[client_counter] = read_net_input(input);

System.out.println(user[client_counter] + " Connected!");
```

The server assigns a thread that reads characters sent to the server from a client, and that "echoes" the characters to the other client. In this case, to support two client programs, the server will use two *reader* threads. As you can see, the function starts the *reader* thread and increments the thread counter. Then, the function must wait while the client is connected. If the function does not wait and lets the *serviceRequest* function complete, that thread will be destroyed, and the local copies of the network input and output will disappear:

```
(new reader(this, client_counter)).start();
int c = client_counter++;

while (user[c] != null)
  try
    Thread.sleep(5000);
  catch (InterruptedException e)
    ;
}
```

The *read_net_input* function, which reads network input from a client, and the *write_net_output* function, which writes network output to a client, now take an extra parameter. This parameter is the stream to use for input or output:

```
String read_net_input(DataInputStream input)
  {
  try
    return input.readLine();
  catch (IOException e)
    return null;
  }

//————————————————————————————

void write_net_output(PrintStream output, String string)
  {
  output.println(string);
  output.flush();
  }
```

The reader Thread

As discussed, the *reader* thread reads the characters from one client and writes them to the second client. The *reader* class runs as a thread, so it extends the *Thread* class:

```
class reader extends Thread
```

The *reader* class uses two variables: one to reference the server object, and an index that tells it which client it supports:

```
server s;
int index;
```

The *reader* class constructor receives these two values and stores them into the member variables:

```
public reader(server s, int index)
   {
     this.s = s;
     this.index = index;
   }
```

When the thread runs, you can set its priority to minimum, because it depends on user input that is rather slow in computer time. The *Thread* class contains the *setPriority* function as a member function, and *MIN_PRIORITY* as a *final* and *static* member variable. By setting the priority of your threads in this way, you can fine-tune your applet's performance:

```
public void run()
   {
     setPriority(MIN_PRIORITY);
```

To start, the server sends a "WAIT" message to the client, and then waits until there are two clients available:

```
s.write_net_output(s.net_output [index], "WAIT");
while (s.client_counter < 2)
   ;
```

When there are two clients connected to the server, the server sends a "GO" message to the client:

```
s.write_net_output(s.net_output [index], "  GO...");
```

Then, the thread starts a loop that gets network input, displays the character input to the console, and sends it to the other client. If the client being serviced disconnects, the *read_net_input* function will return a null, and breaks out of the loop:

```
while (true)
   {
     String string = s.read_net_input(s.net_input [index]);

     if (string == null)
       break;

     System.out.println(s.user[index] + ": " + string);
     s.write_net_output(s.net_output[(index+1)%2], string);
   }
```

When a client disconnects, the server displays a message to the console that the user disconnected, and then resets the username to null, which will end the *serviceRequest* function for the current client:

```
System.out.println(s.user[index] + " has disconnected.");
s.user[index] = null;
```

If both clients have disconnected, the server program exits:

```
  if (—s.client_counter == 0)
    System.exit(0);
}
```

The Client Program

The client program in this chapter contains very few changes to the client program you examined in Chapter 40. The first change is in the class variables of the *network* class. This class adds a variable that keeps track of the characters typed in the current window:

```
String typed_line = "";
```

When a character is typed, the *keyDown* function adds this character to the *typed_line* variable, and then sends the character to the server. If the number of characters exceeds 20, the function removes the first character by resetting the value to start at the second character, using the *String* class *substring* member function. Since Java array indexes start at 0, the function sends a 1 to the *substring* function to get the second character. After sending the character to the server, the function repaints the screen:

```
typed_line = typed_line + (char) key;
if (typed_line.length () > 20)
  typed_line = typed_line.substring(1);
write_net_output("" + (char) key);
repaint();
```

Remember that in the previous chapter, the *net_line* class variable of the *writer* class kept track of the characters echoed to the client by the server. In this program, the characters sent by the server will be the characters typed by the other client. You do not have to change the client program much to reflect this. You just have to draw the typed line in the red box, and the characters received from the server in the green box:

```
public void paint(Graphics g)
  {
    Font f = new Font("TimesRoman", Font.BOLD, 20);
    g.setFont(f);
    g.drawString("Hello " + username, 100, 50);

    g.setColor(Color.red);
    g.fillRect(100, 100, 300, 50);
    g.setColor(Color.white);
    g.drawRect(100, 100, 300, 50);
    g.drawString(typed_line, 120, 125);
```

```
    g.setColor(Color.green);
    g.fillRect(100, 200, 300, 50);
    g.setColor(Color.black);
    g.drawRect(100, 200, 300, 50);
    g.drawString(w.net_line, 120, 225);
}
```

ENHANCEMENTS YOU CAN MAKE TO TWO-WAY CHAT

In this program, the server program ends when the clients disconnect. Modify the server program so the server supports disconnect and reconnect operations.

PUTTING IT ALL TOGETHER

The **Two-Way Chat** program shows you how two clients can chat with each other over the network. In Chapter 42, you will see how to implement the client program as an applet that can run over the Web, and how to use the *Socket* class instead of Sun's undocumented network classes. Before you continue with Chapter 42, however, make sure you understand the following key concepts:

☑ Within a server, you can keep track of the clients in an array.

☑ You can use the *substring* function of the *String* class to get a substring of a string, which starts at the character position that is passed as a parameter.

☑ When the server receives characters from one client of the server, it simply sends them to the other client. This way, each client sees what the other client is typing.

CHAPTER 42

SOCKETS CHAT
A SOCKETS-BASED CHAT PROGRAM

In Chapter 41, you learned how to get two clients to chat over the network by using Sun's networking classes. In this chapter, you will learn how to use the *Sockets* class to implement the networking instead of using Sun's undocumented network classes. This chapter will also show you how to create an applet that contains networking. By the time you finish this chapter, you will understand the following key concepts:

- You can use *ServerSocket* and *Socket* classes instead of *NetworkServer* and *NetworkClient* to create networking programs.

- When you exit an applet, the browser calls the *stop* function.

- You can create an applet that talks to a server on a host computer system.

USING SOCKETS CHAT

The client program is an applet, and it can be run from the HTML file provided. To test the programs in this chapter, you have to run the server, and then run two clients. You can run the server program on a host machine, and set up the applet with its HTML file on two different computers. If you want to run the programs from the same computer, you have to set up the HTML file in two separate directories. If you run the same HTML file twice to run two clients, then, when the server sends a character to one client, the other one will also receive it.

If you use Netscape Navigator 2.0 on Windows 95/NT to browse the HTML file that contains the applet, the default configuration might cause a socket security exception when the client tries to connect to the server. This might happen if the server is running on a computer that is not an IRC server. There are some workarounds available on the Internet for Netscape Navigator; one of them replaces your **moz2_0.zip** file. Supposedly, Netscape is working on user-configurable security options for the Navigator. If you run *appletviewer*, you might also have the same security problem during connect.

The server program is a standalone program that has to run on a host computer. To run the server program using the Java interpreter, type the following command:

```
java server <ENTER>
```

The client program is an applet, so you can use your HTML browser to display the HTML file for this chapter, which contains the client applet. Make sure that your HTML browser is Java aware.

When you run the server program, it waits for exactly two clients to connect to it. When a client connects, the server gets the username and displays it on the console, and sends a "WAIT" message to the client. When both clients have connected, the server sends a "GO" message to both of them. As each client sends a character, it is displayed on the server screen preceded by the username of the client that sent it, and then the character is sent to the other client. When a client disconnects, the server is notified, and it displays the appropriate output on the console. When both clients disconnect, the server program exits. The server's console output after a session with two clients is shown in Figure 42.1.

When you run the client program, the browser will display a graphics screen. There will be two boxes: the red box will contain the characters typed at that screen, and the green box will contain the characters typed at the other client and other messages sent by the server. The client will receive a "WAIT" message when it first connects. When both clients have connected, they will receive a "GO" message. At this point, you can type characters on either client. Make sure that you click on the client where you want to type, so it can get the focus. As you type characters, they are displayed on its red box, and sent to the server. The server will display the characters received and will send them to the other client. On the other client, the characters will be displayed in the green box. When you tell the browser to exit the applet, either by closing the browser or moving to another HTML page, the clients will close the connection to the server.

The screen output of the first client is shown in Figure 42.2, and the screen output of the second client is shown in Figure 42.3.

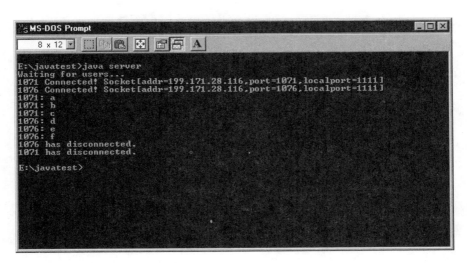

Figure 42.1 *The server console.*

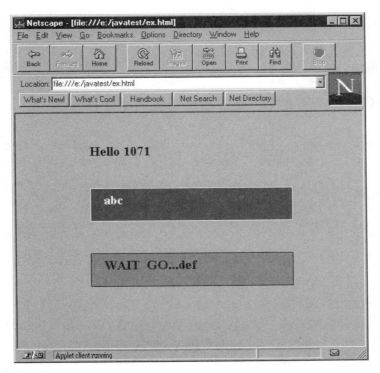

Figure 42.2 *The first client's screen.*

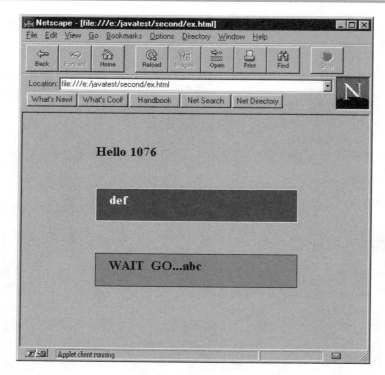

Figure 42.3 *The second client's screen.*

THE HTML FILE

Use the following HTML file to run the *client* applet:

```
<applet code=client.class width=420 height=260>
<param name=host value=sam>
</applet>
```

LOOKING AT SOCKETS CHAT

The **Sockets Chat** program consists of a server program and a client program. This chapter presents the server program first.

The Server Program

As discussed, the server program waits for two clients to connect. The server then echoes the characters the first client types to the second client, and vice-versa. This server program uses the *Socket* class instead of the *NetworkServer* class to implement a server. The following code implements the server:

```
//***********************************************************************
// server.java
//***********************************************************************

import java.io.*;
import java.net.*;
```

```
//*****************************************************************

class server
  {
    ServerSocket server_socket;

    String user[];
    InputStream net_input[];
    OutputStream net_output[];

    static int client_counter = 0;

      //————————————————————

    public static void main(String args[])
      {
        new server();
      }

      //————————————————————

    public server()
      {
        user = new String[2];
        net_input = new InputStream[2];
        net_output = new OutputStream[2];

        try
          server_socket = new ServerSocket(1111);
        catch (IOException e)
          {
            System.out.println("Error in server socket");
            return;
          }

        System.out.println("Waiting for users...");

        while (true)
          {
            try
              {
                Socket socket = server_socket.accept();
                service_request(socket);
              }
            catch (IOException e)
              {
                System.out.println("Exception: <" + e + ">");
                break;
              }
          }
      }

      //————————————————————
```

```java
public void service_request(Socket socket)
  {
    InputStream input;
    OutputStream output;

    try
      {
        input = socket.getInputStream();
        output = socket.getOutputStream();
      }
    catch (IOException e)
      {
        System.out.println("Unable to get input/output streams");
        return;
      }

    if (client_counter >= 2)
      {
        write_net_output(output, "There are already two clients");
        return;
      }

    net_input[client_counter] = input;
    net_output[client_counter] = output;
    user[client_counter] = read_net_input_line(input);

    System.out.println(user[client_counter] + " Connected! " +
                       socket.toString());

    (new reader(this, client_counter)).start();
    client_counter++;
  }

//————————————————————————————

String read_net_input_line(InputStream input)
  {
    String line = "";
    String c;

    c = read_net_input(input);
    while ((byte) c.charAt(0) != 10)
      {
        line = line + c;
        c = read_net_input(input);
      }

    return line;
  }

//————————————————————————————
```

```
    String read_net_input(InputStream input)
      {
        byte bytes[];
        int number_of_bytes;

        try
          {
            bytes = new byte[1];
            number_of_bytes = input.read(bytes, 0, 1);
            if (number_of_bytes > 0)
              return (new String(bytes, 0, 0, number_of_bytes));
            else
              return null;
          }
        catch (IOException e)
          return null;
      }

    //—————————————————————————

    void write_net_output(OutputStream output, String string)
      {
        byte byte_array[];

        int length = string.length();
        byte_array = new byte[length];
        string.getBytes(0, length, byte_array, 0);

        try
          output.write(byte_array);
        catch (IOException e)
          ;
      }
  }

//****************************************************************

class reader extends Thread
  {
    server s;
    int index;

    //—————————————————————————

    public reader(server s, int index)
      {
        this.s = s;
        this.index = index;
      }

    //—————————————————————————
```

```
    public void run ()
      {
        setPriority(MIN_PRIORITY);

        s.write_net_output(s.net_output[index], "WAIT");
        while (s.client_counter < 2)
          ;

        s.write_net_output(s.net_output[index], "  GO...");

        while (true)
          {
            String string = s.read_net_input(s.net_input[index]);

            if (string == null)
              break;

            System.out.println(s.user[index] + ": " + string);
            s.write_net_output(s.net_output[(index+1)%2], string);
          }

        System.out.println(s.user [index] + " has disconnected.");

        if (-s.client_counter == 0)
          System.exit(0);
      }
  }
```

The Client Program

As discussed, the client first connects to the server and then waits for a second client. After two clients are connected to the server, the text a user types at one client appears in the green window on the local system and in the red window of the remote client. This program is an applet, and it uses the *Socket* class instead of the *NetworkClient* class to implement a client:

```
//****************************************************************
// client.java
//****************************************************************

import java.applet.*;
import java.awt.*;
import java.io.*;
import java.net.*;


//****************************************************************

public class client extends Applet
  {
    Socket server;
    InputStream net_input;
    OutputStream net_output;
```

```
String username;
boolean connected = false;
writer w;

String typed_line = "";

String host;

//————————————————————————

public void init()
  {
    host = getParameter("HOST");

    if (connect())
      {
        connected = true;
        w = new writer(this);
        w.start();
      }
    else
      {
        username = "* NOT CONNECTED *";
        return;
      }
  }

//————————————————————————

boolean connect()
  {
    try
      server = new Socket(host, 1111);
    catch (IOException e)
      return false;

    username = "" + server.getLocalPort();

    try
      {
        net_input = server.getInputStream();
        net_output = server.getOutputStream ();
      }
    catch (IOException e)
      return false;

    write_net_output(username + "\n");

    return true;
  }

//————————————————————————
```

```java
    String read_net_input()
      {
        byte bytes[];
        int number_of_bytes;

        try
          {
            bytes = new byte[1];
            number_of_bytes = net_input.read(bytes, 0, 1);
            if (number_of_bytes > 0)
              return(new String(bytes, 0, 0, number_of_bytes));
            else
              return null;
          }
        catch (IOException e)
          return null;
      }

//————————————————————

    void write_net_output(String string)
      {
        byte byte_array[];

        int length = string.length();
        byte_array = new byte[length];
        string.getBytes(0, length, byte_array, 0);

        try
          net_output.write(byte_array);
        catch (IOException e)
          ;
      }

//————————————————————

    void close_server()
      {
        try
          server.close();
        catch (Exception e)
          ;
      }

//————————————————————

    public void stop()
      {
        close_server();
        w.stop();
      }

//————————————————————
```

```
    public boolean keyDown(Event evt, int key)
      {
        if (key == 27)
          {
            if (connected)
              {
                connected = false;
                close_server();
              }
          }

        else if (connected)
          {
            typed_line = typed_line + (char) key;
            if (typed_line.length() > 20)
              typed_line = typed_line.substring(1);
            write_net_output("" + (char) key);
            repaint();
          }

        return true;
      }

    //————————————————————————————


    public void paint(Graphics g)
      {
        Font font = new Font ("TimesRoman", Font.BOLD, 20);
        g.setFont (font);
        g.drawString ("Hello " + username, 100, 50);

        g.setColor (Color.red);
        g.fillRect (100, 100, 300, 50);
        g.setColor (Color.white);
        g.drawRect (100, 100, 300, 50);
        g.drawString (typed_line, 120, 125);

        g.setColor (Color.green);
        g.fillRect (100, 200, 300, 50);
        g.setColor (Color.black);
        g.drawRect (100, 200, 300, 50);
        g.drawString (w.net_line, 120, 225);
      }
  }

//*****************************************************************

class writer extends Thread
  {
    String net_line = "";

    client c;

    //————————————————————————————
```

405

```
      public writer(client c)
        {
          this.c = c;
        }

    //———————————————————————————

      public void run()
        {
          while (true)
            {
              String character = c.read_net_input();

              if (character == null)
                break;

              net_line = net_line + character;

              if (net_line.length() > 20)
                net_line = net_line.substring(1);

              c.repaint();
            }

          net_line = "disconnected";
          c.repaint();
        }
    }
```

BREAKING APART SOCKETS CHAT

In this section, you will examine each program in detail. First, you will examine the server program, and then you will examine the client program.

The Server Program

The server imports two packages: the *java.io* package for streams, and the *java.net* package for sockets:

```
import java.io.*;
import java.net.*;
```

Class Variables

To start, the server creates a server socket. When you later initialize this variable, you will bind it to a specific port on the host computer:

```
ServerSocket server_socket;
```

The server then declares the arrays to hold the usernames, network input streams, and network output streams. The class will use an *OutputStream* object instead of a *PrintStream* object, just so you can see how to use this object. The class also declares a counter which will contain the number of clients currently connected:

```
String user[];
InputStream net_input[];
OutputStream net_output[];

static int client_counter = 0;
```

The main Function

As stated, the server is a standalone program whose execution starts at the *main* function. Within the *main* function, the server creates a new instance of the *server* object:

```
public static void main(String args[])
   {
     new server();
   }
```

The Constructor

The server constructor function first initializes the arrays. Since this program only allows two clients, the function allocates two items for each array:

```
public server()
   {
     user = new String[2];
     net_input = new InputStream[2];
     net_output = new OutputStream[2];
```

Next, the function creates the server socket and binds it to a port. This object throws an exception if it cannot be created. After the function gets a server socket, it waits for clients to connect:

```
try
   server_socket = new ServerSocket(1111);
catch (IOException e)
   {
     System.out.println("Error in server socket");
     return;
   }

System.out.println("Waiting for users...");
```

As you can see, the function starts a loop that waits for a connection. To wait for a connection, the function calls the *accept* member function of the server socket. After the function gets a connection, it calls the *service_request* function and passes to it the socket of the client that connected:

```
while (true)
   {
     try
       {
         Socket socket = server_socket.accept();
         service_request(socket);
       }
```

```
        catch (IOException e)
          {
            System.out.println("Exception: <" + e + ">");
            break;
          }
      }
```

Servicing the Client

To service a client, the *service_request* function needs the socket, which it receives as a parameter. Next, the function gets the input and output streams. The *Socket* class contains two member functions that return those streams: the *getInputStream* function and the *getOutputStream* function:

```
public void service_request(Socket socket)
  {
    InputStream input;
    PrintStream output;

    try
      {
        input = socket.getInputStream();
        output = socket.getOutputStream();
      }
    catch (IOException e)
      {
        System.out.println("Unable to get input/output streams");
        return;
      }
```

The function then checks if it already has two clients. If it has two clients, the function sends a message to the current client and returns:

```
if (client_counter >= 2)
  {
    write_net_output(output, "There are already two clients");
    return;
  }
```

The function stores the input and output streams into their respective arrays for the current client. It then reads a line from the network to get the username:

```
net_input[client_counter] = input;
net_output[client_counter] = output;
user[client_counter] = read_net_input_line(input);
```

After it connects to a client, the function displays to the console the username of the new client. The function then starts a *reader* thread, which will wait for client input, and will then increment the counter that keeps track of how many clients have connected:

```
System.out.println(user[client_counter] + " Connected! " +
                   socket.toString());
```

```
(new reader(this, client_counter)).start();
client_counter++;
```

Network Reading and Writing

The *read_net_input_line* function reads input from the network one line at a time. To do this, the function starts a loop that gets one character at a time. While the character is not a linefeed, the function appends it to the line it is creating. When the function encounters the linefeed character, it returns the string of characters:

```
String read_net_input_line(InputStream input)
  {
    String line = "";
    String c;

    c = read_net_input(input);
    while ((byte) c.charAt(0) != 10)
      {
        line = line + c;
        c = read_net_input(input);
      }

    return line;
  }
```

The input stream has a *read* function that reads characters from the network. To use the *read* function, you pass to it a reference to a byte array, and the number of characters the array can hold. Using the *read* function, the *read_net_input* function reads one character at a time from across the Net. In this case, if the *read* function gets a character, the *read_net_input* function converts the character to a string and returns it. If there are no bytes available, or the *read* function generates an exception, the function returns a null:

```
String read_net_input(InputStream input)
  {
    byte bytes[];
    int number_of_bytes;

    try
      {
        bytes = new byte[1];
        number_of_bytes = input.read(bytes, 0, 1);
        if (number_of_bytes > 0)
          return (new String(bytes, 0, 0, number_of_bytes));
        else
          return null;
      }
    catch (IOException e)
      return null;
  }
```

The *write_net_output* function writes the string to the network. It assumes that the string to be sent contains all the characters that you want to send, including the linefeed characters. Since you are using an *OutputStream* instead of a *PrintStream*, you have to convert the string to a byte array before you can write it to the network:

```
void write_net_output(OutputStream output, String string)
  {
    byte byte_array[];

    int length = string.length();
    byte_array = new byte[length];
    string.getBytes(0, length, byte_array, 0);

    try
      output.write(byte_array);
    catch (IOException e)
      ;
  }
```

The reader Class

This class is the same as the *reader* class in the previous chapter. The only difference is that at the bottom of the *run* function, you do not have to reset the username to a null because the *service_request* function in this program does not have to wait for the client to disconnect before it ends, unlike the *serviceRequest* function in the previous chapter's server program.

The Client Program

The client program imports four packages: the *java.applet* package, because the client runs as an applet; the *java.awt* package, to perform graphics; the *java.io* package, to use input/output streams; and the *java.net* package, to use the networking classes:

```
import java.applet.*;
import java.awt.*;
import java.io.*;
import java.net.*;
```

The main *client* class is an applet, so it must extend the *Applet* class. As you can see, the class defines a *Socket* variable instead of the *NetworkClient* variable, which you used in the previous chapter. The client also defines a *host* variable which will contain the host-computer name that this client will use. Again, the class will use an *OutputStream* object instead of a *PrintStream* object. The other variables the class defines are the same as in the *network* class of the client program in the previous chapter:

```
public class client extends Applet
  {
    Socket server;
    InputStream net_input;
    OutputStream net_output;

    String username;
    boolean connected = false;
    writer w;

    String typed_line = "";

    String host;
```

Initializing the Applet

Within the *init* function, the client first gets the host computer name from the HTML file and then tries to connect to the server. If the function is able to connect, it sets the *connected* variable, creates a new *writer* object, and then starts it. If the function is unable to connect, it sets the *username* variable to "* NOT CONNECTED *" because the username will be displayed on the applet window:

```
public void init()
  {
    host = getParameter("HOST");

    if (connect())
      {
        connected = true;
        w = new writer(this);
        w.start();
      }
    else
      {
        username = "* NOT CONNECTED *";
        return;
      }
  }
```

Connecting to the Server

The *client* class uses the *connect* function to connect to the server. To do so, the *connect* function must create a new *Socket* object. To create a new *Socket* object, the function has to pass to it the host computer name, and the desired port number. You have to catch an exception in case the *Socket* object cannot connect to the server:

```
boolean connect()
  {
    try
      server = new Socket(host, 1111);
    catch (IOException e)
      return false;
```

Then, the function creates a username using the local port number. This will return the local port to which the socket is connected. The function also gets the input and output streams used by the socket. The function uses the *getInputStream* function to get the input stream, and the *getOutputStream* to get the output stream. These functions throw an exception if there is an error. Finally, the function sends the server the username followed by a linefeed, and returns *true*, meaning that it successfully connected:

```
username = "" + server.getLocalPort();

try
  {
    net_input = server.getInputStream();
    net_output = server.getOutputStream ();
  }
```

```
catch (IOException e)
  return false;
write_net_output(username + "\n");

return true;
```

Network Reading and Writing

To read data from the network, the client uses the *read_net_input* function. This function reads input from the network. It is the same as the *read_net_input* function in the server program:

```
String read_net_input()
  {
    byte bytes[];
    int number_of_bytes;

    try
      {
        bytes = new byte[1];
        number_of_bytes = net_input.read(bytes, 0, 1);
        if (number_of_bytes > 0)
          return(new String(bytes, 0, 0, number_of_bytes));
        else
          return null;
      }
    catch (IOException e)
      return null;
  }
```

To write data across the network, the client uses the *write_net_output* function. It is the same as the *write_net_output* function in the server program:

```
void write_net_output(String string)
  {
    byte byte_array[];

    int length = string.length();
    byte_array = new byte[length];
    string.getBytes(0, length, byte_array, 0);

    try
      net_output.write(byte_array);
    catch (IOException e)
      ;
  }
```

Closing the Server

To close the connection to the server, the client simply calls the *Socket* object *close* function. This function throws an exception if an error occurs:

```
void close_server()
  {
  try
    server.close();
  catch (IOException e)
    ;
  }
```

When the Applet Stops

When you tell the browser to exit the applet, either by closing the browser or moving to another HTML page, the client has to close the connection to the server. You can do this because, before an applet exits, it calls the *stop* function to let you clean up. In this function, you can close the server, and stop the *writer* object:

```
public void stop()
  {
  close_server();
  w.stop();
  }
```

Getting Keyboard Input

As you have learned, when the user presses a key, Java calls the *keyDown* function. This function is very similar to the *keyDown* functions used in the previous chapters. In this program, if the user hits the ESCAPE key, the connection to the server will close; otherwise, the character that the user typed will be sent to the server:

```
public boolean keyDown(Event evt, int key)
  {
  if (key == 27)
    {
    if (connected)
      {
      connected = false;
      close_server();
      }
    }

  else if (connected)
    {
    typed_line = typed_line + (char) key;
    if (typed_line.length() > 20)
      typed_line = typed_line.substring(1);
    write_net_output("" + (char) key);
    repaint();
    }

  return true;
  }
```

The paint Function

The *paint* function is the same as in the previous chapter. It simply writes the user input in a red box, and the other client's output in the green box.

```
public void paint(Graphics g)
  {
    Font font = new Font ("TimesRoman", Font.BOLD, 20);
    g.setFont (font);
    g.drawString ("Hello " + username, 100, 50);

    g.setColor (Color.red);
    g.fillRect (100, 100, 300, 50);
    g.setColor (Color.white);
    g.drawRect (100, 100, 300, 50);
    g.drawString (typed_line, 120, 125);

    g.setColor (Color.green);
    g.fillRect (100, 200, 300, 50);
    g.setColor (Color.black);
    g.drawRect (100, 200, 300, 50);
    g.drawString (w.net_line, 120, 225);
  }
```

The writer Class

As you may recall from Chapter 41, the *writer* class is a thread that continually gets characters from the server and displays them in the frame. This class is very similar to the *writer* class in Chapter 41. The only difference is in the *run* function where, if a network input returns a null, the server has disconnected, so, the thread must break out of the loop, and send a "disconnected" message to the screen:

```
public void run()
  {
    while (true)
      {
        String character = c.read_net_input();

        if (character == null)
          break;

        net_line = net_line + character;

        if (net_line.length() > 20)
          net_line = net_line.substring(1);

        c.repaint();
      }

    net_line = "disconnected";
    c.repaint();
  }
```

Enhancements You Can Make to Sockets Chat

Modify the programs to allow three people to chat. Or even an infinite number of users. Of course, for an infinite number, you cannot keep creating different colored boxes. Instead, you have to show a screen within which each client types their message, and the client's username appears on everybody's screen followed by the message. This screen should also be scrollable.

Putting It All Together

The **Sockets Chat** applet shows you how to write a network client applet. In addition to examining sockets, you learned how to use the *stop* function to cleanup an applet before it ends. In Chapter 43, you will learn how to write a Java program that connects to an FTP site and downloads a file. Before you continue with Chapter 43, however, make sure you understand the following key concepts:

- ☑ You can use *ServerSocket* and *Socket* classes instead of *NetworkServer* and *NetworkClient* to create networking programs.

- ☑ When you exit an applet, the browser calls the *stop* function. This gives you a chance to exit from the server.

- ☑ An applet can be created that talks to a server on a host computer system.

Chapter 43

Java FTP
Connect to an FTP Site and Download a File

Before the World Wide Web brought the Internet to the masses, one of the most widely used programs was FTP. The letters FTP are an acronym for File Transfer Protocol — the rules that programs follow to download files across the Net. Using an FTP program, users connect to FTP sites, such as **ftp.microsoft.com**. Once users are connected to a site, they can view directory listings of the available files and then select and download the files they desire. Across the Net, there are several million files users can download using FTP. Therefore, this chapter shows you how you can create a Java program that interacts with FTP. By the time you finish this chapter, you will understand the following key concepts:

◆ You can use the *FtpClient* class (provided in the *sun.net.ftp* package) to connect to an FTP site.

◆ After you connect to a site, you can change directories and download files.

◆ You can use the *TelNetInputStream* class to access characters from the FTP site.

◆ You can write to a file from a standalone program using FTP.

Using Java FTP

The **Java FTP** program is a standalone program. In other words, you do not run the program within a browser or the appletviewer. Instead, to run the **Java FTP** program, you can type the following at the command prompt:

```
java FTP   <Enter>
```

When you run the **Java FTP** program, the program will ask you to enter the name of the FTP site to which you want to connect. After you type the name of the site you want, your screen will look similar to Figure 43.1. Then the program will ask for a filename. At this point, you can either type the name of the file, or you can change directories. To change directories, type "cd" followed by a space, and the directory name, as shown in Figure 43.2. Next, you can change directories again or type in a filename. When you see the file that you want, type in the filename. When you type the filename, the program will download the file to you and you will see the contents of the file on the screen, as shown in Figure 43.3. At this point, the program ends, and you can find the file on your computer, as shown in Figure 43.4.

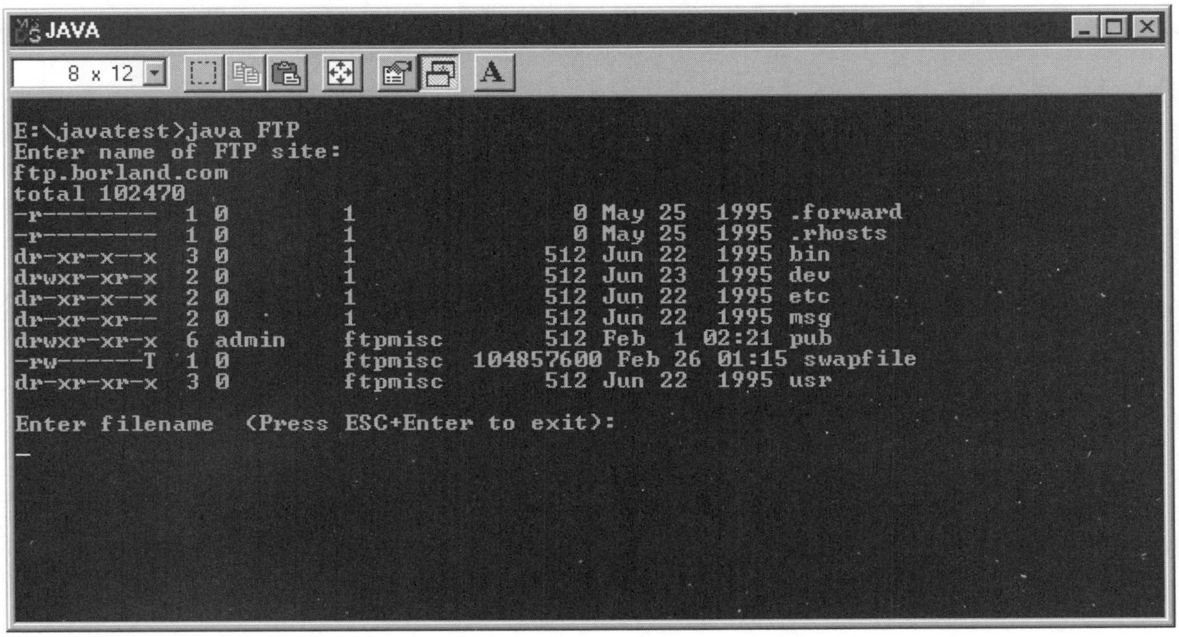

Figure 43.1 The screen after typing the name of the FTP site.

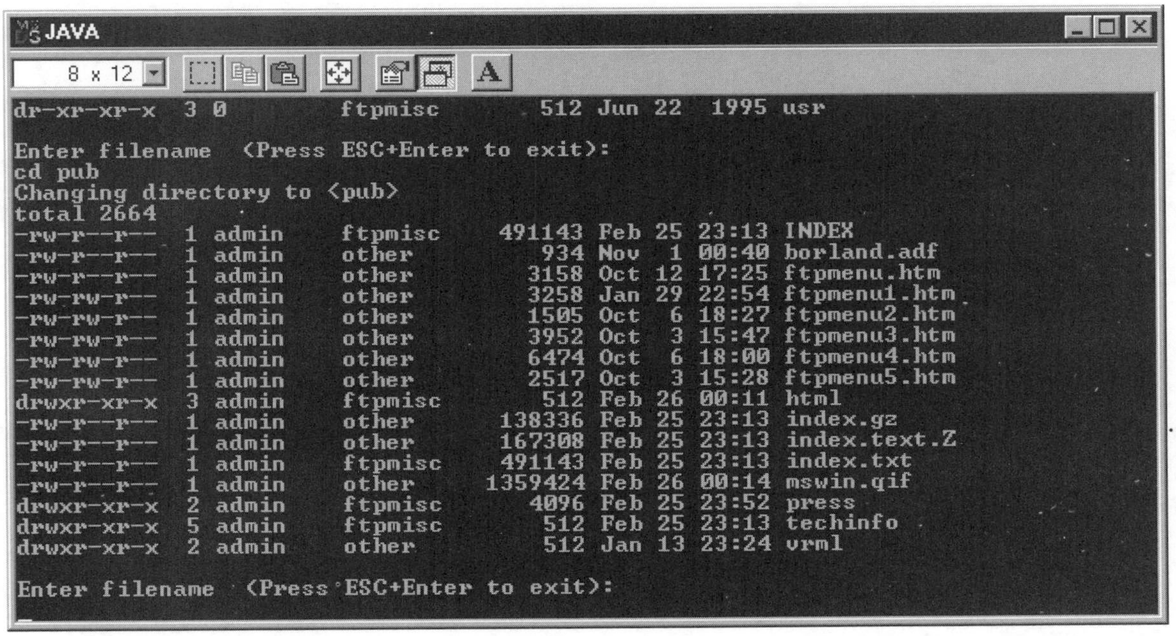

Figure 43.2 The screen after changing to the "pub" directory.

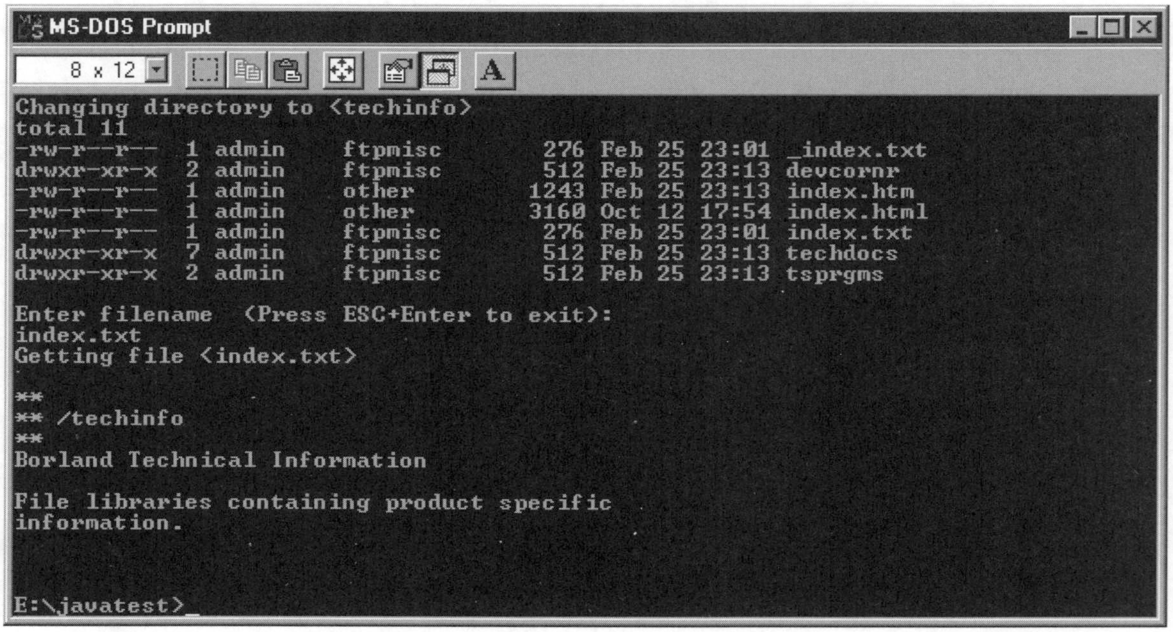

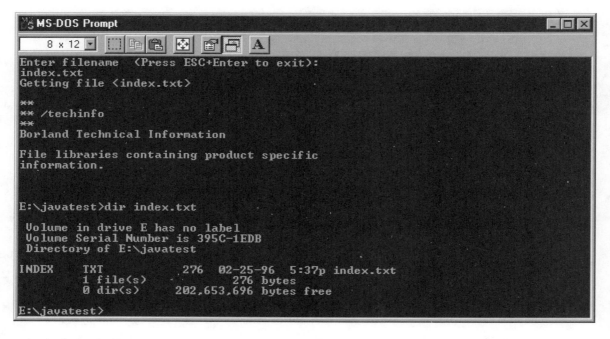

Figure 43.3 *After downloading the "index.txt" file.*

Figure 43.4 *The "index.txt" directory entry on the local computer.*

The HTML File

Because the **Java FTP** program is a standalone program, there is no HTML file for the program.

Looking at Java FTP

The **Java FTP** program uses the *FtpClient* class found in the *sun.net.ftp* package. The following code implements **Java FTP**:

```
//*****************************************************************
// FTP.java
//*****************************************************************

import java.io.*;
import sun.net.ftp.*;
import sun.net.*;

//*****************************************************************

class FTP
  {
    FtpClient ftp;

    //————————————————————————

    public static void main(String args[])
      {
        new FTP();
      }

    //————————————————————————

    public FTP()
      {
        try
          {
            System.out.println("Enter name of FTP site: ");
            String ftp_site = read_line();

            ftp = new FtpClient(ftp_site);
            ftp.login("anonymous", "your@email.com");
            ftp.binary();

            telnet_read();

            get_file();
          }

        catch (IOException e)
          System.out.println("Exception: " + e);
      }

    //————————————————————————
```

```java
String read_line() throws IOException
  {
    DataInputStream s = new DataInputStream(System.in);
    return s.readLine();
  }


//————————————————————————


void telnet_read() throws IOException
  {
    int c;

    TelnetInputStream t = ftp.list();

    while ((c = t.read()) >= 0)
      System.out.print("" + (char) c);

    t.close();
  }


//————————————————————————


void telnet_read_to_file(String filename)
                              throws IOException
  {
    int c;

    TelnetInputStream t = ftp.get(filename);

    RandomAccessFile f = new RandomAccessFile(filename, "rw");

    while ((c = t.read()) >= 0)
      {
        System.out.print("" + (char) c);
        f.writeByte((byte) c);
      }

    f.close();

    t.close();
  }


//————————————————————————


void get_file() throws IOException
  {
    while (true)
      {
        System.out.print("\nEnter filename  ");
        System.out.println("(Press ESC+Enter to exit):");
        String string = read_line();
        if (string.charAt(0) == (char) 27)
          return;
```

```
          try
            {
              if (string.startsWith("cd "))
                {
                  System.out.println("Changing directory to <" +
                                      string.substring(3) + ">");
                  ftp.cd(string.substring(3));
                  telnet_read();
                }
              else
                {
                  System.out.println("Getting file <" +
                                      string + ">");
                  telnet_read_to_file(string);
                  break;
                }
            }
          catch (FileNotFoundException e)
            System.out.println("File not found!  Try again");
        }
    }
}
```

Breaking Apart Java FTP

The **Java FTP** program uses three packages: the *java.io* package for the exceptions and file output, the *sun.net.ftp* package for the *FtpClient* class, and the *sun.net* package for the *TelNetInputStream* class.

```
import java.io.*;
import sun.net.ftp.*;
import sun.net.*;
```

The program creates the *FTP* class, which is really a plain vanilla class. The *FTP* class doesn't extend or implement anything. You can declare a class this way when you are writing a standalone program:

```
class FTP
```

The *FTP* class has only one member variable: the *FtpClient* object:

```
FtpClient ftp;
```

The **Java FTP** program creates an *FtpClient* object, and then uses the client to connect to an FTP server. The *main* function just starts a new instance of the *FTP* class:

```
public static void main(String args[])
  {
    new FTP();
  }
```

Because **Java FTP** creates a standalone program, as opposed to an applet, **Java FTP** uses a *main* function, much like C/C++ (as opposed to the *init* function).

The Constructor

The *FTP* class constructor first prompts the user for the name of the FTP site to which they wish to connect. The function uses *read_line* functions to read the site name the user types. Next, the *FTP* class creates a new *FtpClient* object, passing to it the site name as a parameter. Then, you can login to the FTP site, passing it a username and a password, which is usually your e-mail address. Edit this source file and replace the text **your@email.com** with your e-mail address. After the function logs you to the site, it sets the file transfer protocol to binary.

After the function sets up the FTP site, it can read the information from the site. For example, the local member function *telnet_read* gets a directory listing of the site. After the function displays the list of files, you can call the *get_file* local member function to get a file from the site, or to change directories. If there are any exceptions, the function catches them and displays them to the console window:

```
public FTP()
  {
    try
      {
        System.out.println("Enter name of FTP site: ");
        String ftp_site = read_line();

        ftp = new FtpClient(ftp_site);
        ftp.login("anonymous", "your@email.com");
        ftp.binary();

        telnet_read();

        get_file();
      }

    catch (IOException e)
      System.out.println("Exception: " + e);
  }
```

Read a Line from System Input

As you just saw, the *FTP* class constructor uses the *read_line* function to read the site name the user types. Since the function has access to the *InputStream* object for keyboard entry using *System.in*, it converts the input-stream object to a *DataInputStream* object, which lets it read a line that ends with a linefeed. As you can see, the function uses the *readLine* member function that returns a string:

```
String read_line() throws IOException
  {
    DataInputStream s = new DataInputStream(System.in);
    return s.readLine();
  }
```

Reading from the FTP Site

You can read information from the FTP site by using a *TelnetInputStream* object. For example, the *telnet_read* function reads and displays the list of files that reside in the site's current directory. To start, the function calls the *list* member function of the *FtpClient* object that lists the files on the FTP server, and returns a *TelnetInputStream* object. Then, the function uses this object to read each character from the stream, and displays it to the screen. After the function reads and displays the last character, it closes the stream:

```
void telnet_read() throws IOException
  {
    int c;

    TelnetInputStream t = ftp.list();

    while ((c = t.read()) >= 0)
      System.out.print("" + (char) c);

    t.close();
  }
```

Reading a file from the FTP Site

To read and display a file from the FTP site, the program uses the *telnet_read_to_file* function. First, the function calls the *get* member function of the *FtpClient* object, which gets a file from the FTP server, and returns a *TelnetInputStream* object. Then, the function uses this object to read each character from the stream, save it to a file, and to display it on the screen. After the last character is received, the function closes the stream object.

Before the function can write to a file on your system, it must first create one. To create the file, the function uses the *RandomAccessFile* object, which lets you create a file whose contents you can access in a random fashion. You pass the *RandomAccessFile* object a filename and the mode you are using to open the file. The mode can be "r" to read a file, or "rw" to read-and-write to a file. Because this function writes to the file, it uses the "rw" mode. As it gets each character from the FTP site, the function uses the *writeByte* function to write the character to the file. After the last character, the function closes the file:

```
void telnet_read_to_file(String filename) throws IOException
  {
    int c;

    TelnetInputStream t = ftp.get(filename);

    RandomAccessFile f = new RandomAccessFile(filename, "rw");

    while ((c = t.read()) >= 0)
      {
        System.out.print("" + (char) c);
        f.writeByte((byte) c);
      }

    f.close();

    t.close();
  }
```

Getting the File or Changing Directories

The *FTP* class uses the *get_file* function to get a file when you type in a filename, and change directories if you type in a "cd" followed by a space and a directory name. If, at the prompt to enter a filename, you hit the ESCAPE key and press the ENTER key, the function will return, and the program will end. The entire process of this function is inside a loop, because the user may need to change directories many times before they locate a file:

```
void get_file() throws IOException
  {
    while (true)
      {
        System.out.print("\nEnter filename  ");
        System.out.println("(Press ESC+Enter to exit):");
        String string = read_line();
        if (string.charAt(0) == (char) 27)
          return;
```

If the string the user types starts with a "cd" followed by a space, the function calls the *FtpClient* object *cd* member function to change the directory, passing to the function the directory name that should start in the fourth character position (you use index 3 instead of 4 since Java indexes start from 0). After changing directories, the function calls *telnet_read* to read and display the files that reside in the new directory:

```
try
  {
    if (string.startsWith("cd "))
      {
        System.out.println("Changing directory to <" +
                            string.substring(3) + ">");
        ftp.cd(string.substring(3));
        telnet_read();
      }
```

If the user types a filename, the function calls the *telnet_read_to_file* local member function and passes the filename to it:

```
  else
    {
      System.out.println("Getting file <" +
                          string + ">");
      telnet_read_to_file(string);
      break;
    }
```

Notice that the operation that gets the file might cause an exception. If an exception occurs, the function catches it, displays it to the screen, and then loops, letting the user select another file:

```
catch (FileNotFoundException e)
  System.out.println("File not found!  Try again");
```

ENHANCEMENTS YOU CAN MAKE TO FTP

To start, modify the program to use a graphical screen, as opposed to the screen display. To do so, you can extract the filenames from the directory listing, and display them in a window. Next, allow the user to use the mouse to select the file they want to download.

PUTTING IT ALL TOGETHER

As your programs become more complex, you can reduce your programming significantly by taking advantage of existing Internet protocols, such as FTP and Telnet. Using the **Java FTP** program, you learned how to connect to an FTP site, change directories at the site, and download a file. In Chapter 44, you will revisit the bitmap-font class, this time to create a marquee-like ticker that displays its message using a bitmap-font. Before you continue with Chapter 44, however, make sure you have learned the following key points:

- ☑ Using the *FtpClient* class, you can connect to an FTP site.

- ☑ After you connect to the site, your applet can send text messages to change directories or download a file from the FTP site.

- ☑ Using the *TelNetInputStream* class, you can access characters from the FTP site.

- ☑ Although you can't perform file I/O from within a Java applet, you can write to a file from a standalone program.

CHAPTER 44

TICKER
CREATING A BITMAPPED TICKER

In Chapter 5, you created a marquee appplet that scrolls a message across the screen. In Chapter 34, you learned how to create your own bitmap-font. In this chapter, you will combine the marquee and the bitmap-font to create a message ticker. By the time you finish this chapter, you will understand the following key concepts:

- You can create a ticker font by drawing each bit of the bitmap font smaller. For example, in this chapter, the bits are half as wide and half as high.

- To scroll a message horizontally one bit at a time, you have to keep track of the bit where you are starting, calculate the bit of the last character where to stop, and be able to shift all the characters in the middle.

USING TICKER

When you run the **Ticker** applet, you will see a window with a message that scrolls horizontally, as shown in Figure 44. When you resize the window, the font will also resize to fit inside the window.

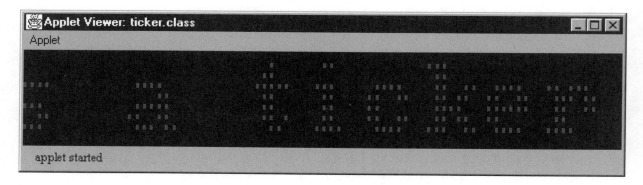

Figure 44 A bitmapped ticker message.

THE HTML FILE

Use the following HTML file to run the **Ticker** applet:

```
<applet code=ticker.class width=600 height=100>
<param name=delay value=200>
<param name=message value="Some ticker message to display">
</applet>
```

As you can see, the HTML parameters specify the ticker's message and a delay value that controls the ticker's speed.

Looking at Ticker

The **Ticker** applet contains two classes: the main *ticker* class, and the old bitmap-font class, slightly modified. This chapter will present the *ticker* class first.

The ticker Class

This class uses a bitmap-font class to display a ticker. It displays 10 characters at a time, and scrolls horizontally through each bit of the character bytes. As it scrolls each bit of the first character off the left side of the screen, it brings in the eleventh character one bit at a time on the right side of the screen. When the first character is off the screen, the 10 characters are then set to the second through the eleventh character. As the second character goes off the left side of the screen, the twelfth character is brought in on the right side of the screen, and so on. After the last character comes in on the right side of the screen, the string is reset to the beginning 10 characters again. The following code implements the *ticker* class:

```
//***************************************************************
// ticker.java
//***************************************************************

import java.applet.*;
import java.awt.*;

//***************************************************************

public class ticker extends Applet implements Runnable
   {
      Graphics g;

      font_8x8 font;

      Thread my_thread;

      int width;
      int height;

      String ticker_string = "This is a ticker test";

      int index;
      int length;

      int delay_amount = 200;

      //——————————————————————————————

      public void init()
         {
            g = getGraphics();
            font = new font_8x8(g);

            String parameter = getParameter("DELAY");
            if (parameter != null)
               delay_amount = Integer.parseInt(parameter);
```

```
        parameter = getParameter("MESSAGE");
        if (parameter != null)
          ticker_string = parameter;

        set_defaults();

        index = 0;
        length = ticker_string.length();
    }

//————————————————————————

void set_defaults()
    {
      width = size().width;
      height = size().height;
    }

//————————————————————————

public void start()
    {
      if (my_thread == null)
        {
          my_thread = new Thread(this);
          my_thread.start();
        }
    }

//————————————————————————

public void stop()
    {
      if (my_thread != null)
        {
          my_thread.stop();
          my_thread = null;
        }
    }

//————————————————————————

void delay()
    {
      try
        {
          Thread.sleep(delay_amount);
        }
      catch (InterruptedException e)
        {
        }
    }

//————————————————————————
```

```
       public void run()
         {
           while (my_thread != null)
             repaint();
         }


       //————————————————————————

       public void update(Graphics _g)
         {
           for (int i = 0; i < 8; i++)
             {
               g.setColor(Color.black);
               g.fillRect(0, 0, width, height);
               g.setColor(Color.red);

               font.draw_string
                         (ticker_string.substring(index, index+11),
                          0, height, width, height, 10, i);

               delay();
             }

           if (++index > length-11)
             index = 0;
         }

       //————————————————————————

       public void paint(Graphics g)
         {
           set_defaults();
           update(g);
         }
     }
```

The Bitmap-Font Class

The bitmap-font class contains the code to define each letter in an 8x8 bitmap. It contains all 256 characters used on an IBM-PC or PC-compatible computer. The methods are modified slightly from Chapter 34 to be able to print ticker-like characters. The following code implements the bitmap-font class:

```
//****************************************************************
// font_8x8.java
//****************************************************************

import java.awt.*;


//****************************************************************

public class font_8x8
  {
    Graphics g;
```

```java
static final int table[][] =
  {
  {0x00, 0x00, 0x00, 0x00, 0x00, 0x00, 0x00, 0x00},
  {0x7e, 0x81, 0xa5, 0x81, 0xbd, 0x99, 0x81, 0x7e},
  {0x7e, 0xff, 0xdb, 0xff, 0xc3, 0xe7, 0xff, 0x7e},
  {0x6c, 0xfe, 0xfe, 0xfe, 0x7c, 0x38, 0x10, 0x00},
  {0x10, 0x38, 0x7c, 0xfe, 0x7c, 0x38, 0x10, 0x00},
  {0x38, 0x7c, 0x38, 0xfe, 0xfe, 0x7c, 0x38, 0x7c},
  {0x10, 0x10, 0x38, 0x7c, 0xfe, 0x7c, 0x38, 0x7c},
  {0x00, 0x00, 0x18, 0x3c, 0x3c, 0x18, 0x00, 0x00},
  {0xff, 0xff, 0xe7, 0xc3, 0xc3, 0xe7, 0xff, 0xff},
  {0x00, 0x3c, 0x66, 0x42, 0x42, 0x66, 0x3c, 0x00},
  {0xff, 0xc3, 0x99, 0xbd, 0xbd, 0x99, 0xc3, 0xff},
  {0x0f, 0x07, 0x0f, 0x7d, 0xcc, 0xcc, 0xcc, 0x78},
  {0x3c, 0x66, 0x66, 0x66, 0x3c, 0x18, 0x7e, 0x18},
  {0x3f, 0x33, 0x3f, 0x30, 0x30, 0x70, 0xf0, 0xe0},
  {0x7f, 0x63, 0x7f, 0x63, 0x63, 0x67, 0xe6, 0xc0},
  {0x99, 0x5a, 0x3c, 0xe7, 0xe7, 0x3c, 0x5a, 0x99},
  {0x80, 0xe0, 0xf8, 0xfe, 0xf8, 0xe0, 0x80, 0x00},
  {0x02, 0x0e, 0x3e, 0xfe, 0x3e, 0x0e, 0x02, 0x00},
  {0x18, 0x3c, 0x7e, 0x18, 0x18, 0x7e, 0x3c, 0x18},
  {0x66, 0x66, 0x66, 0x66, 0x66, 0x00, 0x66, 0x00},
  {0x7f, 0xdb, 0xdb, 0x7b, 0x1b, 0x1b, 0x1b, 0x00},
  {0x3e, 0x63, 0x38, 0x6c, 0x6c, 0x38, 0xcc, 0x78},
  {0x00, 0x00, 0x00, 0x00, 0x7e, 0x7e, 0x7e, 0x00},
  {0x18, 0x3c, 0x7e, 0x18, 0x7e, 0x3c, 0x18, 0xff},
  {0x18, 0x3c, 0x7e, 0x18, 0x18, 0x18, 0x18, 0x00},
  {0x18, 0x18, 0x18, 0x18, 0x7e, 0x3c, 0x18, 0x00},
  {0x00, 0x18, 0x0c, 0xfe, 0x0c, 0x18, 0x00, 0x00},
  {0x00, 0x30, 0x60, 0xfe, 0x60, 0x30, 0x00, 0x00},
  {0x00, 0x00, 0xc0, 0xc0, 0xc0, 0xfe, 0x00, 0x00},
  {0x00, 0x24, 0x66, 0xff, 0x66, 0x24, 0x00, 0x00},
  {0x00, 0x18, 0x3c, 0x7e, 0xff, 0xff, 0x00, 0x00},
  {0x00, 0xff, 0xff, 0x7e, 0x3c, 0x18, 0x00, 0x00},
  {0x00, 0x00, 0x00, 0x00, 0x00, 0x00, 0x00, 0x00},
  {0x30, 0x78, 0x78, 0x30, 0x30, 0x00, 0x30, 0x00},
  {0x6c, 0x6c, 0x6c, 0x00, 0x00, 0x00, 0x00, 0x00},
  {0x6c, 0x6c, 0xfe, 0x6c, 0xfe, 0x6c, 0x6c, 0x00},
  {0x30, 0x7c, 0xc0, 0x78, 0x0c, 0xf8, 0x30, 0x00},
  {0x00, 0xc6, 0xcc, 0x18, 0x30, 0x66, 0xc6, 0x00},
  {0x38, 0x6c, 0x38, 0x76, 0xdc, 0xcc, 0x76, 0x00},
  {0x60, 0x60, 0xc0, 0x00, 0x00, 0x00, 0x00, 0x00},
  {0x18, 0x30, 0x60, 0x60, 0x60, 0x30, 0x18, 0x00},
  {0x60, 0x30, 0x18, 0x18, 0x18, 0x30, 0x60, 0x00},
  {0x00, 0x66, 0x3c, 0xff, 0x3c, 0x66, 0x00, 0x00},
  {0x00, 0x30, 0x30, 0xfc, 0x30, 0x30, 0x00, 0x00},
  {0x00, 0x00, 0x00, 0x00, 0x00, 0x30, 0x30, 0x60},
  {0x00, 0x00, 0x00, 0xfc, 0x00, 0x00, 0x00, 0x00},
  {0x00, 0x00, 0x00, 0x00, 0x00, 0x30, 0x30, 0x00},
  {0x06, 0x0c, 0x18, 0x30, 0x60, 0xc0, 0x80, 0x00},
  {0x7c, 0xc6, 0xce, 0xde, 0xf6, 0xe6, 0x7c, 0x00},
  {0x30, 0x70, 0x30, 0x30, 0x30, 0x30, 0xfc, 0x00},
  {0x78, 0xcc, 0x0c, 0x38, 0x60, 0xcc, 0xfc, 0x00},
  {0x78, 0xcc, 0x0c, 0x38, 0x0c, 0xcc, 0x78, 0x00},
```

```
{0x1c, 0x3c, 0x6c, 0xcc, 0xfe, 0x0c, 0x1e, 0x00},
{0xfc, 0xc0, 0xf8, 0x0c, 0x0c, 0xcc, 0x78, 0x00},
{0x38, 0x60, 0xc0, 0xf8, 0xcc, 0xcc, 0x78, 0x00},
{0xfc, 0xcc, 0x0c, 0x18, 0x30, 0x30, 0x30, 0x00},
{0x78, 0xcc, 0xcc, 0x78, 0xcc, 0xcc, 0x78, 0x00},
{0x78, 0xcc, 0xcc, 0x7c, 0x0c, 0x18, 0x70, 0x00},
{0x00, 0x30, 0x30, 0x00, 0x00, 0x30, 0x30, 0x00},
{0x00, 0x30, 0x30, 0x00, 0x00, 0x30, 0x30, 0x60},
{0x18, 0x30, 0x60, 0xc0, 0x60, 0x30, 0x18, 0x00},
{0x00, 0x00, 0xfc, 0x00, 0x00, 0xfc, 0x00, 0x00},
{0x60, 0x30, 0x18, 0x0c, 0x18, 0x30, 0x60, 0x00},
{0x78, 0xcc, 0x0c, 0x18, 0x30, 0x00, 0x30, 0x00},
{0x7c, 0xc6, 0xde, 0xde, 0xde, 0xc0, 0x78, 0x00},
{0x30, 0x78, 0xcc, 0xcc, 0xfc, 0xcc, 0xcc, 0x00},
{0xfc, 0x66, 0x66, 0x7c, 0x66, 0x66, 0xfc, 0x00},
{0x3c, 0x66, 0xc0, 0xc0, 0xc0, 0x66, 0x3c, 0x00},
{0xf8, 0x6c, 0x66, 0x66, 0x66, 0x6c, 0xf8, 0x00},
{0xfe, 0x62, 0x68, 0x78, 0x68, 0x62, 0xfe, 0x00},
{0xfe, 0x62, 0x68, 0x78, 0x68, 0x60, 0xf0, 0x00},
{0x3c, 0x66, 0xc0, 0xc0, 0xce, 0x66, 0x3e, 0x00},
{0xcc, 0xcc, 0xcc, 0xfc, 0xcc, 0xcc, 0xcc, 0x00},
{0x78, 0x30, 0x30, 0x30, 0x30, 0x30, 0x78, 0x00},
{0x1e, 0x0c, 0x0c, 0x0c, 0xcc, 0xcc, 0x78, 0x00},
{0xe6, 0x66, 0x6c, 0x78, 0x6c, 0x66, 0xe6, 0x00},
{0xf0, 0x60, 0x60, 0x60, 0x62, 0x66, 0xfe, 0x00},
{0xc6, 0xee, 0xfe, 0xfe, 0xd6, 0xc6, 0xc6, 0x00},
{0xc6, 0xe6, 0xf6, 0xde, 0xce, 0xc6, 0xc6, 0x00},
{0x38, 0x6c, 0xc6, 0xc6, 0xc6, 0x6c, 0x38, 0x00},
{0xfc, 0x66, 0x66, 0x7c, 0x60, 0x60, 0xf0, 0x00},
{0x78, 0xcc, 0xcc, 0xcc, 0xdc, 0x78, 0x1c, 0x00},
{0xfc, 0x66, 0x66, 0x7c, 0x6c, 0x66, 0xe6, 0x00},
{0x78, 0xcc, 0xe0, 0x70, 0x1c, 0xcc, 0x78, 0x00},
{0xfc, 0xb4, 0x30, 0x30, 0x30, 0x30, 0x78, 0x00},
{0xcc, 0xcc, 0xcc, 0xcc, 0xcc, 0xcc, 0xfc, 0x00},
{0xcc, 0xcc, 0xcc, 0xcc, 0xcc, 0x78, 0x30, 0x00},
{0xc6, 0xc6, 0xc6, 0xd6, 0xfe, 0xee, 0xc6, 0x00},
{0xc6, 0xc6, 0x6c, 0x38, 0x38, 0x6c, 0xc6, 0x00},
{0xcc, 0xcc, 0xcc, 0x78, 0x30, 0x30, 0x78, 0x00},
{0xfe, 0xc6, 0x8c, 0x18, 0x32, 0x66, 0xfe, 0x00},
{0x78, 0x60, 0x60, 0x60, 0x60, 0x60, 0x78, 0x00},
{0xc0, 0x60, 0x30, 0x18, 0x0c, 0x06, 0x02, 0x00},
{0x78, 0x18, 0x18, 0x18, 0x18, 0x18, 0x78, 0x00},
{0x10, 0x38, 0x6c, 0xc6, 0x00, 0x00, 0x00, 0x00},
{0x00, 0x00, 0x00, 0x00, 0x00, 0x00, 0x00, 0xff},
{0x30, 0x30, 0x18, 0x00, 0x00, 0x00, 0x00, 0x00},
{0x00, 0x00, 0x78, 0x0c, 0x7c, 0xcc, 0x76, 0x00},
{0xe0, 0x60, 0x60, 0x7c, 0x66, 0x66, 0xdc, 0x00},
{0x00, 0x00, 0x78, 0xcc, 0xc0, 0xcc, 0x78, 0x00},
{0x1c, 0x0c, 0x0c, 0x7c, 0xcc, 0xcc, 0x76, 0x00},
{0x00, 0x00, 0x78, 0xcc, 0xfc, 0xc0, 0x78, 0x00},
{0x38, 0x6c, 0x60, 0xf0, 0x60, 0x60, 0xf0, 0x00},
{0x00, 0x00, 0x76, 0xcc, 0xcc, 0x7c, 0x0c, 0xf8},
{0xe0, 0x60, 0x6c, 0x76, 0x66, 0x66, 0xe6, 0x00},
{0x30, 0x00, 0x70, 0x30, 0x30, 0x30, 0x78, 0x00},
```

```
    {0x0c, 0x00, 0x0c, 0x0c, 0x0c, 0xcc, 0xcc, 0x78},
    {0xe0, 0x60, 0x66, 0x6c, 0x78, 0x6c, 0xe6, 0x00},
    {0x70, 0x30, 0x30, 0x30, 0x30, 0x30, 0x78, 0x00},
    {0x00, 0x00, 0xcc, 0xfe, 0xfe, 0xd6, 0xc6, 0x00},
    {0x00, 0x00, 0xf8, 0xcc, 0xcc, 0xcc, 0xcc, 0x00},
    {0x00, 0x00, 0x78, 0xcc, 0xcc, 0xcc, 0x78, 0x00},
    {0x00, 0x00, 0xdc, 0x66, 0x66, 0x7c, 0x60, 0xf0},
    {0x00, 0x00, 0x76, 0xcc, 0xcc, 0x7c, 0x0c, 0x1e},
    {0x00, 0x00, 0xdc, 0x76, 0x66, 0x60, 0xf0, 0x00},
    {0x00, 0x00, 0x7c, 0xc0, 0x78, 0x0c, 0xf8, 0x00},
    {0x10, 0x30, 0x7c, 0x30, 0x30, 0x34, 0x18, 0x00},
    {0x00, 0x00, 0xcc, 0xcc, 0xcc, 0xcc, 0x76, 0x00},
    {0x00, 0x00, 0xcc, 0xcc, 0xcc, 0x78, 0x30, 0x00},
    {0x00, 0x00, 0xc6, 0xd6, 0xfe, 0xfe, 0x6c, 0x00},
    {0x00, 0x00, 0xc6, 0x6c, 0x38, 0x6c, 0xc6, 0x00},
    {0x00, 0x00, 0xcc, 0xcc, 0xcc, 0x7c, 0x0c, 0xf8},
    {0x00, 0x00, 0xfc, 0x98, 0x30, 0x64, 0xfc, 0x00},
    {0x1c, 0x30, 0x30, 0xe0, 0x30, 0x30, 0x1c, 0x00},
    {0x18, 0x18, 0x18, 0x00, 0x18, 0x18, 0x18, 0x00},
    {0xe0, 0x30, 0x30, 0x1c, 0x30, 0x30, 0xe0, 0x00},
    {0x76, 0xdc, 0x00, 0x00, 0x00, 0x00, 0x00, 0x00},
    {0x00, 0x10, 0x38, 0x6c, 0xc6, 0xc6, 0xfe, 0x00},
    {0x78, 0xcc, 0xc0, 0xcc, 0x78, 0x18, 0x0c, 0x78},
    {0x00, 0xcc, 0x00, 0xcc, 0xcc, 0xcc, 0x7e, 0x00},
    {0x1c, 0x00, 0x78, 0xcc, 0xfc, 0xc0, 0x78, 0x00},
    {0x7e, 0xc3, 0x3c, 0x06, 0x3e, 0x66, 0x3f, 0x00},
    {0xcc, 0x00, 0x78, 0x0c, 0x7c, 0xcc, 0x7e, 0x00},
    {0xe0, 0x00, 0x78, 0x0c, 0x7c, 0xcc, 0x7e, 0x00},
    {0x30, 0x30, 0x78, 0x0c, 0x7c, 0xcc, 0x7e, 0x00},
    {0x00, 0x00, 0x78, 0xc0, 0xc0, 0x78, 0x0c, 0x38},
    {0x7e, 0xc3, 0x3c, 0x66, 0x7e, 0x60, 0x3c, 0x00},
    {0xcc, 0x00, 0x78, 0xcc, 0xfc, 0xc0, 0x78, 0x00},
    {0xe0, 0x00, 0x78, 0xcc, 0xfc, 0xc0, 0x78, 0x00},
    {0xcc, 0x00, 0x70, 0x30, 0x30, 0x30, 0x78, 0x00},
    {0x7c, 0xc6, 0x38, 0x18, 0x18, 0x18, 0x3c, 0x00},
    {0xe0, 0x00, 0x70, 0x30, 0x30, 0x30, 0x78, 0x00},
    {0xc6, 0x38, 0x6c, 0xc6, 0xfe, 0xc6, 0xc6, 0x00},
    {0x30, 0x30, 0x00, 0x78, 0xcc, 0xfc, 0xcc, 0x00},
    {0x1c, 0x00, 0xfc, 0x60, 0x78, 0x60, 0xfc, 0x00},
    {0x00, 0x00, 0x7f, 0x0c, 0x7f, 0xcc, 0x7f, 0x00},
    {0x3e, 0x6c, 0xcc, 0xfe, 0xcc, 0xcc, 0xce, 0x00},
    {0x78, 0xcc, 0x00, 0x78, 0xcc, 0xcc, 0x78, 0x00},
    {0x00, 0xcc, 0x00, 0x78, 0xcc, 0xcc, 0x78, 0x00},
    {0x00, 0xe0, 0x00, 0x78, 0xcc, 0xcc, 0x78, 0x00},
    {0x78, 0xcc, 0x00, 0xcc, 0xcc, 0xcc, 0x7e, 0x00},
    {0x00, 0xe0, 0x00, 0xcc, 0xcc, 0xcc, 0x7e, 0x00},
    {0x00, 0xcc, 0x00, 0xcc, 0xcc, 0x7c, 0x0c, 0xf8},
    {0xc3, 0x18, 0x3c, 0x66, 0x66, 0x3c, 0x18, 0x00},
    {0xcc, 0x00, 0xcc, 0xcc, 0xcc, 0xcc, 0x78, 0x00},
    {0x18, 0x18, 0x7e, 0xc0, 0xc0, 0x7e, 0x18, 0x18},
    {0x38, 0x6c, 0x64, 0xf0, 0x60, 0xe6, 0xfc, 0x00},
    {0xcc, 0xcc, 0x78, 0xfc, 0x30, 0xfc, 0x30, 0x30},
    {0xf8, 0xcc, 0xcc, 0xfa, 0xc6, 0xcf, 0xc6, 0xc7},
    {0x0e, 0x1b, 0x18, 0x3c, 0x18, 0x18, 0xd8, 0x70},
```

```
{0x1c, 0x00, 0x78, 0x0c, 0x7c, 0xcc, 0x7e, 0x00},
{0x38, 0x00, 0x70, 0x30, 0x30, 0x30, 0x78, 0x00},
{0x00, 0x1c, 0x00, 0x78, 0xcc, 0xcc, 0x78, 0x00},
{0x00, 0x1c, 0x00, 0xcc, 0xcc, 0xcc, 0x7e, 0x00},
{0x00, 0xf8, 0x00, 0xf8, 0xcc, 0xcc, 0xcc, 0x00},
{0xfc, 0x00, 0xcc, 0xec, 0xfc, 0xdc, 0xcc, 0x00},
{0x3c, 0x6c, 0x6c, 0x3e, 0x00, 0x7e, 0x00, 0x00},
{0x38, 0x6c, 0x6c, 0x38, 0x00, 0x7c, 0x00, 0x00},
{0x30, 0x00, 0x30, 0x60, 0xc0, 0xcc, 0x78, 0x00},
{0x00, 0x00, 0x00, 0xfc, 0xc0, 0xc0, 0x00, 0x00},
{0x00, 0x00, 0x00, 0xfc, 0x0c, 0x0c, 0x00, 0x00},
{0xc3, 0xc6, 0xcc, 0xde, 0x33, 0x66, 0xcc, 0x0f},
{0xc3, 0xc6, 0xcc, 0xdb, 0x37, 0x6f, 0xcf, 0x03},
{0x18, 0x18, 0x00, 0x18, 0x18, 0x18, 0x18, 0x00},
{0x00, 0x33, 0x66, 0xcc, 0x66, 0x33, 0x00, 0x00},
{0x00, 0xcc, 0x66, 0x33, 0x66, 0xcc, 0x00, 0x00},
{0x22, 0x88, 0x22, 0x88, 0x22, 0x88, 0x22, 0x88},
{0x55, 0xaa, 0x55, 0xaa, 0x55, 0xaa, 0x55, 0xaa},
{0xdb, 0x77, 0xdb, 0xee, 0xdb, 0x77, 0xdb, 0xee},
{0x18, 0x18, 0x18, 0x18, 0x18, 0x18, 0x18, 0x18},
{0x18, 0x18, 0x18, 0x18, 0xf8, 0x18, 0x18, 0x18},
{0x18, 0x18, 0xf8, 0x18, 0xf8, 0x18, 0x18, 0x18},
{0x36, 0x36, 0x36, 0x36, 0xf6, 0x36, 0x36, 0x36},
{0x00, 0x00, 0x00, 0x00, 0xfe, 0x36, 0x36, 0x36},
{0x00, 0x00, 0xf8, 0x18, 0xf8, 0x18, 0x18, 0x18},
{0x36, 0x36, 0xf6, 0x06, 0xf6, 0x36, 0x36, 0x36},
{0x36, 0x36, 0x36, 0x36, 0x36, 0x36, 0x36, 0x36},
{0x00, 0x00, 0xfe, 0x06, 0xf6, 0x36, 0x36, 0x36},
{0x36, 0x36, 0xf6, 0x06, 0xfe, 0x00, 0x00, 0x00},
{0x36, 0x36, 0x36, 0x36, 0xfe, 0x00, 0x00, 0x00},
{0x18, 0x18, 0xf8, 0x18, 0xf8, 0x00, 0x00, 0x00},
{0x00, 0x00, 0x00, 0x00, 0xf8, 0x18, 0x18, 0x18},
{0x18, 0x18, 0x18, 0x18, 0x1f, 0x00, 0x00, 0x00},
{0x18, 0x18, 0x18, 0x18, 0xff, 0x00, 0x00, 0x00},
{0x00, 0x00, 0x00, 0x00, 0xff, 0x18, 0x18, 0x18},
{0x18, 0x18, 0x18, 0x18, 0x1f, 0x18, 0x18, 0x18},
{0x00, 0x00, 0x00, 0x00, 0xff, 0x00, 0x00, 0x00},
{0x18, 0x18, 0x18, 0x18, 0xff, 0x18, 0x18, 0x18},
{0x18, 0x18, 0x1f, 0x18, 0x1f, 0x18, 0x18, 0x18},
{0x36, 0x36, 0x36, 0x36, 0x37, 0x36, 0x36, 0x36},
{0x36, 0x36, 0x37, 0x30, 0x3f, 0x00, 0x00, 0x00},
{0x00, 0x00, 0x3f, 0x30, 0x37, 0x36, 0x36, 0x36},
{0x36, 0x36, 0xf7, 0x00, 0xff, 0x00, 0x00, 0x00},
{0x00, 0x00, 0xff, 0x00, 0xf7, 0x36, 0x36, 0x36},
{0x36, 0x36, 0x37, 0x30, 0x37, 0x36, 0x36, 0x36},
{0x00, 0x00, 0xff, 0x00, 0xff, 0x00, 0x00, 0x00},
{0x36, 0x36, 0xf7, 0x00, 0xf7, 0x36, 0x36, 0x36},
{0x18, 0x18, 0xff, 0x00, 0xff, 0x00, 0x00, 0x00},
{0x36, 0x36, 0x36, 0x36, 0xff, 0x00, 0x00, 0x00},
{0x00, 0x00, 0xff, 0x00, 0xff, 0x18, 0x18, 0x18},
{0x00, 0x00, 0x00, 0x00, 0xff, 0x36, 0x36, 0x36},
{0x36, 0x36, 0x36, 0x36, 0x3f, 0x00, 0x00, 0x00},
{0x18, 0x18, 0x1f, 0x18, 0x1f, 0x00, 0x00, 0x00},
{0x00, 0x00, 0x1f, 0x18, 0x1f, 0x18, 0x18, 0x18},
```

```
        {0x00, 0x00, 0x00, 0x00, 0x3f, 0x36, 0x36, 0x36},
        {0x36, 0x36, 0x36, 0x36, 0xff, 0x36, 0x36, 0x36},
        {0x18, 0x18, 0xff, 0x18, 0xff, 0x18, 0x18, 0x18},
        {0x18, 0x18, 0x18, 0x18, 0xf8, 0x00, 0x00, 0x00},
        {0x00, 0x00, 0x00, 0x00, 0x1f, 0x18, 0x18, 0x18},
        {0xff, 0xff, 0xff, 0xff, 0xff, 0xff, 0xff, 0xff},
        {0x00, 0x00, 0x00, 0x00, 0xff, 0xff, 0xff, 0xff},
        {0xf0, 0xf0, 0xf0, 0xf0, 0xf0, 0xf0, 0xf0, 0xf0},
        {0x0f, 0x0f, 0x0f, 0x0f, 0x0f, 0x0f, 0x0f, 0x0f},
        {0xff, 0xff, 0xff, 0xff, 0x00, 0x00, 0x00, 0x00},
        {0x00, 0x00, 0x76, 0xdc, 0xc8, 0xdc, 0x76, 0x00},
        {0x00, 0x78, 0xcc, 0xf8, 0xcc, 0xf8, 0xc0, 0xc0},
        {0x00, 0xfc, 0xcc, 0xc0, 0xc0, 0xc0, 0xc0, 0x00},
        {0x00, 0xfe, 0x6c, 0x6c, 0x6c, 0x6c, 0x6c, 0x00},
        {0xfc, 0xcc, 0x60, 0x30, 0x60, 0xcc, 0xfc, 0x00},
        {0x00, 0x00, 0x7e, 0xd8, 0xd8, 0xd8, 0x70, 0x00},
        {0x00, 0x66, 0x66, 0x66, 0x66, 0x7c, 0x60, 0xc0},
        {0x00, 0x76, 0xdc, 0x18, 0x18, 0x18, 0x18, 0x00},
        {0xfc, 0x30, 0x78, 0xcc, 0xcc, 0x78, 0x30, 0xfc},
        {0x38, 0x6c, 0xc6, 0xfe, 0xc6, 0x6c, 0x38, 0x00},
        {0x38, 0x6c, 0xc6, 0xc6, 0x6c, 0x6c, 0xee, 0x00},
        {0x1c, 0x30, 0x18, 0x7c, 0xcc, 0xcc, 0x78, 0x00},
        {0x00, 0x00, 0x7e, 0xdb, 0xdb, 0x7e, 0x00, 0x00},
        {0x06, 0x0c, 0x7e, 0xdb, 0xdb, 0x7e, 0x60, 0xc0},
        {0x38, 0x60, 0xc0, 0xf8, 0xc0, 0x60, 0x38, 0x00},
        {0x78, 0xcc, 0xcc, 0xcc, 0xcc, 0xcc, 0xcc, 0x00},
        {0x00, 0xfc, 0x00, 0xfc, 0x00, 0xfc, 0x00, 0x00},
        {0x30, 0x30, 0xfc, 0x30, 0x30, 0x00, 0xfc, 0x00},
        {0x60, 0x30, 0x18, 0x30, 0x60, 0x00, 0xfc, 0x00},
        {0x18, 0x30, 0x60, 0x30, 0x18, 0x00, 0xfc, 0x00},
        {0x0e, 0x1b, 0x1b, 0x18, 0x18, 0x18, 0x18, 0x18},
        {0x18, 0x18, 0x18, 0x18, 0x18, 0xd8, 0xd8, 0x70},
        {0x30, 0x30, 0x00, 0xfc, 0x00, 0x30, 0x30, 0x00},
        {0x00, 0x76, 0xdc, 0x00, 0x76, 0xdc, 0x00, 0x00},
        {0x38, 0x6c, 0x6c, 0x38, 0x00, 0x00, 0x00, 0x00},
        {0x00, 0x00, 0x00, 0x18, 0x18, 0x00, 0x00, 0x00},
        {0x00, 0x00, 0x00, 0x00, 0x18, 0x00, 0x00, 0x00},
        {0x0f, 0x0c, 0x0c, 0x0c, 0xec, 0x6c, 0x3c, 0x1c},
        {0x78, 0x6c, 0x6c, 0x6c, 0x6c, 0x00, 0x00, 0x00},
        {0x70, 0x18, 0x30, 0x60, 0x78, 0x00, 0x00, 0x00},
        {0x00, 0x00, 0x3c, 0x3c, 0x3c, 0x3c, 0x00, 0x00},
        {0x00, 0x00, 0x00, 0x00, 0x00, 0x00, 0x00, 0x00},
    };

//————————————————————————————————

public font_8x8(Graphics g)
  {
    this.g = g;
  }

//————————————————————————————————
```

```java
    public void draw_string(String string, int x, int y, int w, int h,
                   int number_of_characters_to_show, int start_bit)
  {
    int string_length = string.length();
    char char_array[] = new char[string_length];
    string.getChars(0, string_length, char_array, 0);

    w /= number_of_characters_to_show;

    draw_char(char_array[0],
            x, y, w, h, start_bit, 8, start_bit);

    for (int i = 1; i < string_length-1; i++)
      {
        x += w;
        draw_char(char_array[i],
                x, y, w, h, 0, 8, start_bit);
      }

    x += w;
    draw_char(char_array[string_length-1],
            x, y, w, h, 0, start_bit, start_bit);
  }

//——————————————————————————————

    public void draw_char(char c, int x, int y, int w, int h, int s,
                      int e, int move)
  {
    int index = (int) c;

    for (int i = 0; i < 8; i++)
      {
        for (int j = s; j < e; j++)
          {
            int bit = table[index][i] >> (7-j);
            if ((bit & 1) == 1)
              g.fillRect(x+(j-move)*w/8, y-(8-i)*h/9, w/16, h/18);
          }
      }
  }
}
```

BREAKING APART TICKER

The **Ticker** applet uses two classes: the *ticker* class and the bitmap-font class. This chapter examines the *ticker* class first.

The ticker Class

The *ticker* class imports two packages: the *java.applet* class, because this class is an applet, and the *java.awt* class, to perform graphics:

```
import java.applet.*;
import java.awt.*;
```

The *ticker* class inherits from the *Applet* class and will run as a thread, so the class is implemented as *Runnable*:

```
public class ticker extends Applet implements Runnable
```

Class Variables

To start, the class declares a variable to store its graphics context. The class will pass this variable to the bitmap-font class so that it can draw to the screen:

```
Graphics g;
```

Next, the class defines a *font* object that it will use to draw the ticker characters:

```
font_8x8 font;
```

As discussed, *ticker* runs as a thread. As such, the class creates a thread object:

```
Thread my_thread;
```

The class then declares the width and height variables to store the current size of the window. The bitmap-font class will use these variables to resize the fonts as the window is resized:

```
int width;
int height;
```

The *ticker_string* variable will contain the string to display on the ticker window. It is initialized here, but the applet can reset its value if there is a MESSAGE parameter in the HTML file:

```
String ticker_string = "This is a ticker test";
```

The class uses the *index* variable to contain the index of the first character in the string that it is displaying in the ticker window. Likewise, the class uses the *length* variable to store the number of characters the message contains:

```
int index;
int length;
```

Lastly, the class declares a variable to store the delay amount that it waits before shifting left one bit of the current string. The applet will override this value if the HTML file contains the DELAY parameter:

```
int delay_amount = 200;
```

Initializing the Applet

Within the *init* function, the applet gets the graphics context for this applet and initializes the bitmap font:

```
public void init()
  {
    g = getGraphics();
    font = new font_8x8(g);
```

Next, the applet gets the parameters from the HTML file:

```
String parameter = getParameter("DELAY");
if (parameter != null)
  delay_amount = Integer.parseInt(parameter);

parameter = getParameter("MESSAGE");
if (parameter != null)
  ticker_string = parameter;
```

Finally, the function sets the default window sizes, sets the index for the first character to display, and gets the length of the string:

```
    set_defaults();

    index = 0;
    length = ticker_string.length();
}
```

Setting the Defaults

The only defaults the applet sets are the width and the height of the window. The applet sets these because the user can resize the window if they run the applet within the *appletviewer*.

```
void set_defaults()
  {
    width = size().width;
    height = size().height;
  }
```

Starting the Applet

After the applet has been initialized, Java calls the *start* function to get the applet started. Within the *start* function, *ticker* creates and starts the thread, which will scroll the message on the ticker window:

```
public void start()
  {
    if (my_thread == null)
      {
        my_thread = new Thread(this);
        my_thread.start();
      }
  }
```

When the Applet Stops

As you have learned, when an applet ends, Java calls the *stop* function. In this case, the function stops the thread that the *ticker* class started in the *start* function:

```
public void stop()
  {
    if (my_thread != null)
      {
        my_thread.stop();
        my_thread = null;
      }
  }
```

Delay between Redraws

As the *ticker* class shifts each character to the left (one bit at a time), it pauses so the scrolling of each bit always takes the same amount of time, no matter how fast or slow the computer is that the applet is running on:

```
void delay()
  {
    try
      {
        Thread.sleep(delay_amount);
      }
    catch (InterruptedException e)
      {
      }
  }
```

Running The Thread

The *run* function is quite simple. As long as the thread is running, it repaints the screen:

```
public void run()
  {
    while (my_thread != null)
      repaint();
  }
```

Updating the Screen

The *update* function updates the screen by using the graphics context set in the *init* function. To do this, the function uses the local member variable *g*, and names the parameter "_g" so it does not use the parameter. This is so the function does not use the parameter, but uses the same graphics context as in the bitmap-font class.

Every time the screen updates, the function shifts the message to the left one bit at a time. To display the message, the function erases the entire screen with the black color, sets the color to red, and draws ten characters at a time. The function passes the bitmap-font class *draw_string* function 11 characters because, as it shifts the first character off the screen, the eleventh character has to come in from the right side:

```
public void update(Graphics _g)
  {
    for (int i = 0; i < 8; i++)
      {
        g.setColor(Color.black);
        g.fillRect(0, 0, width, height);
        g.setColor(Color.red);

        font.draw_string
                 (ticker_string.substring(index, index+11),
                  0, height, width, height, 10, i);

        delay();
      }
```

After shifting left a whole character, the function increments the index so the next update starts at the next character. If the last character has come in from the right side, the function resets the index to 0 to start at the beginning again:

```
if (++index > length-11)
  index = 0;
```

Repainting the Applet

Every time the user resizes the screen, the applet has to set the new defaults for the width and height, and update the screen:

```
public void paint(Graphics g)
  {
    set_defaults();
    update(g);
  }
```

The Bitmap-Font Class

The *draw_string* function and the *draw_char* functions discussed next are the only differences between this class and the bitmap-font class in Chapter 34.

Drawing the String

The *draw_string* function displays a string using the bitmap font. To draw the string, the function needs the string, the x-and-y coordinates, the width and height of the area to use, the number of characters to show, and the bit to start at when drawing the first character:

```
public void draw_string(String string, int x, int y, int w, int h,
             int number_of_characters_to_show, int start_bit)
```

To display characters, the function breaks up the string into individual characters and stores them into a character array:

```
int string_length = string.length();
char char_array[] = new char[string_length];
string.getChars(0, string_length, char_array, 0);
```

Next, the function calculates the width of each character by dividing the width of the entire area by the number of characters to display:

```
w /= number_of_characters_to_show;
```

Then, the function draws the first character starting at the bit specified by the *start_bit* parameter:

```
draw_char(char_array[0],
          x, y, w, h, start_bit, 8, start_bit);
```

Next, the function draws the middle characters. If the number of characters was 10, then the function will draw 9 characters in this loop:

```
for (int i = 1; i < string_length-1; i++)
  {
    x += w;
    draw_char(char_array[i],
              x, y, w, h, 0, 8, start_bit);
  }
```

Lastly, the function draws the last character using the number of bits specified in the *start_bit* parameter:

```
x += w;
draw_char(char_array[string_length-1],
          x, y, w, h, 0, start_bit, start_bit);
```

Drawing Each Character

The *draw_char* function actually displays a character on the screen using the bitmap-font. To draw each character, the function needs the character to draw, the x-and-y coordinates, the width and height of the area you will use for this character, the start bit, the end bit, and the number of bits that the first character has moved:

```
public void draw_char(char c, int x, int y, int w, int h, int s,
                      int e, int move)
```

The function gets the index into the array by converting the character into its integer ASCII equivalent:

```
int index = (int) c;
```

Next, the function draws 8 rows for each horizontal bit-position of the character. For each row, the function starts at the start-bit index provided, and stops at one less than the end-bit index provided. For each bit, the function checks to see if it has to draw it by checking if the bit is set. For each bit that the function has to draw, the width will be half of what it should be and the height will be half of what it should be. Since each character is eight bits wide, each bit's width is $w/8$, so you will use $w/16$; and each character is 9 rows high, each row is $h/9$, so you will use $h/18$. The x-coordinate of the bit to draw has to take into account the start bit of the first character:

```
for (int i = 0; i < 8; i++)
   {
     for (int j = s; j < e; j++)
       {
         int bit = table[index][i] >> (7-j);
         if ((bit & 1) == 1)
           g.fillRect(x+(j-move)*w/8, y-(8-i)*h/9, w/16, h/18);
       }
   }
```

ENHANCEMENTS YOU CAN MAKE TO TICKER

Make a ticker that scrolls vertically instead of horizontally.

PUTTING IT ALL TOGETHER

The **Ticker** applet shows you how to combine a *ticker* class and a bitmap-font object to draw characters used in a ticker marquee. In Chapter 45, you will learn how to create an **Eraser** applet that erases the screen image. The **Eraser** applet not only teaches you considerable graphics programming, it provides the foundation for Chapter 46's **Reveal Image** applet — one of the coolest applets in this book. Before you continue with Chapter 45, however, make sure you have learned the following key concepts:

☑   You can create a ticker font by drawing each bit of the bitmap font smaller. For example, in this chapter, the bits are half as wide and half as high.

☑   To scroll a message horizontally one bit at a time, you have to keep track of the bit where you are starting, calculate the bit of the last character where to stop, and be able to shift all the characters in the middle.

CHAPTER 45

ERASER
USING THE MOUSE TO ERASE AN IMAGE

When you develop a Web site, one of the points you need to keep foremost in your mind is a list of things you can do to get users to come back to your site. In this chapter, you will examine the **Eraser** applet, which lets the user erase an on-screen image by using their mouse. In short, as the user moves their mouse over the image, the **Eraser** applet will erase the image. In Chapter 46, you will modify this applet to let the user erase one image to reveal a second. While the **Eraser** applet is one of the cooler applets in this book, you will find that its code is actually quite simple. However, because your Web site can constantly change the images the user can erase and reveal, you give the user a reason to come back to your site. By the time you finish this chapter, you will understand the following key concepts:

- ◆ Within your applets, you can display a non-destructive cursor (such as an eraser) and move it across the screen by using exclusive or (XOR) operations with the underlying image.

- ◆ To erase an image on the screen, you simply perform an exclusive-or of the image pixels with themselves. In other words, when you exclusive-or an image with itself, the image disappears.

USING ERASER

When you run the **Eraser** applet, you will see a window with an image and a square eraser, as shown in Figure 45. When you press the mouse button, the area under the eraser will erase. As you drag the mouse with the button pressed, you will erase more of the image. Eventually, you can use your mouse to erase the entire image.

Figure 45 An image with an eraser.

THE HTML FILE

Use the following HTML file to run the **Eraser** applet:

```
<applet code=eraser.class width=300 height=400>
<param name=eraser_size value=20>
</applet>
```

If you examine the HTML file, you will find that the file includes a setting for *eraser_size* that defines the size of the eraser, in pixels. The larger the eraser, the faster it will erase an image on your screen.

LOOKING AT ERASER

As discussed, the **Eraser** applet lets you erase a background image by holding down your mouse key and dragging your mouse. The following code implements the **Eraser** applet:

```
//*****************************************************************
// eraser.java
//*****************************************************************

import java.applet.*;
import java.awt.*;

//*****************************************************************

public class eraser extends Applet
   {
      Graphics g;

      Image background;

      int width;
      int height;

      boolean done_loading_image = false;
      boolean first_time = true;

      int eraser_size = 50;

      int old_x;
      int old_y;

      //————————————————————————————

      public void init()
        {
          g = getGraphics();

          width = size().width;
          height = size().height;
```

```java
      String parameter = getParameter("ERASER_SIZE");
      if (parameter != null)
        eraser_size = Integer.parseInt(parameter);

      background = getImage(getCodeBase(), "image.gif");

      Image offscreen_image = createImage(300, 400);
      Graphics offscreen_GC = offscreen_image.getGraphics();
      offscreen_GC.drawImage(background, 0, 0, this);
    }

    //————————————————————————————

    public boolean mouseMove(Event evt, int x, int y)
      {
        Graphics g2 = g.create();
        g2.setXORMode(Color.white);

        if (first_time)
          first_time = false;
        else
          g2.drawRect(old_x, old_y, eraser_size, eraser_size);

        g2.drawRect(x, y, eraser_size, eraser_size);
        old_x = x;
        old_y = y;
        return true;
      }

    //————————————————————————————

    public boolean mouseDown(Event evt, int x, int y)
      {
        replace_image(x, y);
        return true;
      }

    //————————————————————————————

    public boolean mouseDrag(Event evt, int x, int y)
      {
        replace_image(x, y);
        return true;
      }

    //————————————————————————————

    public void replace_image(int x, int y)
      {
        Graphics g2 = g.create();
        g2.setXORMode(Color.white);
```

```
        if (!first_time)
          {
            g2.drawRect(old_x, old_y, eraser_size, eraser_size);
            first_time = true;
          }

        g2.setPaintMode();
        g2.setColor(Color.lightGray);
        g2.fillRect(x, y, eraser_size, eraser_size);
      }

    //————————————————————————

    public boolean imageUpdate(Image img, int infoflags, int x, int y,
                               int w, int h)
      {
        if (infoflags == ALLBITS)
          {
            done_loading_image = true;
            repaint();

            return false;
          }
        else
          return true;
      }

    //————————————————————————

    public void paint(Graphics _g)
      {
        if (!done_loading_image)
          showStatus("Eraser:  loading image");

        else
          {
            width = size().width;
            height = size().height;
            first_time = true;
            showStatus("Eraser:  done");
            g.drawImage(background, 0, 0, width, height, this);
          }
      }
  }
```

Breaking Apart Eraser

Much of the **Eraser** applet's initial processing is very similar to the applets you have examined throughout this book. The applet, for example, declares variables to hold the graphics context, the applet window width and height, and so on. Within the *init* function, the applet loads its background image and processes HTML parameters. The **Eraser** applet performs much of the key processing when the user moves the mouse, as discussed next.

Moving the Mouse

As you know, when the user moves their mouse within an applet, Java calls the applet's *mouseMove* function, passing the x-and-y coordinates of the mouse to the function:

```
public boolean mouseMove(Event evt, int x, int y)
```

Within *mouseMove*, the function first makes a copy of the graphics context (because the function will change the paint mode). Next, the function sets the paint mode to XOR (pronounced exclusive-or) using the white color. When you paint a pixel in XOR mode, the current pixel colors are exclusive-or'ed (XORed) with your selected color. In this case, the existing colors are XORed with the color white.

When you perform an exclusive-or operation on two values, the result of the operation depends on two values. For example, if you exclusive-or two values that are 0, the result is 0. If you exclusive-or a 1 and a 0, the result is 1. Lastly, if you exclusive-or a 1 and a 1, the result is 0.

Within a white image, all the image bits are one. To erase an image, an applet can draw the white cursor block on the screen (actually displaying the white block). Next, if the applet draws the white block a second time, using an XOR operation, the white block will disappear, leaving only the original background. The following statements create a new graphics context and then select the XOR paint mode for the new context:

```
Graphics g2 = g.create();
g2.setXORMode(Color.white);
```

The first time this function executes, there is no white block to erase; therefore, the applet simply resets the *first_time* boolean's value. If this is not the first time, the applet will erase the old white block by redrawing it. When the user has erased an area by clicking and dragging the mouse, there is also no white block to erase, because the *replace_image* function will have erased it and will have set the *first_time* variable to *true*:

```
if (first_time)
  first_time = false;
else
  g2.drawRect(old_x, old_y, eraser_size, eraser_size);
```

Then, the function draws the eraser in the new position, and saves the position's coordinates as *old_x* and *old_y*, which the applet will use to erase the white block next time. The function then returns the value *true* to Java to indicate that it handled the mouse event:

```
g2.drawRect(x, y, eraser_size, eraser_size);
old_x = x;
old_y = y;
return true;
```

Clicking the Mouse

When the user presses the mouse button within the applet, Java calls the *mouseDown* function, passing to the function the x-and-y coordinates of the mouse where the user pressed the mouse button. In the case of the **Eraser** applet, when the user presses a mouse key, the applet replaces the background image at that location with a light-gray box:

```
public boolean mouseDown(Event evt, int x, int y)
  {
    replace_image(x, y);
    return true;
  }
```

Dragging the Mouse

When the user drags their mouse within the applet, Java calls the *mouseDrag* function, passing to the function the current mouse's x-and-y coordinates. If the user drags the mouse very quickly, the applet will not get every x-and-y coordinate the mouse crosses, because Java can't possibly keep up with very fast mouse movement. In the case of the **Eraser** applet, if the user drags their mouse, the *mouseDrag* function erases the corresponding background image:

```
public boolean mouseDrag(Event evt, int x, int y)
  {
    replace_image(x, y);
    return true;
  }
```

Replacing the Image

As you have learned, the **Eraser** applet uses the *replace_image* function to erase an image from the screen. As the user clicks and drags the mouse, this function will replace the erase box with a light-gray box at the x-and-y coordinates provided as parameters:

```
public void replace_image(int x, int y)
```

To start, the function makes a copy of the graphics context (because the function will change the paint mode). Then, the function selects the XOR paint mode with the color white:

```
Graphics g2 = g.create();
g2.setXORMode(Color.white);
```

If this is not the first time, you have to erase the eraser from the old position and reset the *first_time* variable to *true*. You must do this because, after the image is replaced with the background, you will not have an eraser that needs to be erased on the screen next time:

```
if (!first_time)
  {
    g2.drawRect(old_x, old_y, eraser_size, eraser_size);
    first_time = true;
  }
```

Then, to erase the image, the function sets the paint mode to overwrite the destination, sets the color to the background color of light-gray, and fills a rectangle the size of the eraser:

```
g2.setPaintMode();
g2.setColor(Color.lightGray);
g2.fillRect(x, y, eraser_size, eraser_size);
```

ENHANCEMENTS YOU CAN MAKE TO ERASER

To start, allow the user to change the size of the eraser interactively. For example, each time the user double-clicks their mouse, the applet can toggle between a small and large eraser. Also, let the user select the color that the applet will use to erase the image. You can set up the color choices on the right or the bottom of the image, and use the techniques learned in the **Cyber Zoo** applet in Chapter 13, "Cyber Zoo," to make the selections.

PUTTING IT ALL TOGETHER

The **Eraser** applet shows you how to move the eraser by using exclusive-or operations, and how to erase the screen when the user clicks and drags the mouse. When you create Java applets that perform animations by moving objects, you can use exclusive-or operations to move and erase images. In Chapter 46, you will enhance the **Eraser** applet so that as you erase one image, the applet displays an underlying image. Before you continue with Chapter 46, however, make sure you understand the following key concepts:

☑ To move images across the screen, many programs perform exclusive-or graphics operations.

☑ To erase an item that has been drawn in the exclusive-or graphics mode, an applet simply redraws the item in the same spot, using the same mode.

CHAPTER 46

REVEAL IMAGE
ERASING ONE IMAGE TO REVEAL A SECOND IMAGE

In Chapter 45, using the **Eraser** applet, you learned how to make the mouse an eraser and erase an image on the screen. In this chapter, you will create the **Reveal Image** applet that lets you erase an image to reveal an image underneath. For example, a Web site for a car dealership might let you erase a picture of the car to reveal a picture of the car's interior, or more likely, the car's great price. Likewise, the Playboy home page might . . . well, you probably get the picture. As you will learn, erasing one image to reveal a second is pretty cool and pretty easy. By the time you finish this chapter, you will understand the following key concept:

♦ To erase one image and reveal a second image, your applet simply overwrites the image it is erasing with the second image, which gives the illusion that the user is revealing the second image.

USING REVEAL IMAGE

When you run the **Reveal Image** applet, you will see a window with an image and a square eraser, as shown in Figure 46.1. When you press the mouse button, the area under the eraser will erase to a second image. As you drag the mouse with the button pressed, you will erase more of the first image, which will reveal more of the second image, as shown in Figure 46.2.

Figure 46.1 The original image with an eraser.

Figure 46.2 *The second image starts to appear as you erase the old image.*

THE HTML FILE

Use the following HTML file to run the **Reveal Image** applet:

```
<applet code=eraser.class width=300 height=300>
<param name=eraser_size value=20>
</applet>
```

As did the **Eraser** applet, the **Reveal Image** applet lets you specify the eraser size in the HTML file. The larger the eraser size, the faster the applet can erase the image.

LOOKING AT REVEAL IMAGE

The **Reveal Image** applet lets you erase one image to reveal a second image. The following code implements the **Reveal Image** applet:

```
//******************************************************************
// eraser.java
//******************************************************************

import java.applet.*;
import java.awt.*;


//******************************************************************
```

```java
public class eraser extends Applet
   {
     Graphics g;

     Image image_1;
     Image image_2;

     int width;
     int height;

     boolean done_loading_image = false;
     boolean first_time = true;

     int eraser_size = 50;

     int old_x;
     int old_y;

     //————————————————————————————————

     public void init()
       {
         g = getGraphics();

         width = size().width;
         height = size().height;

         String parameter = getParameter("ERASER_SIZE");
         if (parameter != null)
           eraser_size = Integer.parseInt(parameter);

         image_1 = getImage(getCodeBase(), "image1.gif");
         image_2 = getImage(getCodeBase(), "image2.gif");

         offscreen_image = createImage(300, 400);
         Graphics offscreen_GC = offscreen_image.getGraphics();
         offscreen_GC.drawImage(image_1, 0, 0, this);
       }

     //————————————————————————————————

     public boolean mouseMove(Event evt, int x, int y)
       {
         Graphics g2 = g.create();
         g2.setXORMode(Color.white);

         if (first_time)
           first_time = false;
         else
           g2.drawRect(old_x, old_y, eraser_size, eraser_size);

         g2.drawRect(x, y, eraser_size, eraser_size);
```

```
        old_x = x;
        old_y = y;
        return true;
    }

//————————————————————

public boolean mouseDrag(Event evt, int x, int y)
    {
        replace_image(x, y);
        return true;
    }

//————————————————————

public boolean mouseDown(Event evt, int x, int y)
    {
        replace_image(x, y);
        return true;
    }

//————————————————————

public void replace_image(int x, int y)
    {
        Graphics g2 = g.create();
        g2.setXORMode(Color.white);

        if (!first_time)
          {
            g2.drawRect(old_x, old_y, eraser_size, eraser_size);
            first_time = true;
          }

        g2.setPaintMode();
        g2.clipRect(x, y, eraser_size, eraser_size);
        g2.drawImage(image_2, 0, 0, width, height, this);
    }

//————————————————————

public boolean imageUpdate(Image img, int infoflags, int x, int y,
                           int w, int h)
    {
        if (infoflags == ALLBITS)
          {
            done_loading_image = true;
            repaint();

            return false;
          }
        else
          return true;
    }

//————————————————————
```

```
    public void paint(Graphics _g)
      {
        if (!done_loading_image)
          showStatus("Eraser:  loading image");

        else
          {
            width = size().width;
            height = size().height;
            first_time = true;
            showStatus("Eraser:  done");
            g.drawImage(image_1, 0, 0, width, height, this);
          }
      }
  }
```

Breaking Apart Reveal Image

The **Reveal Image** applet is very similar to the **Eraser** applet you examined in Chapter 45. The following sections, therefore, will only examine the code that differs between the two applets.

The **Reveal Image** applet uses two images: the starting image that you erase, and the ending image that you reveal. If you examine the applet's class member variables, you will find two image objects: *image1* corresponds to the starting image, and *image2* corresponds to the ending image:

```
Image image_1;
Image image_2;
```

Within the *init* function, the applet must get and load two images. The applet loads the first image as an offscreen image, so you can use the *imageUpdate* function to determine when the image has loaded:

```
image_1 = getImage(getCodeBase(), "image1.gif");
image_2 = getImage(getCodeBase(), "image2.gif");

offscreen_image = createImage(300, 400);
Graphics offscreen_GC = offscreen_image.getGraphics();
offscreen_GC.drawImage(image_1, 0, 0, this);
```

The mouse-movement functions are the same in this applet as they were in the previous chapter's **Eraser** applet. However, in the *replace_image* function, you do not want to simply replace the image with the background. Instead, you replace it with the second image. To do this, you still have to set the paint mode to overwrite the destination. Then, you set up the clip rectangle (so only the portion of the eraser gets overwritten) and then draw the second image:

```
g2.setPaintMode();
g2.clipRect(x, y, eraser_size, eraser_size);
g2.drawImage(image_2, 0, 0, width, height, this);
```

You do not have to change anything else from the **Eraser** applet.

ENHANCEMENTS YOU CAN MAKE TO REVEAL IMAGE

To start, create an applet that emulates the "scratch to win prizes" games. For example, display one or more covered items. Depending on which item the user erases, the user can win a certain prize. If you are creating a clothing store Web site, you might create images of a model in the same pose, but wearing different clothes. As the user erases, different clothes appear on the model.

PUTTING IT ALL TOGETHER

The **Reveal Image** applet has shown you how to erase one image to reveal a second image. As you learned, the applet only gives the perception that you are revealing a second image as you erase. Instead, the applet actually overwrites the first image with the second as the user erases. In Chapter 47, you will create a **Poorman's Photoshop** applet that lets you display a color image, and then drain all the color from the image. Before you continue with Chapter 47, however, make sure you have learned the following key concept:

☑ To reveal a second image as you erase an image, the applet actually overwrites the first image with the second.

Chapter 47

Poorman's Photoshop
Adding and Removing Image Color

In Chapter 46, using the **Reveal Image** applet, you learned how to work with two images to produce an illusion that as the user erased one image, they revealed a second image. In this chapter, using the **Poorman's Photoshop** applet, you will again use two images. This time, however, the images are identical, with one exception—one image is in color, while the second is in black-and-white. By slowly overwriting one image with the other, you create the illusion that the applet is adding color to, or draining color from, an image.

- Using two identical images, one in color, and the other in black-and-white, your applet can replace one image with the second to create cool effects.

- As you replace the first image with the second image, it will seem as though the image is losing color; then, when you restore the first image, it will seem as though the image is gaining its color back. In reality, however, the applet is simply displaying two identical images—one that is in color, and the second that is in black-and-white.

Using Poorman's Photoshop

When you run the **Poorman's Photoshop** applet, you will see a window with a picture, as shown in Figure 47. Then, the picture will seem to lose its color as a second image starts to display from the left side of the window. When the entire second image is in view, the screen will contain a black-and-white picture. Then, the color will start to reappear from the right side of the window as the original image starts to appear. When the original picture is completely displayed, the entire picture will be in color. The applet will continue this process of adding and removing image colors until you close the applet window.

Figure 47 The original picture.

THE HTML FILE

Use the following HTML file to run the **Poorman's Photoshop** applet:

```
<applet code=replace.class width=350 height=350>
<param name=delay_amount value=50>
</applet>
```

As you can see, within the HTML file, you can specify a setting for the *delay_amount* entry that determines how long the applet delays, in milliseconds, each time it adds or removes a color band from the image. The smaller the delay value, the faster the applet will convert a color image to black-and-white, or a black-and-white image to color.

LOOKING AT POORMAN'S PHOTOSHOP

The **Poorman's Photoshop** applet displays a picture, slowly removes its color, and then slowly restores its color. By specifying the delay between drawing the vertical-image scan lines, you can control how fast the applet updates the image. The following code implements the **Poorman's Photoshop** applet:

```
//*******************************************************************
// replace.java
//*******************************************************************

import java.applet.*;
import java.awt.*;

//*******************************************************************

public class replace extends Applet implements Runnable
  {
    Graphics g;

    Image image_1;
    Image image_2;

    int width;
    int height;

    boolean done_loading_image = false;

    int delay_amount = 0;

    //——————————————————————————————

    public void init()
      {
        g = getGraphics();

        width = size().width;
        height = size().height;

        String parameter = getParameter("DELAY_AMOUNT");
        if (parameter != null)
          delay_amount = Integer.parseInt(parameter);
```

```
         image_1 = getImage(getCodeBase(), "image1.gif");
         image_2 = getImage(getCodeBase(), "image2.gif");

         Image offscreen_image = createImage(300, 400);
         Graphics offscreen_GC = offscreen_image.getGraphics();
         offscreen_GC.drawImage(image_1, 0, 0, this);
     }

// ————————————————————————————

public void start()
   {
     (new Thread(this)).start();
   }

// ————————————————————————————

void delay()
   {
     try
       Thread.sleep(delay_amount);
     catch (InterruptedException e)
       ;
   }

// ————————————————————————————

public void run()
   {
     while (!done_loading_image)
       ;

     while (true)
       {
         for (int x = 0; x < width; x++)
           {
             Graphics g2 = g.create();
             g2.clipRect(x, 0, 1, height);
             g2.drawImage(image_2, 0, 0, width, height, this);
             delay();
           }

         for (int x = width-1; x >= 0; x—)
           {
             Graphics g2 = g.create();
             g2.clipRect(x, 0, 1, height);
             g2.drawImage(image_1, 0, 0, width, height, this);
             delay();
           }
       }
   }

// ————————————————————————————
```

```
        public boolean imageUpdate(Image img, int infoflags, int x, int y,
                                   int w, int h)
   {
     if (infoflags == ALLBITS)
       {
          done_loading_image = true;
          repaint();

          return false;
       }
     else
       return true;
   }

   //————————————————————

   public void paint(Graphics _g)
     {
       if (!done_loading_image)
         showStatus("Replace:  loading image");

       else
         {
           width = size().width;
           height = size().height;
           showStatus("Replace:  started");
           g.drawImage(image_1, 0, 0, width, height, this);
         }
     }
}
```

BREAKING APART POORMAN'S PHOTOSHOP

The **Poorman's Photoshop** applet is very similar to many of the applets presented throughout this text. To start, the applet imports its packages and then implements a *Runnable* interface so it can use a thread to update the images. Next, the applet declares its class variables. If you examine the class variables, you will find that the applet supports two image objects: one for the color image, and one for the black-and-white image.

Initializing the Applet

Within the *init* function, the applet gets the graphics context and the width and height of the applet window. Then, the applet gets the delay-value setting from the HTML file. The *init* function then gets and loads the first graphics image as an offscreen image:

```
public void init()
  {
    g = getGraphics();

    width = size().width;
    height = size().height;
```

```
      String parameter = getParameter("DELAY_AMOUNT");
      if (parameter != null)
        delay_amount = Integer.parseInt(parameter);


      image_1 = getImage(getCodeBase(), "image1.gif");
      image_2 = getImage(getCodeBase(), "image2.gif");


      Image offscreen_image = createImage(300, 400);
      Graphics offscreen_GC = offscreen_image.getGraphics();
      offscreen_GC.drawImage(image_1, 0, 0, this);
   }
```

Starting the Thread

As briefly discussed, the **Poorman's Photoshop** applet uses a thread to continually update the image. To create the thread, the applet creates a new instance of the *Thread* class by using this applet, and then calls its *start* function:

```
public void start()
   {
     (new Thread(this)).start();
   }
```

Running the Thread

Within the thread's *run* function, the applet must first wait until it has loaded the first image:

```
public void run()
   {
     while (!done_loading_image)
       ;
```

Then, the function starts a loop that will loop forever, or until the applet is stopped. This loop will contain two *for* loops: the first, which will draw the second image one vertical scan line at a time, from the left until the whole image is done; and the second, which will draw the first image one vertical scan line at a time, from the right side until it is done.

The function creates a new graphics context every time through the loop, because the clip rectangle changes every time through the loop:

```
for (int x = 0; x < width; x++)
   {
     Graphics g2 = g.create();
     g2.clipRect(x, 0, 1, height);
     g2.drawImage(image_2, 0, 0, width, height, this);
     delay();
   }
```

The second *for* loop differs from the first loop in that it starts at the right-hand side of the image and goes to the left, decrementing the x-coordinate until it gets to zero:

```
for (int x = width-1; x >= 0; x-)
  {
    Graphics g2 = g.create();
    g2.clipRect(x, 0, 1, height);
    g2.drawImage(image_1, 0, 0, width, height, this);
    delay();
  }
```

Updating the Image

This function is the same as in the previous chapter. It just waits for the image to finish loading and then repaints the applet window:

```
public boolean imageUpdate(Image img, int infoflags, int x, int y,
                           int w, int h)
  {
    if (infoflags == ALLBITS)
      {
        done_loading_image = true;
        repaint();

        return false;
      }
    else
      return true;
  }
```

ENHANCEMENTS YOU CAN MAKE TO POORMAN'S PHOTOSHOP

To start, modify the program so the image is replaced from top-to-bottom instead of left-to-right. You could also modify it so the replacement image comes in from the left and the right, like a curtain closing, and then starts to replace the original image from the middle again, like a curtain opening. Lastly, change the applet so it starts its update from the middle of the image and works outward.

PUTTING IT ALL TOGETHER

This applet demonstrated how to show an image, replace it with a black-and-white duplicate, and then restore the original image. In Chapter 48, you will learn how to build a drag-and-drop pizza. Before continuing with Chapter 48, however, make sure you understand the following key concepts:

☑ You can create two images, one in color, and the other in black-and-white, and then merge the images to create cool effects.

☑ As you replace the first image with the second image, it will seem as though the image is losing color, and then when you restore the first image, it will seem as though the image is gaining its color back. In reality, however, the applet simply overwrites one image with the other.

Chapter 48

Pizza Site
Building Drag-and-Drop Pizza

If you watched the early evolution of the World Wide Web, you may have noticed that several of the first "interactive" sites were those of the pizza companies. Using these sites, users could order their pizzas online and in 30 minutes (or less) the pizza-delivery person was at their door. In this chapter, you will build the ultimate online pizza site. Using the site's default pizza, users can drag-and-drop the toppings they desire onto the pizza. By the time you finish this chapter, you will understand the following key concepts:

- ◆ Using mouse operations, you can drag-and-drop items on top of another image.

- ◆ You can keep track of which items have been dropped on the image, and which have not.

- ◆ You can calculate the price of the pizza according to how many toppings the user has selected.

- ◆ You can create your own buttons that will respond to mouse clicks and perform specific actions.

Using Pizza Site

When you run the **Pizza Site** applet, you will see a window with a pizza, some toppings, and buttons, as shown in Figure 48.1. You can select toppings and drag them on top of the pizza. Then, when you click on "Price," you will get the price of the pizza with the toppings selected. Clicking on "Order" will place an order for the pizza with the toppings selected. Clicking on "Reset" will clear the pizza and move all the toppings back to their original places.

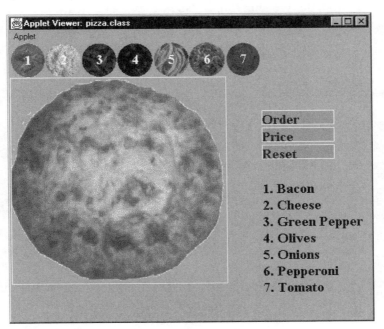

Figure 48.1 A pizza with selectable toppings.

When you drag toppings to the pizza, the screen will look like the one shown in Figure 48.2.

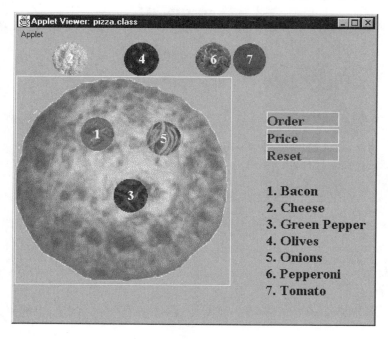

Figure 48.2 The screen after dragging three toppings to the pizza.

When you hit the "Price" button, the program calculates the total amount of the pizza by taking the base amount, and adding the amounts for each pizza topping to it. The output of the button-press is sent to the console, as shown in Figure 48.3. If this program was written to interact with a server, this button would initiate a connection with the server and send the selected toppings, and the server would respond with the total price of the pizza.

When you hit the "Order" button, this program simply sends a message to the console saying that the pizza has been ordered, as shown in Figure 48.4. If this program was written to interact with a server, this button would initiate a connection with the server and send an order for the pizza that includes the items that you have selected.

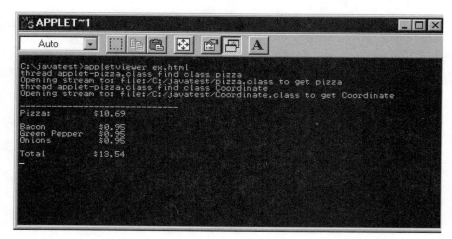

Figure 48.3 The output on the console when you hit the "Price" button.

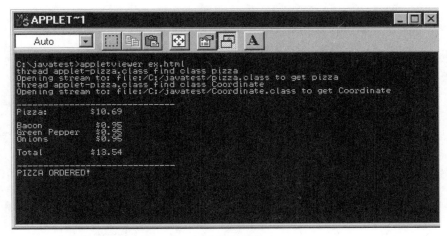

Figure 48.4 *The output on the console when you hit the "Order" button.*

The HTML File

Use the following HTML file to run the **Pizza Site** applet:

```
<applet code=pizza.class width=500 height=380> </applet>
```

Looking at Pizza Site

The **Pizza Site** applet displays the pizza and seven toppings. To add a topping to the pizza, the user simply drag-and-drops the topping. As the user adds toppings, the applet keeps track of the pizza price. After the user has added the toppings they desire, they can click on the "Order" button to initiate the pizza order. The following code implements the **Pizza Site**:

```java
//*****************************************************************
// pizza.java
//*****************************************************************

import java.applet.*;
import java.awt.*;

//*****************************************************************

class Coordinate
  {
    public int x;
    public int y;

    public Coordinate(int x, int y)
      {
        this.x = x;
        this.y = y;
      }
  }

//*****************************************************************
```

```
public class pizza extends Applet
  {
    static final int TOTAL_TOPPINGS = 7;
    static final int ORDER          = TOTAL_TOPPINGS;
    static final int PRICE          = ORDER + 1;
    static final int RESET          = PRICE + 1;
    static final int TOTAL_ITEMS    = RESET + 1;

    Graphics g;
    Image background;
    Image topping_gif[];

    boolean done_loading_image = false;

    Coordinate coordinate[];
    String topping_name[];

    FontMetrics font_metrics;

    int current_topping = 0;

    int new_x;
    int new_y;
    int width;
    int height;

    int size_of_toppings =  50;
    int point_size       =  20;
    int button_position  = 350;
    int size_of_pizza    = 300;

    //————————————————————————————

    public void init()
      {
        g = getGraphics();

        Font font = new Font("TimesRoman", Font.BOLD, point_size);
        g.setFont(font);
        font_metrics = g.getFontMetrics();

        width = size().width;
        height = size().height;

        background = getImage(getCodeBase(), "pizza.gif");

        topping_gif = new Image[TOTAL_TOPPINGS];
        for (int i = 0; i < TOTAL_TOPPINGS; i++)
          topping_gif[i] = getImage(getCodeBase(), "t" + (i+1) + ".gif");

        get_coordinates();
        get_topping_names();
```

```
        Image offScrImage = createImage(width, height);
        Graphics offScrGC = offScrImage.getGraphics();
        offScrGC.drawImage(background, 0, 0, this);

        for (int i = 0; i < TOTAL_TOPPINGS; i++)
          {
             showStatus("Pizza:  loading image " + i);
             while (!done_loading_image)
                ;
             done_loading_image = false;
             offScrGC.drawImage(topping_gif [i], 0, 0,
                                size_of_toppings, size_of_toppings, this);
          }

        showStatus("Pizza:  loading last image");
        while (!done_loading_image)
           ;
        repaint();
    }

//————————————————————

void get_coordinates()
  {
     coordinate = new Coordinate[TOTAL_ITEMS];

     for (int i = 0; i < TOTAL_TOPPINGS; i++)
        coordinate[i] = new Coordinate(i * size_of_toppings, 0);

     coordinate[ORDER] = new Coordinate(button_position, 100);
     coordinate[PRICE] = new Coordinate(button_position, 125);
     coordinate[RESET] = new Coordinate(button_position, 150);
  }

//————————————————————

void get_topping_names()
  {
     topping_name = new String[TOTAL_ITEMS];

     topping_name[0] = new String("Bacon       ");
     topping_name[1] = new String("Cheese      ");
     topping_name[2] = new String("Green Pepper");
     topping_name[3] = new String("Olives      ");
     topping_name[4] = new String("Onions      ");
     topping_name[5] = new String("Pepperoni   ");
     topping_name[6] = new String("Tomato      ");
  }

//————————————————————
```

```java
void draw_items()
  {
    int font_height = font_metrics.getHeight();

    g.setColor(Color.white);

    for (int i = 0; i < TOTAL_TOPPINGS; i++)
      {
        g.drawImage(topping_gif[i],
                    coordinate[i].x,
                    coordinate[i].y,
                    size_of_toppings,
                    size_of_toppings,
                    null);

        String number = "" + (i+1);
        g.drawString(number,
                     coordinate[i].x + (size_of_toppings -
                       font_metrics.stringWidth(number))/2,
                     coordinate[i].y + font_metrics.getAscent() +
                       (size_of_toppings - font_height)/2);
      }

    g.setColor(Color.cyan);

    g.fillRect(coordinate[ORDER].x, coordinate[ORDER].y,
               100, point_size);
    g.fillRect(coordinate[PRICE].x, coordinate[PRICE].y,
               100, point_size);
    g.fillRect(coordinate[RESET].x, coordinate[RESET].y,
               100, point_size);

    g.setColor(Color.blue);

    g.drawString("Order",
                 coordinate[ORDER].x,
                 coordinate[ORDER].y + point_size);

    g.drawString("Price",
                 coordinate[PRICE].x,
                 coordinate[PRICE].y + point_size);

    g.drawString("Reset",
                 coordinate[RESET].x,
                 coordinate[RESET].y + point_size);

    g.setColor(Color.white);

    g.drawRect(coordinate[ORDER].x, coordinate[ORDER].y,
               100, point_size);
    g.drawRect(coordinate[PRICE].x, coordinate[PRICE].y,
               100, point_size);
    g.drawRect(coordinate[RESET].x, coordinate[RESET].y,
               100, point_size);
```

```
        int x = button_position;
        int y = 220;

        g.setColor(Color.black);
        for (int i = 0; i < TOTAL_TOPPINGS; i++)
          {
            g.drawString ((i+1) + ". " + topping_name[i], x, y);
            y += font_height;
          }
    }


//————————————————————————————


void move_topping(int index)
  {
        int old_x = coordinate[index].x;
        int old_y = coordinate[index].y;
        int dx    = new_x - old_x;
        int dy    = new_y - old_y;
        int end   = Math.max(Math.abs(dx), Math.abs(dy));

        for (int i = 0; i < end; i++)
          {
            int x = old_x + dx * i / end;
            int y = old_y + dy * i / end;

            Graphics g2;
            g2 = g.create();

            g2.clipRect(coordinate [index].x, coordinate [index].y,
                        size_of_toppings, size_of_toppings);

            g2.setColor(Color.white);
            g2.drawRect(0, size_of_toppings,
                        size_of_pizza, size_of_pizza);

            g2.drawImage(background, 0, size_of_toppings,
                         size_of_pizza, size_of_pizza, null);

            coordinate[index].x = x;
            coordinate[index].y = y;

            g.drawImage(topping_gif[index],
                        coordinate[index].x,
                        coordinate[index].y,
                        size_of_toppings,
                        size_of_toppings,
                        null);
          }
    }


//————————————————————————————
```

```
    public boolean mouseDown(Event evt, int x, int y)
      {
        if (x > coordinate[ORDER].x         &&
            x < coordinate[ORDER].x + 100 &&
            y > coordinate[ORDER].y         &&
            y < coordinate[ORDER].y + point_size)
          {
            g.setColor(Color.black);
            g.fillRect(coordinate[ORDER].x, coordinate[ORDER].y,
                       100, point_size);

            g.setColor(Color.white);
            g.drawString("Order",
                         coordinate [ORDER].x,
                         coordinate [ORDER].y + point_size);

            order();
            return true;
          }

        if (x > coordinate[PRICE].x         &&
            x < coordinate[PRICE].x + 100 &&
            y > coordinate[PRICE].y         &&
            y < coordinate[PRICE].y + point_size)
          {
            g.setColor(Color.black);
            g.fillRect(coordinate[PRICE].x, coordinate[PRICE].y,
                       100, point_size);
            g.setColor(Color.white);
            g.drawString("Price",
                         coordinate[PRICE].x,
                         coordinate[PRICE].y + point_size);
            price();
            return true;
          }

        if (x > coordinate[RESET].x         &&
            x < coordinate[RESET].x + 100 &&
            y > coordinate[RESET].y         &&
            y < coordinate[RESET].y + point_size)
          {
            g.setColor(Color.black);
            g.fillRect(coordinate[RESET].x, coordinate[RESET].y,
                       100, point_size);

            g.setColor (Color.white);
            g.drawString("Reset",
                         coordinate[RESET].x,
                         coordinate[RESET].y + point_size);

            get_coordinates();
            return true;
          }
```

```
        for (int i = 0; i < TOTAL_TOPPINGS; i++)
          {
            if (x > coordinate[i].x                        &&
                x < coordinate[i].x + size_of_toppings &&
                y > coordinate[i].y                        &&
                y < coordinate[i].y + size_of_toppings)
              {
                current_topping = i + 1;
              }
          }

        return true;
      }

//————————————————————

public boolean mouseDrag(Event evt, int x, int y)
  {
    if (current_topping != 0)
      {
        new_x = x - size_of_toppings/2;
        new_y = y - size_of_toppings/2;

        if (new_x < 0)
          new_x = 0;

        if (new_y < 0)
          new_y = 0;

        move_topping(current_topping - 1);
      }

    return true;
  }

//————————————————————

public boolean mouseUp(Event evt, int x, int y)
  {
    current_topping = 0;
    repaint();
    return true;
  }

//————————————————————

void price()
  {
    double total = 10.69;
    boolean no_items = true;

    System.out.println("\n————————————\n" +
                       "Pizza:          $" + total + "\n");
    for (int i = 0; i < TOTAL_TOPPINGS; i++)
```

```
              {
              if (coordinate[i].x > 0 &&
                  coordinate[i].x < size_of_pizza &&
                  coordinate[i].y > size_of_toppings &&
                  coordinate[i].y < size_of_pizza + size_of_toppings)
                {
                no_items = false;
                total += 0.95;
                System.out.println(topping_name[i] + "   $0.95");
                }
              }

          if (no_items)
            System.out.println("   NO TOPPINGS");

          System.out.println("\nTotal          $" + total);
        }

//─────────────────────────────────────

void order()
    {
      System.out.println("\n───────────────\n" +
                         "PIZZA ORDERED!\n");
    }

//─────────────────────────────────────

public boolean imageUpdate(Image img, int infoflags, int x, int y,
                           int width, int height)
    {
      if (infoflags == ALLBITS)
        {
          done_loading_image = true;
          repaint();
          return false;
        }
      else
        return true;
    }

//─────────────────────────────────────

public void paint(Graphics g)
    {
      if (done_loading_image)
        {
          showStatus("");

          width = size().width;
          height = size().height;

          g.setColor(Color.lightGray);
          g.fillRect(0, 0, width, height);
```

```
            g.drawImage(background, 0, size_of_toppings,
                        size_of_pizza, size_of_pizza, this);

            g.setColor(Color.white);
            g.drawRect(0, size_of_toppings,
                        size_of_pizza, size_of_pizza);

            draw_items();
        }
    }
}
```

BREAKING APART PIZZA SITE

The **Pizza Site** applet uses two classes: *pizza* and *Coordinate*. The main class is the *pizza* class. The applet uses the *Coordinate* class to keep track of the x-and-y coordinates of the toppings.

The Coordinate Class

Since the applet has toppings that it needs to keep track of, it must store coordinates for each topping. To store coordinates, the applet uses the *Coordinate* class that you have seen in previous chapters. This class contains two member variables: the x-coordinate and the y-coordinate. The constructor accepts as arguments the item's initial x-and-y coordinates, and stores them as values of the member variables:

```
class Coordinate
  {
    public int x;
    public int y;

    public Coordinate(int x, int y)
      {
        this.x = x;
        this.y = y;
      }
  }
```

The pizza Class

Within the *pizza* class, you will create an array of the coordinates of each item the user can select with the mouse. These items include the toppings and the three buttons. To access the coordinates of these items, you need the indexes into the array of the toppings and each of the buttons. The *pizza* class defines these indexes as *final* constants:

```
static final int TOTAL_TOPPINGS = 7;
static final int ORDER          = TOTAL_TOPPINGS;
static final int PRICE          = ORDER + 1;
static final int RESET          = PRICE + 1;
static final int TOTAL_ITEMS    = RESET + 1;
```

Next, the class declares variables to store the graphics context, and the images for the pizza, and the toppings, along with a variable that will let the class know when the images have been loaded:

```
    Graphics g;
    Image background;
    Image topping_gif[];

    boolean done_loading_image = false;
```

The class then defines variables to store the coordinates for each of the items, the name of each topping, and the font metrics to use with the buttons:

```
    Coordinate coordinate[];
    String topping_name[];

    FontMetrics font_metrics;
```

Next, as the user drags a topping, the applet needs to know which topping they are moving, the new x-and-y coordinates to which the user is moving the topping, and the width and the height of the window. As you can see, the applet uses some defaults (like the size of the topping) that you will use as the width and the height of each topping, the point size to use for the buttons, the x-coordinate of the positions of the buttons, and the size of the pizza, which you will use as the width and the height of the pizza:

```
    int current_topping = 0;

    int new_x;
    int new_y;
    int width;
    int height;

    int size_of_toppings  =  50;
    int point_size        =  20;
    int button_position   = 350;
    int size_of_pizza     = 300;
```

Initializing the Applet

Within the *init* function, the applet first gets the graphics context, then gets the font that you will use for the buttons, the topping names, and the topping numbers:

```
    public void init()
      {
        g = getGraphics();

        Font font = new Font("TimesRoman", Font.BOLD, point_size);
        g.setFont(font);
        font_metrics = g.getFontMetrics();
```

Next, the function determines the width and the height of the applet window, and then gets the images that it will use for the pizza and toppings, the coordinates of all the items, and the names of all the toppings:

```
    width = size().width;
    height = size().height;
```

```
background = getImage(getCodeBase(), "pizza.gif");
topping_gif = new Image[TOTAL_TOPPINGS];
for (int i = 0; i < TOTAL_TOPPINGS; i++)
  topping_gif[i] = getImage(getCodeBase(), "t" + (i+1) + ".gif");

get_coordinates();
get_topping_names();
```

As you know, when you initialize the image variables, the actual images are not loaded into memory until you use the image. So, to stop the flashing as the images load on the screen, the function loads these images into the offscreen image, one at a time, and displays a status showing which image it is loading:

```
Image offScrImage = createImage(width, height);
Graphics offScrGC = offScrImage.getGraphics();
offScrGC.drawImage(background, 0, 0, this);

for (int i = 0; i < TOTAL_TOPPINGS; i++)
  {
    showStatus("Pizza:  loading image " + i);
    while (!done_loading_image)
      ;
    done_loading_image = false;
    offScrGC.drawImage(topping_gif [i], 0, 0, this);
  }

showStatus("Pizza:  loading last image");
while (!done_loading_image)
  ;
```

Finally, when all the images have been loaded, the function calls the *repaint* function to paint the screen:

```
  repaint();
}
```

Getting the Coordinates

Within the *get_coordinates* function, you allocate the space for the coordinates, and then define the coordinate pairs for each item. The applet will place the toppings all in one row at the top of the window, and the x-coordinates will be at the increments of the size of each topping. The applet will then place the buttons at the right side of the screen, and the x-coordinate will be at the button position that you defined as a member variable:

```
void get_coordinates()
  {
    coordinate = new Coordinate[TOTAL_ITEMS];

    for (int i = 0; i < TOTAL_TOPPINGS; i++)
      coordinate[i] = new Coordinate(i * size_of_toppings, 0);

    coordinate[ORDER] = new Coordinate(button_position, 100);
    coordinate[PRICE] = new Coordinate(button_position, 125);
    coordinate[RESET] = new Coordinate(button_position, 150);
  }
```

Getting the Topping Names

The *get_topping_names* function first allocates the space for the array, and then defines the name for each topping. You should pad the name with blanks at the end so that when you press the "Price" button, the topping names and the prices which print to the right of the names will line up:

```
void get_topping_names()
  {
    topping_name = new String[TOTAL_ITEMS];

    topping_name[0] = new String("Bacon        ");
    topping_name[1] = new String("Cheese       ");
    topping_name[2] = new String("Green Pepper");
    topping_name[3] = new String("Olives       ");
    topping_name[4] = new String("Onions       ");
    topping_name[5] = new String("Pepperoni    ");
    topping_name[6] = new String("Tomato       ");
  }
```

Drawing the Items

Within the *draw_item* function, the applet will draw each of the screen images except for the pizza, which the applet draws in the *paint* function:

```
void draw_items()
```

To start, the function gets the height of the font, which it will use to center the topping numbers inside the toppings images. In addition, the function sets the color that it will use to print the number. Then, the function starts a loop that will print the topping images on the applet and draw the number centered on the image:

```
int font_height = font_metrics.getHeight();

g.setColor(Color.white);

for (int i = 0; i < TOTAL_TOPPINGS; i++)
  {
    g.drawImage(topping_gif[i],
                coordinate[i].x,
                coordinate[i].y,
                size_of_toppings,
                size_of_toppings,
                null);

    String number = "" + (i+1);
    g.drawString(number,
                coordinate[i].x + (size_of_toppings -
                  font_metrics.stringWidth(number))/2,
                coordinate[i].y + font_metrics.getAscent() +
                  (size_of_toppings - font_height)/2);
  }
```

Next, the function draws the rectangles that represent the three buttons. The function places each rectangle at the coordinates for the respective button:

```
g.setColor(Color.cyan);

g.fillRect(coordinate[ORDER].x, coordinate[ORDER].y,
           100, point_size);
g.fillRect(coordinate[PRICE].x, coordinate[PRICE].y,
           100, point_size);
g.fillRect(coordinate[RESET].x, coordinate[RESET].y,
           100, point_size);
```

Next, the function draws the words on the buttons. The function uses the point-size to determine the y-coordinate of the baseline of the font:

```
g.setColor(Color.blue);

g.drawString("Order",
             coordinate[ORDER].x,
             coordinate[ORDER].y + point_size);

g.drawString("Price",
             coordinate[PRICE].x,
             coordinate[PRICE].y + point_size);

g.drawString("Reset",
             coordinate[RESET].x,
             coordinate[RESET].y + point_size);
```

Then, the function draws a border around each button:

```
g.setColor(Color.white);

g.drawRect(coordinate[ORDER].x, coordinate[ORDER].y,
           100, point_size);
g.drawRect(coordinate[PRICE].x, coordinate[PRICE].y,
           100, point_size);
g.drawRect(coordinate[RESET].x, coordinate[RESET].y,
           100, point_size);
```

Finally, the function draws the topping names on the window so the user knows what they are, in case they have trouble figuring out the topping by looking at the images. The function sets the x-coordinate to the same value as the x-coordinate for the buttons:

```
    int x = button_position;
    int y = 220;

    g.setColor(Color.black);
    for (int i = 0; i < TOTAL_TOPPINGS; i++)
      {
        g.drawString ((i+1) + ". " + topping_name[i], x, y);
        y += font_height;
      }
}
```

Moving the Selected Topping

The *move_topping* function will move a topping to wherever the mouse takes it. As the function moves the topping, it has to erase the old topping by redrawing the pizza in that area. The function uses an index into the arrays to track information for each topping:

```
void move_topping(int index)
```

First, the *move_topping* function defines the *old_x* and *old_y* variables, which contain the coordinates of the topping before it is moved:

```
int old_x = coordinate[index].x;
int old_y = coordinate[index].y;
```

Second, the function gets the difference between the old and the new coordinates:

```
int dx = new_x - old_x;
int dy = new_y - old_y;
```

Then, the function determines the larger of the two differences and stores the value in the variable *end*, which will be used as the ending value of the following *for* loop:

```
int end = Math.max(Math.abs(dx), Math.abs(dy));
```

The function uses the *for* loop to iterate through each pixel of the larger difference. The function uses the larger difference because, if it selects the smaller difference, you might see big jumps instead of small movements for the toppings:

```
for (int i = 0; i < end; i++)
```

To get the new coordinates, the function adds a percentage of the difference to the old coordinates. The function obtains the percentage by dividing the loop counter *i* by the total distance:

```
int x = old_x + dx * i / end;
int y = old_y + dy * i / end;
```

Next, the function creates a new graphics context it will use to create a clip rectangle to redraw the pizza in the topping's old position:

```
Graphics g2;
g2 = g.create();

g2.clipRect(coordinate [index].x, coordinate [index].y,
            size_of_toppings, size_of_toppings);
```

Before redrawing the pizza, the function redraws the pizza border:

```
g2.setColor(Color.white);
g2.drawRect(0, size_of_toppings,
            size_of_pizza, size_of_pizza);

g2.drawImage(background, 0, size_of_toppings,
            size_of_pizza, size_of_pizza, null);
```

Then, the function resets the topping's new coordinates and redraws the topping at the new position:

```
coordinate[index].x = x;
coordinate[index].y = y;

g.drawImage(topping_gif[index],
            coordinate[index].x,
            coordinate[index].y,
            size_of_toppings,
            size_of_toppings,
            null);
```

Clicking the Mouse Button

As you have learned, when you click the mouse button, Java calls the *mouseDown* function and gives it the x-and-y coordinates of where the mouse button was clicked:

```
public boolean mouseDown(Event evt, int x, int y)
```

Within the *mouseDown* function, the code first checks to see if the mouse click was on the "Order" button. If so, the function redraws the button in the pushed state, which uses white lettering on top of a black rectangle. Then, it calls the *order* function. After ordering, the function returns *true* to Java to indicate you processed the event:

```
if (x > coordinate[ORDER].x       &&
    x < coordinate[ORDER].x + 100 &&
    y > coordinate[ORDER].y       &&
    y < coordinate[ORDER].y + point_size)
  {
    g.setColor(Color.black);
    g.fillRect(coordinate[ORDER].x, coordinate[ORDER].y,
               100, point_size);

    g.setColor(Color.white);
    g.drawString("Order",
                 coordinate [ORDER].x,
                 coordinate [ORDER].y + point_size);

    order();
    return true;
  }
```

If the user did not click on the "Order" button, the function checks to see if the mouse click was on the "Price" button. If so, the function redraws the button in the pushed state, and then calls the *price* function. Then, the function returns *true* to Java to indicate that you processed the event:

```
if (x > coordinate[PRICE].x        &&
    x < coordinate[PRICE].x + 100 &&
    y > coordinate[PRICE].y        &&
    y < coordinate[PRICE].y + point_size)
  {
    g.setColor(Color.black);
    g.fillRect(coordinate[PRICE].x, coordinate[PRICE].y,
               100, point_size);
    g.setColor(Color.white);
    g.drawString("Price",
                 coordinate[PRICE].x,
                 coordinate[PRICE].y + point_size);
    price();
    return true;
  }
```

If the user did not click on the "Price" button, the function checks to see if the mouse click was on the "Reset" button. If so, the function redraws the button in the pushed state, and then calls *get_coordinates* to get the original coordinates of all the items. The function then returns *true* to Java to indicate you processed the event. You do not have to repaint the screen here, because when you release the mouse button, Java will call the *mouseUp* function, which repaints the screen:

```
if (x > coordinate[RESET].x        &&
    x < coordinate[RESET].x + 100 &&
    y > coordinate[RESET].y        &&
    y < coordinate[RESET].y + point_size)
  {
    g.setColor(Color.black);
    g.fillRect(coordinate[RESET].x, coordinate[RESET].y,
               100, point_size);

    g.setColor (Color.white);
    g.drawString("Reset",
                 coordinate[RESET].x,
                 coordinate[RESET].y + point_size);

    get_coordinates();
    return true;
  }
```

Finally, the function checks to see if the mouse click was on a topping. If so, the function sets the *current_topping* variable to point to the topping. The function adds 1 to the index, because a value of 0 means that there is no topping selected. However, you have to make sure that you subtract 1 whenever you need the index for the topping:

```
for (int i = 0; i < TOTAL_TOPPINGS; i++)
  {
    if (x > coordinate[i].x                    &&
        x < coordinate[i].x + size_of_toppings &&
```

```
            y > coordinate[i].y                         &&
            y < coordinate[i].y + size_of_toppings)
        {
          current_topping = i + 1;
        }
    }
```

Lastly, the function returns *true* to Java to indicate that you handled the event:

```
    return true;
```

Dragging the Mouse

As you know, Java calls the *mouseDrag* function when the user moves the mouse while the button is pressed. Because the button has already been pressed by the user, the *mouseDown* function has already been called to determine which item has been selected. If the item that was selected was a topping, the *current_topping* variable will not be 0:

```
    public boolean mouseDrag(Event evt, int x, int y)
      {
        if (current_topping != 0)
          {
```

In this case, you want the x-and-y coordinates given to be the position in the middle of the topping. To get the x-and-y coordinates of the top-left of the topping image, the function has to subtract half of the size of the topping:

```
    new_x = x - size_of_toppings/2;
    new_y = y - size_of_toppings/2;
```

If the coordinates become less than zero, the function resets them to 0. Then, the function moves to the current topping by calling the *move_topping* function. As you will recall, you have to subtract 1 from the *current_topping* variable to get the index of the topping into the *coordinate* array:

```
    if (new_x < 0)
      new_x = 0;

    if (new_y < 0)
      new_y = 0;

    move_topping(current_topping - 1);
  }
```

Lastly, the function returns *true* to Java to indicate you handled the event:

```
    return true;
```

Releasing the Mouse Button

As you know, when the user releases the mouse button, Java calls the *mouseUp* function. When you release the mouse button, the function resets the current topping to 0 (meaning that no topping has been selected), and then repaints the screen:

```
public boolean mouseUp(Event evt, int x, int y)
  {
    current_topping = 0;
    repaint();
    return true;
  }
```

Getting the Price

When the user clicks their mouse on the "Price" button, the applet calls the *price* function, which prints the price of the pizza, the price of each of the toppings, and the total price to the console window:

```
void price()
```

To start, the function initializes the total price to the base price of the pizza, and assumes that no toppings have been selected by setting the *no_items* variable to zero:

```
double total = 10.69;
boolean no_items = true;
```

Next, the function displays a header to the console with the base price of the pizza:

```
System.out.println("\n————————————\n" +
               "Pizza:          $" + total + "\n");
```

Next, the function iterates through each topping, checking whether the user has dropped the topping on the pizza. If the topping is in the coordinate space of the pizza, the function sets *no_items* to *false*, adds the price of the topping (in this case, you will assume that each topping is 95 cents), and then prints out a line for the current topping:

```
for (int i = 0; i < TOTAL_TOPPINGS; i++)
  {
  if (coordinate[i].x > 0 &&
      coordinate[i].x < size_of_pizza &&
      coordinate[i].y > size_of_toppings &&
      coordinate[i].y < size_of_pizza + size_of_toppings)
    {
      no_items = false;
      total += 0.95;
      System.out.println(topping_name[i] + "   $0.95");
    }
  }
```

If the user did not select any items, the function displays a message stating so to the console:

```
if (no_items)
  System.out.println("   NO TOPPINGS");
```

Finally, the function prints out the total price of the pizza:

```
System.out.println("\nTotal            $" + total);
```

Ordering the Pizza

When the user clicks the mouse on the "Order" button, the applet calls the *order* function. This program simply prints a message to the console that the pizza has been ordered. If you were to make this program into a client/server application, you would include in this function the code to order the pizza:

```
void order()
  {
    System.out.println("\n————————————\n" +
                       "PIZZA ORDERED!\n");
  }
```

Updating the Image

The *imageUpdate* function, as it has been described in many chapters of this book, lets you know when the image that you are drawing has completed. When the image is completed, the function repaints the screen:

```
public boolean imageUpdate(Image img, int infoflags, int x, int y,
                           int width, int height)
  {
    if (infoflags == ALLBITS)
      {
        done_loading_image = true;
        repaint();
        return false;
      }
    else
      return true;
  }
```

The paint Function

To start, the *paint* function waits for all the images to finish loading. Then, the function erases the status message, and gets the width and the height of the window:

```
public void paint(Graphics g)
  {
    if (done_loading_image)
      {
        showStatus("");

        width = size().width;
        height = size().height;
```

Next, the function clears the screen. As you can see, the function uses the light-gray color to erase the screen (because that is used as the default color for many applets):

```
g.setColor(Color.lightGray);
g.fillRect(0, 0, width, height);
```

Now the function draws the pizza on the window. The y-coordinate of the pizza has to be below the toppings. The function uses the size of the topping as the y-coordinate:

```
g.drawImage(background, 0, size_of_toppings,
            size_of_pizza, size_of_pizza, this);
```

Lastly, the function draws a white border around the pizza and draws all the toppings and the buttons on the screen:

```
g.setColor(Color.white);
g.drawRect(0, size_of_toppings,
           size_of_pizza, size_of_pizza);

draw_items();
```

ENHANCEMENTS YOU CAN MAKE TO PIZZA SITE

To start, modify the program to have different prices for different toppings. Next, allow the user to select a small, medium, or large pizza by providing buttons for the three options. Then, convert this applet into a client/server program. You will have to write a server program, but you can use a server program from one of the networking chapters and modify it. Allow the user to select a topping by typing the digit which corresponds to a topping. If the digit is pressed again, reset the topping back to the top.

PUTTING IT ALL TOGETHER

The **Pizza Site** applet shows you how to drag-and-drop toppings on top of a pizza, get its price, and place an order. It also shows you how to create your own buttons that will respond to mouse clicks. Although this applet used a pizza and toppings, you could easily change the applet to let a user add features to a new car, or plants and trees to their landscape. In Chapter 49, you will learn how to display a deck of playing cards. Before you continue with Chapter 49, however, make sure you understand the following key concepts:

- ☑ You can drag-and-drop items on top of another image.
- ☑ Using an array, you can keep track of which items have been dropped on the image, and which items have not.
- ☑ By trapping mouse operations, you can create your own buttons that will respond to mouse clicks and perform actions.

CHAPTER 49

PLAYING CARDS
SHOWING A BASIC DECK OF CARDS

In this chapter, you will use the Java *Graphics* class to draw a deck of playing cards. Over the next three chapters, you will enhance the card deck to create a Blackjack program. As you will learn, drawing a card deck requires you to combine and track multiple graphics images. By the time you finish this chapter, you will understand the following key concepts:

- ◆ You can create a class that will display 54 playing cards, including jokers.

- ◆ You can use the *fillRoundRect* class to fill rectangles with rounded corners.

USING PLAYING CARDS

When you run the **Playing Cards** applet, you will see a window that displays one card at a time and some statistics at the right, as shown in Figure 49. The applet will update the screen once a second, changing the screen to another random card, and updating the statistics on the right. The status bar at the bottom of the applet window shows the total number of cards that have been dealt from the current deck. When the deck runs out, the applet resets it, and starts all over again.

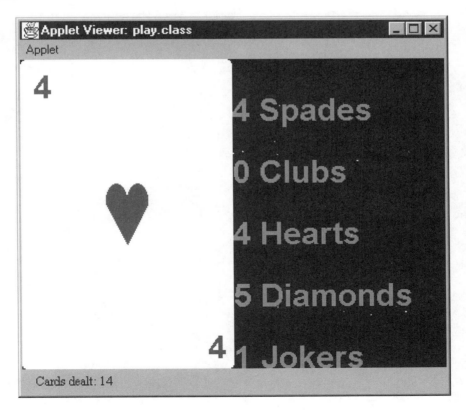

Figure 49 Displaying one card at a time.

THE HTML FILE

Use the following HTML file to run the **Playing Cards** applet:

```
<applet code=play.class width=400 height=300>
</applet>
```

LOOKING AT PLAYING CARDS

The **Playing Cards** applet contains two classes: the main *play* class, and the *cards* class.

The play Class

The *play* class applet uses the *cards* class to display one card at a time, in random order on the screen, one card per second. The class keeps track of each card as it is dealt, and does not display the same card twice for a deck. When the entire deck has been displayed, it resets the deck and starts over. The following code implements the *play* class:

```
//******************************************************************
// play.java
//******************************************************************

import java.applet.*;
import java.awt.*;

//******************************************************************

public class play extends Applet implements Runnable
  {
    Graphics g;
    cards card_deck;

    Thread my_thread;

    int width;
    int height;

    boolean card_displayed[];
    int suits[];

    int card_count;

    //————————————————————————

    public void init()
      {
        g = getGraphics();

        card_deck = new cards(g);

        card_displayed = new boolean[54];
        suits = new int[5];      // 5th is for counting jokers
        reset_cards();
```

```
        card_deck.joker = getImage(getCodeBase(), "joker.gif");

        set_defaults();

        card_deck.draw_joker(0, 0, width/4, height/2);
    }

//————————————————————————

void reset_cards()
    {
        int i;

        for (i = 0; i < 54; i++)
            card_displayed[i] = false;

        for (i = 0; i < 5; i++)
            suits[i] = 0;

        card_count = 0;
    }

//————————————————————————

void set_defaults()
    {
        width = size().width;
        height = size().height;
    }

//————————————————————————

public void start()
    {
        if (my_thread == null)
            {
                my_thread = new Thread(this);
                my_thread.start();
            }
    }

//————————————————————————

public void stop()
    {
        if (my_thread != null)
            {
                my_thread.stop();
                my_thread = null;
            }
    }

//————————————————————————
```

```java
void delay(int amount)
  {
    try
      {
        Thread.sleep(amount);
      }
    catch (InterruptedException e)
      {
      }
  }

//———————————————————————

public void run()
  {
    while (my_thread != null)
      {
        repaint();
        delay(1000);
      }
  }

//———————————————————————

public void update(Graphics _g)
  {
    g.setColor(Color.black);
    g.fillRect(0, 0, width, height);

    int card = (int) (Math.random() * 54);

    do
      {
        if (!card_displayed[card])
          {
            card_displayed[card] = true;
            break;
          }
        else if (++card == 54)
          card = 0;

      } while (true);

    card_deck.draw(card, 0, 0, width/2, height);

    g.setColor(Color.black);
    g.fillRect(width/2, 0, width, height);
    g.setColor(Color.green);

    int suit = card / 13;
    ++suits[suit];

    g.drawString("" + suits[0] + " Spades",
                 width/2, (height*1)/5);
```

```
        g.drawString("" + suits[1] + " Clubs",
                     width/2, (height*2)/5);

        g.drawString("" + suits[2] + " Hearts",
                     width/2, (height*3)/5);

        g.drawString("" + suits[3] + " Diamonds",
                     width/2, (height*4)/5);

        g.drawString("" + suits[4] + " Jokers",
                     width/2, (height*5)/5);

        card_count++;
        showStatus("Cards dealt: " + card_count);

        if (card_count == 54)
          {
            delay(2000);
            g.setColor(Color.black);
            g.fillRect(0, 0, width, height);
            g.setColor(Color.green);
            g.drawString("Resetting", 0, height/2);
            reset_cards();
            delay(2000);
          }
      }

  //————————————————————————————

  public void paint(Graphics g)
     {
       set_defaults();
     }
  }
```

The cards Class

The *cards* class draws a playing card on the screen. To draw a card, the applet calls the *draw* function with parameters that specify which card, the x-and-y coordinates of the top-left corner of the card, and the width and the height of the card. For simplicity, the class draws each card with only one suit that appears in the middle of the card. In Chapter 50, you will expand the class to draw the correct number of suits for a given card. The following code implements the *cards* class:

```
//****************************************************************
// cards.java
//****************************************************************

import java.awt.*;

//****************************************************************
```

```java
public class cards
  {
    Graphics g;
    Image joker;

    //————————————————————————————

    public cards(Graphics g)
      {
        this.g = g;
      }

    //————————————————————————————

    public void draw_spades(int x, int y, int w, int h)
      {
        int xx[] = new int[3];
        int yy[] = new int[3];

        xx[0] = x + w/2;  yy[0] = y          ;
        xx[1] = x       ;  yy[1] = y + h/2;
        xx[2] = x + w  ;  yy[2] = y + h/2;

        g.fillPolygon(xx, yy, 3);

        g.fillOval(x    , y+h/3, w/2, h/2);
        g.fillOval(x+w/2, y+h/3, w/2, h/2);

        g.fillRect(x+(w*3)/7, y+h/3, w/7, (h*2)/3);
      }

    //————————————————————————————

    public void draw_clubs(int x, int y, int w, int h)
      {
        g.fillOval(x    , y+(h*2)/5, w/2, h/2);
        g.fillOval(x+w/2, y+(h*2)/5, w/2, h/2);
        g.fillOval(x+w/4, y        , w/2, h/2);

        g.fillRect(x+(w*3)/7, y+h/3, w/7, (h*2)/3);
      }

    //————————————————————————————

    public void draw_hearts(int x, int y, int w, int h)
      {
        int xx[] = new int[3];
        int yy[] = new int[3];

        xx[0] = x + w/2;  yy[0] = y + h  ;
        xx[1] = x       ;  yy[1] = y + h/3;
        xx[2] = x + w  ;  yy[2] = y + h/3;
```

```
        g.fillPolygon(xx, yy, 3);

        g.fillOval(x      , y, w/2, h/2);
        g.fillOval(x+w/2, y, w/2, h/2);
    }

    //————————————————————

    public void draw_diamonds(int x, int y, int w, int h)
    {
        int xx[] = new int[4];
        int yy[] = new int[4];

        xx[0] = x + w/2;  yy[0] = y + h  ;
        xx[1] = x      ;  yy[1] = y + h/2;
        xx[2] = x + w/2;  yy[2] = y      ;
        xx[3] = x + w  ;  yy[3] = y + h/2;

        g.fillPolygon(xx, yy, 4);
    }

    //————————————————————

    public void draw_joker(int x, int y, int w, int h)
    {
        g.drawImage(joker, x, y, w, h, null);
    }

    //————————————————————

    public void draw(int card, int x, int y, int w, int h)
    {
        g.setColor(Color.white);
        g.fillRoundRect(x, y, w, h, w/20, h/20);
        Font font = new Font("Helvetica", Font.BOLD, h/10);
        g.setFont(font);
        FontMetrics font_metrics = g.getFontMetrics();

        String string;
        int number;
        int suit = 4;

        if (card > 51)
        {
            string = "JOKER";
            g.setColor(Color.green);
        }
        else
        {
            number = card % 13;
            suit = card / 13;
```

```
            if (number == 0)
              string = "A";
            else if (number == 10)
              string = "J";
            else if (number == 11)
              string = "Q";
            else if (number == 12)
              string = "K";
            else
              string = "" + (number+1);

            if (suit/2 == 0)
              g.setColor(Color.black);
            else
              g.setColor(Color.red);
        }

        int string_width = font_metrics.stringWidth(string);
        g.drawString(string, x+(w*31)/32-string_width, y+(h*31)/32);
        g.drawString(string, x+w/15, y+h/8);

        if (suit == 0)
          draw_spades(x+(w*2)/5, y+(h*2)/5, w/5, h/5);
        else if (suit == 1)
          draw_clubs(x+(w*2)/5, y+(h*2)/5, w/5, h/5);
        else if (suit == 2)
          draw_hearts(x+(w*2)/5, y+(h*2)/5, w/5, h/5);
        else if (suit == 3)
          draw_diamonds(x+(w*2)/5, y+(h*2)/5, w/5, h/5);
        else
          draw_joker(x+w/4, y+h/4, w/2, h/2);
    }
}
```

BREAKING APART PLAYING CARDS

The **Playing Cards** applet uses two classes: the *play* class and the *cards* class. This section will examine the *play* class first, followed by the *cards* class.

The play Class

The *play* class imports two packages: the *java.applet* package, because it is an applet; and the *java.awt* package, to perform graphics:

```
import java.applet.*;
import java.awt.*;
```

The class inherits from the *Applet* class, and since it will be run as a thread, implements the *Runnable* interface:

```
public class play extends Applet implements Runnable
```

Member Variables

To start, the class declares variables to store the graphics context, an instance of the *cards* class, and the thread variable for the thread that will run the applet:

```
Graphics g;
cards card_deck;

Thread my_thread;
```

Next, the class defines variables that will store the width and the height of the applet window, an array that keeps track of whether or not a card has been displayed, and another array that keeps track of how many cards of each suit have been dealt, including jokers as a fifth suit. And, lastly, a variable that keeps track of how many cards have been dealt:

```
int width;
int height;

boolean card_displayed[];
int suits[];

int card_count;
```

Initializing the Applet

Within the *init* function, the class gets the graphics context, creates a new deck of cards, and passes to the *cards* class the graphics context. The function then allocates space for the array of cards that have been displayed, and the array that keeps track of the suits:

```
public void init()
  {
    g = getGraphics();

    card_deck = new cards(g);

    card_displayed = new boolean[54];
    suits = new int[5];     // 5th is for counting jokers
```

Next, the function resets the cards, gets the joker image, and sets the defaults for the applet window. Finally, the function draws the joker. If you do not draw the joker, the first time the joker is drawn on the screen the applet will have to load it, and the user will not see it on the screen. You might, for example, comment out that line and see what happens when the joker is displayed the first time. The function has to pass the *draw_joker* function of the *card_deck* object the exact same width and height that will be used by the joker card when the applet is running:

```
reset_cards();

card_deck.joker = getImage(getCodeBase(), "joker.gif");

set_defaults();

card_deck.draw_joker(0, 0, width/4, height/2);
```

Resetting the Cards

The *play* class uses an array to keep track of which cards have been dealt, and an array that tracks the suits that have been played. In addition, the class tracks the number of cards that have been played. The *reset_cards* function initializes these values to 0. (In other words, no cards have been played.) The *play* class calls the *reset_cards* function when the applet first starts, and when it has dealt the entire deck and is ready to start again:

```
void reset_cards()
  {
    int i;

    for (i = 0; i < 54; i++)
      card_displayed[i] = false;

    for (i = 0; i < 5; i++)
      suits[i] = 0;

    card_count = 0;
  }
```

Setting the Defaults

The *set_defaults* function sets the defaults for the applet window's width and height. The class sets these defaults because the size of the cards and the size of the font used for statistics will be recalculated based on their values:

```
void set_defaults()
  {
    width = size().width;
    height = size().height;
  }
```

Starting the Thread

The *play* class uses a thread to display the cards continuously on the screen. The *start* function creates and starts the thread. After Java calls the *init* function, it calls the *start* function. Within the *start* function, the applet checks to make sure that its thread has not been previously initialized, then sets the thread variable to a new instance of the *Thread* class, and passes it a reference to this applet. Finally, the function starts the thread:

```
public void start()
  {
    if (my_thread == null)
      {
        my_thread = new Thread(this);
        my_thread.start();
      }
  }
```

Stopping the Applet

As you have learned, Java calls the *stop* function when the applet is closed. Within the *stop* function, if the thread has been started, the function stops it and resets the thread variable to null:

```
public void stop()
  {
    if (my_thread != null)
      {
        my_thread.stop();
        my_thread = null;
      }
  }
```

Running the Thread

Within the *run* function, the thread enters a loop within which it will display a card every second. Within the *while* loop, the thread calls the *repaint* function that draws the new card. The thread then delays one second, and the process repeats:

```
public void run()
  {
    while (my_thread != null)
      {
        repaint();
        delay(1000);
      }
  }
```

Updating the Screen

Each time the applet calls *repaint*, the *repaint* function, in turn, calls the *update* function and the graphics context is passed to it. Since the class already has a graphics context that you are using in this applet (defined as a member variable *g*), make sure you call the parameter something different, like "*_g*" or something else that you will not use. This is to make sure that this function uses the same graphics context as the one that has been initialized in the *init* function and used in the rest of the applet's functions:

```
public void update(Graphics _g)
```

To start, the *update* function clears the window to black. Next, the function gets a random number between 0 and 53, which gives it access to the 54 cards:

```
g.setColor(Color.black);
g.fillRect(0, 0, width, height);

int card = (int) (Math.random() * 54);
```

After the function gets a card, it has to make sure that the card has not been displayed. If the card has been displayed, the function increments the number and checks the next card. The function repeats this process until it finds an unplayed card. If the count reaches 54, the function resets the card to 0. After the function finds a card that has not been displayed, it exits the loop:

```
do
  {
    if (!card_displayed[card])
```

```
      {
        card_displayed[card] = true;
        break;
      }
    else if (++card == 54)
      card = 0;

  } while (true);
```

At this point, the function can draw the card on the screen by calling the *card* object *draw* function. To draw the card, you must pass the *draw* function the card to draw, and the area to use for the card. As you saw in Figure 49, this program uses the left-hand side of the applet window to draw the card:

```
card_deck.draw(card, 0, 0, width/2, height);
```

Next, the function displays the statistics about the deck. To do so, the function clears the right hand side of the screen to black, and sets the foreground color to green:

```
g.setColor(Color.black);
g.fillRect(width/2, 0, width, height);
g.setColor(Color.green);
```

The function then determines which card it played. Cards 0-12 are spades, 13-25 are clubs, 26-38 are hearts, and 39-51 are diamonds. Cards 52 and 53 are the jokers. As you can see, the function increments the number of cards displayed for this card's suit.

```
int suit = card / 13;
++suits[suit];

g.drawString("" + suits[0] + " Spades", width/2, (height*1)/5);

g.drawString("" + suits[1] + " Clubs", width/2, (height*2)/5);

g.drawString("" + suits[2] + " Hearts", width/2, (height*3)/5);

g.drawString("" + suits[3] + " Diamonds", width/2, (height*4)/5);

g.drawString("" + suits[4] + " Jokers", width/2, (height*5)/5);
```

Next, the function increments the total number of cards played, and displays a status showing this count. If the function has displayed all 54 cards, it waits for two seconds, clears the whole screen to black, displays "Resetting" in green, resets the cards, and waits another two seconds. The function will then repeat this process, randomly dealing and displaying the deck again:

```
card_count++;
showStatus("Cards dealt: " + card_count);

if (card_count == 54)
  {
    delay(2000);
    g.setColor(Color.black);
```

```
      g.fillRect(0, 0, width, height);
      g.setColor(Color.green);
      g.drawString("Resetting", 0, height/2);
      reset_cards();
      delay(2000);
  }
```

Painting the Screen

If the *update* function exists, the only time the *paint* function is called is when the entire screen has to be repainted, for instance, when the screen is resized. Within the *paint* function, the code sets the default variables for the current size of the window. As you will recall, the size of the playing cards and the statistics font are based on the window size:

```
public void paint(Graphics g)
  {
    set_defaults();
  }
```

The cards Class

The *cards* class draws a card on the screen at a specific x-and-y coordinate. The class imports one package, the *java.awt* package, to perform graphics:

```
import java.awt.*;
```

You must define the *cards* class as *public* so your main applet, the *play* class, can access it:

```
public class cards
```

Member Variables

To start, the *cards* class declares variables to show the graphics context and the image it uses for the joker.

```
Graphics g;
Image joker;
```

The Constructor

The constructor function for the *cards* class simply stores the card's graphics context as a local member variable. The graphics context corresponds to the graphics context of the object that created the instance of the *cards* class, which, in this case, is the main *play* class object:

```
public cards(Graphics g)
  {
    this.g = g;
  }
```

Drawing the Spades Suit

The function receives the x-and-y coordinates of the top-left corner of the area to use for this suit, and the width and the height of the area. The class uses a unique function to draw each suit. For example, to draw the spades suit, the class calls the *draw_spades* function:

```
public void draw_spades(int x, int y, int w, int h)
```

To draw a spade, the function draws a triangle, two circles at the bottom of the triangle, and then a small rectangle between the circles as the stem of the spade suit:

```
int xx[] = new int[3];
int yy[] = new int[3];

xx[0] = x + w/2;  yy[0] = y        ;
xx[1] = x      ;  yy[1] = y + h/2;
xx[2] = x + w  ;  yy[2] = y + h/2;

g.fillPolygon(xx, yy, 3);

g.fillOval(x     , y+h/3, w/2, h/2);
g.fillOval(x+w/2, y+h/3, w/2, h/2);

g.fillRect(x+(w*3)/7, y+h/3, w/7, (h*2)/3);
```

Drawing the Clubs Suit

To draw the clubs suit, the class calls the *draw_clubs* function. This function receives the same parameters as the *draw_spades* function. To create the club, the function draws three circles, and then a stem at the bottom:

```
public void draw_clubs(int x, int y, int w, int h)
  {
    g.fillOval(x     , y+(h*2)/5, w/2, h/2);
    g.fillOval(x+w/2, y+(h*2)/5, w/2, h/2);
    g.fillOval(x+w/4, y            , w/2, h/2);

    g.fillRect(x+(w*3)/7, y+h/3, w/7, (h*2)/3);
  }
```

Drawing the Hearts Suit

To draw the hearts suit, the class calls the *draw_hearts* function. To create the hearts suit, the function draws an upside-down triangle, and then two circles at the top:

```
public void draw_hearts(int x, int y, int w, int h)
  {
    int xx[] = new int[3];
    int yy[] = new int[3];

    xx[0] = x + w/2;  yy[0] = y + h  ;
    xx[1] = x      ;  yy[1] = y + h/3;
    xx[2] = x + w  ;  yy[2] = y + h/3;
```

```
      g.fillPolygon(xx, yy, 3);

      g.fillOval(x    , y, w/2, h/2);
      g.fillOval(x+w/2, y, w/2, h/2);
   }
```

Drawing the Diamonds Suit

To draw the diamond suit, the class calls the *draw_diamond* function. To draw a diamond, the function draws just that, a diamond:

```
public void draw_diamonds(int x, int y, int w, int h)
   {
     int xx[] = new int[4];
     int yy[] = new int[4];

     xx[0] = x + w/2;  yy[0] = y + h  ;
     xx[1] = x      ;  yy[1] = y + h/2;
     xx[2] = x + w/2;  yy[2] = y      ;
     xx[3] = x + w  ;  yy[3] = y + h/2;

     g.fillPolygon(xx, yy, 4);
   }
```

Drawing the Joker

To draw a joker, the class calls the *draw_joker* function. The joker image was loaded in the *init* function of the *play* class. The function draws the joker image at the x-and-y coordinates given as parameters, and uses the width and height, also given as parameters:

```
public void draw_joker(int x, int y, int w, int h)
   {
     g.drawImage(joker, x, y, w, h, null);
   }
```

Drawing the Card

As discussed, to display a card, the *play* class calls the *draw* function. This function receives as parameters, the card to draw, the x-and-y coordinates of the top-left of the card, and the width and the height of the area you have to use for the card:

```
public void draw(int card, int x, int y, int w, int h)
```

To start, the function fills a white rounded rectangle by using the *fillRoundRect* function. The function passes to the *fillRoundRect* function the x-and-y coordinates, the width and the height of the rectangle, the width of the arcs to be used at the corners, and the height of the arcs:

```
g.setColor(Color.white);
g.fillRoundRect(x, y, w, h, w/20, h/20);
```

Next, the function gets the font it will use for numbering the cards. The size of the font depends on the height of the area the function can use for the card:

```
Font font = new Font("Helvetica", Font.BOLD, h/10);
g.setFont(font);
FontMetrics font_metrics = g.getFontMetrics();
```

Next, the function defines a *String* object, which will contain the string to use for drawing the numbers at the corners of the cards, the number for the card if it is not a face card, and the suit, set to assume that the card is a joker. The values for *suit* are: 0 for spades, 1 for clubs, 2 for hearts, 3 for diamonds, and 4 for jokers:

```
String string;
int number;
int suit = 4;
```

If the card is number 52 or 53, it is a joker. As you can see, for a joker, the function displays the word "JOKER" in green on the card's top-left and bottom-right corners:

```
if (card > 51)
  {
    string = "JOKER";
    g.setColor(Color.green);
  }
```

If the card is not a joker, the function gets the number of the card by using the modulus function with the value 13, and gets the suit of the card by dividing by 13. If the number is 0, the card is an ace. One through nine are the numbers 2-10. Face card numbers are 10 for a jack, 11 for a queen, and 12 for a king. The first two suits, spades and clubs, are black, and the next two suits are red:

```
else
  {
    number = card % 13;
    suit = card / 13;

    if (number == 0)
      string = "A";
    else if (number == 10)
      string = "J";
    else if (number == 11)
      string = "Q";
    else if (number == 12)
      string = "K";
    else
      string = "" + (number+1);

    if (suit/2 == 0)
      g.setColor(Color.black);
    else
      g.setColor(Color.red);
  }
```

Then, the function determines the x-and-y coordinates for the bottom-right of the card and the top-left of the card, and draws the string at those coordinates. The function uses the string width to draw the string at the bottom-right corner, so it knows how much to subtract from the right side of the card:

```
int string_width = font_metrics.stringWidth(string);
g.drawString(string, x+(w*31)/32-string_width, y+(h*31)/32);
g.drawString(string, x+w/15, y+h/8);
```

Finally, the function draws the card's suit. Remember, if the suit is 0 through 3, the suit is one of the four normal suits, but if the suit is 4, then the function has to draw the joker:

```
if (suit == 0)
   draw_spades(x+(w*2)/5, y+(h*2)/5, w/5, h/5);
else if (suit == 1)
   draw_clubs(x+(w*2)/5, y+(h*2)/5, w/5, h/5);
else if (suit == 2)
   draw_hearts(x+(w*2)/5, y+(h*2)/5, w/5, h/5);
else if (suit == 3)
   draw_diamonds(x+(w*2)/5, y+(h*2)/5, w/5, h/5);
else
   draw_joker(x+w/4, y+h/4, w/2, h/2);
```

ENHANCEMENTS YOU CAN MAKE TO PLAYING CARDS

One of the best ways to improve the appearance of the cards is to use GIF images instead of drawing the card suits. You could also create GIF files for the numbers and the letters to use. In real cards, the number or letter at the bottom-right of the card is upside down; so, if you are using GIF files for these values, you need one that is right-side-up and one that is upside-down for each value.

PUTTING IT ALL TOGETHER

The **Playing Cards** applet has shown you how to create a sample deck of cards by using the Java *Graphics* class. As you have learned, you can create shapes such as spades, hearts, clubs, and diamonds by combining images you can create using the standard *Graphics* class functions. In Chapter 50, you will expand the card deck to draw the proper number of suits on each card. Before you continue with Chapter 50, however, make sure you understand the following key concepts:

☑ You can create a class that will display 54 playing cards, including jokers.

☑ You can use the *fillRoundRect* class to fill rectangles with rounded corners.

CHAPTER 50

CARDS WITH SUITS
SHOWING A CARD DECK WITH THE RIGHT NUMBER OF SUITS

In Chapter 49, you learned how to display a basic deck of cards. In this chapter, you will learn how to create a deck of cards that includes the correct number of suits for each card. For example, if the card is a 5 of clubs, as shown in Figure 50, the card will display 5 clubs on its face. By the time you finish this chapter, you will understand the following key concepts:

♦ By making a few changes to the **Playing Cards** applet you created in Chapter 49, you can draw the right number of suits for each card.

♦ You do not have to modify the main applet to change how the cards look.

USING CARDS WITH SUITS

When you run the **Cards with Suits** applet, you will see a window that displays one card at a time and some statistics at the right of the card, as shown in Figure 50. The applet changes the card on the screen to another random card every second, and updates the statistics on the right. The status bar at the bottom shows the total number of cards dealt from the current deck. When the deck runs out of cards, the applet resets the deck, and starts over again.

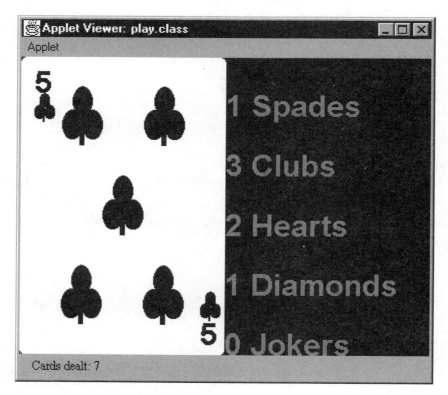

Figure 50 *Displaying one card at a time.*

THE HTML FILE

Use the following HTML file to run the **Cards with Suits** applet:

```
<applet code=play.class width=400 height=300> </applet>
```

LOOKING AT CARDS WITH SUITS

The *play* class is exactly the same as the one in the previous chapter. Therefore, this chapter will not present the source code. However, if you examine the CD-ROM that accompanies this book, you will find the complete source code for the *play* class in both the CHAP49 and CHAP50 subdirectories. As you will recall from Chapter 49, the *play* class randomly displays one card at a time, one card per second, until the entire deck has been displayed. The class then recycles the deck and starts again.

The cards Class

As you will recall from Chapter 49, the *cards* class draws a playing card within the applet window at a specific height and width, and at specific x-and-y coordinates. The one main difference between this class and the *cards* class presented in Chapter 49 is the addition of the *draw_suit* function. This function determines which card to draw, and then draws the correct number of suits for that card. Also, instead of the *draw* function calling the individual functions to draw spades, clubs, hearts, or diamonds, it calls the *draw_suit* function. The following code implements the *cards* class:

```java
//*********************************************************************
// cards.java
//*********************************************************************

import java.awt.*;

//*********************************************************************

public class cards
  {
    Graphics g;
    Image joker;

    int x;
    int y;
    int w;
    int h;
    int number;
    int suit;

    //─────────────────────────────────

    public cards(Graphics g)
      {
        this.g = g;
      }

    //─────────────────────────────────
```

```java
    public void draw_spades(int x, int y, int w, int h)
      {
        int xx[] = new int[3];
        int yy[] = new int[3];

        xx[0] = x + w/2;  yy[0] = y      ;
        xx[1] = x      ;  yy[1] = y + h/2;
        xx[2] = x + w  ;  yy[2] = y + h/2;

        g.fillPolygon(xx, yy, 3);

        g.fillOval(x     , y+h/3, w/2, h/2);
        g.fillOval(x+w/2, y+h/3, w/2, h/2);

        g.fillRect(x+(w*3)/7, y+h/3, w/7, (h*2)/3);
      }

    //—————————————————————————

    public void draw_clubs(int x, int y, int w, int h)
      {
        g.fillOval(x     , y+(h*2)/5, w/2, h/2);
        g.fillOval(x+w/2, y+(h*2)/5, w/2, h/2);
        g.fillOval(x+w/4, y        , w/2, h/2);

        g.fillRect(x+(w*3)/7, y+h/3, w/7, (h*2)/3);
      }

    //—————————————————————————

    public void draw_hearts(int x, int y, int w, int h)
      {
        int xx[] = new int[3];
        int yy[] = new int[3];

        xx[0] = x + w/2;  yy[0] = y + h  ;
        xx[1] = x      ;  yy[1] = y + h/4;
        xx[2] = x + w  ;  yy[2] = y + h/4;

        g.fillPolygon(xx, yy, 3);

        g.fillOval(x     , y, w/2, h/2);
        g.fillOval(x+w/2, y, w/2, h/2);
      }

    //—————————————————————————

    public void draw_diamonds(int x, int y, int w, int h)
      {
        int xx[] = new int[4];
        int yy[] = new int[4];

        xx[0] = x + w/2;  yy[0] = y + h  ;
        xx[1] = x      ;  yy[1] = y + h/2;
```

```java
      xx[2] = x + w/2;   yy[2] = y         ;
      xx[3] = x + w  ;   yy[3] = y + h/2;

      g.fillPolygon(xx, yy, 4);
  }

//————————————————————————

public void draw_joker(int x, int y, int w, int h)
  {
    g.drawImage(joker, x, y, w, h, null);
  }

//————————————————————————

public void draw(int card, int x, int y, int w, int h)
  {
    this.x = x;
    this.y = y;
    this.w = w;
    this.h = h;

    g.setColor(Color.white);
    g.fillRoundRect(x, y, w, h, w/20, h/20);
    Font font = new Font("Helvetica", Font.BOLD, h/10);
    g.setFont(font);
    FontMetrics font_metrics = g.getFontMetrics();

    String string;
    number = -1;
    suit = -1;

    if (card > 51)
      {
        string = "JOKER";
        g.setColor(Color.green);
      }
    else
      {
        number = card % 13;
        suit = card / 13;

        if (number == 0)
          string = "A";
        else if (number == 10)
          string = "J";
        else if (number == 11)
          string = "Q";
        else if (number == 12)
          string = "K";
        else
          string = "" + (number+1);
```

```
            if (suit/2 == 0)
              g.setColor(Color.black);
            else
              g.setColor(Color.red);
        }

    int string_width = font_metrics.stringWidth(string);
    g.drawString(string, x+(w*31)/32-string_width, y+(h*31)/32);
    g.drawString(string, x+w/15, y+h/8);

    draw_suit(x+w/15, y+h/8,
              x+(w*31)/32-string_width, y+(h*31)/32,
              3 * font_metrics.getHeight () / 2);
  }


//————————————————————————————

void draw_suit(int x1, int y1, int x2, int y2, int hh)
  {
    switch (suit)
      {
        case 0:
          draw_spades(x1, y1    , w/10, h/10);
          draw_spades(x2, y2-hh, w/10, h/10);

          switch (number+1)
            {
              case 1:
              case 11:
              case 12:
              case 13:
                draw_spades(x+(w*2)/5, y+(h*2)/5, w/5, h/5);
                break;

              case 2:
                draw_spades(x+(w*2)/5, y+(h*1)/10, w/5, h/5);
                draw_spades(x+(w*2)/5, y+(h*7)/10, w/5, h/5);
                break;

              case 3:
                draw_spades(x+(w*2)/5, y+(h*1)/10, w/5, h/5);
                draw_spades(x+(w*2)/5, y+(h*4)/10, w/5, h/5);
                draw_spades(x+(w*2)/5, y+(h*7)/10, w/5, h/5);
                break;

              case 4:
                draw_spades(x+(w*1)/5, y+(h*1)/10, w/5, h/5);
                draw_spades(x+(w*3)/5, y+(h*1)/10, w/5, h/5);
                draw_spades(x+(w*1)/5, y+(h*7)/10, w/5, h/5);
                draw_spades(x+(w*3)/5, y+(h*7)/10, w/5, h/5);
                break;
```

```
case 5:
  draw_spades(x+(w*2)/5, y+(h*2)/5 , w/5, h/5);
  draw_spades(x+(w*1)/5, y+(h*1)/10, w/5, h/5);
  draw_spades(x+(w*3)/5, y+(h*1)/10, w/5, h/5);
  draw_spades(x+(w*1)/5, y+(h*7)/10, w/5, h/5);
  draw_spades(x+(w*3)/5, y+(h*7)/10, w/5, h/5);
  break;

case 6:
  draw_spades(x+(w*1)/5, y+(h*1)/10, w/5, h/5);
  draw_spades(x+(w*1)/5, y+(h*4)/10, w/5, h/5);
  draw_spades(x+(w*1)/5, y+(h*7)/10, w/5, h/5);
  draw_spades(x+(w*3)/5, y+(h*1)/10, w/5, h/5);
  draw_spades(x+(w*3)/5, y+(h*4)/10, w/5, h/5);
  draw_spades(x+(w*3)/5, y+(h*7)/10, w/5, h/5);
  break;

case 7:
  draw_spades(x+(w*1)/5, y+(h*1)/10, w/5, h/5);
  draw_spades(x+(w*1)/5, y+(h*4)/10, w/5, h/5);
  draw_spades(x+(w*1)/5, y+(h*7)/10, w/5, h/5);
  draw_spades(x+(w*3)/5, y+(h*1)/10, w/5, h/5);
  draw_spades(x+(w*3)/5, y+(h*4)/10, w/5, h/5);
  draw_spades(x+(w*3)/5, y+(h*7)/10, w/5, h/5);
  draw_spades(x+(w*2)/5, y+(h*5)/10, w/5, h/5);
  break;

case 8:
  draw_spades(x+(w*1)/5, y+(h*1)/10, w/5, h/5);
  draw_spades(x+(w*1)/5, y+(h*4)/10, w/5, h/5);
  draw_spades(x+(w*1)/5, y+(h*7)/10, w/5, h/5);
  draw_spades(x+(w*3)/5, y+(h*1)/10, w/5, h/5);
  draw_spades(x+(w*3)/5, y+(h*4)/10, w/5, h/5);
  draw_spades(x+(w*3)/5, y+(h*7)/10, w/5, h/5);
  draw_spades(x+(w*2)/5, y+(h*5)/10, w/5, h/5);
  draw_spades(x+(w*2)/5, y+(h*2)/10, w/5, h/5);
  break;

case 9:
  draw_spades(x+(w*1)/5, y+(h*1)/10, w/5, h/5);
  draw_spades(x+(w*1)/5, y+(h*3)/10, w/5, h/5);
  draw_spades(x+(w*1)/5, y+(h*5)/10, w/5, h/5);
  draw_spades(x+(w*1)/5, y+(h*7)/10, w/5, h/5);
  draw_spades(x+(w*3)/5, y+(h*1)/10, w/5, h/5);
  draw_spades(x+(w*3)/5, y+(h*3)/10, w/5, h/5);
  draw_spades(x+(w*3)/5, y+(h*5)/10, w/5, h/5);
  draw_spades(x+(w*3)/5, y+(h*7)/10, w/5, h/5);
  draw_spades(x+(w*2)/5, y+(h*2)/5 , w/5, h/5);
  break;

case 10:
  draw_spades(x+(w*1)/5, y+(h*1)/10, w/5, h/5);
  draw_spades(x+(w*1)/5, y+(h*3)/10, w/5, h/5);
  draw_spades(x+(w*1)/5, y+(h*5)/10, w/5, h/5);
```

```
                    draw_spades(x+(w*1)/5, y+(h*7)/10, w/5, h/5);
                    draw_spades(x+(w*3)/5, y+(h*1)/10, w/5, h/5);
                    draw_spades(x+(w*3)/5, y+(h*3)/10, w/5, h/5);
                    draw_spades(x+(w*3)/5, y+(h*5)/10, w/5, h/5);
                    draw_spades(x+(w*3)/5, y+(h*7)/10, w/5, h/5);
                    draw_spades(x+(w*2)/5, y+(h*5)/10, w/5, h/5);
                    draw_spades(x+(w*2)/5, y+(h*2)/10, w/5, h/5);
                    break;
                }

            break;

        case 1:
            draw_clubs(x1, y1   , w/10, h/10);
            draw_clubs(x2, y2-hh, w/10, h/10);

            switch (number+1)
              {
                case 1:
                case 11:
                case 12:
                case 13:
                    draw_clubs(x+(w*2)/5, y+(h*2)/5, w/5, h/5);
                    break;

                case 2:
                    draw_clubs(x+(w*2)/5, y+(h*1)/10, w/5, h/5);
                    draw_clubs(x+(w*2)/5, y+(h*7)/10, w/5, h/5);
                    break;

                case 3:
                    draw_clubs(x+(w*2)/5, y+(h*1)/10, w/5, h/5);
                    draw_clubs(x+(w*2)/5, y+(h*4)/10, w/5, h/5);
                    draw_clubs(x+(w*2)/5, y+(h*7)/10, w/5, h/5);
                    break;

                case 4:
                    draw_clubs(x+(w*1)/5, y+(h*1)/10, w/5, h/5);
                    draw_clubs(x+(w*3)/5, y+(h*1)/10, w/5, h/5);
                    draw_clubs(x+(w*1)/5, y+(h*7)/10, w/5, h/5);
                    draw_clubs(x+(w*3)/5, y+(h*7)/10, w/5, h/5);
                    break;

                case 5:
                    draw_clubs(x+(w*2)/5, y+(h*2)/5 , w/5, h/5);
                    draw_clubs(x+(w*1)/5, y+(h*1)/10, w/5, h/5);
                    draw_clubs(x+(w*3)/5, y+(h*1)/10, w/5, h/5);
                    draw_clubs(x+(w*1)/5, y+(h*7)/10, w/5, h/5);
                    draw_clubs(x+(w*3)/5, y+(h*7)/10, w/5, h/5);
                    break;

                case 6:
                    draw_clubs(x+(w*1)/5, y+(h*1)/10, w/5, h/5);
                    draw_clubs(x+(w*1)/5, y+(h*4)/10, w/5, h/5);
```

```
            draw_clubs(x+(w*1)/5, y+(h*7)/10, w/5, h/5);
            draw_clubs(x+(w*3)/5, y+(h*1)/10, w/5, h/5);
            draw_clubs(x+(w*3)/5, y+(h*4)/10, w/5, h/5);
            draw_clubs(x+(w*3)/5, y+(h*7)/10, w/5, h/5);
            break;

        case 7:
            draw_clubs(x+(w*1)/5, y+(h*1)/10, w/5, h/5);
            draw_clubs(x+(w*1)/5, y+(h*4)/10, w/5, h/5);
            draw_clubs(x+(w*1)/5, y+(h*7)/10, w/5, h/5);
            draw_clubs(x+(w*3)/5, y+(h*1)/10, w/5, h/5);
            draw_clubs(x+(w*3)/5, y+(h*4)/10, w/5, h/5);
            draw_clubs(x+(w*3)/5, y+(h*7)/10, w/5, h/5);
            draw_clubs(x+(w*2)/5, y+(h*5)/10, w/5, h/5);
            break;

        case 8:
            draw_clubs(x+(w*1)/5, y+(h*1)/10, w/5, h/5);
            draw_clubs(x+(w*1)/5, y+(h*4)/10, w/5, h/5);
            draw_clubs(x+(w*1)/5, y+(h*7)/10, w/5, h/5);
            draw_clubs(x+(w*3)/5, y+(h*1)/10, w/5, h/5);
            draw_clubs(x+(w*3)/5, y+(h*4)/10, w/5, h/5);
            draw_clubs(x+(w*3)/5, y+(h*7)/10, w/5, h/5);
            draw_clubs(x+(w*2)/5, y+(h*5)/10, w/5, h/5);
            draw_clubs(x+(w*2)/5, y+(h*2)/10, w/5, h/5);
            break;

        case 9:
            draw_clubs(x+(w*1)/5, y+(h*1)/10, w/5, h/5);
            draw_clubs(x+(w*1)/5, y+(h*3)/10, w/5, h/5);
            draw_clubs(x+(w*1)/5, y+(h*5)/10, w/5, h/5);
            draw_clubs(x+(w*1)/5, y+(h*7)/10, w/5, h/5);
            draw_clubs(x+(w*3)/5, y+(h*1)/10, w/5, h/5);
            draw_clubs(x+(w*3)/5, y+(h*3)/10, w/5, h/5);
            draw_clubs(x+(w*3)/5, y+(h*5)/10, w/5, h/5);
            draw_clubs(x+(w*3)/5, y+(h*7)/10, w/5, h/5);
            draw_clubs(x+(w*2)/5, y+(h*2)/5 , w/5, h/5);
            break;

        case 10:
            draw_clubs(x+(w*1)/5, y+(h*1)/10, w/5, h/5);
            draw_clubs(x+(w*1)/5, y+(h*3)/10, w/5, h/5);
            draw_clubs(x+(w*1)/5, y+(h*5)/10, w/5, h/5);
            draw_clubs(x+(w*1)/5, y+(h*7)/10, w/5, h/5);
            draw_clubs(x+(w*3)/5, y+(h*1)/10, w/5, h/5);
            draw_clubs(x+(w*3)/5, y+(h*3)/10, w/5, h/5);
            draw_clubs(x+(w*3)/5, y+(h*5)/10, w/5, h/5);
            draw_clubs(x+(w*3)/5, y+(h*7)/10, w/5, h/5);
            draw_clubs(x+(w*2)/5, y+(h*5)/10, w/5, h/5);
            draw_clubs(x+(w*2)/5, y+(h*2)/10, w/5, h/5);
            break;
    }

    break;
```

```
            case 2:
              draw_hearts(x1, y1    , w/10, h/10);
              draw_hearts(x2, y2-hh, w/10, h/10);

              switch (number+1)
                {
                  case 1:
                  case 11:
                  case 12:
                  case 13:
                    draw_hearts(x+(w*2)/5, y+(h*2)/5, w/5, h/5);
                    break;

                  case 2:
                    draw_hearts(x+(w*2)/5, y+(h*1)/10, w/5, h/5);
                    draw_hearts(x+(w*2)/5, y+(h*7)/10, w/5, h/5);
                    break;

                  case 3:
                    draw_hearts(x+(w*2)/5, y+(h*1)/10, w/5, h/5);
                    draw_hearts(x+(w*2)/5, y+(h*4)/10, w/5, h/5);
                    draw_hearts(x+(w*2)/5, y+(h*7)/10, w/5, h/5);
                    break;

                  case 4:
                    draw_hearts(x+(w*1)/5, y+(h*1)/10, w/5, h/5);
                    draw_hearts(x+(w*3)/5, y+(h*1)/10, w/5, h/5);
                    draw_hearts(x+(w*1)/5, y+(h*7)/10, w/5, h/5);
                    draw_hearts(x+(w*3)/5, y+(h*7)/10, w/5, h/5);
                    break;

                  case 5:
                    draw_hearts(x+(w*2)/5, y+(h*2)/5 , w/5, h/5);
                    draw_hearts(x+(w*1)/5, y+(h*1)/10, w/5, h/5);
                    draw_hearts(x+(w*3)/5, y+(h*1)/10, w/5, h/5);
                    draw_hearts(x+(w*1)/5, y+(h*7)/10, w/5, h/5);
                    draw_hearts(x+(w*3)/5, y+(h*7)/10, w/5, h/5);
                    break;

                  case 6:
                    draw_hearts(x+(w*1)/5, y+(h*1)/10, w/5, h/5);
                    draw_hearts(x+(w*1)/5, y+(h*4)/10, w/5, h/5);
                    draw_hearts(x+(w*1)/5, y+(h*7)/10, w/5, h/5);
                    draw_hearts(x+(w*3)/5, y+(h*1)/10, w/5, h/5);
                    draw_hearts(x+(w*3)/5, y+(h*4)/10, w/5, h/5);
                    draw_hearts(x+(w*3)/5, y+(h*7)/10, w/5, h/5);
                    break;

                  case 7:
                    draw_hearts(x+(w*1)/5, y+(h*1)/10, w/5, h/5);
                    draw_hearts(x+(w*1)/5, y+(h*4)/10, w/5, h/5);
                    draw_hearts(x+(w*1)/5, y+(h*7)/10, w/5, h/5);
                    draw_hearts(x+(w*3)/5, y+(h*1)/10, w/5, h/5);
                    draw_hearts(x+(w*3)/5, y+(h*4)/10, w/5, h/5);
```

```
              draw_hearts(x+(w*3)/5, y+(h*7)/10, w/5, h/5);
              draw_hearts(x+(w*2)/5, y+(h*5)/10, w/5, h/5);
              break;

          case 8:
              draw_hearts(x+(w*1)/5, y+(h*1)/10, w/5, h/5);
              draw_hearts(x+(w*1)/5, y+(h*4)/10, w/5, h/5);
              draw_hearts(x+(w*1)/5, y+(h*7)/10, w/5, h/5);
              draw_hearts(x+(w*3)/5, y+(h*1)/10, w/5, h/5);
              draw_hearts(x+(w*3)/5, y+(h*4)/10, w/5, h/5);
              draw_hearts(x+(w*3)/5, y+(h*7)/10, w/5, h/5);
              draw_hearts(x+(w*2)/5, y+(h*5)/10, w/5, h/5);
              draw_hearts(x+(w*2)/5, y+(h*2)/10, w/5, h/5);
              break;

          case 9:
              draw_hearts(x+(w*1)/5, y+(h*1)/10, w/5, h/5);
              draw_hearts(x+(w*1)/5, y+(h*3)/10, w/5, h/5);
              draw_hearts(x+(w*1)/5, y+(h*5)/10, w/5, h/5);
              draw_hearts(x+(w*1)/5, y+(h*7)/10, w/5, h/5);
              draw_hearts(x+(w*3)/5, y+(h*1)/10, w/5, h/5);
              draw_hearts(x+(w*3)/5, y+(h*3)/10, w/5, h/5);
              draw_hearts(x+(w*3)/5, y+(h*5)/10, w/5, h/5);
              draw_hearts(x+(w*3)/5, y+(h*7)/10, w/5, h/5);
              draw_hearts(x+(w*2)/5, y+(h*2)/5 , w/5, h/5);
              break;

          case 10:
              draw_hearts(x+(w*1)/5, y+(h*1)/10, w/5, h/5);
              draw_hearts(x+(w*1)/5, y+(h*3)/10, w/5, h/5);
              draw_hearts(x+(w*1)/5, y+(h*5)/10, w/5, h/5);
              draw_hearts(x+(w*1)/5, y+(h*7)/10, w/5, h/5);
              draw_hearts(x+(w*3)/5, y+(h*1)/10, w/5, h/5);
              draw_hearts(x+(w*3)/5, y+(h*3)/10, w/5, h/5);
              draw_hearts(x+(w*3)/5, y+(h*5)/10, w/5, h/5);
              draw_hearts(x+(w*3)/5, y+(h*7)/10, w/5, h/5);
              draw_hearts(x+(w*2)/5, y+(h*5)/10, w/5, h/5);
              draw_hearts(x+(w*2)/5, y+(h*2)/10, w/5, h/5);
              break;
          }

      break;

  case 3:
      draw_diamonds(x1, y1    , w/10, h/10);
      draw_diamonds(x2, y2-hh, w/10, h/10);

      switch (number+1)
        {
          case 1:
          case 11:
          case 12:
          case 13:
              draw_diamonds(x+(w*2)/5, y+(h*2)/5, w/5, h/5);
              break;
```

```
            case 2:
              draw_diamonds(x+(w*2)/5, y+(h*1)/10, w/5, h/5);
              draw_diamonds(x+(w*2)/5, y+(h*7)/10, w/5, h/5);
              break;

            case 3:
              draw_diamonds(x+(w*2)/5, y+(h*1)/10, w/5, h/5);
              draw_diamonds(x+(w*2)/5, y+(h*4)/10, w/5, h/5);
              draw_diamonds(x+(w*2)/5, y+(h*7)/10, w/5, h/5);
              break;

            case 4:
              draw_diamonds(x+(w*1)/5, y+(h*1)/10, w/5, h/5);
              draw_diamonds(x+(w*3)/5, y+(h*1)/10, w/5, h/5);
              draw_diamonds(x+(w*1)/5, y+(h*7)/10, w/5, h/5);
              draw_diamonds(x+(w*3)/5, y+(h*7)/10, w/5, h/5);
              break;

            case 5:
              draw_diamonds(x+(w*2)/5, y+(h*2)/5 , w/5, h/5);
              draw_diamonds(x+(w*1)/5, y+(h*1)/10, w/5, h/5);
              draw_diamonds(x+(w*3)/5, y+(h*1)/10, w/5, h/5);
              draw_diamonds(x+(w*1)/5, y+(h*7)/10, w/5, h/5);
              draw_diamonds(x+(w*3)/5, y+(h*7)/10, w/5, h/5);
              break;

            case 6:
              draw_diamonds(x+(w*1)/5, y+(h*1)/10, w/5, h/5);
              draw_diamonds(x+(w*1)/5, y+(h*4)/10, w/5, h/5);
              draw_diamonds(x+(w*1)/5, y+(h*7)/10, w/5, h/5);
              draw_diamonds(x+(w*3)/5, y+(h*1)/10, w/5, h/5);
              draw_diamonds(x+(w*3)/5, y+(h*4)/10, w/5, h/5);
              draw_diamonds(x+(w*3)/5, y+(h*7)/10, w/5, h/5);
              break;

            case 7:
              draw_diamonds(x+(w*1)/5, y+(h*1)/10, w/5, h/5);
              draw_diamonds(x+(w*1)/5, y+(h*4)/10, w/5, h/5);
              draw_diamonds(x+(w*1)/5, y+(h*7)/10, w/5, h/5);
              draw_diamonds(x+(w*3)/5, y+(h*1)/10, w/5, h/5);
              draw_diamonds(x+(w*3)/5, y+(h*4)/10, w/5, h/5);
              draw_diamonds(x+(w*3)/5, y+(h*7)/10, w/5, h/5);
              draw_diamonds(x+(w*2)/5, y+(h*5)/10, w/5, h/5);
              break;

            case 8:
              draw_diamonds(x+(w*1)/5, y+(h*1)/10, w/5, h/5);
              draw_diamonds(x+(w*1)/5, y+(h*4)/10, w/5, h/5);
              draw_diamonds(x+(w*1)/5, y+(h*7)/10, w/5, h/5);
              draw_diamonds(x+(w*3)/5, y+(h*1)/10, w/5, h/5);
              draw_diamonds(x+(w*3)/5, y+(h*4)/10, w/5, h/5);
              draw_diamonds(x+(w*3)/5, y+(h*7)/10, w/5, h/5);
              draw_diamonds(x+(w*2)/5, y+(h*5)/10, w/5, h/5);
              draw_diamonds(x+(w*2)/5, y+(h*2)/10, w/5, h/5);
              break;
```

```
                        case 9:
                          draw_diamonds(x+(w*1)/5, y+(h*1)/10, w/5, h/5);
                          draw_diamonds(x+(w*1)/5, y+(h*3)/10, w/5, h/5);
                          draw_diamonds(x+(w*1)/5, y+(h*5)/10, w/5, h/5);
                          draw_diamonds(x+(w*1)/5, y+(h*7)/10, w/5, h/5);
                          draw_diamonds(x+(w*3)/5, y+(h*1)/10, w/5, h/5);
                          draw_diamonds(x+(w*3)/5, y+(h*3)/10, w/5, h/5);
                          draw_diamonds(x+(w*3)/5, y+(h*5)/10, w/5, h/5);
                          draw_diamonds(x+(w*3)/5, y+(h*7)/10, w/5, h/5);
                          draw_diamonds(x+(w*2)/5, y+(h*2)/5 , w/5, h/5);
                          break;

                        case 10:
                          draw_diamonds(x+(w*1)/5, y+(h*1)/10, w/5, h/5);
                          draw_diamonds(x+(w*1)/5, y+(h*3)/10, w/5, h/5);
                          draw_diamonds(x+(w*1)/5, y+(h*5)/10, w/5, h/5);
                          draw_diamonds(x+(w*1)/5, y+(h*7)/10, w/5, h/5);
                          draw_diamonds(x+(w*3)/5, y+(h*1)/10, w/5, h/5);
                          draw_diamonds(x+(w*3)/5, y+(h*3)/10, w/5, h/5);
                          draw_diamonds(x+(w*3)/5, y+(h*5)/10, w/5, h/5);
                          draw_diamonds(x+(w*3)/5, y+(h*7)/10, w/5, h/5);
                          draw_diamonds(x+(w*2)/5, y+(h*5)/10, w/5, h/5);
                          draw_diamonds(x+(w*2)/5, y+(h*2)/10, w/5, h/5);
                          break;
                    }

                  break;

                default:
                  draw_joker(x+w/4, y+h/4, w/2, h/2);
              }
          }
      }
```

Breaking Apart Cards with Suits

Since the *play* class is exactly the same as the *play* class in the previous chapter, this section will not discuss it. However, the *cards* class does contain some differences from the previous chapter, and the following section will discuss those differences.

Member Variables

To start, the *play* class declares member variables to keep track of some of the values that are used in the *draw* function. The class declares these member variables so you do not have to pass the values to the *draw_suit* function, which keeps the parameter list from getting too long. These variables are the card's x-and-y coordinates, the card's width and the height, the card's number value, and the card's suit:

```
int x;
int y;
int w;
int h;
int number;
int suit;
```

The draw Function

To start, the *draw* function stores its parameters in the new class member variables:

```
public void draw(int card, int x, int y, int w, int h)
  {
    this.x = x;
    this.y = y;
    this.w = w;
    this.h = h;
```

At the end of the function, instead of calling the appropriate function to draw the card's suit, the function has to call the *draw_suit* function, and passes to it five parameters that will be described in the next section:

```
draw_suit(x+w/15, y+h/8, x+(w*31)/32-string_width, y+(h*31)/32,
          3 * font_metrics.getHeight () / 2);
```

Drawing the Suits

As discussed, the *draw_suit* function draws a card's suit. The function accepts five parameters: the x-and-y coordinates of the suit to draw under the top-left card value, the x-and-y coordinates of the suit to draw above the bottom-right card value, and the height to use for the card's bottom-right positions:

```
void draw_suit(int x1, int y1, int x2, int y2, int hh)
```

To start, the function must determine which suit to draw. Remember, the *cards* class represents the suit as follows: 0 is spades, 1 is clubs, 2 is hearts, 3 is diamonds, and 4 is jokers. To determine the card's suit, the *draw_suit* function uses a switch statement:

```
switch (suit)
  {
    case 0:
```

For each suit, the function first draws the suit in the two positions for which you received parameters: under the top-left card value, and above the bottom-right card value:

```
draw_spades(x1, y1   , w/10, h/10);
draw_spades(x2, y2-hh, w/10, h/10);
```

Next, the function must determine the card's value to determine how many suits to draw. For the ace, king, queen, and jack, the function draws one suit in the middle of the card:

```
switch (number+1)
  {
    case 1:
    case 11:
    case 12:
    case 13:
      draw_spades(x+(w*2)/5, y+(h*2)/5, w/5, h/5);
      break;
```

For the two of spades, the function draws the spades at the x-coordinate, which is two-fifths of the width of the card from the left. The y-coordinates are one-tenth of the height of the card from the top, and seven-tenths of the height of the card from the top:

```
case 2:
    draw_spades(x+(w*2)/5, y+(h*1)/10, w/5, h/5);
    draw_spades(x+(w*2)/5, y+(h*7)/10, w/5, h/5);
    break;
```

The function draws the rest of the cards in a similar fashion, determining the x-and-y coordinates for each position of the suits. For the joker, however, the function calls the *draw_joker* function, just as it did in the previous chapter.

```
draw_joker(x+w/4, y+h/4, w/2, h/2);
```

ENHANCEMENTS YOU CAN MAKE TO PLAYING CARDS

In a real deck of cards, the suits on the bottom half of the card are upside down. As such, no matter which way you hold up the cards, they look like they are right-side-up. Modify the program so the suits on the bottom half are drawn backwards. If you want to use GIF files, make sure that you create suits that are backwards.

PUTTING IT ALL TOGETHER

The **Cards with Suits** applet shows you how to display a deck of cards with each card containing the correct number of suits. In Chapter 51, you will use the *cards* class to create a Blackjack game. Before you continue with Chapter 51, however, make sure you understand the following key concepts:

☑ The *draw_suits* function draws the right number of suits for each card.

☑ You do not have to modify the main applet to change how the cards look. This is one of the advantages of object-oriented programming.

CHAPTER 51

BLACKJACK
USING THE CARD CLASS TO PLAY A GAME

For the past two chapters, you have developed a deck of cards you can display in a window. In this chapter, you will use the card deck to create an interactive Blackjack game. By the time you finish the chapter, you will understand the following key concepts:

◆ You can use the *cards* class to create the popular game of Blackjack.

◆ You can create a class of your own type of buttons, which the user can click to perform a specific action.

USING BLACKJACK

When you run the **Blackjack** applet, you will see a window with two cards for the dealer at the top, and two cards for you at the bottom, as shown in Figure 51.1. Notice that the first card for the dealer is face-down. At this point, you have two options: "Hit Me," which will give you another card; and "Stay," which means you do not want another card. When you stay, the dealer's face down card will turn over. Then, the dealer will hit as long as it has 16 or less, and will stay at 17 or more. However, if you have busted (gone over 21), then the dealer's face-down card will turn over, but the dealer will not take any cards.

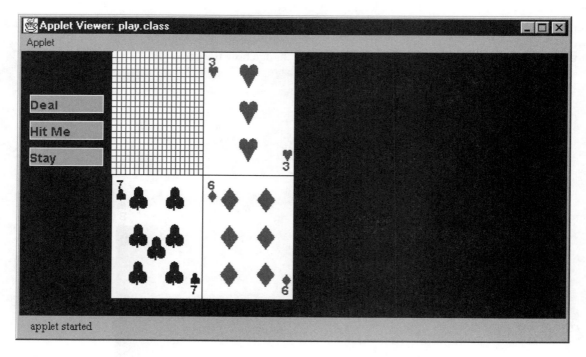

Figure 51.1 A typical opening Blackjack screen.

If the player's total is greater than the dealer's total, the player wins, and a green message will show up under the buttons that says "Player WINS", as shown in Figure 51.2.

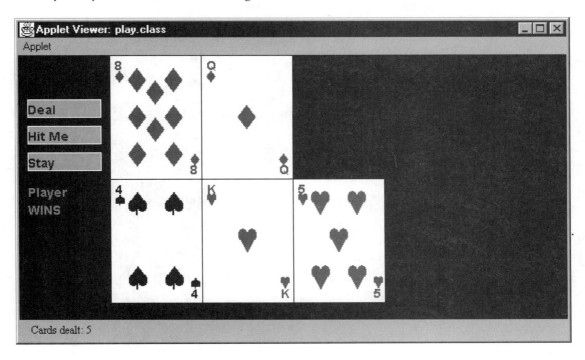

Figure 51.2 The player wins!

If the totals for the player and the dealer are the same, it is a push, and a yellow message will say "PUSH", as shown in Figure 51.3.

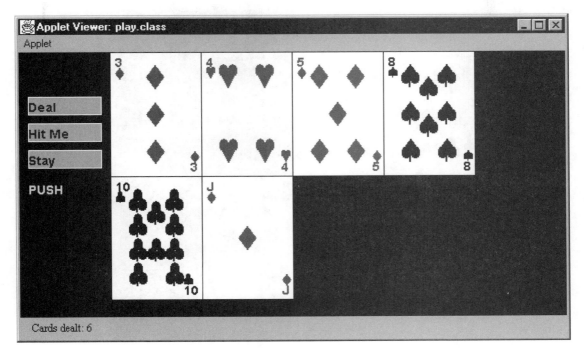

Figure 51.3 A push.

If the dealer's total is greater than the player's total, the dealer wins, and a red message will say "Dealer WINS", as shown in Figure 51.4.

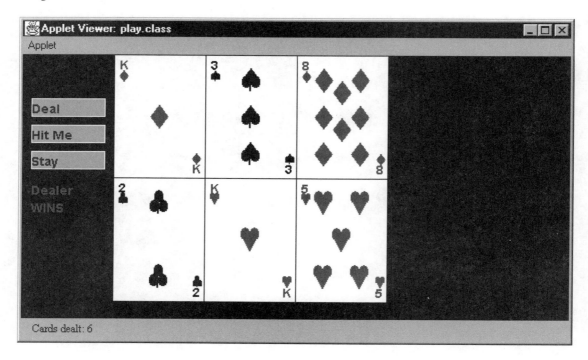

Figure 51.4 *The dealer wins.*

If the player's total exceeds 21, the dealer wins, and a red message will say "Player Busted Dealer WINS", as shown in Figure 51.5.

Figure 51.5 *The player busted, so the dealer wins.*

If the dealer's total exceeds 21, the player wins, and a green message will say "Dealer Busted Player WINS", as shown in Figure 51.6.

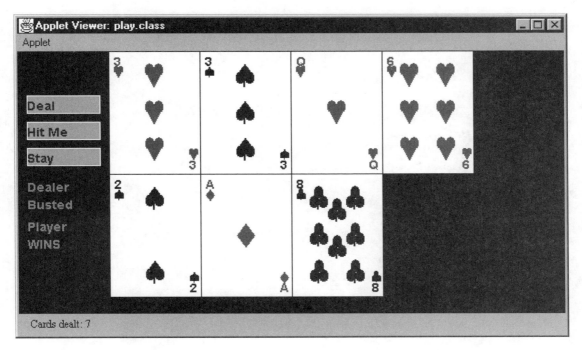

Figure 51.6 The dealer busted, so the player wins.

The HTML File

Use the following HTML file to run the **Blackjack** applet:

```
<applet code=play.class width=600 height=300> </applet>
```

Looking at Blackjack

The **Blackjack** applet uses four classes in three files. The "play.java" file contains the *play* class, the "cards.java" file contains the *cards* class, and the "buttons.java" file contains the *buttons* class and the *button_info* class. This section examines each of the classes.

The "play.java" File

The "play.java" file contains the **Blackjack** applet. In other words, it contains the code that plays the game. The following code implements the applet:

```
//*************************************************************
// play.java
//*************************************************************


import java.applet.*;
import java.awt.*;


//*************************************************************
```

```java
public class play extends Applet
  {
    Graphics g;
    cards card_deck;

    int width;
    int height;
    int card;
    int number;
    int suit;

    boolean card_displayed[];
    int dealer_cards[];
    int player_cards[];

    int card_count;
    int card_width = 100;
    int card_height = 140;

    int number_of_dealer_cards;
    int number_of_player_cards;

    boolean hand_done = true;

    //─────────────────────────────────

    public void init()
      {
        g = getGraphics();

        card_deck = new cards(g);

        card_displayed = new boolean [52];
        dealer_cards   = new int      [10];
        player_cards   = new int      [10];

        new buttons(g, "Deal"  , 10,  50, 80, 20);
        new buttons(g, "Hit Me", 10,  80, 80, 20);
        new buttons(g, "Stay"  , 10, 110, 80, 20);

        deal();
      }

    //─────────────────────────────────

    void reset_cards()
      {
        int i;

        for (i = 0; i < 52; i++)
          card_displayed[i] = false;

        card_count = 0;
```

```
                  number_of_dealer_cards = 0;
                  number_of_player_cards = 0;
          }

       //————————————————————————

       void set_defaults()
          {
             width = size().width;
             height = size().height;
          }

       //————————————————————————

       void get_card()
          {
             card = (int) (Math.random() * 52);

             do
                {
                   if (!card_displayed[card])
                      {
                         card_displayed[card] = true;
                         break;
                      }
                   else if (++card == 52)
                      card = 0;

                } while (true);

             get_number_and_suit(card);
          }

       //————————————————————————

       void get_number_and_suit(int card)
          {
             number = card % 13;
             suit = card / 13;
          }

       //————————————————————————

       void deal()
          {
             hand_done = false;

             reset_cards();

             for (int x = 0; x < 2; x++)
                {
                   for (int y = 0; y < 2; y++)
                      {
                         get_card();
```

```
                        if (y == 0)
                          dealer_cards[number_of_dealer_cards++] = card;
                        else
                          player_cards[number_of_player_cards++] = card;

                        if (x == 0 && y == 0)
                          card_deck.draw_back(card_width, 0,
                                              card_width, card_height);
                        else
                          card_deck.draw(card,
                                         (x+1)*card_width, y*card_height,
                                         card_width, card_height);

                        card_count++;
                        showStatus("Cards dealt: " + card_count);
                    }
                }
        }

//————————————————————————————

void hit_me()
  {
    if (hand_done)
      return;

    get_card();

    player_cards[number_of_player_cards++] = card;

    card_deck.draw(card,
                   number_of_player_cards*card_width, card_height,
                   card_width, card_height);

    card_count++;
    showStatus("Cards dealt: " + card_count);

    int player_total = get_total(player_cards,
                                 number_of_player_cards);

    if (player_total > 21)
      done();
  }

//————————————————————————————

int get_total(int cards[], int number_of_cards)
  {
    int total = 0;
    int aces = 0;

    for (int i = 0; i < number_of_cards; i++)
      {
        get_number_and_suit(cards[i]);
```

```
        switch (number)
          {
            case 10:
            case 11:
            case 12:
              total += 10;
              break;

            case 0:
              aces++;
              total += 1;
              break;

            default:
              total += number + 1;
          }
      }

    for (int a = 0; a < aces; a++)
      {
        if (total + 10 > 21)
          break;
        else
          total += 10;
      }

    return total;
  }

//─────────────────────────────────

void done()
  {
    if (hand_done)
      return;

    hand_done = true;
    card_deck.draw(dealer_cards [0], card_width, 0,
                   card_width, card_height);

    int player_total = get_total(player_cards,
                                 number_of_player_cards);

    int dealer_total = get_total(dealer_cards,
                                 number_of_dealer_cards);

    if (player_total > 21)
      {
        g.setColor(Color.red);
        g.drawString("Player", 10, 160);
        g.drawString("BUSTED", 10, 180);
        g.drawString("Dealer", 10, 205);
        g.drawString("WINS"  , 10, 225);
        return;
      }
```

```java
        while (dealer_total < 17)
          {
            get_card();

            dealer_cards[number_of_dealer_cards++] = card;

            card_deck.draw(card, number_of_dealer_cards*card_width, 0,
                        card_width, card_height);

            card_count++;
            showStatus("Cards dealt: " + card_count);

            dealer_total = get_total(dealer_cards,
                                   number_of_dealer_cards);
          }

      if (dealer_total > 21)
        {
          g.setColor(Color.green);
          g.drawString("Dealer", 10, 160);
          g.drawString("Busted", 10, 180);
          g.drawString("Player", 10, 205);
          g.drawString("WINS"  , 10, 225);
        }
      else if (player_total > dealer_total)
        {
          g.setColor(Color.green);
          g.drawString("Player", 10, 160);
          g.drawString("WINS"  , 10, 180);
        }
      else if (dealer_total == player_total)
        {
          g.setColor(Color.yellow);
          g.drawString("PUSH", 10, 160);
        }
      else
        {
          g.setColor(Color.red);
          g.drawString("Dealer", 10, 160);
          g.drawString("WINS"  , 10, 180);
        }
  }

//————————————————————————————

public boolean mouseUp(Event evt, int x, int y)
  {
    buttons.draw_items();
    return true;
  }

//————————————————————————————
```

```
public boolean mouseDown(Event evt, int x, int y)
  {
    int button_pushed = buttons.push_button(x, y);

    switch (button_pushed)
      {
      case 0:
        if (!hand_done)
          break;

        clear();
        deal();
        repaint();
        break;

      case 1:
        hit_me();
        break;

      case 2:
        done();
        break;
      }

    return true;
  }
```

//————————————————————

```
void clear()
  {
    g.setColor(Color.black);
    g.fillRect(0, 0, width, height);
  }
```

//————————————————————

```
public void update(Graphics _g)
  {
    clear();

    if (hand_done)
      card_deck.draw(dealer_cards[0], card_width, 0,
                     card_width, card_height);
    else
      card_deck.draw_back(card_width, 0, card_width, card_height);

    for (int i = 1; i < number_of_dealer_cards; i++)
      card_deck.draw(dealer_cards[i], (i+1)*card_width, 0,
                     card_width, card_height);

    for (int i = 0; i < number_of_player_cards; i++)
      card_deck.draw(player_cards[i],
                     (i+1)*card_width, card_height,
                     card_width, card_height);
```

```
        buttons.draw_items();
    }


    //————————————————————————————————————


    public void paint(Graphics g)
      {
        set_defaults();
        update(g);
      }
  }
```

The "cards.java" File

The "cards.java" file contains the *card* class you created in Chapter 49. In this case, the class makes one small change that is described later in this chapter. Because you examined the *cards* class in detail in Chapter 49, we will not present the code here. Instead, you can find the complete source code for the *cards* class in the directory JAVABOOK\CHAP51 on the CD-ROM that accompanies this book.

The "buttons.java" File

Within the "buttons.java" file, you will find code for the custom buttons the **Blackjack** program uses. The following code implements "buttons.java":

```
//******************************************************************
// buttons.java
//******************************************************************


import java.awt.*;
import java.util.*;


//******************************************************************


class button_info extends Object
  {
    public String s;
    public int x;
    public int y;
    public int w;
    public int h;

    public button_info(String s, int x, int y, int w, int h)
      {
        this.s = s;
        this.x = x;
        this.y = y;
        this.w = w;
        this.h = h;
      }
  }


//******************************************************************
```

```
public class buttons
  {
    static Graphics g;
    static boolean first_time = true;
    static int total_buttons = 0;

    static Vector coordinate;

    static FontMetrics font_metrics;

    static int point_size = 20;
    static int baseline =   0;

    //————————————————————————

    public buttons(Graphics g, String s, int x, int y, int w, int h)
      {
        if (first_time)
          {
            first_time = false;
            this.g = g;

            Font font = new Font("TimesRoman", Font.BOLD, point_size);
            g.setFont(font);
            font_metrics = g.getFontMetrics();
            baseline = font_metrics.getAscent();

            coordinate = new Vector();
          }

        total_buttons++;
        coordinate.addElement(new button_info(s, x, y, w, h));
        draw_items();
      }

    //————————————————————————

    static void draw_items()
      {
        for (int i = 0; i < total_buttons; i++)
          {
            button_info b = (button_info) coordinate.elementAt(i);

            g.setColor(Color.cyan);
            g.fillRect(b.x, b.y, b.w, b.h);

            g.setColor(Color.blue);
            g.drawString(b.s, b.x, b.y + baseline - 1);

            g.setColor(Color.white);
            g.drawRect(b.x, b.y, b.w, b.h);
          }
      }

    //————————————————————————
```

```
      static int push_button(int x, int y)
    {
      for (int i = 0; i < total_buttons; i++)
        {
          button_info b = (button_info) coordinate.elementAt(i);

          if (x > b.x && x < b.x + b.w &&
              y > b.y && y < b.y + b.h)
          {
              g.setColor(Color.black);
              g.fillRect(b.x, b.y, b.w, point_size);
              g.setColor(Color.white);
              g.drawString(b.s, b.x, b.y + baseline);

              return (i);
          }
        }

      return (-1);
    }
  }
```

BREAKING APART BLACKJACK

The following sections examine the four classes that make up the **Blackjack** applet. Some of the code may be the same as code in previous chapters, and those pieces of code will be mentioned but not explained here.

The play Class

The *play* class imports two packages: the *java.applet* package, because this class is an applet; and the *java.awt* package, to perform graphics:

```
import java.applet.*;
import java.awt.*;
```

As you can see, the *play* class is public and extends the *Applet* class:

```
public class play extends Applet
```

Member Variables

To start, the *play* class defines member variables to store the graphics context, a deck of cards the width and height of the window, a variable to keep track of the current card, the number value of the card, and the suit for the card:

```
Graphics g;
cards card_deck;

int width;
int height;
int card;
int number;
int suit;
```

The *play* class uses arrays to keep track of which cards have been displayed, the dealer's cards, and the player's cards. The class also uses variables to keep track of how many cards have been played, the card width, and the card height. Finally, the class defines variables to store the number of dealer cards, the number of player cards, and a status value that contains the status of when a hand is done:

```
boolean card_displayed[];
int dealer_cards[];
int player_cards[];

int card_count;
int card_width = 100;
int card_height = 140;

int number_of_dealer_cards;
int number_of_player_cards;

boolean hand_done = true;
```

Initializing the Applet

As you can see, the *init* function first gets the graphics context, and then creates a new deck of cards:

```
public void init()
  {
    g = getGraphics();

    card_deck = new cards(g);
```

The function then initializes the arrays that keep track of the cards that have been displayed, the dealer's cards, and the player's cards. Notice that there will only be 52 cards in this program, because you do not use jokers in Blackjack:

```
card_displayed = new boolean [52];
dealer_cards   = new int     [10];
player_cards   = new int     [10];
```

Lastly, the *init* function creates the buttons that you need for this program, and then deals the cards:

```
new buttons(g, "Deal"  , 10,  50, 80, 20);
new buttons(g, "Hit Me", 10,  80, 80, 20);
new buttons(g, "Stay"  , 10, 110, 80, 20);

deal();
```

Resetting all the Cards

The *reset_cards* function prepares the card deck for a new game. To reset all the cards, the function resets all the cards in the *card_displayed* array to *false*, sets the card count to 0, and sets the number of dealer's cards and the number of player's cards to 0:

```
void reset_cards()
  {
    int i;

    for (i = 0; i < 52; i++)
      card_displayed[i] = false;

    card_count = 0;

    number_of_dealer_cards = 0;
    number_of_player_cards = 0;
  }
```

Setting the Defaults

The class uses the *set_defaults* function to set the variables containing the width and the height of the window. As you will learn, the *cards* class draws its cards based on the window size:

```
void set_defaults()
  {
    width = size().width;
    height = size().height;
  }
```

Getting a Random Card

To select the dealer and player cards, the program gets cards randomly using the *get_card* function. The function gets a random number from 0 to 51. First, the function checks to see if the card has already been displayed. If it has, the function increments the index to point to the next card in sequence, and checks that card. If the function gets to 52, it starts from the top again by resetting the card to 0. After the function finds a card, it breaks out of the loop, and gets the card's number and suit:

```
void get_card()
  {
    card = (int) (Math.random() * 52);

    do
      {
        if (!card_displayed[card])
          {
            card_displayed[card] = true;
            break;
          }
        else if (++card == 52)
          card = 0;

      } while (true);

    get_number_and_suit(card);
  }
```

Getting the Number and Suit of a Card

The *get_number_and_suit* function assigns the card number and suit to the corresponding member functions. The program orders cards as follows: 0-12 are spades, 13-25 are clubs, 26-38 are hearts, and 39-51 are diamonds. To get the number of the card, perform a modulus with 13; and to get the suit, divide by 13:

```
void get_number_and_suit(int card)
  {
    number = card % 13;
    suit = card / 13;
  }
```

Dealing the Cards

The *deal* function deals the player's and dealer's initial hands. To deal the cards, the function first sets the variable, which tells the applet whether the hand is done, to *false*. Then, the function resets the cards for a new game:

```
void deal()
  {
    hand_done = false;

    reset_cards();
```

The function then deals two cards for the dealer and two cards for the player:

```
for (int x = 0; x < 2; x++)
  {
    for (int y = 0; y < 2; y++)
      {
```

For each card that the function deals, it has to get the card. Then, if you are dealing the dealer's cards, add the card to the dealer's card array; otherwise, add the card to the player's card array:

```
get_card();

if (y == 0)
  dealer_cards[number_of_dealer_cards++] = card;
else
  player_cards[number_of_player_cards++] = card;
```

If this is the first card for the dealer, the function displays the back of the card. Otherwise, it displays the card face up:

```
if (x == 0 && y == 0)
  card_deck.draw_back(card_width, 0, card_width, card_height);
else
  card_deck.draw(card, (x+1)*card_width, y*card_height,
              card_width, card_height);
```

Next, the function increments the total number of cards dealt so far, and displays the count in the status bar:

```
card_count++;
showStatus("Cards dealt: " + card_count);
```

Giving a Card to the Player

If the player selects the "Hit Me" button, the applet calls the *hit_me* function. First, the function checks to see if the hand is already done. If it is, the function ignores the button press and returns:

```
void hit_me()
  {
    if (hand_done)
      return;
```

Otherwise, the function gets a card and adds it to the player's card array. Then, the function draws the card on the screen, increments the total card count, and displays the count on the status bar:

```
get_card();

player_cards[number_of_player_cards++] = card;

card_deck.draw(card,
               number_of_player_cards*card_width, card_height,
               card_width, card_height);

card_count++;
showStatus("Cards dealt: " + card_count);
```

Then, the function gets the current total of the player's cards, and if the total is greater than 21, the player has busted:

```
int player_total = get_total(player_cards,
                             number_of_player_cards);

if (player_total > 21)
  done();
```

Getting the Total

The applet calls the *get_total* function to get the total (the score) of a user's hand. To get a hand's total, the function needs the card array for which it will calculate the total, and the number of cards in this card array:

```
int get_total(int cards[], int number_of_cards)
```

To start, the function resets the total to 0, and the number of aces to 0. Remember, in Blackjack, an ace can count as either 1 or 11. You have to select the value that will give the hand the greatest number without exceeding 21. If you have multiple aces, you might have to have a combination of 1s and 11s:

```
int total = 0;
int aces = 0;
```

The function uses a *for* loop to step through each card. Within the loop, the function first has to get the number and suit of the card. The suit is irrelevant, but you need the number. The function uses a *switch* statement to determine each card's value:

```
for (int i = 0; i < number_of_cards; i++)
  {
    get_number_and_suit(cards[i]);

    switch (number)
      {
```

If the current card is a face card or a 10, the function adds 10 to the total:

```
case 10:
case 11:
case 12:
  total += 10;
  break;
```

If the card is an ace, the function increments the number of aces and adds 1 to the total:

```
case 0:
  aces++;
  total += 1;
  break;
```

Otherwise, the function adds the value of the card to the total. Remember that cards 2 through 9 are numbered 1 through 8, so you have to add 1 to the number:

```
default:
  total += number + 1;
```

Each ace has already been counted with the value of 1. The function can add a value of 10 more per ace until you go through all the aces, or the total exceeds 21. If the total exceeds 21, the function does not add the last value of 10 and breaks out of the loop, returning the total:

```
for (int a = 0; a < aces; a++)
  {
    if (total + 10 > 21)
      break;
    else
      total += 10;
  }

return total;
```

Figuring Out Who Won

To determine who won the game, the function calls the *done* function. If the hand is already done, that means that the applet has already performed this calculation, so the function returns without recalculating:

```
void done()
  {
    if (hand_done)
      return;
```

Otherwise, the function sets the *hand_done* variable to *true*, because the function will calculate the total here. To start, the function turns the dealer's first card face up:

```
hand_done = true;
card_deck.draw(dealer_cards [0], card_width, 0,
               card_width, card_height);
```

Next, the function uses the *get_total* function to get the total of the player's cards and the total of the dealer's cards:

```
int player_total = get_total(player_cards, number_of_player_cards);

int dealer_total = get_total(dealer_cards, number_of_dealer_cards);
```

If the player's total exceeds 21, the player busted and the dealer wins. Therefore, the function will display the results on the screen:

```
if (player_total > 21)
  {
    g.setColor(Color.red);
    g.drawString("Player", 10, 160);
    g.drawString("BUSTED", 10, 180);
    g.drawString("Dealer", 10, 205);
    g.drawString("WINS"  , 10, 225);
    return;
  }
```

If the player has not busted, then the dealer has to get more cards while his total is less than 17. The dealer has to take a card if he has 16 or less, and has to stay if he has 17 or more. The function gets a random card, adds to the dealer's card array, draws the card on the screen, increments the card count, and displays the count on the screen. Then, the function gets the dealer's total, to see if he has to get more cards:

```
while (dealer_total < 17)
  {
    get_card();

    dealer_cards[number_of_dealer_cards++] = card;

    card_deck.draw(card, number_of_dealer_cards*card_width, 0,
                   card_width, card_height);

    card_count++;
    showStatus("Cards dealt: " + card_count);

    dealer_total = get_total(dealer_cards, number_of_dealer_cards);
  }
```

When the dealer is done taking cards, the function checks to see if its total exceeds 21. If it does, the function shows a green message saying "Dealer Busted Player WINS":

```
if (dealer_total > 21)
  {
```

```
        g.setColor(Color.green);
        g.drawString("Dealer", 10, 160);
        g.drawString("Busted", 10, 180);
        g.drawString("Player", 10, 205);
        g.drawString("WINS"  , 10, 225);
    }
```

Otherwise, if the player's total exceeds the dealer's total, the function shows a green message saying "Player WINS":

```
    else if (player_total > dealer_total)
      {
        g.setColor(Color.green);
        g.drawString("Player", 10, 160);
        g.drawString("WINS"  , 10, 180);
      }
```

Or, if the dealer's total is equal to the player's total, the function shows a yellow message saying "PUSH". When there is a push in Blackjack, neither player wins:

```
    else if (dealer_total == player_total)
      {
        g.setColor(Color.yellow);
        g.drawString("PUSH", 10, 160);
      }
```

If none of the above conditions are met, that means that the dealer wins, and the function shows a red message saying "Dealer WINS":

```
    else
      {
        g.setColor(Color.red);
        g.drawString("Dealer", 10, 160);
        g.drawString("WINS"  , 10, 180);
      }
```

Processing a Mouse Button Click

As you have learned, when the user presses a mouse button, Java calls the *mouseDown* function. To start, the function checks if the user clicked the mouse on one of the applet's buttons. To do this, the function calls the *buttons* class *push_button* method, and passes the x-and-y coordinates of where the mouse button was clicked. The function uses a *switch* statement to see which button was pressed, if any:

```
public boolean mouseDown(Event evt, int x, int y)
  {
    int button_pushed = buttons.push_button(x, y);

    switch (button_pushed)
      {
```

If the user clicked the "Deal" button, the function checks to see if the hand is already done. If the hand is active, the function cannot deal another hand. The hand has to be done before the game can deal again. If the hand is done, the function clears the screen, deals the cards, and repaints the screen:

```
case 0:
  if (!hand_done)
    break;

  clear();
  deal();
  repaint();
  break;
```

If the user clicked on the "Hit Me" button, the function calls the *hit_me* function, which will give the user another card:

```
case 1:
  hit_me();
  break;
```

If the user clicked on the "Stay" button, the function calls the *done* function to figure out who won:

```
case 2:
  done();
  break;
```

Finally, the function returns *true* to Java to indicate that you processed the event:

```
return true;
```

Processing the Release of a Mouse Button

As you know, when the user releases a mouse button, Java calls the *mouseUp* function. When the user releases the mouse button, the applet redraws all the button items on the screen so they appear in the unpressed state, which is blue lettering on a cyan rectangle. (The pressed state is white lettering on a black rectangle):

```
public boolean mouseUp(Event evt, int x, int y)
  {
    buttons.draw_items();
    return true;
  }
```

Clearing the Screen

To clear the screen, the function sets the color to black and fills a rectangle the size of the entire screen:

```
void clear()
  {
    g.setColor(Color.black);
    g.fillRect(0, 0, width, height);
  }
```

Updating the Window

Whenever the screen has to be updated, Java calls the *update* function. Since you already have the graphics context, name this parameter something other than *g*, like "*_g*" for example. In this function, you have to redraw all the items:

```
public void update(Graphics _g)
```

To start, the function clears the screen. Then, it checks whether to draw the dealer's first card face-up or face-down. If the hand is done, the function can draw it face-up. The function then draws the rest of the dealer's cards:

```
clear();

if (hand_done)
  card_deck.draw(dealer_cards[0], card_width, 0,
                card_width, card_height);
else
  card_deck.draw_back(card_width, 0, card_width, card_height);

for (int i = 1; i < number_of_dealer_cards; i++)
  card_deck.draw(dealer_cards[i], (i+1)*card_width, 0,
                card_width, card_height);
```

Next, the function draws the player's cards on the screen:

```
for (int i = 0; i < number_of_player_cards; i++)
  card_deck.draw(player_cards[i], (i+1)*card_width, card_height,
                card_width, card_height);
```

Finally, the function draws all the buttons:

```
buttons.draw_items();
```

The paint Function

When the entire screen has to be repainted, Java calls the *paint* function. In this function, you just have to set the defaults, and update the screen by calling the *update* function, which will draw all the cards and the buttons on the screen:

```
public void paint(Graphics g)
  {
    set_defaults();
    update(g);
  }
```

The cards Class

The only difference between this class and the class in the previous chapter is the addition of the *draw_back* function. This function draws the back-side of the cards. It accepts four parameters: the x-and-y coordinates, and the width and the height of the card:

```
public void draw_back(int x, int y, int w, int h)
```

To start, the function fills a rounded rectangle with white. Next, the function draws 20 horizontal red lines, and 20 vertical red lines:

```
g.setColor(Color.white);
g.fillRoundRect(x, y, w, h, w/20, h/20);

g.setColor(Color.red);

int x_end = x + w;
int x_inc = w/20;
int y_end = y + h;
int y_inc = h/20;

for (int i = x + x_inc; i < x_end; i += x_inc)
  g.drawLine(i, y, i, y_end);

for (int j = y + y_inc; j < y_end; j += y_inc)
  g.drawLine(x, j, x_end, j);
```

The Buttons File

As discussed, within the *buttons* class, you will find code for the custom buttons that appear in the **Blackjack** game. The class uses two packages: the *java.awt* package to perform graphics that draw the buttons; and the *java.util* package, to store the buttons in the *Vector* class:

```
import java.awt.*;
import java.util.*;
```

This file contains two classes: the *button_info* class and the *buttons* class. Each of them will be described separately in the following sections.

The button_info Class

The *button_info* class is used by the *buttons* class to hold information for each button, such as the string to be used as the label. The class has to inherit from the *Object* class because you will store objects of this type in a *Vector* object. Notice that the class is not declared *public* because you will use it from the *buttons* class, which is in the same file:

```
class button_info extends Object
```

The information that the *button_info* class holds is the string you will use as the button label, the x-and-y coordinates of the top-left of the button, and the width and the height of the button:

```
public String s;
public int x;
public int y;
public int w;
public int h;
```

The *button_info* constructor just takes the parameters passed to it and stores them in the member variables:

```
public button_info(String s, int x, int y, int w, int h)
  {
    this.s = s;
    this.x = x;
    this.y = y;
    this.w = w;
    this.h = h;
  }
```

The buttons Class

The *buttons* class defines and controls the custom buttons that appear in the **Blackjack** game. The class is *public* because you will use it from the *play* class, which you define outside this file:

```
public class buttons
```

As in any program, there are many ways to implement this class. In this program, you will define everything as *static* so that you can use the functions and the member variables without having to use a variable of this class. There will be multiple buttons, with multiple button information objects stored in the vector, but there will only be one vector.

Member Variables

The *button* class defines member variables to store the graphics context, a flag that tells the constructor that this is the first object of this class, and the total number of buttons:

```
static Graphics g;
static boolean first_time = true;
static int total_buttons = 0;
```

Next, the class declares the vector, which will hold the button information for each button:

```
static Vector coordinate;
```

To draw the labels, the class needs the font metrics for the font, the point size, and the baseline offset from the top of the button:

```
static FontMetrics font_metrics;

static int point_size = 20;
static int baseline =  0;
```

The Constructor

The *buttons* class constructor takes as parameters the graphics context, the x-and-y coordinates, and the width and the height of the button it is to create:

```
public buttons(Graphics g, String s, int x, int y, int w, int h)
```

If this is the first button you are creating, the constructor sets the graphics-context member variable, sets the font to use, gets the font metrics for this font, and gets the offset of the baseline of the font from the top of the button. Then, the function creates a new *Vector* object where you will store all the button information:

```
if (first_time)
  {
    first_time = false;
    this.g = g;

    Font font = new Font("TimesRoman", Font.BOLD, point_size);
    g.setFont(font);
    font_metrics = g.getFontMetrics();
    baseline = fm.getAscent();

    coordinate = new Vector();
  }
```

Next, the function increments the count for the total number of buttons, adds the button information for the current button to the vector, and redraws all the buttons on the window:

```
total_buttons++;
coordinate.addElement(new button_info(s, x, y, w, h));
draw_items();
```

Drawing the Button Items

The class uses the *draw_items* function to display a button. Since the class knows how many buttons there are, it uses a *for* loop to iterate through each button. Within the loop, the function gets the button information, then draws a rectangle that will represent the button in the cyan color, draws the button label stored as a string and, lastly, draws a white border around the button:

```
static void draw_items()
  {
    for (int i = 0; i < total_buttons; i++)
      {
        button_info b = (button_info) coordinate.elementAt(i);

        g.setColor(Color.cyan);
        g.fillRect(b.x, b.y, b.w, b.h);

        g.setColor(Color.blue);
        g.drawString(b.s, b.x, b.y + baseline - 1);

        g.setColor(Color.white);
        g.drawRect(b.x, b.y, b.w, b.h);
      }
  }
```

Processing Button Pushes

The class uses the *push_button* function to determine if the x-and-y coordinate of a mouse-click operation corresponds to a button's coordinates. The actual mouse click is processed in the *play* class. Here, the *push_button* function will receive the x-and-y coordinates of the mouse-click position:

```
static int push_button(int x, int y)
```

Using a *for* loop, the function iterates through each button to determine if the x-and-y coordinates of the mouse operation correspond to the button region:

```
for (int i = 0; i < total_buttons; i++)
  {
    button_info b = (button_info) coordinate.elementAt(i);

    if (x > b.x && x < b.x + b.w &&
        y > b.y && y < b.y + b.h)
```

If the function finds the button that was pressed, it fills the button rectangle in black and writes the label in white. The function then returns the index value of the button:

```
g.setColor(Color.black);
g.fillRect(b.x, b.y, b.w, point_size);
g.setColor(Color.white);
g.drawString(b.s, b.x, b.y + baseline);

return (i);
```

If the function finds that the mouse click did not occur inside any buttons stored in this class, it returns a value of a negative one:

```
return (-1);
```

ENHANCEMENTS YOU CAN MAKE TO BLACKJACK

To improve the program's appearance, create a GIF image for each card and a GIF image for the back of the cards. In addition to improving the program's appearance, using GIF files will simplify the code because you won't have to draw each number and suit. However, using GIFs will make the program slower, especially in the beginning when the images have not been loaded.

PUTTING IT ALL TOGETHER

This applet demonstrates how to use the *cards* class to create a game of Blackjack. The applet is also your final applet of the **Java Programmer's Library**. We hope you had as much fun reading the book as we had writing it. As you examine other Java applets, take time to experiment with them. If you find something cool, let us know about it, too. Before you continue on your way with Java, make sure you understand the following key concepts:

☑ You can use the *cards* class to create the popular game of Blackjack.

☑ You can create a class of your own type of buttons, which you can click to perform some action.

INDEX